Ending Childhood Obesity

ELGAR STUDIES IN HEALTH AND THE LAW

Series Editor: Professor Amandine Garde, *University of Liverpool, UK*

This new and exciting series will tackle and explore important issues around Health and the Law as they become increasingly entwined in today's world. Public interest issues sparked by the media and new spaces of information and communication engage society on a more hands-on level, which inevitably impacts many aspects of the Law and Policies that we live by. As a field of study, Health and the Law will encompass the legal and political ramifications of various health issues within national and international law. The various and numerous aspects relating to these broad areas include healthcare law, non-communicable diseases, prevention strategies, health policies, reproductive justice, social and mental health law, bioethics, and medicinal law. Elgar Studies in Health and the Law will also be an excellent forum to discuss and debate the diverse and growing range of issues that remain unexplored. The primary mission of the series is to stimulate the development of original thinking across Health and the Law and to foster the best theoretical and empirical scholarship in the field. With valuable insights, open-minded approaches, and high quality authored and edited collections; this series will be of interest to academics and practitioners alike.

Titles in the series include:

The Law and Policy of Healthcare Financing
An International Comparison of Models and Outcomes
Edited by Wolf Sauter, Jos Boertjens, Johan van Manen and Misja Mikkers

The Regulation of E-cigarettes
International, European and National Challenges
Edited by Lukasz Gruszczynski

Human Rights and Tobacco Control
Edited by Marie Elske Gispen and Brigit Toebes

Ending Childhood Obesity
A Challenge at the Crossroads of International Economic and Human Rights Law
Edited by Amandine Garde, Joshua Curtis and Olivier De Schutter

Ending Childhood Obesity
A Challenge at the Crossroads of International Economic and Human Rights Law

Edited by

Amandine Garde

University of Liverpool, UK

Joshua Curtis

University of Liverpool, UK

Olivier De Schutter

Catholic University of Louvain, Belgium

ELGAR STUDIES IN HEALTH AND THE LAW

Cheltenham, UK • Northampton, MA, USA

© The Editors and Contributors Severally 2020

All rights reserved. No part of this publication may be reproduced, stored in a retrieval system or transmitted in any form or by any means, electronic, mechanical or photocopying, recording, or otherwise without the prior permission of the publisher.

Published by
Edward Elgar Publishing Limited
The Lypiatts
15 Lansdown Road
Cheltenham
Glos GL50 2JA
UK

Edward Elgar Publishing, Inc.
William Pratt House
9 Dewey Court
Northampton
Massachusetts 01060
USA

A catalogue record for this book
is available from the British Library

Library of Congress Control Number: 2020950155

This book is available electronically in the Elgaronline
Law subject collection
http://dx.doi.org/10.4337/9781788114028

ISBN 978 1 78811 401 1 (cased)
ISBN 978 1 78811 402 8 (eBook)

Printed and bound by CPI Group (UK) Ltd, Croydon, CR0 4YY

Contents

List of contributors		vii
1	Ending childhood obesity: Introducing the issues and the legal challenge ***Amandine Garde, Joshua Curtis and Olivier De Schutter***	1
PART I	HUMAN RIGHTS APPROACH TO CHILDHOOD OBESITY PREVENTION	
2	International human rights and childhood obesity prevention ***Sarah A Roache and Oscar A Cabrera***	30
3	The child's right to health as a tool to end childhood obesity ***Katharina Ó Cathaoir and Mette Hartlev***	57
4	Human rights, childhood obesity and health inequalities ***Marine Friant-Perrot and Nikhil Gokani***	86
PART II	UTILISING THE SPACE AVAILABLE FOR REGULATORY MEASURES UNDER INTERNATONAL ECONOMIC LAW	
5	Sugar as commodity or health risk: The unmaking or remaking of international trade law? ***Gregory Messenger***	112
6	Using food labelling laws to combat childhood obesity: Lessons from the EU, the WTO and Codex ***Caoimhín MacMaoláin***	138
7	Investment protection agreements, regulatory chill, and national measures on childhood obesity prevention ***Mavluda Sattorova***	161
8	International trade and childhood obesity: A Caribbean perspective ***Nicole Foster***	185

PART III   ADDITIONAL TOOLS AVAILABLE UNDER
          HUMAN RIGHTS LAW

9   Can the United Nations system be mobilized to promote
     human rights-based approaches in preventing and ending
     childhood obesity?   219
     Asbjørn Eide and Wenche Barth Eide

10   Combatting obesogenic commercial practices through the
     implementation of the best interests of the child principle   251
     Amandine Garde and Seamus Byrne

11   Multinational food corporations and the right to health:
     Achieving accountability through mandatory human rights
     due diligence?   282
     Oliver Bartlett

12   Bridging governance gaps with extraterritorial human
     rights obligations: Accessing home State courts to end
     childhood obesity   309
     Joshua Curtis

13   Overcoming the legal challenge to end childhood obesity:
     Pathways towards positive harmonization in law and governance   339
     Joshua Curtis and Amandine Garde

Index   370

Contributors

Oliver Bartlett, Maynooth University, Ireland

Dr Oliver Bartlett is Assistant Professor of Law at Maynooth University. He graduated from Durham University with L.L.B, MJur, and PhD degrees. He wrote his PhD thesis on the role of EU law in preventing addiction. Before joining Maynooth in 2018, Oliver lectured at the University of Liverpool. Oliver's recent research has focussed on EU law and health policy, alcohol policy, and public health ethics.

Seamus Byrne, University of Liverpool, UK

Seamus Byrne is a Lecturer in Law in the School of Law and Social Justice at the University of Liverpool. Seamus's research interests lie in the areas of children's socio-economic rights, education rights and the application of a children's rights-based approach to the interface between law and non-communicable diseases. Seamus also adopts participatory methodological approaches within his research and is interested in progressive methodological approaches regarding children's rights issues.

Oscar A. Cabrera, Georgetown University, US

Oscar A. Cabrera, *Abogado* (JD equivalent), LL.M., is the Program Director of the Healthy Families Initiative at the O'Neill Institute for National and Global Health Law and a Visiting Professor of Law at Georgetown Law. Previously, Oscar served as the Executive Director of the O'Neill Institute for over seven years. He earned his law degree in Venezuela, and his Master of Laws (LL.M.), with concentration in Health Law and Policy, at the University of Toronto. Oscar regularly works on projects with external partners, such as the World Health Organization, the Centers for Disease Control and Prevention, and the Campaign for Tobacco Free Kids. He also collaborates with NGOs, and currently is a board member of the Inter-American Heart Foundation, and the president of the board of the Inter-American Heart Foundation Argentina. His interests include health and human rights, sexual and reproductive rights, tobacco control and modifiable risk factors for NCDs.

Joshua Curtis, University of Liverpool, UK

Dr Joshua Curtis is a Lecturer in Law in the School of Law and Social Justice at the University of Liverpool. His work is located at the intersection of human rights, international economic law and development economics. He has written, for example, on human rights and foreign investment, the nature of legal obligations on States to cooperate internationally, and the application of human rights law to the process of economic policy-making. He has advised the Irish Department of Foreign Affairs, the Irish Cancer Society, Amnesty International, and the International Federation for Human Rights, and is currently an academic member of the Extraterritorial Human Rights Obligations (ETO) Consortium. His present research is on 'The EU, the BRICS, Extraterritorial Human Rights Obligations and International Economic Governance'.

Olivier De Schutter, University of Louvain, Belgium

Olivier De Schutter is a Professor of Law at UCLouvain and at SciencesPo (Paris). Olivier is also a member of the Global Law School Faculty at New York University. He holds an LL.M. from Harvard University, a diploma cum laude from the International Institute of Human Rights (Strasbourg) and a Ph.D. in Law from UCLouvain. In 2013, he was awarded the prestigious Francqui Prize for his contribution to international human rights law and to the theory of governance. He is a past UN Special Rapporteur on the Right to Food and Member of the United Nations Committee on Economic, Social and Cultural Rights. He is the first chair of the Belgian Advisory Council on Policy Coherence for Development and he co-chairs the International Panel of Experts on Sustainable Food Systems (IPES-Food). In March 2020, he was appointed UN Special Rapporteur on extreme poverty and human rights.

Asbjørn Eide, University of Oslo, Norway

Asbjørn Eide, dr.juris h.c. Lund University, born 1933. Professor Emeritus and Senior Fellow, Norwegian Centre for Human Rights, University of Oslo, founder and first Director of the Centre. Member, UN Sub-Commission on the Promotion and Protection of Human Rights for 20 years, Special rapporteur on The Right to Adequate Food as a Human Right, Special rapporteur on Peaceful and Constructive Ways of Handling Situations Involving Minorities. Chairman of UN working group on rights of indigenous peoples (1982–1983) and UN working group on minorities (1995–2004). President of the Council of Europe's Advisory Committee on the Rights of National Minorities. Chairman FAO Panel of Eminent Experts on Ethics in Food and Agriculture (2000–2007). He is a Knight of The Royal Norwegian St Olav's Order for his work in peace and conflict research and human rights promotion.

Wenche Barth Eide, Department of Nutrition, University of Oslo, Norway; coordinator of the interdisciplinary research and action network FoHRC (Food, Human Rights and Corporations)

Wenche Barth Eide is affiliated with the Public Health Nutrition research group at the Department of Nutrition of the University of Oslo in *emerita* position. She also coordinates the research and action network Food, Human Rights and Corporations (*https://www.jus.uio.no/ smr/english/research/projects/fohrc*). Her research and teaching have linked international human rights norms and practice with public health nutrition policy and action. She served as the first nutrition adviser to the International Fund for Agricultural Development (IFAD) in Rome in the first half of the 1990s, and has been associated with many other parts of the UN regarding food security and nutrition and human rights-based development. She has been adviser to the Norwegian government and board member of the Norwegian Institute of International Affairs (NUPI), International Food Policy Research Institute (IFPRI), and the International Foundation for Science (IFS). Being among the early pioneers in giving content to the human right to adequate food, she was in 2015 made Commander of the Royal Norwegian Order of Merit for her contributions to the development of the right to food as a human right.

Nicole Foster, University of the West Indies, Barbados

Nicole Foster (née Clarke) is a Lecturer at the Faculty of Law, University of the West Indies, Barbados where she teaches public international law and WTO law. Mrs. Foster is an Attorney-at-Law and holds L.L.M degrees in international law and international organizations from Cambridge University and Washington College of Law, American University, respectively. From 1999–2005 she was Counsellor with Barbados' Permanent Mission to the United Nations Office and other International Organisations at Geneva with responsibility for WTO, WIPO and UNCTAD matters. Mrs Foster is also a Policy Adviser with Healthy Caribbean Coalition, a regional not-for-profit organization advocating on NCD prevention and control. She has acted as a consultant to the government of Barbados on WTO matters and as a regional consultant for the WTO, and is a member of the Indicative List of Arbitrators to hear disputes under the CARIFORUM - EC Economic Partnership Agreement.

Marine Friant-Perrot, University of Nantes, France

Marine Friant-Perrot is maître de conférences at the Faculty of Law and Political Science at the University of Nantes. She specializes in consumer law, food law and public health law. With Professor Amandine Garde she published a major policy report in 2015 with the French National Health

Agency (INPES) on the regulation of food marketing to prevent childhood obesity and related non-communicable diseases. She has worked with the French Institute of Medical and Health Research (Inserm) (2016) and for the Higher Council of Public Health (Haut conseil de la santé publique). She is a member of the working group "Droit sciences et technique" of the "Trans Europe Expert" network, of the International Association of Consumer Law and of the Research Centre on recherche en droit sur la diversité et la sécurité alimentaires dirigée par G. Parent (Université Laval à Québec).

Amandine Garde, University of Liverpool, UK

Amandine Garde is Professor of Law at the University of Liverpool. She is an expert in the legal aspects of obesity prevention and other non-communicable diseases (NCD) risk factors. Her book *EU Law and Obesity Prevention* (Kluwer Law International, 2010) was the first to offer a critical analysis of the EU's Obesity Prevention Strategy, and she is co-editor (with Alberto Alemanno) of *Regulating Lifestyle Risks: the EU, Alcohol, Tobacco and Unhealthy Diets* (Cambridge University Press, 2015). She is the founding director of the Law and NCD Research Unit at the University of Liverpool, which regularly advises international organizations, NGOs, public health agencies and governments worldwide. She has written numerous policy reports and developed several training courses on law, NCDs, childhood obesity, healthy diets and food marketing. She was a member of the Ad Hoc Working Group on Science and Evidence to the WHO Commission on Ending Childhood Obesity in 2014–2016 and is now a member of the *Lancet* Chatham House Commission on improving population health post COVID-19.

Nikhil Gokani, University of Essex, UK

Nikhil Gokani is a Lecturer in Law at the University of Essex. His research explores the role of local, national, supranational and international law in preventing non-communicable diseases and reducing health inequalities through tackling the risk factors of unhealthy diets, excessive alcohol consumption, tobacco use and exposure to air pollution. Nikhil is a regular presenter at national and international conferences and has published widely in both peer-reviewed journals and non-academic publications. Nikhil regularly works with governments, charities and other non-governmental organisations at national and international levels as part of his advisory and consultancy work, and is a member of several national committees on health policy. Nikhil is also a member of the Advisory Board of the Law & NCD Unit at the University of Liverpool, and a Fellow of the Royal Society of Public Health.

Mette Hartlev, University of Copenhagen, Denmark

Mette Hartlev is Professor, PhD, LL.D, at the Faculty of Law, University of Copenhagen. She is specialized in health law, public health law and patients' rights with a special interest in how a human rights-based approach can contribute to the intersection and balancing of public health interests and patients' fundamental rights in regard to non-communicable diseases. She has been involved in several interdisciplinary research projects including projects concerned with governing obesity. Public health policies impact on stigmatization of individuals has been a special focus for her research in these projects. Mette Hartlev's research network includes researchers from Europe, the US and Canada. Her publication list includes more than 120 articles and monographies, and she is co-editor of the editorial board of *European Journal of Health Law*.

Caoimhín MacMaoláin, Trinity College Dublin, Ireland

Dr Caoimhín MacMaoláin is an Associate Professor in the School of Law, Trinity College Dublin, Ireland. He is a graduate of UCD (BCL, L.L.M) and DCU (PhD). He previously lectured at the University of Northampton and held a Jean Monnet Chair in EU Integration at the University of Exeter. His research focuses on the way in which the production and sale of food is regulated by EU and International law. He has written two books on this subject, both published by Hart: Bloomsbury. He is currently researching and writing a third book, which is specifically on Irish Food Law. He has also published a number of book chapters and articles in the leading international journals in the field, including the *European Law Review*, the *Common Market Law Review*, the *European Journal of Consumer Law*, *European Public Law* and the *Food and Drug Law Journal*.

Gregory Messenger, University of Liverpool, UK

Dr Gregory Messenger is Senior Lecturer in Law at the University of Liverpool where he teaches world trade law, constitutional law, and administrative law. He was previously Junior Research Fellow in Law at the Queen's College, University of Oxford. Greg's research examines challenges arising from the development and application of international economic law. His research interests are principally in: public health and trade, the interface between sustainable development and trade, and the regulation of commodities in international law. Through his work at the University of Liverpool Law & NCD Unit, Greg has worked with the WHO and UNICEF on strategies to prevent non-communicable diseases within the framework of world trade law. He has also worked on a number of projects consulting governments on international law matters, from border delimitation to trade concessions. Since 2018, Greg has been working on trade issues in the UK Foreign and Commonwealth Office as an AHRC-ESRC FCO Knowledge Exchange Fellow.

Katharina Ó Cathaoir, University of Copenhagen, Denmark

Katharina Ó Cathaoir, PhD, is assistant professor at the Faculty of Law, University of Copenhagen, where she lectures in health and human rights law. Her PhD thesis analyses children's rights to freedom from obesogenic food marketing, and the corresponding responsibilities of states, parents and businesses. Katharina's research interests lie in the interplay between health law and human rights law, in particular, the collective right to health, children's rights, the prevention and treatment of non-communicable diseases, and the interplay between states and individuals' responsibilities for health.

Sarah A. Roache, Georgetown University, US

Sarah Roache is the Director of Health Law Programs and Visiting Professor, O'Neill Institute for National and Global Health Law at Georgetown University Law Center. She also leads the O'Neill Institute's broader health law capacity building programs, including developing health law trainings for government officials working at the intersection of law and health. Sarah's expertise includes non-communicable disease law and policy, health and human rights, and public interest litigation. Prior to joining the O'Neill Institute, Sarah worked as a complex class action litigator and a legal policy adviser to government and NGOs. She holds an L.L.M. in Global Health Law from Georgetown University, where she received the Thomas Bradbury Chetwood, S.J. Prize for the most distinguished academic record, and an L.L.B. (Hons) and a B.A. from the University of Melbourne. She is admitted to the New York Bar and to the Supreme Court of Victoria, Australia.

Mavluda Sattorova, University of Liverpool, UK

Dr Sattorova specializes in international economic law broadly defined, with particular focus on international investment law and investor-state arbitration. Her most recent work examines the impact of investment treaty law on national policy-making and governance. She works closely with international organizations and government agencies involved in the design and reform of international investment treaties and national investment policies. Dr Sattorova has published extensively on international investment law and worked in an expert capacity with the UNCTAD Investment Division and the World Health Organisation. She was a rapporteur for the Moscow meeting on law and NCD prevention organized by the WHO Regional Office for Europe in 2016. She is a member of the Law and NCD Unit and director of Liverpool Economic Governance Unit, University of Liverpool. Since 2019, Mavluda has been working on investment issues in the UK Foreign and Commonwealth Office as an AHRC-ESRC FCO Knowledge Exchange Fellow.

1. Ending childhood obesity: Introducing the issues and the legal challenge

Amandine Garde, Joshua Curtis and Olivier De Schutter

In June 2014, in advance of the Second United Nations (UN) High Level Meeting on NCDs, the Director-General of the World Health Organization (WHO) established the Commission on Ending Childhood Obesity (ECHO), noting that progress in tackling childhood obesity had been 'slow and inconsistent'. ECHO was entrusted with producing a report specifying which approaches and combinations of interventions were likely to be most effective in tackling childhood and adolescent obesity in different contexts around the world.[1] In May 2016, the 69th World Health Assembly (WHA) welcomed ECHO's report and asked the WHO to develop an action plan for the implementation of its recommendations.[2] Following consultation with member States and relevant stakeholders, an implementation plan was submitted to the 70th WHA in May 2017,[3] which the member States welcomed.[4] Using the Commission's report as its starting point, this edited collection reflects on the problem of childhood obesity as a legal challenge and calls for the robust, evidence-based regulation of the food industry, not least multinational

---

[1] Two ad hoc working groups were convened to provide guidance to the Commission, focusing respectively on the science and evidence for ending childhood obesity and on implementation, monitoring and accountability frameworks. On ECHO and its working groups, see www.who.int/end-childhood-obesity/en (accessed 15 May 2020).

[2] WHA, 'Report of the Commission on Ending Childhood Obesity', Resolution A69/8, World Health Organization, 24 March 2016. Following consultation with member States and relevant stakeholders, an implementation plan was submitted to the 70th WHA in May 2017 ('Report of the Commission on Ending Childhood Obesity: Implementation Plan Report by the Secretariat', EB140/30, 13 January 2017), which the member States welcomed: Resolution WHA 70.31.

[3] In this regard, the WHO Secretariat has submitted a report to the 140th session of the Executive Board: WHO, Executive Board.

[4] Resolution WHA 70.31.

corporations that operate at a global level and have been identified as major contributors to the problem.

1. CHILDHOOD OBESITY AS A GROWING PUBLIC HEALTH CHALLENGE

1.1 The Global Rise of Childhood Obesity

Many children are growing up in 'obesogenic' environments that encourage weight gain and deter weight loss.[5] The WHO estimates that the prevalence of worldwide obesity has nearly tripled in the last four decades. It is fuelled by the rising prevalence of overweight among children. In 2016, over 340 million children and adolescents aged five–19 were overweight or obese – an increase from 4 per cent in 1975 to around 18 per cent in 2016; whilst an estimated 38.2 million children under the age of five years were overweight or obese in 2019.[6]

Once considered a problem only for high-income countries, overweight and obesity rates are rising rapidly in low- and middle-income countries (LMICs). The vast majority of overweight or obese children now live in developing countries, where the rate of increase has been more than 30 per cent higher than that of developed countries.[7] Consequently, several LMICs face the 'double burden' of malnutrition. While they continue to deal with infectious diseases and undernutrition, they are experiencing a rapid upsurge in chronic disease risk factors such as overweight and obesity. It is increasingly common to find undernutrition and obesity existing side by side within the same country, the same community and even within the same household. This double burden may reflect inadequate prenatal and infant nutrition predisposing individuals to weight gain and metabolic risks from later exposure to unhealthy food[8] and lack of physical activity. It also reflects the 'nutrition transition',[9] character-

---

[5] G Egger and B Swinburn, 'An "Ecological" Approach to the Obesity Pandemic' (1997) 315 *British Medical Journal* 477.
[6] WHO, 'Obesity and Overweight: Key Facts and Figures', WHO, Geneva, 1 April 2020.
[7] WHO, 'Obesity and Overweight: Key Facts and Figures', WHO, Geneva, 16 April 2018.
[8] The term 'unhealthy food', which is used increasingly in WHO documents, means highly processed, nutritiously poor food and non-alcoholic beverages which are high in fat, sugar or salt. ECHO has urged States to 'develop nutrient-profiles to identify unhealthy foods and beverages' (recommendation 1.4).
[9] B Popkin, 'Nutrition, Agriculture and the Global Food System in Low- and Middle-Income Countries' (2014) *Food Policy* 91; C Monteiro and G Cannon, 'The Impact of Transnational "Big Food" Companies on the South: A View from Brazil' (2012) 9 *PLoS Medicine* e1001252.

ized by the shift to processed food richer in salt, sugar and saturated fats – food that has a long shelf life and is attractive to urban populations and younger generations, but is often less nutritious.[10]

1.2 The Costs Associated with Obesity

In addition to their psychological consequences and the risks of harassment and bullying children with severe overweight face, overweight and obesity are major risk factors for a broad range of non-communicable diseases (NCDs), including high blood pressure and cardiovascular diseases, diabetes and resistance to insulin, musculoskeletal disorders, and some forms of cancer.[11] Obese children also experience breathing difficulties, increased risk of fractures, hypertension, early markers of cardiovascular disease, insulin resistance and psychological effects. Childhood obesity is also associated with increased future risks of obesity, premature death and disability in adulthood.[12] It therefore has the potential to reverse many of the health benefits that are contributing to increased life expectancy,[13] whilst undermining the physical, social and psychological well-being of children.

Obesity is a threat to sustainable development, with high economic, social and ecological costs, directly affecting each element in the 'triple bottom line' of development.[14] It is associated with inequality, low social cohesion, low economic status, poor quality of life, reduced mobility, poorer employment opportunities, poor health and a lower life expectancy.[15] Obesity gives rise to high economic costs, with its high toll on public health systems and budgets and negative impact on labour markets due to lower productivity, premature death and lower employment rates.[16]

---

[10] O De Schutter, 'The Transformative Potential of the Right to Food', Final Report to the UN General Assembly, UN Doc A/HRC/25/57, 24 January 2014, 7.

[11] WHO, 'Obesity and Overweight: Key Facts and Figures', WHO, Geneva, 1 April 2020.

[12] ECHO Report, n2, 40.

[13] Ibid., 2.

[14] UN Standing Committee on Nutrition, 'Nutrition and the Post-2015 Sustainable Development Goals', Technical Note, UNSCN Secretariat, October 2014; B Swinburn, et al., 'The Global Obesity Pandemic: Shaped by Global Drivers and Local Environments' (2011) 378 *Lancet* 815; World Bank, 'Non-Communicable Diseases in the Caribbean: The New Challenge for Productivity and Growth', World Bank LAC Caribbean Knowledge Series, June 2013.

[15] Political Declaration of the UN High-Level Meeting on the Prevention and Control of Non-Communicable Diseases, 20 September 2011, Document A/66/L 1.

[16] The current costs of obesity are estimated at about US $2 trillion annually from direct healthcare costs and lost economic productivity. These costs represent

1.3 Calls from the International Community to End Childhood Obesity

In the late 1990s, the WHO recognized obesity as a major global health problem.[17] However, it was only in September 2011 that the issue of childhood obesity and NCDs became prominent on the global scene, when the UN General Assembly convened the first High Level meeting on Non-Communicable Diseases[18] and the international community acknowledged the scope of the challenge it was facing.[19] This meeting paved the way for the adoption of a series of global declarations, action plans and recommendations, as well as the establishment of commissions, working groups and taskforces committed to addressing NCDs, including ECHO.

The WHO Global Action Plan for the Prevention and Control of Non-communicable Diseases 2013–2020 includes a monitoring framework with nine voluntary global targets to be reached by 2025, including three that are particularly relevant to this book: a 25 per cent reduction in the overall mortality from cardiovascular diseases, cancer, diabetes or chronic respiratory diseases; a 30 per cent relative reduction in mean population intake of salt/sodium; and a halt in the rise of diabetes and obesity.[20] Since then, the UN

2.8% of the world's gross domestic product (GDP) and are roughly the equivalent of the costs of smoking or armed violence and war.

[17] See the WHO Consultation on Obesity carried out in 1999 and published in *Obesity: Preventing and Managing the Global Epidemic* (WHO, first published in 2000 and reprinted in 2004), Technical Report Series 894.

[18] President of the General Assembly, 'Political Declaration of the High-Level Meeting of the General Assembly on the Prevention and Control of Non-Communicable Diseases', A/66/L.1, UN, New York, 16 September 2011.

[19] In 2000, the WHA adopted the WHO Global Strategy for the Prevention and Control of NCDs: Resolution WHA 53.14, whilst in September 2007, the Heads of Government of the Caribbean Community (CARICOM) adopted the Port of Spain NCD Summit Declaration, in which they committed to provide the critical leadership required for implementing strategies for the reduction of and which was influential in setting a global agenda on NCDs: J Kirton, et al., 'Controlling NCDs through Summitry: The CARICOM Case', 2011. On obesity and healthy diets more specifically, note the adoption of the Strategy on Diet, Physical Activity and Health in 2004 which called on States and other 'stakeholders' to improve nutrition and help tackle obesity prevention: WHA Resolution WHA 57.17.

[20] WHO, 'Global Action Plan for the Prevention and Control of Noncommunicable Diseases, 2013–2020', Resolution WHA66.10, WHO, Geneva, 2013, 5.

General Assembly has held two further meetings devoted specifically to the prevention and control of NCDs, in 2014[21] and in 2018.[22]

In November 2014, the Food and Agriculture Organization (FAO) and the WHO convened the Second International Conference on Nutrition (ICN2). ICN2 led to the adoption of the Rome Declaration on Nutrition, in which ministers and representatives of the member States acknowledge that all forms of malnutrition – including overweight and obesity – not only affect people's health and well-being, but in addition carry a high burden in the form of negative social and economic consequences to individuals, families, communities and countries.[23] In April 2016, the UN General Assembly endorsed the ICN2 declaration and proclaimed 2016–2025 the UN Decade of Action on Nutrition.[24]

In September 2015, the UN General Assembly also adopted the 2030 Agenda and the Sustainable Development Goals (SDGs). In sharp contrast with their predecessors, the Millennium Development Goals, the SDGs address concerns such as NCDs and malnutrition, thus reflecting the increasing attention that obesity, and childhood obesity more specifically, has received over the last 20 years.[25] In particular, SDG 2 urges 'all countries and all stakeholders' to 'end hunger, achieve food security and improved nutrition and promote sustainable agriculture', while SDG 3 calls on them to 'ensure healthy lives and promote well-being for all at all ages'.[26]

---

[21] Resolution 68/300 of 17 July 2014 (A/68/L.53) adopting the outcome document of the high-level meeting of the General Assembly held on 10 and 11 July on the comprehensive review and assessment of the progress achieved in the prevention and control of non-communicable diseases.

[22] Resolution 73/2 of 10 October 2018 (A/73/L.2) adopting the Political declaration of the third high-level meeting of the General Assembly on the prevention and control of NCDs, following the High-level meeting held on 27 September 2018 to undertake a comprehensive review of the prevention and control of NCDs.

[23] Second International Conference on Nutrition, 'Rome Declaration on Nutrition', Conference Outcome Document, ICN2 2014/2, FAO and WHO, Rome, November 2014, para 4.

[24] UN General Assembly, 'United Nations Decade of Action on Nutrition (2016–2025)', A/RES/70/259, 15 April 2016.

[25] The MDGs called for the eradication of hunger and extreme poverty, and Target 1.c more specifically called for halving between 1990 and 2015 the number of people who suffer from hunger. The focus therefore was on undernutrition rather than malnutrition more broadly defined.

[26] UN General Assembly, 'Transforming Our World: The 2030 Agenda for Sustainable Development', UN Doc A/RES/70/1, 25 September 2015.

2. THE MULTISECTORAL RESPONSE REQUIRED TO ADDRESS CHILDHOOD OBESITY EFFECTIVELY

Widespread changes in food type, availability, affordability and marketing, as well as a decline in physical activity, with more time being spent on screen-based and sedentary leisure activities, have resulted in an 'energy imbalance', with the ingestion of more calories than the body can use effectively. However, because the problem is multifactorial, there is no 'magic' or 'silver' bullet, to coin the phrases often used in this context, and unravelling the complex combination of factors is key to tackling the problem effectively.[27] As ECHO has noted, 'it is only by taking a multisectoral approach through a comprehensive, integrated package of interventions that address the obesogenic environment, the life-course dimension and the education sector, that sustained progress can be made'.[28] ECHO therefore recommends that States 'coordinate contributions of all government sectors and institutions responsible for policies, including, but not limited to: education; food, agriculture; commerce and industry; development; finance and revenue; sport and recreation; communication; environmental and urban planning; transport and social affairs; and trade'.[29]

The WHO Global Action Plan on NCDs, the ECHO Report and related WHO and other UN documents urge States around the world to adopt a broad range of measures with a view to promoting healthy diets and ending childhood obesity. Some of these measures are intended to ensure that consumers are well informed and therefore 'empowered' to make healthier choices.[30] Several other recommendations call for measures going beyond informational rules, addressing more radically the food environment, to promote the availability, accessibility and affordability of healthier food, whilst reducing that of unhealthy food. Priority areas which member States should consider as part of effective obesity prevention strategies should include the promotion

---

[27] For a very striking map of the causal web of obesity, see Fig. 5.2 'The full obesity system map with thematic clusters' in the Foresight Project Report, *'Tackling Obesities: Future Choices'* (UK Government Office for Science 2007) 84.

[28] ECHO Report, n2, 40.

[29] Ibid., xii.

[30] For example, ECHO has called on States to 'implement a standardized global nutrient labelling system' (ibid., recommendation 1.6) and 'implement interpretive front-of-pack labelling supported by public education of both adults and children for nutrition literacy' (ibid., recommendation 1.7).

of breastfeeding[31] and the regulation of food marketing,[32] the use of economic instruments such as food subsidies and food taxes,[33] food reformulation, food procurement,[34] and, more broadly, trade and agricultural policy.[35]

Overall, however, inertia has prevailed. Despite years of mounting concern for growing rates of child obesity and related NCDs, progress has been slow and inadequate. As the 2018 UN Political Declaration states: 'The world has yet to fulfil its promise of implementing, at all levels, measures to reduce the risk of premature death and disability from NCDs.'[36] Ending childhood obesity and related NCDs requires 'enhanced political leadership to advance strategic, outcome-oriented action across sectors and policy coherence for the prevention and control of NCDs, in line with whole-of-government and health-in-all policies approaches'.[37]

3. CHILDHOOD OBESITY AS A LEGAL CHALLENGE

In October 2017, States gathered in Montevideo to prepare the Third UN High Level Meeting on NCDs where they reiterated their 'commitment to take bold action and accelerate progress to, by 2030, reduce by one-third the premature mortality from [NCDs] in line with the 2030 Agenda for Sustainable

---

[31] In light of evidence that exclusive breastfeeding for the first six months of life is a significant factor in reducing the risk of obesity, ECHO has called on States to promote breastfeeding; to this effect, they should in particular implement the Code of Marketing of Breastmilk Substitutes and subsequent WHA resolutions (recommendation 4.1) and 'support mothers to breastfeed, through regulatory measures such as maternity leave, facilities and time for breastfeeding in the work place' (recommendation 4.4).

[32] ECHO has called on States to 'implement the Set of Recommendations on the Marketing of Foods and Non-alcoholic Beverages to Children to reduce the exposure of children and adolescents to, and the power of, the marketing of unhealthy foods' (recommendation 1.3).

[33] ECHO recommendation 1.2 calls for the implementation of an effective tax on sugar-sweetened beverages.

[34] ECHO recommendations 5.1 to 5.3 focus on increasing the availability of healthy food and water fountains, whilst eliminating the provision or sale of unhealthy food in schools.

[35] See also C Hawkes, et al., 'Smart Food Policies for Obesity Prevention' (2015) 385 *Lancet* 2410.

[36] Resolution 73/2 of 10 October 2018, at para 4.

[37] WHO Montevideo Road Map 2018–2030 on NCDs as a Sustainable Development Priority, 18–20 October 2017, para 3 (emphasis added).

Development'. For the first time, they explicitly acknowledged the need for legal expertise in this field:

> We will enhance policy and legal expertise to develop NCDs responses in order to achieve the SDGs. We call upon the UN Inter-Agency Task Force on the Prevention and Control of NCDs and its Members, within their mandates, to scale up and broaden intersectoral work integrating expertise relevant to public health-related legal issues into NCD country support, including by providing evidence, technical advice, and case studies relevant to legal challenges. We encourage the UN Inter-Agency Task Force on the Prevention and Control of NCDs to explore the relationship between NCDs and the law to improve support to Member States in this area and to raise the priority it gives to this work.[38]

Law as an Opportunity: The Added Value of a Human rights-Based Approach to Childhood Obesity

With an increased focus on 'NCD promoting' environments, the question of the role of law has gained prominence in the obesity and NCD prevention debate. Not only do the international commitments of States to reduce obesity often call for a legislative or regulatory intervention, but there is a growing recognition that law as a discipline has a major role to play in the development and implementation of effective obesity and NCD prevention strategies at global, regional, national and local levels.

The importance of reflecting on the role that law can play in promoting healthier diets becomes even more acute when the issue of childhood obesity is framed as a children's rights issue. Policy documents increasingly refer to the added value of a human rights approach to the prevention and control of NCDs, which the WHO NCD Global Action Plan mentions as one of its nine overarching principles.[39] ECHO highlighted that the child's right to health should be the first guiding principle of interventions intended to end childhood obesity:

> Government and society have a moral responsibility to act on behalf of the child to reduce the risk of obesity. Tackling childhood obesity resonates with the universal acceptance of the rights of the child to a healthy life as well as the obligations assumed by State Parties to the Convention of the Rights of the Child.[40]

---

[38] Ibid, para 21.
[39] It should be recognized that the enjoyment of the highest attainable standard of health is one of the fundamental rights of every human being, without distinction of race, colour, sex, language, religion, political or other opinion, national or social origin, property, birth or other status, as enshrined in the Universal Declaration of Human Rights.
[40] ECHO Report, n2, 8, see also 10 and 40.

A children's rights approach to obesity and NCD prevention implies that the UN Convention on the Rights of the Child (CRC)[41] – the most ratified human rights instrument in the world – and other international human rights instruments should guide all policies that have a foreseeable impact on children, including the regulation of commercial practices that negatively affect them. Adopting such an approach has several benefits:

- Accountability – A children's rights approach guarantees a degree of State accountability, making effective remedies more likely where rights are violated. This, in turn, facilitates the translation of the commitments and obligations established in the CRC into practicable, long-lasting and realizable entitlements, guaranteed by independent monitoring bodies, including courts and national human rights institutions.
- Empowerment – Once the concept of 'rights' is introduced in policy-making, the rationale for preventing childhood obesity no longer comes only from the fact that children have needs but also from the fact that they have rights – entitlements that give rise to legal obligations on the part of States.
- Legitimacy – Because children's rights are inalienable and universal, there is an inherent legitimacy to the language of human rights. Consequently, arguments based on children's rights can ensure that an issue is given special consideration and that competing interests lose legitimacy if they are incompatible with children's rights.
- Advocacy – An approach based on human rights provides an opportunity to build strategic alliances, coalitions and networks with other actors who share a similar vision and pursue common objectives. In relation to childhood obesity, a children's rights approach is likely to encourage the involvement of a broad range of actors who may not have viewed marketing of unhealthy food to children as a concern of children's rights. In turn, this is likely to help galvanize political will and increase pressure on governments to ensure that they comply with their human rights obligations, particularly under the CRC.[42]

The CRC was adopted 40 years ago, when obesity was not seen as a major global public health problem. Like other human rights instruments, however, it should be interpreted in order to provide guidance to States facing new challenges: as noted by the Committee on the Rights of the Child, which is

---

[41] United Nations, 'Convention on the Rights of the Child', adopted and opened for signature, ratification and accession by General Assembly resolution 44/25 of 20 November 1989, entry into force 2 September 1990.
[42] *A Child Rights-Based Approach to Food Marketing: A Guide for Policy Makers* (Unicef 2018), at para 3.1.2.

entrusted with the interpretation and monitoring of the CRC, 'children's health is affected by a variety of factors, many of which have changed during the past 20 years and are likely to continue to evolve in the future'.[43] States should therefore prioritize issues, such as the availability of 'safe and nutritionally adequate food' and the shaping of 'a healthy and safe environment', which have gained in prominence in recent years.[44] It has also been argued that the set of WHO recommendations on the marketing of foods and non-alcoholic beverages to children should guide the interpretation of what the CRC requires from countries to ensure that they uphold their legal obligation to protect children's rights from harmful business practices.[45] More generally, global health law and policy should guide the interpretation of what the CRC and other international human rights instruments require from State Parties to ensure that they uphold their legal obligation to respect, protect and fulfil human rights, including where necessary by regulating the food industry and prohibiting harmful commercial practices.[46]

Nevertheless, despite the growing interest in, and potential of, human rights-based approaches to obesity and NCD prevention, few States are likely to meet their commitment to halt the rise of obesity given existing policies and practices.

4. THE GLOBAL AGRI-FOOD INDUSTRY AND CHANGING FOOD SYSTEMS: MOVING TARGETS FOR EFFECTIVE REGULATORY INTERVENTION

The incidence of obesity is directly related to the nature of food environments,[47] and to food systems at the local and national levels that have been

---

[43] CRC, General Comment No. 15, on the right of the child to the enjoyment of the highest attainable standard of health, UN Doc CRC/C/GC/15, 17 April 2013, para 5.

[44] Office of the United Nations High Commissioner for Human Rights, 'The Right of the Child to the Enjoyment of the Highest Attainable Standard of Health', Geneva, 2013, para 99.

[45] Unicef, n42. See also K Ó Cathaoir, *A Children's Rights Approach to Obesogenic Marketing* (2017) PhD thesis (mimeo), University of Copenhagen.

[46] A Garde, 'Global Health Law and Non-communicable Disease Prevention: Maximizing Opportunities by Understanding Constraints', in G Burci and B Toebes, *Research Handbook on Global Health Law* (Edward Elgar 2018), 420. See also Unicef, *Advocacy Brief for 30th Anniversary of the CRC: Protecting Children's Right to a Healthy Food Environment*, Geneva, November 2019.

[47] K Witten and J Pierce (eds), *Geographies of Obesity: Environmental Understandings of the Obesity Epidemic* (Routledge 2010).

described as 'toxic'.[48] These environments are heavily shaped by the operations of multinational agricultural and food corporations (agri-food MNCs) at the global level.[49] Taken collectively, agri-food MNCs have structured food production, distribution and retail systems around the world that promote the increased consumption of processed and ultra-processed food,[50] and the widespread westernization of diets.[51] Such 'international forces' are key drivers of the 'obesity engine'.[52] As Swinburn and colleagues have noted, obesity results mainly from 'changes in the global food system', making it a 'predictable outcome of market economies predicated on consumption-based growth'.[53]

This form of growth has been promoted by decades of economic policies at national and international levels, prioritizing trade and investment liberalization, marketization and deregulation. The resulting globalized food system has, in turn, catalysed the growth of obesity,[54] through intensified trade in a broadened range of food commodities, global sourcing, foreign investment, global food marketing, retail restructuring and the rise of supermarkets, urbanization, westernization, and the development of global economic rules

---

[48] K Brownell and K Horgen, *Food Fight: The Inside Story of the Food Industry, America's Obesity Crisis and What We Can Do About It* (McGraw-Hill 2003). On obesogenic environments see also, A Lake (et al. eds), *Obesogenic Environments: Complexities, Perceptions and Objective Measures* (Wiley-Blackwell 2010).

[49] C Hawkes and S Murphy, 'An Overview of Global Food Trade' in C Hawkes (et al. eds), *Trade, Food, Diet and Health: Perspectives and Policy Options* (Wiley-Blackwell 2010).

[50] C Monteiro, et al., 'Ultra-Processed Products are Becoming Dominant in the Global Food System' (2013) 14 *Obesity Reviews* 21; J Wilkinson, 'The Food Processing Industry, Globalization and Developing Countries' (2004) 1 *e-Journal of Agricultural and Development Economics* 184; C Monteiro, 'The Big Issue is Ultra-Processing' (2010) 1 *World Nutrition* 237.

[51] P Pingali, 'Westernization of Asian Diets and the Transformation of Food Systems: Implications for Research and Policy' (2006) 32 *Food Policy* 281. As Etilé and Oberlander have noted, the concerns relating to trade openness are compounded by the social aspects of globalization, such as exposure to foreign cultures, which are important in explaining the change in dietary habits: 'The Economics of Diet and Obesity: Understanding the Global Trends', Oxford Research Encyclopaedia of Economics and Finance, March 2019.

[52] B Popkin, 'Global Dynamics in Childhood Obesity: Reflections on a Life of Work in the Field' in M Freemark (ed.), *Paediatric Obesity: Etiology, Pathogenesis and Treatment* (Springer 2010), 3.

[53] B Swinburn, et al. 'The Global Obesity Pandemic: Shaped by Global Drivers and Local Environments' (2011) 378 *Lancet* 804, 804

[54] C Hawkes, 'Uneven Dietary Development: Linking the Policies and Processes of Globalization with the Nutrition Transition, Obesity and Diet-Related Chronic Diseases' (2006) 2 *Global Health* 4.

and governance institutions conducive to the emergence of the transnational agri-food industry.⁵⁵

This industry is now highly concentrated;⁵⁶ 50 large food manufacturers, mostly controlled by firms from the global North, account for half of global food sales,⁵⁷ and the prevailing trend is currently towards even greater concentration.⁵⁸ The biggest year ever for mergers and acquisitions globally in the agri-business field was 2015,⁵⁹ seeing 42,300 known deals with a total value of US$ 4.7 trillion.⁶⁰ In 2017, the four largest manufacturers of breakfast cereals controlled 62 per cent of the global market and the four largest baby food producers controlled 60 per cent.⁶¹ The power of the industry has been enhanced by the intense lobbying of agri-food MNCs in Northern policy-making centres such as Brussels and Washington DC, backed by capacious budgets and economic power.⁶²

The intense re-structuring of local food systems in line with global demands, led by increasingly concentrated and powerful agri-food MNCs, strengthens the industrial and processed food model.⁶³ Local food environments are more obesogenic as a result and efforts to protect public health undermined.⁶⁴ In

---

⁵⁵ Ibid., 5; M Qaim, 'Globalisation of Agrifood Systems and Sustainable Nutrition' (2017) 76 *Proceedings of the Nutrition Society* 12, 19; A Drewnowski, et al., 'International Trade, Food and Diet Costs, and the Global Obesity Epidemic' in C Hawkes (et al. eds), n49.

⁵⁶ T Weis, *The Global Food Economy: The Battle for the Future of Farming* (Zed Books 2007).

⁵⁷ *Agrifood Atlas: Facts and Figures about the Corporations that Control What We Eat* (Heinrich Böll Foundation 2017), 28.

⁵⁸ Ibid., 6–12.

⁵⁹ M Farrell, '2015 Becomes the Biggest M&A Year Ever', *Wall Street Journal*, 3 December 2015.

⁶⁰ 'Mergers and Acquisitions Review: Financial Advisors – Full Year 2015', Thomson Reuters, 2015.

⁶¹ *Agrifood Atlas*, n57, 29. These figures might be compared to a general rule of thumb accepted by most economists that a market is no longer competitive when four actors control more than 40 per cent of it, at which point collusive and coercive behaviour is deemed to have become 'unproductive'. See, P Howard, *Concentration and Power in the Food System: Who Controls What We Eat* (Bloomsbury 2016).

⁶² *Agrifood Atlas*, n57, 44–5. On the soda industry more specifically, see M Nestle, *Soda Politics: Taking on Big Soda (and Winning)* (OUP 2015); and A Taylor and M Jacobson, 'Carbonating the world: the marketing and health impact of sugar drinks in low-and-middle income countries', Center for Science in the Public Interest, Washington DC, 2016.

⁶³ G Kennedy, et al., *Globalization of Food Systems in Developing Countries: Impact on Food Security and Nutrition* (Food and Agricultural Organization 2004).

⁶⁴ W James, et al., 'An International Perspective on Obesity and Obesogenic Environments' in A Lake (et al eds), n48.

particular, LMICs are undergoing a significant nutrition transition as a result of their increased reliance on food imports, and the incidence of obesity and other NCDs is forecast to continue to rise sharply due to a homogenization of the global food system and the restructuring of traditional production, markets and diets.[65]

Incessant and aggressive expansion into developing markets is driven by a fall in the profits of agri-food MNCs in the developed North due to market saturation, and by some change in consumption patterns towards healthier products.[66] To maintain desired levels of shareholder value and the rates of profit needed to sustain it, many of the leading agri-food MNCs have adopted business models that rely heavily on rapid expansion into developing countries.[67] As a result, for example, in the Latin American and Caribbean (LAC) region overall sales from fast food chains roughly doubled in the period 2008–16, from US$ 8.9 billion to 16.3 billion.[68] Similar patterns are replicated across the developing world.[69] Obesogenic food environments are therefore intensifying in the wake of major transformations aligning local food systems with the needs of the global agri-food industry.[70] Ubiquitous policies of liberalization and agri-food privatization throughout the LAC and other developing regions have realigned local goals and practices to the demands of a global economy, ushering in 'the rapid rise of supermarkets, large processors, fast food chains and food logistics firms'.[71] Government control of the food system has been routinely dismantled without any effective regulation to replace it, leading to the creation of a largely unmanaged private system with serious social consequences and health impacts.[72]

---

[65] S Anand, et al., 'Food Consumption and its Impact on Cardiovascular Disease: Importance of Solutions Focused on the Globalized Food System' (2015) 66 *Journal of the American College of Cardiology* 1590, 1591.

[66] M Christian and G Gereffi, 'Fast-Food Value Chains and Childhood Obesity: A Global Perspective' in M Freemark (ed.), *Paediatric Obesity: Etiology, Pathogenesis and Treatment* (2nd edn, Springer 2018), 723–6; *Agrifood Atlas*, n57, 28.

[67] Nestlé generated 70 per cent of its sales outside Europe and North America in 2015, and the figure for Unilever was 75 per cent. *Agrifood Atlas*, n57, 42.

[68] B Popkin and T Reardon, 'Obesity and the Food System Transformation in Latin America' (2018) 19(8) *Obesity Reviews* 1028.

[69] For further discussion on China and Russia, e.g., see Christian and Gereffi, n66, 723–5; D Berman, 'When Global Value Chains are Not Global: Case Studies from the Russian Fast-Food Industry' (2011) 15 *Competition and Change* 274; G Gereffi and M Christian, 'Trade, Transnational Corporations and Food Consumption: A Global Value Chain Approach' in C Hawkes (et al. eds) n49, 99.

[70] Popkin and Reardon, n68, 1.

[71] Ibid.

[72] See further, R Vogli, et al., 'The Influence of Deregulation on Fast Food Consumption and Body Mass Index: A Cross-National Time Series Analysis' (2014) 92 *Bulletin of the World Health Organization* 99.

The 'global value chains' (GVCs) on which the agri-food industry relies are among the most important drivers of obesity; therefore the responses, including the legal responses, should be transnational in nature.[73] A GVC perspective clarifies how 'corporate strategies and international processes relating to the production, distribution and marketing of fast-food (and agri-food) companies are linked to childhood obesity as a health problem'.[74] In short, the main features of a GVC approach place the macro-level of operations and processes within the global economy in the foreground,[75] through identification and analysis of 'lead' agri-food MNCs as major actors and drivers in the field. It then links this analysis to a theoretical framework on 'dietary dependence'. The latter framework refers to the mode of integration of a particular country or locality into the global economy via GVCs. It assesses the extent to which local diets are dependent on imported products and processed food supplied by agri-food MNCs and otherwise heavily shaped by their practices,[76] fundamentally determining patterns of local food availability, consumption, habits and food choices in favour of unhealthy options.[77]

The observed power differential between agri-food MNCs and local institutional actors, including regulators, consumers and producers, also tilts the balance of social, political and even legal decision-making in favour of an economic rationale (jobs, investment, growth, reduced prices…) over public health. This, again, privileges the interests of agri-food MNCs, expands their reach and further entrenches their influence. Importantly, agri-food MNCs can systematically take advantage, through their cross-border GVCs, of weaker regulatory environments in developing markets, enabling resistance, avoidance or the undermining of nationally based initiatives to combat obesogenic environments and control harmful business practices.

---

[73] See Gereffi and Christian, n69; G Gereffi, et al., 'US-Based Food and Agricultural Value Chains and Their Relevance to Healthy Diets' (2009) 4 *Journal of Hunger Environment and Nutrition* 357. See also, T Sturgeon, 'From Commodity Chains to Value Chains: Interdisciplinary Theory-Building in the Age of Globalization' in J Bair (ed.), *Frontiers of Commodity Chain Research* (Stanford University Press 2009).
[74] Christian and Gereffi, n66, 726.
[75] Ibid., 719.
[76] D Stuckler, et al., 'Manufacturing Epidemics: The Role of Global Producers in Increased Consumption of Unhealthy Commodities Including Processed Foods, Alcohol and Tobacco' (2012) 9 *Policy Forum* 1.
[77] G Rayner, et al., 'Trade Liberalization and the Diet Transition: A Public Health Response' (2006) 21 *Health Promotion International* 67.

The Need to Address the Globalization of Food Systems Through International Cooperation

The causes of, and the structure of appropriate solutions to, growing rates of childhood obesity cannot be approached without a fundamental appreciation of this global, cross-border context.[78] Yet, insufficient attention has been paid to the global dimension of the fight against obesity. As Hawkes and Popkin have noted, while many countries are taking actions to promote healthier eating at the national level, few of them are truly taking on the broader food system, its priorities and its entire structure.[79] The search for solutions must be attentive to the power imbalance that now applies between agri-food MNCs and many public institutions, particularly in LMICs.

The cross-border dimension of childhood obesity is now increasingly acknowledged,[80] and so is the need for transnational cooperation to address it. For example, ECHO has called for the implementation of 'a standardized global nutrient labelling system', as recommended by the Codex Alimentarius Commission[81] (Recommendation 1.6) and to 'establish cooperation between member States to reduce the impact of cross-border marketing of unhealthy foods and beverages' (Recommendation 1.5). To date, however, little has been done to effectively address the transnational impact of agri-food MNCs on the scale that this challenge demands.

The Ambiguous Status of MNCs in the Development and Implementation of obesity and NCD

In part, the difficulties encountered may stem from the ability of agri-food MNCs to capture State power and use it to their advantage. Certain WHO instruments seek to address the risk of corporate capture and conflicts of interests. Most notably, the Framework Convention on Tobacco Control (FCTC) contains a specific and unequivocal prohibition against the involvement of the tobacco industry in the development and implementation of tobacco control

---

[78] Qaim, n55, 12.
[79] C Hawkes and B Popkin, 'Can the Sustainable Development Goals Reduce the Burden of Nutrition-Related Non-Communicable Diseases Without Truly Addressing Major Food System Reforms?' (2015) 13 *BMC Medicine* 143, 145.
[80] Lancet Report, n16.
[81] Resolution WHA 56.23 Joint FAO/WHO evaluation of the work of the Codex Alimentarius Commission. In May 2019, the Codex Alimentarius Committee on Food Labelling began formal negotiations on guiding principles for the development of front-of-pack nutrition labelling.

policies.⁸² Similarly, the International Code of Marketing of Breast-milk Substitutes calls upon member States to ban all commercial marketing of breast-milk substitutes in consideration of the special vulnerabilities of mothers to commercial influence, implicitly recognizing that governments had been hitherto insufficiently willing to challenge the ability for food manufacturers to shape consumers' choices.⁸³ Similarly, the WHO set of recommendations on the marketing of foods and non-alcoholic beverages to children also highlight that Governments should be the key stakeholders in the development of policy and that they should protect the public interest and avoiding conflict of interest.⁸⁴

However, the 2004 WHO Strategy on Diet, Physical Activity and Health is less clear on the role that it envisages for the food industry in the prevention and control of overweight and obesity.⁸⁵ The main aim of the WHO strategy was to encourage the food and beverage sectors primarily in Europe and the USA to do far more to improve nutrition and help tackle obesity prevention. Led by both European and US sugar trade lobbyists, these powerful sectors had adopted confrontational positions. Prior to the WHO Executive Board meeting in Geneva where the draft strategy was to be considered, they appeared to have secured strong support from the US Government. This attempt to derail the WHO Strategy was effectively blocked by an open letter from Professor Kaare Norum, the Norwegian chair of the WHO's strategy reference group.⁸⁶ The wording of the WHO Strategy nonetheless remains ambiguous concerning the involvement it foresees for food companies and their associations. Not only does it explicitly encourage governments to consult stakeholders on policy, including the private sector and the media, but it also encourages them to establish mechanisms to promote their participation in activities related to diet, physical activity and health,⁸⁷ thus increasing the risk that conflicts of interest impede change. It also provides that '[WHO] will hold discussions with the transnational food industry and other parts of the private sector in support of the aims of the Strategy, and of implementing the recommendations in countries'.⁸⁸ In other words, it starts from the premise that the food industry

---

⁸² FCTC, Art 5(3).
⁸³ WHO International Code of Marketing of Breast-milk Substitutes, Art 5(1).
⁸⁴ Resolution WHA 63.14, Recommendation 6. Discussed in A Garde et al., 'Implementing the WHO Recommendations whilst Avoiding Real, Perceived or Potential Conflicts of Interest' (2017) 8(2) *European Journal of Risk Regulation* 237.
⁸⁵ WHO, n19.
⁸⁶ K Norum, 'World Health Organization's Global Strategy on Diet, Physical Activity and Health: The Process Behind the Scenes' (2005) 49 *Scandinavian Journal of Nutrition* 83.
⁸⁷ WHO, n19, para 44.
⁸⁸ Ibid., para 50.

can play a positive role in the prevention and control of overweight and obesity worldwide, even though it has not defined in any specific terms what this role could be. Of course, hearing from industry is, of itself, not problematic. However, putting already powerful and influential companies in an institutionally privileged position to shape opinions, advice, or standards upon which governments rely may be seen as an abdication of responsibility against the public interest.[89]

A 2018 UN Political Declaration on NCDs calls on States and the international community to:

> [e]ngage with the private sector, taking into account national health priorities and objectives for its meaningful and effective contribution to the implementation of national responses to non-communicable diseases in order to reach Sustainable Development Goal target 3.4 on non-communicable diseases, while giving due regard to managing conflicts of interest.[90]

Unfortunately, however, the specific terms of engagement with the food industry remain undefined. There is still no consensus on what the phrase 'giving due regard to managing conflicts of interest' should mean. Clear rules are needed to ensure that real, potential and perceived conflicts of interest are acknowledged and carefully managed.[91]

In this ambiguous context, States and international institutions have often relied extensively on 'agri-food' MNCs to take the organizational lead, drive change and solve problems through public-private food 'partnerships'.[92] Even the most powerful States, such as the US, feel compelled to do so by the influence of the industry.[93] As a result, not only food production and delivery but also the response to childhood obesity becomes overwhelmingly designed according to the needs of the agri-food industry rather than the requirements of the environment, sustainability or public health.[94] In fact, given the dominant

---

[89] A Garde et al., n84.

[90] Political declaration of the 3rd High-Level Meeting of the General Assembly on the Prevention and Control of Non-Communicable Diseases, UN Doc A/RES/73/2, 17 October 2018, para 43.

[91] Note that some WHO instruments use the language of conflicts of interest avoidance rather than conflicts of interest management. See, e.g., the set of WHO recommendations on the marketing of food and non-alcoholic beverages to children, n84.

[92] Monteiro and Cannon, n9, 3.

[93] E Fried, 'The Potential for Policy Initiatives to Address the Obesity Epidemic: A Legal Perspective from the United States' in D Crawford (et al. eds), *Obesity Epidemiology: From Aetiology to Public Health* (OUP 2010) 324.

[94] Anand, et al., n65, 1593.

form of development shaped by economic globalization, 'obesity and serious chronic diseases can be seen as an integral part of economic development'.[95]

This ambiguity concerning the role agri-food MNCs may be able to play in preventing childhood obesity has systematically been used by the industry: it explains the adoption of 'pledges' and voluntary commitments, ostensibly to 'partner' in addressing the challenge, in fact to remove the need for more robust regulatory interventions. However, and as Anand Grover, UN Special Rapporteur on the right to the highest attainable standard of health between 2008 and 2014, stated:

> Owing to the inherent problems associated with self-regulation and public–private partnerships, there is a need for States to adopt laws that prevent companies from using insidious marketing strategies. The responsibility to protect the enjoyment of the right to health warrants State intervention in situations when third parties, such as food companies, use their position to influence dietary habits by directly or indirectly encouraging unhealthy diets, which negatively affect people's health. Therefore, States have a positive duty to regulate unhealthy food advertising and the promotion strategies of food companies. Under the right to health, States are especially required to protect vulnerable groups such as children from violations of their right to health.[96]

More work is urgently needed to determine what role the food industry should have and what would amount to conflicts of interest.[97] The assumption cannot be that because food is different from tobacco, partnerships with the food industry in addressing unhealthy diets are appropriate and likely to be

---

[95] Monteiro and Cannon, n9, 3.

[96] Report of the Special Rapporteur on the Right of Everyone to the Enjoyment of the Highest Attainable Standard of Physical and Mental Health, Anand Grover, 'Unhealthy Foods, Non-communicable Diseases and the Right to Health', UN Doc A/HRC/26/31, 1 April 2014, para 25. This statement follows from an earlier statement made by Olivier De Schutter, the UN Special Rapporteur on the Right to Food, in 2011:
> It is unacceptable that when lives are at stake, we go no further than soft, promotional measures that ultimately rely on consumer choice, without addressing the supply side of the food chain. […] Food advertising is *proven* to have a strong impact on children and must be strictly regulated in order to avoid the development of bad eating habits early in life.

'World Leaders Must Take Binding Steps to Curb Unhealthy Food Industry – UN Expert', *UN News*, 16 September 2011. See further, Report Submitted by the Special Rapporteur on the Right to Food, Olivier De Schutter, UN Doc A/HRC/1/9/59, 26 December 2011. More recently, see also Unicef, n46.

[97] Some work has been done, in particular: WHO, 'Addressing and Managing Conflicts of Interest in the Planning and Delivery of Nutrition Programmes at Country Level', WHO, Geneva, 2016; and M Mwatsama (ed.), *Public Health and the Food and Drinks Industry: The Governance and Ethics of Interaction. Lessons from Research, Policy and Practice* (UK Health Forum 2018).

effective. Public-private partnerships with the food and alcohol industries have inherent limits. States should adopt laws and regulations that will allow them to provide the level-playing field that MNCs require to operate fairly in a globalized world, whilst meeting their obligation to ensure the enjoyment of the highest attainable standard of health for all.

5. INTERNATIONAL ECONOMIC LAW AS A CATALYST TO CHILDHOOD OBESITY AND A CONSTRAINT ON STATES

As Magnusson has put it, 'with large profits at stake, there is a struggle for regulatory control',[98] and history has shown that the tobacco, alcohol and food industries deploy a broad range of corporate tactics,[99] including legal challenges against measures which could reduce their profit margins. In particular, they have argued that a range of NCD prevention policies adopted by States, as part of their attempts to promote public health, infringe international trade and/or investment law. Such legal arguments are based on claims that State policy in the public interest unjustifiably reduces the consumption of goods freely traded across the world, including tobacco products, alcoholic beverages and unhealthy food – the products most directly implicated in growing rates of NCDs around the world.

Obesity and Economic Liberalization

International trade and investment law rests on the premise that economic liberalization, by allocating resources efficiently, leads to greater competition and lower prices, and therefore increases opportunities for States, consumers and businesses alike.[100] However, several empirical studies have established

---

[98] R Magnusson, 'What's Law Got to Do with It? Part 1: A Framework for Obesity Prevention' (2008) 5 *Australia and New Zealand Health* Policy.

[99] The tactics used by the food industries, and their comparison with those used by the tobacco industries, are increasingly well documented. See, e.g., R Moodie et al., 'Profits and Pandemics: Prevention of Harmful Effects of Tobacco, Alcohol, and Ultra-Processed Food and Drink Industries', (2013) 381 *The Lancet* 670; S Steele, et al., 'The Role of Public Law-Based Litigation in Tobacco Companies' Strategies in High-Income, FCTC Ratifying Countries, 2004–14' (2016) 38 Journal of Public Health 516; and M Nestle, n63; A Taylor and M Jacobson, n63; R Moodie, 'What Public Health Practitioners Need to Know About Unhealthy Industry Tactics' (2017) 107 *American Journal of Public Health* 1047.

[100] For an introduction to international trade law and its rationale, see M Trebilcock, *Advanced Introduction to International Trade Law* (Edward Elgar 2015). See also, V Lowe, *International Law* (OUP 2007) chapter 6.

a link between trade liberalization and increasing rates of obesity[101] and the expansion of processed food markets in developing countries.[102] Although this is a general phenomenon, Small Island Developing States (SIDS) in the Pacific and the Caribbean regions are spectacular illustrations, due to their high reliance on imports of processed and semi-processed food which have grown much faster than imports of raw foodstuffs, and have led to a dramatic increase in obesity and related NCDs.[103]

Heightened dependence on food imports seriously threatens the viability of local food systems, a phenomenon that is particularly worrisome in LMICs. The UN has predicted that for developing countries as a whole the deficit between food imports and exports will widen markedly by 2030, to an overall net import level of US$ 31 billion.[104] ECHO highlighted the impact of trade policies and the globalization of the food system on food affordability, availability and quality at national and local levels,[105] calling for the consideration

---

[101] See A Thow and W Snowdon, 'The Effect of Trade and Trade Policy on Diet and Health in the Pacific Islands' in C Hawkes et al. (eds), n49, 147–68.

[102] A Thow and C Hawkes, 'The Implications of Trade Liberalization for Diet and Health: A Case Study from Central America' (2009) 5 *Global Health*. See also P Baker, A Kay and H Walls, 'Trade and Investment Liberalization and Asia's Non-communicable Disease Epidemic: A Synthesis of Data and Existing Literature' 92014) 10(1) *Globalization and Health* 66; A Schram, et al., 'The Role of Trade and Investment Liberalization and the Sugar-sweetened Carbonated Beverages Market: A Natural Experiment Contrasting Vietnam and the Philippines', *Globalization and Health* 11(1) (2015) 41; and P Baker, et al., 'Trade and Investment Liberalization, Food Systems Change and Highly Processed Food Consumption: A Natural Experiment Contrasting the Soft-drink Markets of Peru and Bolivia' (2016) 12(1) *Globalization and Health* 24.

[103] For Caribbean SIDS, see A Yearwood and A Samuels, 'Evidence Brief: Improving the Healthiness of Food Environments in the Caribbean', Caribbean Public Health Agency, June 2016. On the evaluation of the Port of Spain Declaration on NCDs, see A Samuels and N Unwin, 'Accelerating Action on NCDs', PAHO/WHO and CARICOM, September 2016. For Pacific SIDS, see A Thow, et al., 'Trade and Food Policy: Case Studies from Three Pacific Island Countries' (2010) 35 *Food Policy* 6.

[104] J Bruinsma (ed.), *World Agriculture: Towards 2015/2030 – An FAO Perspective* (FAO/Earthscan 2003) 235–6. See further, P Pingali, n51, 286–7. The islands of Trinidad and Tobago demonstrate how an entire country's food supply system can become dependent on imports; Gereffi and Christian, n69, 101–2.

[105] See ECHO Report, n2, 8. For more detail, see also: WHO, *Consideration of the Evidence on Childhood Obesity for the Commission on Ending Childhood Obesity: Report of the Ad hoc Working Group on Science and Evidence for Ending Childhood Obesity* (WHO 2016) 117.

of the health and equity impacts of national and international economic agreements and policies.[106]

> The Commission has noted the important influence that trade policies can have on the obesogenic environment. This is particularly the case for [SIDS] that are highly dependent on imported foods and where the nature of the food supply and pricing are largely determined by the trade dynamics. The Commission acknowledges the complexity of international trade, particularly in food and agricultural products, but urges member States and those involved in international trade arrangements to seek ways to address the trade issues that impact on child obesity.[107]

International Economic Law and Childhood Obesity Prevention

Notwithstanding its complexity, the fact remains that international trade law does recognize that member States can invoke public interest objectives, not least public health protection, to justify exceptions to the general principle that goods should move freely across national borders.[108] In particular, World Trade Organization (WTO) agreements (not least the 1994 General Agreement on Tariffs and Trade) acknowledge that WTO Members are primarily responsible for protecting the health of their citizens, and should therefore have a broad margin of discretion as to both the level of protection they intend to achieve and the means they intend to use to do so.

However, this discretion is subject to compliance with WTO rules, including the principles of non-discrimination and proportionality. First, WTO Members must ensure that the measures they take to protect public health are non-discriminatory, i.e., they must not distort free trade by putting imported goods at a disadvantage over domestic goods in a competitive relationship. Health promoting measures must be neutral in this regard and should not favour domestic producers – except when there is a health rationale for doing so, as opposed to a protectionist intent.[109] Secondly, when a State adopts

---

[106] ECHO Report, n2, 17. ECHO referred to the work of the Commission on Social Determinants of Health: Closing the gap in a generation: health equity through action on the social determinants of health. Final Report of the Commission on Social Determinants of Health. Geneva, WHO, 2008.

[107] ECHO Report, n2, 37.

[108] See, inter alia: B McGrady, *Trade and Public Health: The WTO, Tobacco, Alcohol, and Diet* (CUP 2011). See also T Voon, 'WTO Law and Risk Factors for Non-Communicable Diseases: A Complex Relationship', in G Van Calster and D Prevost (eds), Research Handbook on Environment, Health and the WTO (Edward Elgar 2013); O De Schutter, *Trade in the Service of Sustainable Development* (Hart 2015).

[109] The notion of discrimination has been construed broadly to cover both direct and indirect discrimination.

a potentially trade-restrictive measure, it must ensure that this measure pursues a legitimate objective (such as the protection of public health) and is necessary to achieve it. The means employed must therefore be proportionate, or in other words adapted to the policy objective, as defined by the State, and free trade may only be restricted to the extent necessary to achieve this objective.[110] International investment law also requires a similar attention to principles of non-discrimination and proportionality with respect to the treatment of foreign investors, as well as adherence to an evidence-based and legitimate policy objective. There are some additional considerations, however, in relation to investment law, including the need for States to clarify that investors may face future regulation as may be required to adhere to human rights and other State obligations mandating the protection of the population. These issues are discussed thoroughly in Part II and recapped in the Conclusion.[111]

Therefore, and importantly, the opportunities highlighted above that the law offers to promote healthier food environments and regulate agri-food MNCs will only be maximized if the constraints that international economic law imposes are well understood.[112] The more robust the regulatory rules and their evidence base, the less likely it is that agri-food MNCs will be able to challenge them successfully. The developing global consensus on what should be done to tackle NCDs, and child obesity more specifically, provides a solid foundation of evidence that States could adduce to support their regulatory strategies and, where necessary, defend any challenges to national rules that may restrict free trade and foreign investment. Global health law, international human rights and international economic law should be complementary and mutually supportive with a view to ensuring an optimal balance between potentially competing interests, putting the SDGs and the rights of the child at their heart.[113]

6.   STRUCTURE OF THIS EDITED COLLECTION

The contributions this volume brings together discuss the role of law in promoting healthier diets and the interaction between international human rights

---

[110] In the absence of a detailed set of principles against which to test the necessity of regulatory action, the scope of this principle has largely been defined by the Dispute Settlement System of the WTO.

[111] On the interaction between international investment law and NCD prevention, see also A Garde and J Zrilic (eds), Special Issue, *Journal of World Investment and Trade* (forthcoming, autumn 2020). See in particular the contribution by Marcelo Campbell on the challenges to Chile's food labelling and advertising legislation.

[112] A Garde, n46.

[113] Ibid, 418.

and economic law in the protection of children and the prevention of childhood obesity. This collection does not purport to offer a comprehensive account of all the legal issues relevant to childhood obesity: in particular, it does not focus on physical activity (e.g., local planning laws, employment law...) or on the medical treatment of obesity and related NCDs (access to medicines...). These omissions should not be read as suggesting that these issues are not important components of health promotion and childhood obesity prevention strategies. The emphasis of this book, however, is on the regulation of the food industry as an essential component of a broader strategy to halt the rise of childhood obesity. We have aimed to provide a range of tools that States and other policy actors may want to use in the development and implementation of obesity prevention strategies at national, regional or global levels, including those intended to promote a more systematic reliance on human rights discourses and enforcement mechanisms.

We believe that part of the originality of this volume mirrors some of the difficulty encountered in constructing it: we have tried to reflect not only on international human rights law and on international economic law in isolation, but also on their relationship. This is difficult because there tends to be little overlap between human rights lawyers and international economic lawyers. Nevertheless, we have attempted to bridge the gap in order to demonstrate how human rights instruments can shed light on inherently economic issues. If we accept that business activities do have an impact on children's rights, then such engagement is indeed paramount. We hope that our complementary expertise and interests will have helped bring a wider range of issues and ideas to the fore than each one of us could have done alone.

This book should therefore be seen as complementing existing literature on the relationship between NCD prevention and international economic law, on the one hand, and NCD prevention and human rights law, on the other. As such, it is intended to contribute – modestly – to the ongoing efforts deployed to build legal capacity to address NCDs, and childhood obesity more specifically. There is a large spectrum of regulatory measures that States may take in order to combat child obesity. The potential for legal reform in this area is largely untapped, however. This is due, in part, to the powerful lobbying efforts of the food industry. It is also the result of an ideological belief in the virtues of 'consumer sovereignty', and in the correlative suspicion towards what libertarians call the 'nanny State'. Nevertheless, even where the democratic process is protected from undue influence by economic actors and where the libertarian ethos – individualistic, market-oriented, and suspicious of governmental intervention – is weak, States are hesitant to adopt a number of legal measures that could effectively transform the food environment and ensure that children adopt healthier eating habits: they may fear, indeed, that the regulation of food marketing or food composition, or the reshaping of food environments to encourage people to eat fresh and locally produced foods, violate commitments under free trade or investment agreements, for instance because they will be seen as discriminatory or as violating the rights of foreign investors. In many cases, a 'chilling effect' operates: even though certain regulatory measures would be perfectly compatible with their international undertakings, States may be hesitant to adopt such measures, in order to avoid the risk to its reputation that would result from being sued before an international court or an arbitral tribunal. Thus, a clear understanding of the relationship between the human rights duties of States, including their duty to protect the right to health, and international trade and investment law is a first and essential step towards a child obesity prevention strategy that uses the regulatory toolbox to its full potential. This book aims to contribute to this objective.

This book primarily addresses the role of law in preventing obesity. We are convinced, however, of the need for a broader interdisciplinary engagement to meet this challenge. Obesity is multifactorial, and as such it necessarily requires a trans-sectoral response. Interdisciplinarity must therefore be the foundation to meaningful work in this area, and it permeates the following collection. Nevertheless, we feel that the role of law is often insufficiently acknowledged and promoted, sometimes leading to an impoverished understanding and some confusion in the response to obesity. Our primary focus on the law is aimed at remedying this perception. However, law can only make an effective contribution if it properly incorporates existing evidence gathered and analysed by other disciplines. This book should therefore be seen as an attempt to promote the role of law; not to limit in any way the role of other disciplines or the role of non-legal tools, such as economic incentives, public information campaigns and the use of 'nudges' to encourage healthy diets and the promotion of a different, healthier food culture.

Chapter Outlines

The book follows a tripartite structure with respect to combatting childhood obesity: from an overarching treatment of the role of human rights law, to an in-depth appreciation of the nature and scope of international economic law, and finally to a more detailed examination of some regulatory aspects and actors suggested by a thorough commitment to human rights in the face of an ascendant global agri-food industry.

Three chapters in Part I highlight the essential contribution and distinct nature of a human rights approach to ending childhood obesity, and in particular the added value of adopting an approach grounded in human rights, and how such an approach can be complementary to approaches based in health science, behavioural science and economics.

Oscar Cabrera and Sarah Roache introduce the broad relevance of international human rights law, enumerating and expanding on the rights most relevant to this inquiry, not least the rights to health and food. They explain the different levels of obligation involved in the duties of States towards human rights, and they clarify the mutually supportive relationship between rights and obesity prevention. The chapter then digs deeper into the precise manner by which human rights interact and are balanced with each other, attending to conflicts between individual autonomy and the right to health or consumer's human rights and corporate claims to their own 'human' rights.

Katharina Ó Cathaoir and Mette Hartlev narrow the focus to specific health aspects of child rights. They draw on and meld together the CRC and the ECHO final report, proposing a child rights approach exhorting States to pursue three key policy goals: providing an enabling environment, pursuing empowerment through societal and legal transformation, and ensuring accountability. They conclude that human rights and public health can be mutually reinforcing, arguing that the WHO provides evidence-based technical guidance, while the CRC legally binds states. The WHO's recommendations can therefore concretize States' sometimes vague obligations under the child's right to health.

Marine Friant-Perrot and Nikhil Gokani then shine a spotlight on the relevance of human rights within the existing context of health inequality both across and within States. Widespread, systematic and entrenched inequalities in childhood obesity are noted between and within societies. Corrective action is required as a matter of social justice to restore children's autonomy, dignity and freedom in food choices. Friant-Perrot and Gokani argue that the right to non-discrimination offers an effective avenue to promote the protection of children from the causes of inequalities in obesity, obliging States to create an environment which grants every child the capacity to choose healthy food.

Part II turns to the precise nature of international economic law, teasing out the scope of the legal space available for States to implement regulatory and other measures to prevent obesity, both through analysis of theory and by providing important empirical context. The four chapters address some misunderstandings and oversimplifications often encountered in debates on economic law and public health policy, seeking a clarity that should encourage government action. This part also aims to indicate where the re-design of international economic law may be warranted to allow greater space for governments to end childhood obesity where it is needed.

Gregory Messenger clarifies the legal limits and nature of international trade law, in large part through a historical treatment of the regulation of sugar markets, from their colonial heritage to their current regulation by international institutions. Messenger questions the often-heard view according to which trade law presents an insurmountable barrier to the introduction of public health measures related to obesogenic goods. He argues that trade law has developed to accommodate the pursuit of legitimate public policy objectives and identifies sugar, in particular, as a possible catalyst for further accommodation in trade law between the pursuit of economic liberalization and public health policies by governments.

Caoimhín MacMaoláin then focuses on food labelling laws and guidelines, ascertaining which measures have been, or could be, effective in the context of restrictions imposed by trade law. He argues that existing trade obligations can act more as an impediment than as an aid to the use of labelling laws. Individual States have devised their own national labelling schemes, but trade obligations may make it difficult for them to compel or encourage anyone to use these schemes. MacMaoláin identifies which labelling types might therefore be the best ones to use to help to reduce childhood obesity in the current legal environment and points to alternative approaches that could facilitate the application of more meaningful and successful measures.

Mavluda Sattorova clarifies the effects of international investment law on potential government measures intended to prevent childhood obesity. She does so by revisiting an ongoing debate over the 'chilling effect' of investment treaties, situating the debate within some recent empirical case-studies. It is often argued that investment treaties may cause governments to abandon the adoption of public health regulations – 'regulatory chill' – but this may be avoided through reforms of investment treaty provisions as well as national laws on foreign investment. The chapter concludes by outlining the key issues that those implementing national childhood obesity measures need to be aware of in order to overcome any possible chilling factor and to ensure that new regulations are immune to legal challenges from affected investors.

Nicole Foster concludes this part by examining the problem of childhood obesity from a regional perspective using the experience of members of the Caribbean Community (CARICOM). The chapter explores whether CARICOM States' regional and multilateral trade commitments constitute significant legal obstacles to regional efforts to tackle childhood obesity, and comments on the potential role of international human rights law in accelerating action in this area. Foster ultimately concludes that while trade obligations do constrain their choice of public health measures and how they implement them, sufficient policy space still remains to take meaningful action. She also recommends leveraging international human rights and its enforcement mechanisms to push Caribbean governments to act more promptly and decisively, while still respecting their international trade obligations.

Following on from Foster's suggestion, Part III addresses certain additional tools provided by human rights law (and associated bodies and mechanisms) to move States in a regulatory direction and to provide them with useful and appropriate institutional and theoretical frameworks through which to act, particularly in controlling global agri-food MNCs and reshaping the global food system. Aside from expectations that States will act within the space allowed by economic law, human rights law suggests, and in some cases may require, additional regulatory, procedural, technical and institutional measures should States and other stakeholders choose to prioritize a human rights approach to childhood obesity prevention.

Wenche Barth Eide and Asbjørn Eide describe a broad set of institutional responses to childhood obesity that should be implemented within the UN system to maximize the benefits of a human rights approach. The chapter describes some obstacles within the UN to ensuring a coherent and effective human rights-based approach to development, emphasizing differences in the orientation of UN agencies. The authors focus on the WHO and the Food and Agriculture Organization (FAO), and argue that the General Assembly's proclamation of the UN Decade of Action on Nutrition 2016–2025 provides a new and promising impetus. They conclude with some ideas for further action which require new and reinforced alliances to strengthen the UN's work with a rights-based approach to malnutrition and childhood obesity.

Amandine Garde and Seamus Byrne pursue in further detail the balance of competing rights earlier introduced in the chapter by Cabrera and Roache. They elaborate on how a thorough and progressive implementation of the principle of the best interests of the child could provide an important device for balancing the competing interests of children and industry operators. The chapter demonstrates the importance of the principle of the best interests of the child in framing an acceptable legal space for regulatory measures, arguing that children's rights should be used throughout the policy process – from policy formulation to policy implementation, monitoring and evaluation – not only as a 'shield' against food industry challenges but also as a 'sword' to carve out space for appropriate regulation.

Oliver Bartlett considers the responsibility resting on MNCs to respect the right to health. Although international human rights law is addressed to States and does not impose direct legal obligations on corporate entities, the UN Guiding Principles on Business and Human Rights adopted by the Human Rights Council in June 2011 require MNCs to conduct human rights due diligence to reduce the risks that their business practices pose to the enjoyment of human rights. Bartlett argues that MNCs have a responsibility to engage in right to health due diligence, to address the ways in which their business practices contribute to the creation of obesogenic environments undermining the child's right to health. He also takes the position that if MNCs are unwilling to voluntarily conduct right to health due diligence, States should oblige them to do so. Furthermore, the 'horizontal effects' of constitutional rights to health on private actors might even provide grounding for courts to mandate such State regulation.

Maintaining Bartlett's focus on the primary corporate actors in the global food system, Joshua Curtis elaborates on the transnational procedures necessary to provide an effective legal remedy for the acts of agri-food MNCs in cross-border contexts that violate children's rights to be free from obesogenic environments. Strengthened transnational corporate accountability is a necessary element in the fight against childhood obesity given the global structure of the agri-food industry. Open and effective access of victims to courts in the home State of agri-food MNCs is a necessary element in such accountability. This chapter explores the feasibility and obstacles to the further opening of access to home State courts through a potential transnational case against Nestlé in Switzerland for aggressive marketing of breast-milk substitutes in the Philippines. Curtis argues that evolving conceptions of extraterritoriality and the development of extraterritorial human rights obligations provide a crucial normative framework supporting calls for the mandatory opening of home State courts and the broader construction of an international order capable of controlling corporate power.

Joshua Curtis and Amandine Garde's Concluding chapter draws out and weaves together the major themes and findings of the collection as a whole, with a particular eye to policy relevance and future orientation. This chapter takes an expressly forward-looking stance, reflecting specifically on the added value of a WHO Framework Convention on Obesity Prevention.

We are most grateful to our colleagues who have contributed to this volume, many of whom have been long-standing friends of the Law & NCD Unit[114] and without whom this endeavour would not have been possible. It has been a pleasure working with you all and we thank you for your patience: this project has been much longer in the making than we originally anticipated. We hope that you are nonetheless pleased with the result. We would also like to thank Edward Elgar for their support and for publishing this book in their Health and the Law series.

---

[114] For information on the activities of the Law & NCD Unit which sits in the School of Law and Social Justice at the University of Liverpool, see: https://www.liverpool.ac.uk/law/research/law-and-non-communicable-diseases/ (accessed 15 May 2020).

PART I

Human rights approach to childhood obesity prevention

2. International human rights and childhood obesity prevention

Sarah A Roache and Oscar A Cabrera[1]

1. INTRODUCTION

Human rights are generally understood as expressing a set of ethical requirements and as a set of rules embodied in international law. The Universal Declaration of Human Rights (UDHR),[2] which recognizes the 'inherent dignity' and 'inalienable rights' of all human beings, is widely accepted as one of the foundational instruments of international human rights law. Adopted in 1948 as a resolution of the United Nations General Assembly, the UDHR has informed and influenced a rich body of treaties, declarations, regional conventions, and domestic human rights protections, which form a legally binding framework for protecting and realizing human rights. The International Covenant on Civil and Political Rights[3] (ICCPR) and the International Covenant on Economic, Social and Cultural Rights[4] (ICESCR) have been ratified by more than 80 per cent of the world's countries.[5] Instruments such as the European Convention for the Protection of Human Rights and Fundamental Freedoms (also known as the European Convention on Human Rights)[6] or the

---

[1] The authors would like to thank Benny Chan for his contribution to researching and drafting this chapter, as well as Andrés Constantin for his editing support.
[2] Universal Declaration of Human Rights, G.A. Res. 271 (III) A (10 December 1948).
[3] International Covenant on Civil and Political Rights, 16 December 1966, 999 U.N.T.S. 171.
[4] International Covenant on Economic, Social and Cultural Rights, 16 December 1966, 993 U.N.T.S 3.
[5] United Nations Office of the High Commissioner (OHCHR), Status of Ratification Interaction Dashboard: International Covenant on Economic, Social and Cultural Rights, http://indicators.ohchr.org/ (last access date 28 September 2020).
[6] European Convention for the Protection of Human Rights and Fundamental Freedoms (ECHR) as amended by Protocols No. 11 and No. 14, 1 June 2010, E.T.S. No. 5.

European Social Charter[7] have allowed different regions of the world to articulate human rights in a manner sensitive to their culture and history. Recently, more specialized human rights treaties have emerged, focusing on issues such as torture[8] and vulnerable groups such as people with disabilities,[9] women[10] and children.[11]

This chapter analyzes the relevance of international human rights law to childhood obesity prevention. It explores the obligations and responsibilities flowing from the most relevant human rights, to health and food, and the rights of the child. A comparison of international human rights law with global strategies to promote healthier diets and physical activity demonstrate these approaches as inherently linked and mutually supportive. This chapter also explores tensions between rights-based interventions to promote healthier diets and competing rights and interests. An individual's right to freedom of choice and personal autonomy may conflict with another's right to health. Consumer's rights to information and health may interfere with corporate or industry claims to their own 'human' rights to free commerce or expression, requiring mutual awareness and balance. Finally, an illustrative selection of relevant human rights case law demonstrates how courts balance competing rights and interests. While often complex and costly, rights-based litigation shows potential to promote human rights and reduce childhood obesity by driving systematic changes in our food environments.

2. HUMAN RIGHTS AND CHILDHOOD OBESITY PREVENTION

Globally, childhood overweight and obesity have reached epidemic proportions, with rapid increases in low- and middle-income countries.[12] Childhood obesity is associated with increased risk of non-communicable diseases and premature death and disability in adulthood.[13] Although the cases of childhood

---

[7] European Social Charter (Revised), 3 May 1966, E.T.S. No. 163.
[8] Convention Against Torture and Other Cruel, Inhuman or Degrading Treatment or Punishment (CAT), 10 December 1984, 1465 U.N.T.S 85.
[9] Convention on the Rights of Persons with Disabilities (CRPD), 24 January 2007, 2515 U.N.T.S. 3.
[10] Convention on the Elimination of All Forms of Discrimination Against Women (CEDAW), 18 December 1979, 1249 U.N.T.S 13.
[11] Convention on the Rights of the Child (CRC), 20 November 1989, 1577 U.N.T.S. 3.
[12] T Lobstein, et al., 'Child and Adolescent Obesity: Part of a Bigger Picture' (2015) 385 *The Lancet* 2510, 2510.
[13] W Dietz, 'Health Consequences of Obesity in Youth: Childhood Predictors of Adult Disease' (1998) 101 *Pediatrics* 518, 522–3.

obesity are complex and varied, obesity is largely preventable. The global rise in overweight and obesity among children is associated with increased prevalence of heavily advertised, inexpensive foods and beverages high in fat, salt, and sugars, and lack of physical activity.[14] These obesogenic environments contribute to ill-health and are inconsistent with the right to health, the right to food, and children's rights.

2.1 The Right to Health

The right to health was first elucidated in the preamble of the Constitution of the World Health Organization (WHO) in 1948. The preamble of WHO's Constitution declares that 'the enjoyment of the highest attainable standard of health is one of the fundamental right of every human being'.[15] That same year, the UN General Assembly adopted the Universal Declaration of Human Rights, which also recognized the right to health as a fundamental human right.[16] The right to health was codified seminally in the ICESCR, as the 'right of everyone to the enjoyment of the highest attainable standard of physical and mental health'.[17] The substance and scope of the right to health was interpreted by the UN Committee on Economic, Social, and Cultural Rights (CESCR) in General Comment No. 14, which notes that the right to health encompasses health care, preventative programmes, and the underlying socioeconomic determinants of health, including 'an adequate supply of safe food' and nutrition.[18] The 2014 Report of the UN Special Rapporteur on the Right to Health highlights the importance of adequate and nutritious food to the realization of the right to health, identifying an urgent need for States to 'address the structural flaws in food production, marketing and retail that promote the availability and accessibility of unhealthy foods over healthier options'.[19]

According to the Covenant, States Parties have an obligation to progressively realize economic, social, and cultural rights. The progressive nature of this obligation is an acknowledgement of resource constraints that may prevent

---

[14] B Popkin, et al., 'Now and Then: The Global Nutrition Transition: The Pandemic of Obesity in Developing Countries' (2012) 70 *Nutrition Rev* 3, 8.

[15] Constitution of the World Health Organization, 7 April 1948, 14 U.N.T.S. 185, preamble.

[16] UDHR, n2, Art. 25.

[17] ICESCR, n4, Art. 12.1.

[18] CESCR, General Comment No. 14: The Right to the Highest Attainable Standard of Health (Art. 12 of the Covenant), U.N. Doc. E/C.12/2000/4, 11 August 2000, 11, 36.

[19] Report of the Special Rapporteur on the right of everyone to the enjoyment of the highest attainable standard of physical and mental health, Anand Grover, Unhealthy foods, non-communicable disease and the right to health, U.N. Doc. A/HRC/26/31, 1 April 2014, 63.

immediate realization. States must take steps that are 'deliberate, concrete and targeted as clearly as possible towards meeting the obligations recognized in the Covenant'.[20] However, certain obligations take effect immediately, including the deployment of the maximum available resources to realize rights free of any discrimination.[21] States also have a 'specific and continuing obligation to move as expeditiously and effectively as possible towards... full realization' meaning that governments cannot take regressive action in the absence of extenuating circumstances.[22]

2.2 The Right to Food

The right to food sufficient to support an adequate standard of living is recognized in the Universal Declaration of Human Rights and the ICESCR.[23],[24] Article 11.2 of the ICESCR articulates 'the fundamental right of everyone to be free from hunger'. The CESCR unpacks the 'core content' of the right to food as comprising the 'availability of good food in a quantity and quality sufficient to satisfy the dietary needs of individuals, free from adverse substances, and acceptable within a given culture' and the 'accessibility of such food in ways that are sustainable and that do not interfere with the enjoyment of other human rights'.[25] For food to meet dietary needs, it must contain 'a mix of nutrients that further physical and mental growth, development and maintenance, and physical activity that are in compliance with human physiological needs at all stages throughout the life cycle and according to gender and occupation'.[26] As with other economic, social, and cultural rights, the right to food is subject to progressive realization, in accordance with available resources.[27]

The right to food has traditionally been associated with hunger and undernutrition. However, in the context of the global obesity epidemic, there is increasing recognition of overnutrition as a dimension of malnutrition that negatively impacts the right to food.[28] In a 2011 Report to the UN Human Rights Council, for example, the UN Special Rapporteur on the Right to Food criticized the

---

[20] CESCR, General Comment No. 3: The Nature of States Parties' Obligations (Art. 2, Para. 1, of the Covenant), U.N. Doc. E/1991/23, 14 December 1990, 2.
[21] CESCR, General Comment No. 14, n18, 30.
[22] Ibid., 31.
[23] UDHR, n2, Art. 25.
[24] ICESCR, n4, Art. 11.
[25] CESCR, General Comment No. 12: The Right to Adequate Food (Art. 11 of the Covenant), U.N. Doc. E/C.12/1999/5, 12 May 1999, 8.
[26] Ibid., 9.
[27] CESCR, General Comment No. 3, n20, 9.
[28] K Schefer, 'The International Law of Overweight and Obesity' (2014) 9 *Asian J. WTO and Int'l Health L. and Pol'y* 1, 32–5.

development of 'obesogenic environments and ... food systems that often work against, rather than facilitate, making healthier choices'.[29] The Special Rapporteur recommended systematic changes, including aligning agricultural subsidies with the requirement of adequate diets[30] and restricting the promotion of foods high in fats, salt, and sugar, especially to children.[31] In a 2019 Interim Report to the UN General Assembly, the Special Rapporteur noted that 'easy access to cheap, processed foods which are high in sugar, salt and fat, is contributing to all forms of malnutrition and the spread of non-communicable diseases among children'.[32] She lamented 'sporadic' State measures to address the systematic drivers of unhealthy diets, calling for 'a more active regulatory role to monitor and enforce industry compliance'.[33]

2.3 Children's Rights

Childhood obesity has serious implications for children's rights, in particular, the right to health and the right to play. Article 24(1) of the Convention on the Rights of the Child provides for the 'right of the child to the enjoyment of the highest attainable standard of health'.[34] Article 24(2) requires States to work towards full implementation of this right, including by combating disease and malnutrition, providing adequate nutritious food, and ensuring that all members of society, especially parents and children, receive education and support on child health and nutrition.[35] This right should be understood holistically as 'a right [of children] to grow and develop to their full potential and live in conditions that enable them to attain the highest standards of health through the implementation of programmes that address the underlying determinants of health'.[36] Also relevant to obesity prevention, the convention recognizes the child's right to engage in play, recreation, and leisure.[37]

---

[29] Report submitted by the Special Rapporteur on the right to food, Olivier De Schutter, U.N. Doc. A/HRC/19/59, 26 December 2011, 26.
[30] Ibid., 48.
[31] Ibid., 50.
[32] Interim report of the Special Rapporteur on the right to food, Hilal Elver, U.N. Doc. A/74/164, 15 July 2019, 30.
[33] Ibid.
[34] CRC, n11, Art. 24(1).
[35] Ibid., Art. 24(2).
[36] Committee on the Rights of the Child, General Comment No. 15 (2013) on the right of the child to the enjoyment of the highest attainable standard of health (Art. 24), U.N. Doc. CRC/C/GC/15, 17 April 2013, 2.
[37] CRC, n11, Art. 31.

3. OBLIGATIONS UNDER INTERNATIONAL HUMAN RIGHTS LAW

3.1 Obligations of States to Respect, Protect, and Fulfil Human Rights

Under international law, States and non-State actors have different obligations and responsibilities regarding the rights to health and food, and children's rights. Traditionally, international human rights law has been understood to bind States only. States are obliged to respect, protect, and fulfil human rights obligations. The obligation to respect means that States are prohibited from taking measures that prevent or interfere with access to the enjoyment of rights.[38] States are thus prohibited from limiting equal access to health-related goods and services, including access to adequate and nutritious foods.[39]

The obligation to protect, on the other hand, requires governments to prevent third-party interference with enjoyment of rights. In the context of the right to health, States are obliged to take measures to ensure 'equal access to health care and health-related services provided by third parties'.[40] The obligation also requires the government to exercise a range of regulatory functions. For instance, the obligation to protect the right to health requires adopting measures to ensure that the privatization of health care does not jeopardize the 'availability, accessibility, acceptability, and quality of health care facilities, goods and services'.[41] States must also ensure that 'advertisements and promotion by food corporations convey accurate and easily understandable information on possible ill effects of their food products'.[42]

Pursuant to the obligation to fulfil, States must adopt laws, policies, and programmes that enable individuals and communities to enjoy their rights. In the context of the rights to food and health, States are obliged to ensure that everyone has access to adequate and nutritious foods. To fulfil these rights, States should proactively strengthen food security and provide adequate food to those who, for reasons beyond their control, lack access to food, for example, victims of disasters.[43] Additionally, States should formulate multisectoral policies that promote the 'availability and accessibility of healthy foods',[44] including agricultural, trade, and fiscal policies tailored to reducing the neg-

---

[38] CESCR, General Comment No. 14, n18, 34.
[39] Ibid.; CESCR, General Comment No. 12, n25, 15.
[40] CESCR, General Comment No. 14, n18, 35.
[41] Ibid.
[42] Report of the Special Rapporteur on the right to health, n19, 15.
[43] CESCR, General Comment No. 12, n25, at 15.
[44] Report of the Special Rapporteur on the right to health, n19, 16.

ative health impacts of foods and beverages high in fats, salt, and sugars in local food environments.[45] The UN Special Rapporteur on the Right to Health, for example, recommends the adoption of agricultural and fiscal policies that discourage the production of unhealthy products and a regulatory framework that restricts the advertising, marketing, and promotion of unhealthy foods, particularly to children.[46] Similarly, the Committee on the Rights of the Child, in its General Comment No. 15, recommends regulating the marketing of unhealthy foods and beverages, including restrictions in schools and other places frequented by children.[47] This obligation is rooted in Article 24(2)(c) of the Convention on the Rights of the Child, which requires States to 'combat disease and malnutrition'.

3.2 Obligations of Corporations

Non-State actors (NSAs), such as corporations, are not traditionally understood to be legally bound or directly accountable for human rights violations.[48] In recent decades, however, there has been debate among scholars, advocates, and international organizations on corporations' responsibilities to respect human rights law and avoid detrimental human rights impacts. The CESCR recognized in General Comment No. 14 that all members of society – including intergovernmental organizations, civil society organizations, and private businesses – have responsibilities when it comes to the realization of the right to health[49] and has recently acknowledged that 'businesses play an important role in the realization of economic, social and cultural rights'.[50] Others have gone further, proposing that corporations be held accountable to human rights in the same way that States are. Steven Ratner, for example, argued in 2001 that businesses have responsibilities for human rights protection insofar as they cooperate with States – the principal subjects of human rights law – and

---

[45] Ibid., 64.
[46] Ibid.
[47] Committee on the Rights of the Child, General Comment No. 15, n36, 47.
[48] This traditional view holds that NSAs are accountable to international human rights instruments only indirectly, i.e., to the extent that the human rights obligations accepted by States can be applied to the NSAs by these States. See M Ssenyonjo, *Economic, Social and Cultural Rights in International Law* (Hart 2009) 159.
[49] CESCR, General Comment No. 14, n18, 53.
[50] CESCR, General Comment No. 24 on State obligations under the International Covenant on Economic, Social and Cultural Rights in the context of business activities, U.N. Doc. E/C.12/GC/24, 10 August 2017, 1.

insofar as their activities 'infringe upon the human dignity of those with whom they have special ties'.[51]

This debate reached its zenith in 2004, when the Sub-Commission of the then UN Commission on Human Rights proposed a set of norms that would have essentially subjected companies to international human rights law. This proposal met with vehement opposition from the business community, while some human rights groups were strongly in favour.[52] In 2005, Professor John Ruggie was appointed by the UN Secretary-General, as Special Representative tasked with reporting on the relationship between business and human rights. After three years of consultation with relevant stakeholders, Professor Ruggie presented a framework to the UN Council of Human Rights that sought to clarify the relevant actors' responsibilities and provide a foundation for future reflection on the matter (the UN Framework). The framework rests on three pillars: the State duty to protect against human rights abuses by third parties; the corporate responsibility to respect human rights; and greater access by victims to effective remedy.[53] Building on the 'Respect, Protect, and Remedy' Framework, Professor Ruggie drafted the UN Guiding Principles on Business and Human Rights (the Guiding Principles), which were endorsed by the UN Human Rights Council in 2011.[54]

The fundamental idea behind the Guiding Principles is that business activities can impact virtually all human rights. This is not just limited to labour rights; there are documented cases where corporate activity has impacted the right to an adequate standard of living, including the right to food.[55] As such, corporations have responsibilities in relation to human rights that are distinct from those of States.[56] Not only must corporations respect human rights, they must practice due diligence by taking steps including 'assessing actual and potential human rights impacts, integrating and acting upon the findings, track-

---

[51] S Ratner, 'Corporations and Human Rights: A Theory of Legal Responsibility' (2001) 111 *Yale L. J.* 443, 449.

[52] Human Rights Council, The UN 'Protect, Respect and Remedy' Framework for Business and Human Rights: Background (September 2010) https://business-humanrights.org/sites/default/files/reports-and-materials/Ruggie-protect-respect-remedy-framework.pdf (last access date 28 September 2020).

[53] Report of the Special Representative of the Secretary-General on the issue of human rights and transnational corporations and other business enterprises, John Ruggie, U.N. Doc. A/HRC/8/5, 7 April 2008.

[54] Human rights and transnational corporations and other business enterprises, Human Rights Council Res. A/HRC/RES/17/4, 6 July 2011.

[55] Report of the Special Representative, n53, 52.

[56] Ibid.

ing responses, and communicating how impacts are addressed'.[57] Businesses should pay 'particular attention to the rights and needs of ... individuals from groups or populations that may be at heightened risk of becoming vulnerable or marginalized'.[58]

If fully adopted and implemented, the Guiding Principles may have a significant effect on how the food industry conducts its business activities. The duty of due diligence obligates businesses to take necessary steps to prevent or mitigate adverse human rights impacts.[59] Pursuant to this duty, producers of unhealthy food and beverage products should assess the impact of their business activities on the right to health, the right to food, and children's rights. In particular, food and beverage companies should assess impact on vulnerable groups, including children, low-socioeconomic groups, and communities with limited access to healthy food. The responsibility to mitigate adverse human rights impacts may include reformulating products to reduce harmful ingredients, ceasing or restricting advertising, or decreasing the availability of unhealthy products.[60]

More recently, the CESCR in General Comment No. 24 emphasizes that the human rights responsibilities of corporations coexist alongside the duty on States to protect against potential corporate human rights abuses.[61] While human rights law has evolved to include responsibilities on the part of private actors, this in no way detracts from the State duty to protect. In fact, many of the measures that States can adopt to protect the rights to health and food involve regulating corporate behavior, such as restrictions on marketing unhealthy food products or setting maximum levels of salt in processed foods. In other words, corporations have the responsibility to respect human rights and States have an obligation and possess unique authority to require corporations to do so. Together with Ruggie's third pillar of strengthening access by victims to effective remedies, the duty to protect and the responsibility to respect have the potential to make a profound impact on improving population nutrition and health.

---

[57] Report of the Special Representative of the Secretary-General on the issue of human rights and transnational corporations and other business enterprises, John Ruggie, Guiding Principles on Business and Human Rights: Implementing the United Nations 'Protect, Respect and Remedy' Framework, U.N. Doc. A/HRC/17/31, 21 March 2011, 17.
[58] Ibid., General Principles.
[59] Ibid., 13.
[60] Report of the Special Rapporteur on the right to health, n19, 29.
[61] CESCR, General Comment No. 24, n50, 7.

4. MUTUALLY SUPPORTIVE RELATIONSHIP BETWEEN HUMAN RIGHTS AND OBESITY PREVENTION

States' efforts to promote healthier diets and prevent childhood obesity are guided by global strategies, targets, and recommendations, many under the auspices of the WHO. In 2004, the World Health Assembly (WHA) endorsed the Global Strategy on Diet, Physical Activity and Health.[62] The WHA subsequently endorsed a set of recommendations on the marketing of foods and non-alcoholic beverages to children in 2010[63] and, in 2012, the WHO released a framework providing practical guidance on implementation.[64] Building on and reinforcing the Global Strategy, the WHO released its Global Action Plan for the Prevention and Control of Noncommunicable Diseases 2013–20 in 2013.[65] The Global Action Plan incorporates a series of nine voluntary targets, including halting the rise in diabetes and obesity, a 30 per cent relative reduction in population salt intake, and a 10 per cent relative reduction in the prevalence of physical inactivity.[66] WHO's Global Monitoring Framework on NCDs is tracking implementation of the plan and progress towards the attainment of the targets by 2025.[67] Most recently, the Sustainable Development Goals (SDGs) include a one-third reduction in premature mortality from NCDs by 2030.[68]

In 2016, the Commission on Ending Childhood Obesity published a report containing recommendations specifically focused on childhood and adolescent obesity. The Commission was formed in 2014 to 'review, build upon and address gaps in existing mandates and strategies'.[69] The Commission consulted

---

[62] Global strategy on diet, physical activity and health, World Health Assembly Res. 57.172, 22 May 2004.

[63] Marketing of food and non-alcoholic beverages to children, Resolution of the Sixty-third World Health Assembly, WHA63.14, adopted 21 May 2010.

[64] WHO, A framework for implementing the set of recommendations on the marketing of foods and non-alcoholic beverages to children (2012), http://apps.who.int/iris/bitstream/10665/80148/1/9789241503242_eng.pdf (last access date 28 September 2020).

[65] WHO, Global Action Plan for the Prevention and Control of Noncommunicable Diseases 2013–2020 (2013), http://apps.who.int/iris/bitstream/10665/94384/1/9789241506236_eng.pdf (last access date 28 September 2020).

[66] Ibid., 9, 37, 40.

[67] See WHO, NCD Global Monitoring Framework, http://www.who.int/nmh/global_monitoring_framework/en/ (last access date 28 September 2020).

[68] 2030 Agenda for Sustainable Development, G.A. Res. A/RES/70/1, 21 October 2015, 76.

[69] WHO, Report of the Commission on Ending Childhood Obesity, xi (2016), http://apps.who.int/iris/bitstream/10665/204176/1/9789241510066_eng.pdf (last access date 28 September 2020).

with over 100 WHO Member States and received 180 online comments. The report pays special attention to the involuntary nature of childhood obesity, cautioning that upstream causal factors should not be equated with voluntary lifestyle choices. Rather, causal factors are a function of biology and social context. As such, the Commission notes that 'governments must address these issues by providing public health guidance, education and establishing regulatory frameworks to address developmental and environmental risks, in order to support families' efforts to change behaviours'.[70] Addressing childhood obesity is a responsibility of both government and civil society, being one that resonates with a child's right to a healthy life. This responsibility, the Commission notes, is provided for in the Convention of the Rights of the Child and elucidated by General Comment No. 15.[71]

Cognizant of the health and economic impacts of overweight and obesity, many national governments are accelerating implementation of global recommendations on diet and health, which help promote and protect the right to health. The case of Mexico provides an illustrative example of innovative, practical steps that governments can take to promote healthier diets, as well as of some of the challenges.

Mexico has some of the highest rates of overweight and obesity in the world. A 2013 estimate placed the overweight and obesity rate at 69.4 per cent for men and 73 per cent for women.[72] Child obesity rates are also concerning: in 2012, 19.5 per cent of boys and 20.2 per cent of girls were overweight while 17.4 per cent of boys and 11.8 per cent of girls were obese.[73] The Mexican government, in response to what it has acknowledged to be an epidemic, formulated a national obesity strategy titled *Acuerdo Nacional para la Salud Alimentaria: Estrategia contra el sobrepeso y la obesidad* (ANSA) in 2010. The agreement, signed by 15 government agencies (including health, economics, education, agriculture, and social welfare), NGOs, academia, and the food and beverage industry, aimed to implement multisectoral actions to address the obesity epidemic in Mexico. The agreement contained a set of targets for 2012, including reversing the rising trend in overweight and obesity in children two–five years old. Government agencies were allocated 117 activities and 249 actions. Under the auspices of the agreement, the Secretariat of Health and the Secretariat of Public Education issued the General Guidelines for the Sale

---

[70] Ibid., 7.
[71] Ibid., 8, 15.
[72] European Association for the Study of Obesity, Obesity Perception and Policy: Multi-Country Review and Survey of Policy Makers, May 2014, 25, https://seedo.es/images/site/C3_EASO_Survey_A4_Web-FINAL.pdf (last access date 28 September 2020).
[73] Ibid.

or Distribution of Food and Drinks in School Consumption Facilities in Basic Education Schools, a binding regulation setting criteria for the types of food and beverages in schools.[74]

The agreement and guidelines, considered some of the most comprehensive efforts to address overweight and obesity, have successfully promoted multisectoral dialogue and negotiation, raised the profile, and achieved some meaningful actions towards addressing the obesity epidemic. According to the National Health and Nutrition Surveys, obesity rose more slowly between 2006 and 2012 (0.3 per cent) than between 2000 and 2006 (1 per cent), but levels remain very high.[75]

The ANSA has also been criticized for its limitations, including lack of costing and budgetary resources for the agreed actions of government agencies and industry, the lack of a monitoring and evaluation system, and the absence of effective enforcement of the binding guidelines for food in schools.[76] Among these deficiencies was the ANSA's lack of a legal framework (*marco jurídico*) capable of ensuring that the measures set out by the strategy would come into effect. The ANSA also failed to articulate crucial accountability mechanisms such as goals, timeframes, and process and result indicators. These absences placed restrictions on the ability to obtain evidence that would demonstrate progress in achieving ANSA's objectives.

In response to these deficiencies, the Mexican government released a new anti-obesity plan in 2013, titled the *Estrategia Nacional Para la Prevención y el Control del Sobrepeso, la Obesidad y la Diabetes*.[77] The National Strategy comprises three pillars: public health promotion; health care; and health regulation and tax policy. Under this third pillar, the Mexican government has gained attention for its tax on sugar-sweetened beverages (SSB tax). The 1-peso-per-liter tax took effect on January 1, 2014. A 2017 study found that SSB sales dropped by 5.5 per cent in the first year and 9.7% in the second year

---

[74] Secretaría de Salud (Mex.), Acuerdo Nacional para la Salud Alimentaria: Estrategia contra el sobrepeso y la obesidad, (2010), https://activate.gob.mx/Documentos/ACUERDO%20NACIONAL%20POR%20LA%20SALUD%20ALIMENTARIA.pdf (last access date: 9/28/2020).

[75] European Association for the Study of Obesity, n72, 12, 26.

[76] E Rodriguez, 'Mexico: National Agreement on Food Health, Strategy against Overweight and Obesity', in M Bonilla-Chacin (ed.), *Promoting Healthy Living in Latin America and the Caribbean Governance of Multisectoral Activities to Prevent Risk Factors for Noncommunicable Diseases* (World Bank 2014) 166–76.

[77] Secretaría de Salud (Mex.), Estrategia Nacional Para la Prevención y el Control del Sobrepeso, la Obesidad y la Diabetes, (2013), http://www.cenaprece.salud.gob.mx/descargas/pdf/EstrategiaNacionalSobrepeso.pdf (last access date 28 September 2020).

(compared to pre-tax sales figures).[78] Consistent with the tax's public health objectives, purchases of untaxed beverages increased 2.1 per cent over the same period.[79]

Although not always framed as human rights issues, global recommendations and national laws and policies to reduce obesity clearly help protect, respect, and fulfil the rights to health and food, and children's rights. These fundamental rights require and justify promotion of healthier diets and prevention and treatment of overweight and obesity. Indeed, human rights and obesity prevention are inherently linked and mutually supportive. In the case of ANSA, which did not contain explicit reference to human rights, resulting advancements appear to be collateral. The National Strategy however, refers to the right to health as enshrined in the Mexican Constitution and cites the Political Declaration of the High-level Meeting of the General Assembly on the Prevention and Control of NCDs.[80] As seen with the National Strategy, governments and advocates seeking to adopt health promotion measures should consider human rights bases and approaches to advance their cause.

5. RIGHTS IN TENSION

Government efforts to implement the Framework Convention on Tobacco Control (FCTC) and global recommendations on alcohol and unhealthy diets raise tensions between protection of the public's health, commercial actors' interests in marketing their products, and personal autonomy (Table 2.1 below). Consumers have rights and interests relating to receiving information about products through advertising and choosing which products they consume. Industry actors have a commercial interest in selling and maximizing profits from legal products. This is especially true in a competitive retail environment where producers, distributors, and retailers stake their survival on maximizing consumer exposure to and consumption of their goods. In this competitive environment, corporations employ a range of strategies, including aggressive marketing and promotion of unhealthy products and lobbying for favourable policies.[81]

The notion of personal autonomy may legitimize approaches that emphasize individual responsibility in addressing obesity, as opposed to approaches

---

[78] M Cochero, et al., 'In Mexico, Evidence of Sustained Consumer Response Two Years After Implementing a Sugar-Sweetened Beverage Tax' (2017) 36 *Health Aff.* 564, 567.
[79] Ibid.
[80] Secretaría de Salud, n77, 32, 37.
[81] I Kickbusch, et al., 'The Commercial Determinants of Health' (2016) 4 *The Lancet Global Health* e895.

Table 2.1 Commercial interests and individual rights implicated by NCD interventions

Intervention point	Example interventions	Rights implicated
Sales	• Ban on sales of tobacco products to minors	• Freedom of commerce
	• Ban on sodas in schools	• Personal autonomy
Use	• Smoke-free place laws	• Personal autonomy
	• Drink-driving laws	
Advertising, promotion, sponsorship	• Ban on advertising junk food during children's programing	• Freedom of speech/ expression
	• Plain packaging for tobacco products	• Right to information
		• Intellectual property rights
Product contents	• Restrictions on salt content in processed foods	• Freedom of commerce
		• Personal autonomy
	• Ban on flavors in tobacco products	
Price	• Excise tax on sugary drinks	• Freedom of commerce
	• Bans on discounts and bulk pricing	• Personal autonomy
Packaging and labelling	• Warning labels on junk food	• Compelled speech
	• Content disclosure requirements on tobacco product packages	• Intellectual property rights

that emphasize the duty of States to reduce obesity through systemic, structural changes. Indeed, when government measures to create healthier food environments threaten commercial profits, the food and beverage industry often frame government actions as paternalistic government interference that encroaches on personal freedoms and commercial interests.[82] Public health advocates have been less active in framing obesity and food environments in the context of fundamental rights, which provide strong bases for adoption and defence of structural changes to help ensure access to adequate and nutritious foods.[83]

---

[82] M Grynbaum, 'Fighting Soda Rule, Industry Focuses on Personal Choice', *New York Times*, 1 July 2012, A10.

[83] A Alemanno and A Garde, 'Regulating Lifestyles in Europe: How to Prevent and Control Non-communicable Diseases Associated with Tobacco, Alcohol and Unhealthy Diets?', Report for the Swedish Institute for European Policy Studies (2013), 46, http://www.sieps.se/en/publications/2013/regulating-lifestyles-in-europe-how-to-prevent-and-control-non-communicable-diseases-associated-with-tobacco-alcohol-and-unhealthy-diets-20137 (last access date 28 September 2020). See further, chapter by Garde and Byrne in this volume.

When competing rights and interests come into tension, lawmakers and ultimately, courts, are required to determine which prevails. In the absence of a clear or formal hierarchy of rights, the legal principle of proportionality is often applied to determine the appropriate balance.[84] Although there are jurisdictional variations, the proportionality test typically requires that the intervention adopted by the government be appropriately tailored to the specific public health objective. The proportionality test comprises two components. The intervention must be suitable to achieve its aims and it must not exceed what is necessary to do so. To establish suitability, the government must establish that the measure is effective in achieving its public health objectives. Governments must also establish necessity, by showing that there are no other, less intrusive means, of achieving the objectives.

The Court of Justice of the European Union's recent decision in *Philip Morris Brands SARL and Others v the Secretary of State for Health*[85] provides an illustrative example of application of the proportionality test. While recognizing conflicting rights and interests in the context of tobacco regulation, the Court found that the protection of health took precedence over industry actors' rights to freedom of speech and freedom of commerce. A key part of the dispute concerned the validity of provisions of a European Union directive prohibiting labels on tobacco products that promoted use, for example, by suggesting that a product is less harmful than others, by making reference to the cigarette's taste or flavour, or by implying that a product has environmental advantages such as biodegradability.[86]

In its reasoning, the Court acknowledged that the prohibition interfered with a business's freedom, guaranteed under Article 11 of the EU Charter of Fundamental Rights,[87] to disseminate information in pursuit of commercial interests.[88] This freedom, the Court noted, is not absolute, and a balance must be struck between the 'fundamental rights and legitimate general interest objectives' protected by the directive.[89] The Court held that, given the scientific consensus on the harms and dangers of tobacco consumption, the protection of human health takes precedence over the interests put forward by the tobacco

---

[84] A Garde, 'Law, Healthy Diets and Obesity Prevention', in M Frelut (ed.), *The ECOG Free Obesity eBook* (2015), 3.

[85] *Philip Morris Brands SARL and Others v. Sec'y of State for Health* (2016), Case C-547/14, EU:C:2016:325.

[86] Ibid., 146.

[87] Charter of Fundamental Rights of the European Union, 2007/C 303/01), pmbl, O.J.E.U. (C303) 50 (2007).

[88] *Philip Morris Brands*, n85, 147.

[89] Ibid., 155.

companies.[90] Less restrictive measures, such as regulating the marketing elements (e.g., flavour, biodegradability) instead of prohibiting them, would 'not be as effective for ensuring the protection of consumer's health'.[91] As such, the prohibition struck a proportional balance between protecting freedom of expression and the overwhelming interest in protecting human health.[92]

The application of the proportionality test will vary depending on the levels of protection afforded to competing rights within the jurisdiction's legal system. In the US, where freedom of speech is afforded strong protections within the Bill of Rights (and the right to health is not protected), the Supreme Court applies a demanding proportionality test[93] and the industry has been particularly successful in using rights-based arguments as a shield against health-promoting regulations. For instance, in the case of *Lorillard Tobacco Company v Reilly*, the Court ruled that a Massachusetts law prohibiting tobacco signage within 1,000 feet of schools unduly infringed on the tobacco company's ability to advertise to adults. The legislation was found to be in violation of the First Amendment's protection of free speech.[94]

As in the case of tobacco regulation, courts are faced with the challenge of striking a proper balance between competing rights and interests when it comes to assessing the legality of rights-infringing measures that seek to prevent and reduce obesity. Actors in the food industry, like their tobacco counterparts, assert that laws regulating labelling and advertising constitute infringements of their rights to freedom of expression and commerce, among other rights.[95]

Courts have long expressed openness to the idea that freedom of expression can be restricted in the context of advertising to children. In the 1987 Canadian case of *Irwin Toy v. Quebec (Attorney General)*, the Supreme Court of Canada upheld the constitutionality of provisions in Quebec's Consumer Protection Act, which prohibited commercial advertising to children under 13 years of age.[96] The Court acknowledged that the provisions infringed the freedom of expression guaranteed in the Canadian Charter of Rights and Freedoms[97] and the Quebec Charter of Human Rights and Freedoms.[98] However, the infringe-

---

[90] Ibid., 156.
[91] Ibid., 160.
[92] Ibid., 161.
[93] Garde, n84, 3.
[94] *Lorillard Tobacco Co. v. Thomas F. Reilly*, 533 U.S. 525 (2001).
[95] Garde, 'The "Obesity Risk": For an Effective Use of Law to Prevent Non-Communicable Diseases' (2017) 8 *Eur. J. Risk Reg.* 77, 80. See also, MacMaoláin's chapter in this volume.
[96] *Irwin Toy Ltd. v. Quebec* (Attorney General), [1989] 1 S.C.R. 927. (Can.).
[97] Canadian Charter of Rights and Freedoms, The Constitution Act, 1982, being Schedule B to the Canada Act, 1982, c 11 (U.K.).
[98] Charter of Human Rights and Freedoms (Quebec), CQLR c C-12 (Canada).

ment met the Court's test for justifying the limitation of a right or freedom under the saving provision of the Canadian Charter.[99] For the restriction to freedom of expression to be permitted under this provision, it must further a sufficiently important objective and meet the test of proportionality. The provisions furthered the pressing and substantive objective of protecting a group that is vulnerable to commercial manipulation. As the Court noted, children 'are not as equipped as adults to evaluate the persuasive force of advertising and advertisements' directed at them.[100] As such, the provisions reasonably precluded advertisers from 'taking advantage of children both by inciting them to make purchases and by inciting them to their parents make purchases'.[101] The ban on advertising also met the test of proportionality: given the broad objective of protecting children from manipulation, the Court ruled that the ban was proportional to the legislative objective.

In the decades since *Irwin Toy* was decided, additional scientific evidence has emerged to strengthen the conclusion that children are vulnerable to commercial advertising and, as such, require special protection. A 2009 systematic review, for example, found a statistically significant association between food advertising and children's attitudes, behaviours, and health status. It confirmed that advertising increases children's consumption of advertised products and other diet-related outcomes.[102] As noted by Graff et al., recent cognitive research has established that children are unable to master any of the concepts that are key to understanding advertising and are incapable of distinguishing between advertising and other content. Studies have shown that most children up to the age of five are unaware that the content of commercial advertising is 'independent and disconnected from the programming that surrounds it'.[103] The consequence of this is that children are more likely to uncritically accept information conveyed in advertisements to be true and accurate. Furthermore, children under the age of eight generally lack the ability to recognize the persuasive intent behind advertising. While children above this age do generally have a comprehension of persuasive intent, studies show that early adolescents in the age range of 11–14 are still in the process of developing a sense of scepticism and awareness of inherent bias in advertising messages.[104] For these

---

[99] Canadian Charter, n97.
[100] *Irwin Toy Ltd*, n96, 933.
[101] Ibid., 990–91.
[102] G Cairns, et al., *The Extent, Nature and Effects of Food Promotion to Children: A Review of the Evidence to December 2008* (WHO 2009) 32.
[103] S Graff, et al., 'Government Can Regulate Food Advertising to Children Because Cognitive Research Shows That It Is Inherently Misleading' (2012) 31 *Health Aff.* 392, 395.
[104] Ibid.

reasons, Graff et al. conclude that advertising is inevitably misleading for children under the age of 12 as they 'generally lack effective understanding of advertising tactics such as exaggeration, embellishment, and "puffery"'.[105]

Such instances of conflicting rights remind us that neither freedom of expression nor the right to health are absolute. Empirical evidence therefore plays an especially crucial role in order to allow courts to properly assess and balance rights.[106]

6. HUMAN RIGHTS CASE LAW

As governments increasingly adopt measures to prevent NCDs, courts are often called upon to balance the impact of laws and policies on competing rights and interests. Traditionally, rights-based arguments have been put forward by industry operators seeking to challenge measures designed to reduce the consumption or health impact of their products. More recently, plaintiffs have begun harnessing the power of human rights-based litigation to demand that governments and corporations take steps to prevent and reduce NCDs and their risk factors.

6.1 Industry Litigation

Commercial actors, particularly tobacco companies, have a long history of challenging government interventions, often arguing that the impugned measures unjustifiably infringe on commercial and consumer rights. From the perspective of defendant governments, litigation against well-resourced industry operators is likely to be lengthy and expensive. In *Philip Morris v. Uruguay,* an industry-sponsored investment law challenge to innovative tobacco control measures, the parties' legal costs (approximately $27.2 million) exceeded the plaintiff's compensation claim.[107]

The threat of litigation or presence of similar litigation in other jurisdictions can exert a 'chilling effect' on governments seeking to enact laws to reduce NCD risk factors. The Canadian government begun considering plain packaging for tobacco products in 1994, but was deterred from taking legislative action by a legal memo sent by R J Reynolds and Philip Morris to the House of Commons Standing Committee on Health. This memo argued that plain pack-

---

[105] Ibid., 396.
[106] T Baytor and O Cabrera, 'International Human Rights Law', in T Voon (et al. eds), *Regulating Tobacco, Alcohol and Unhealthy Foods: The Legal Issues* (Routledge 2014) 65, 79.
[107] *Philip Morris Brands Sàrl et al. v. Oriental Republic of Urugua*, ICSID Case No. ARB/10/7, Award, 8 July 2016.

aging would constitute an illegal expropriation of the company's trademark under the North American Free Trade Agreement's investment chapter, and could result in the Canadian government paying hundreds of millions of dollars in compensation.[108] More recently, the New Zealand government delayed adoption of plain packaging legislation pending the outcome of challenges to Australia's Tobacco Plain Packaging Act 2011 under the Australia-Hong Kong Bilateral Investment Treaty and under World Trade Organization law.[109]

To overcome the challenges associated with industry litigation, governments need to anticipate and prepare for industry lawsuits. In particular, they must ensure they have sufficient evidence to pass the proportionality test. In *Irwin Toy*,[110] for instance, the Supreme Court of Canada noted the need to assess conflicting scientific evidence in determining whether the government's prohibition on advertising to children strikes a proper balance between the claims of competing groups. The Court went on to frame the test of minimal impairment (a key component of proportionality) as one of 'whether the government had a reasonable basis, on the evidence tendered, for concluding that the ban on all advertising directed at children impaired freedom of expression as little as possible given the government's pressing and substantial objective'.[111] On this question, the Court relied heavily on a Federal Trade Commission report showing that a ban on all advertisements towards children would be the only effective remedy. Less stringent measures such as implementing a ban based on audience composition data would not, according to the data presented in the report, sufficiently overcome the cognitive limitations that children are naturally subject to.[112]

Where governments are well prepared and sufficiently resourced, industry litigation may yield results that reinforce the legality of the impugned measure and of public health interventions more broadly.[113] In the field of tobacco control, for example, an industry-sponsored lawsuit in Peru resulted in innovative arguments and judicial recognition of international and constitutional obligations to advance domestic tobacco control efforts. In *5,000 Citizens*

---

[108] M Porterfield and C Byrnes, 'Philip Morris v. Uruguay: Will Investor-State Arbitration Send Restrictions on Tobacco Marketing up in Smoke?', Investment Treaty News, 12 July 2011, http://www.iisd.org/itn/2011/07/12/philip-morris-v-uruguay-will-investor-state-arbitration-send-restrictions-on-tobacco-marketing-up-in-smoke (last access date 28 September 2020).

[109] J Kelsey, 'Regulatory Chill: Learnings from New Zealand's Plain Packaging Tobacco Law' (2017) *Queens. U. Tech. L. Rev.* 21, 21.

[110] *Irwin Toy Ltd*, n96, 927.

[111] Ibid., 993.

[112] Ibid., 994.

[113] O Cabrera and J Carballo, 'Tobacco Control Litigation: Broader Impacts on Health Rights Adjudication' (2013) 41 *J. L. Med. & Ethics* 147, 157.

Against Article 3 of Law No. 28705,[114] the plaintiffs challenged Peru's law that bans smoking in 'establishments dedicated to health or education, in public offices, in the interiors of work places, in enclosed public spaces and on any means of public transportation'. The plaintiffs argued that, due to its absolute character, the ban violated the constitutionally protected right to personal autonomy, and that designated smoking areas should have been permitted. In addition, the plaintiffs argued that the impugned provision violated the rights to free enterprise and free private initiative.

The Constitutional Tribunal of Peru upheld the law, in accordance with the constitutional right to health and the WHO FCTC,[115] which the Peruvian congress approved in 2004. The Court noted that human rights treaties, of which the FCTC is one, have constitutional rank, meaning legislators can neither regulate in contravention of these treaties, nor reject them. Having been incorporated into Peru's legal framework, the FCTC serves as an interpretive standard vis-à-vis other laws in the same manner as the Constitution.[116] As such, measures that further the aims of the FCTC – including continually and substantially reducing the prevalence of tobacco use as well as exposure to tobacco smoke – are not only constitutionally valid but constitutionally obligatory.[117]

Insofar as the ban infringed on protected rights, the Court found that this infringement was proportionate to the important objective of protecting health. The Court considered the infringement of the ban on smokers' rights to personal autonomy, noting that tobacco use is a non-essential interest that does not contribute to any basic need and is intrinsically damaging.[118] In response to the plaintiffs' claim that the bans disproportionately limit the right to free enterprise and free initiative, the majority opinion referred to numerous empirical studies showing that similar bans in other jurisdictions have had a neutral or positive impact on businesses.[119]

The Court's decision upholding Peru's smoke-free place law yielded positive outcomes for the adjudication of tobacco control measures under domestic and international law. First, the Court recognized the government's 'obligation to protect the right to health through a … national policy that continually and substantially reduces the prevalence of tobacco use and the

---

[114] 5,000 Citizens Against Article 3 of Law No. 28705, Constitutional Court of Peru (19 July 2011).
[115] Ibid., 69.
[116] Ibid., 78.
[117] Ibid., 79–80.
[118] Ibid., 131.
[119] Ibid., 136–38.

exposure to tobacco smoke'.[120] Further, the Court opined that the principle of progressive realization means that, except in exceptional circumstances, retrogressive government actions that pull back from existing tobacco control measures would be constitutionally invalid.[121] The incorporation of the principle of non-retrogression into tobacco control jurisprudence is an important step forward in rights-based tobacco control litigation.

Following decades of litigation by the tobacco industry, it is now the soda industry that appears to be escalating its fight against growing government measures to reduce consumption. In 2016, a group of plaintiffs, led by the American Beverage Association (ABA) filed the first lawsuit challenging a public health-based soda tax. Soda taxes are gaining momentum as cost-effective means of discouraging consumption, incentivizing product reformulation to reduce sugar content, and raising revenue for government programs and services.[122] Soda taxes are recommended by the WHO[123] and were identified by the Special Rapporteur on the Right to Food's report to the Human Rights Council as a key method to protect and promote adequate diets.[124]

Following the City of Philadelphia's adoption of a 1.5 cent per ounce tax on sodas, plaintiffs brought a suit seeking to invalidate the measure. The plaintiffs argued that the tax contravened the Sterling Act,[125] the operation of

---

[120] Ibid., 81–2. In support of this line of reasoning, the Court referenced the Georgetown Law Center O'Neill Institute's amicus brief which put forward the claim that the impugned measure is required 'from the International Human Rights Law perspective and the obligation to protect the right to health' (See also O'Neill amicus brief, 5,000 Citizens Against Article 3 of Law No. 28705).

[121] Ibid., 146. The Court also referred to the fact that Peru is a signatory to the International Accord on Economic, Social and Cultural Rights (IAESCR), which commits States to '[t]he prevention and treatment of epidemic diseases' (Art. 12, s. 2). Both the international community and the Peruvian government have recognized smoking to be an epidemic. In addition, the IAESCR imposes an obligation on States to enact measures that will lead to the progressive realization of the right to health. This obligation is also present in other international instruments to which the Peruvian government is a signatory such as the San Salvador Protocol (Arts 1, 2), the American Convention on Human Rights (Art. 26), the ICESCR (General Comment No. 9), and the FCTC (Art. 3).

[122] S Roache and L Gostin, 'The Untapped Power of Soda Taxes: Incentivizing Consumers, Generating Revenue, and Altering Corporate Behavior' (2017) 6 *Int'l J. Health Pol'y Mgmt* 489, 490.

[123] WHO, 'Fiscal Policies for Diet and Prevention of Noncommunicable Diseases: Technical Meeting Report', 5–6 May 2015, http://apps.who.int/iris/bitstream/10665/250131/1/9789241511247-eng.pdf (last access date 28 September 2020).

[124] Report submitted by the Special Rapporteur on the right to food, n29, 39.

[125] Sterling Act (First Class City Taxation). Act of Aug. 5, 1932, Special Session 1, P.L. 45, No. 45 Cl. 53. Special Session No. 1 of 1932. No. 1932-45 §1.

which pre-empts a political subdivision (e.g., a city) from taxing an aspect of a business that is already taxed by the Commonwealth of Pennsylvania. As the Commonwealth previously imposed a sales tax on sodas, the plaintiffs argued that the tax was duplicative and thus pre-empted. The Court of Common Pleas of Philadelphia County rejected this argument, holding that the city's soda tax and the Commonwealth's sales tax 'apply to two different transactions, have two different measures and are paid by different taxpayers'.[126] The soda tax is imposed on the distributor while the sales tax is applied at the retail level on the consumer. Although the plaintiff argued that the tax has duplicative effect because the economic burden is eventually passed to the consumer, the Court held that the structure of the tax is determinative, not what private actors do in response.[127] The Commonwealth Court[128] and the Pennsylvania Supreme Court affirmed the lower court's decision upholding the validity of Philadelphia's soda tax.[129]

In the Philadelphia soda tax litigation, the plaintiffs' arguments and the governments' response focused on questions of tax law and statutory interpretation. An *amicus curiae* brief filed by the American Heart Association (AHA) and other public health organizations discussed the far-reaching public health implications of overturning Philadelphia's soda tax. The brief noted that an overly broad reading of the Sterling Act or the doctrine of pre-emption would place severe limits on the city's ability to impose public health measures that deter the consumption of SSBs such as soda taxes, prohibitions on the sale of SSBs in schools, and menu-labelling regulations.[130] This case shows the potential for industry litigation to undermine governments' capacity to take measures to protect and fulfil human rights. Although the AHA's health-based arguments were not referenced in the judgments, they provide an example of the use of health and rights-based arguments to respond to a wide range of industry litigation.

---

[126] *Williams, et al. v. City of Philadelphia, et al.*, No. 16100940 of 2016, 6 (Philadelphia Ct. Com. Pl. 2016).

[127] Ibid., 7.

[128] *Williams, et al. v. City of Philadelphia, et al.*, No. 2077 C.D. 2016, No. 2078 C.D. 2016 (Pa. Commw. Ct. 2017).

[129] *Williams, et al. v. City of Philadelphia, et al.*, Nos 2 & 3 EAP 2018 (Pa. Ct. 2018).

[130] Brief of American Heart Association et al. for Appellees in *Williams, et al. v. City of Philadelphia, et al.*, No. 2077 C.D. 2016, No. 2078 C.D. 2016, 22–25 (Pa. Commw. Ct. 2017).

6.2 Rights-based Litigation to Advance Obesity Prevention

Increasingly, public health advocates are harnessing the power of rights-based litigation to drive systematic changes in food environments. Ideally, States would regulate and take other steps necessary to respect, protect, and fulfil their human rights obligations, rendering lengthy and expensive litigation unnecessary. However, in many instances the food and beverage industry has captured the political process,[131] preventing or weakening government efforts to decrease consumption of unhealthy products. In these circumstances, litigation is emerging as a powerful tool to compel governments and the food industry to take steps to promote nutritious consumption patterns and prevent childhood obesity.

As seen in tobacco control litigation, lawsuits could be structured to demand adoption, enforcement or compliance with evidence-based interventions to promote healthier diets, including restrictions on advertising unhealthy products, comprehensive nutrition information on product labels, and warnings on nutrient-poor foods and beverages.[132] Depending on the litigant's objectives, there are a range of defendants, legal grounds, and fora available (Figure 2.1).

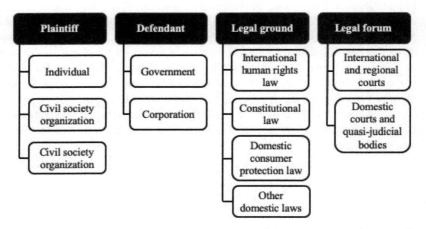

Figure 2.1   *Potential parties, legal grounds, and legal fora in litigation to advance obesity prevention*

---

[131] M Gilens and B Page, 'Testing Theories of American Politics: Elites, Interest Groups, and Average Citizens' (2014) 12 *Perspect. Politics* 564, 574.

[132] Cabrera and Carballo, n113, 150–51.

Following the traditional conceptualization of international human rights actors, an individual could bring proceedings against his or her government for failing to prevent third-party interference (by food and beverage company/ies) with the right to health or children's rights. More innovative structures include actions alleging that corporations are violating constitutionally protected rights. Domestic rights-based actions allow potential plaintiffs, including individuals and civil society organizations, to hold corporations directly accountable, which is not presently feasible before international human rights bodies. Such actions are only available in countries where relevant rights are enshrined in national constitutions and where procedural rules facilitate constitutional litigation. In 2013, 36 per cent of countries guaranteed the right to health within national constitutions.[133] In countries without constitutional protections, or where the constitutional right to health does not extend to healthy food environments, domestic consumer protection laws may constitute another legal basis for litigation.

While proactive litigation is relatively novel, cases seeking to strengthen tobacco control and promote healthier diets illustrate the potential for litigation to drive improvements in NCD prevention. In *Murli S. Deora v. Union of India and Others*,[134] a former member of the Indian Parliament brought a suit demanding that the Indian government adopt a ban on smoking in public places. The Supreme Court of India agreed with the petitioner, who argued that non-smokers exposed to second-hand smoke in public places amounted to deprivation of life without due process, in contravention of Article 21 of the Constitution of India.[135] The Court issued an interim order prohibiting smoking in public places and directed State and local governments to adopt smoke-free place laws.

Rights-based litigation is also emerging as a powerful tool to address some of the underlying drivers of obesity, including advertising of unhealthy food and beverage products to children. In 2007, a Brazilian food company Pandurata Alimentos Ltda, known as Bauducco, ran an advertising campaign based on the computer-animated children's film, *Shrek 3*. Consumers who collected and redeemed five packages from a product line comprising cookies and cakes, could purchase a Shrek-themed watch for R$5.00 Brazilian Reais. The Alana Institute, a Brazilian children's advocacy organization submitted a complaint to the State prosecutor's office in São Paulo, alleging that the

---

[133] See J Heymann, et al., 'Constitutional Rights to Health, Public Health and Medical Care: The Status of Health Protections in 191 Countries' (2013) 8 *Global Pub. Health* 639, 645.
[134] *Murli S. Deora v. Union of India and Others*, (2001) 8 SCC 765 (India).
[135] Indian Constitution, Art. 21.

advertising campaign breached the Consumer Protection Code,[136] the Child and Adolescent Statute,[137] Resolution 163 of the National Council for the Rights of Children and Adolescents,[138] and the Federal Constitution.

In 2016, the Superior Court of Justice[139] upheld a lower court judgment against Bauducco, including orders that the company pay a fine, cease the advertising campaign, and desist from all advertising to children. The Court found that Bauducco's campaign constituted tie-in sales, meaning sales conditional on the purchase of additional unneeded or unwanted goods, in breach of Article 39§1 of the Consumer Protection Code. The Court also held that the campaign was directed at children, which constitutes abusive advertising in breach of Article 37§2. Although the Bauducco decision is based on domestic consumer law, the relevant sections of the Consumer Protection Code are based on, and must be interpreted in accordance with, constitutional protections for consumers and children, including the principle of the best interests of the child.[140] In 2017, the Superior Tribunal of Justice declined to hear Bauducco's appeals.[141]

In the US, a public health group and representatives of religious organizations sued a soda manufacturer, alleging false and misleading marketing of sugar-sweetened beverages[142] under consumer protection laws.[143] The complaint alleges that the defendant misled and confused the public about the health impacts of sugary beverages and advertised to children on a massive scale, despite undertaking not to do so. The claim seeks injunctive relief, including prohibiting the defendants from engaging in unfair and deceptive marketing and requiring the company to fund a corrective public education

---

[136] Consumer Protection Code [Código de Defesa do Consumidor] (Law 8.078/90) (Braz.).

[137] Child and Adolescent Statute [Estatuto da Criança e do Adolescente] (Law 8.069/90) (Braz.).

[138] Resolution of the National Council of the Rights of the Child and the Adolescent [Resolução Conselho Nacional dos Direitos da Criança e do Adolescente] No. 163, (Mar. 13, 2014) (Braz.).

[139] *Pandurata Alimentos Ltda v. Ministério Público do Estado De São Paulo* (Mar. 10, 2016), Superior Tribunal de Justiça, Recurso Especial N° 1.558.086 - SP (2015/0061578-0) (Braz.).

[140] Constitution of Brazil [Constituição Federal], Art. 227 (Braz.).

[141] *Pandurata Alimentos Ltda v. Ministério Público do Estado De São Paulo* (Mar. 10, 2016), Superior Tribunal de Justiça, Recurso Especial N° 1.558.086 - SP (2015/0061578-0) (Braz.).

[142] Complaint in the matter of *Pastor William H. Lamar IV, et al. v. the Coca-Cola Company et al.*, No. 2017 CA 004801B (D.C. Mun. Ct. filed, Jul. 1, 2017).

[143] Consumer Protection Procedures Act, D.C. CODE, §§ 28-3901 to 28-3913 (2013).

campaign on the health impacts of sugar-sweetened beverages.[144] The plaintiffs' claims against the soda industry bear resemblance to litigation brought by several US State attorneys general against major cigarette manufacturers. The tobacco suit resulted in the largest civil litigation settlement in US history, including annual payments in perpetuity to cover the cost of health care, restrictions on tobacco advertising, and the public disclosure of millions of tobacco industry documents.[145]

In addition to mandating specific actions on the part of government or corporations, litigation can have a range or indirect and symbolic impacts[146] that may further the cause of promoting healthier diets and preventing obesity. Publicity of high-profile litigation concerning tobacco and unhealthy foods and beverages may increase public awareness of the health impacts of consumption and illegal industry actions. Litigation often promotes civil society engagement with public health issues, either as parties, as advocates promoting dialogue and deliberation, or as partners in implementing and monitoring outcomes. Perhaps most importantly, litigation to promote healthier diets has potential to frame the proliferation of unhealthy food and beverages as human rights issues and analyze government and industry actions in the context of the right to health, the right to food, and children's rights, bringing the benefits of all three aspects of human rights; moral, legal and political.

7. CONCLUSION

The proliferation of heavily advertised, inexpensive foods high in fat, salt, and sugar is seriously impacting children's rights to health, food, and development. Although many governments are taking steps to promote healthier diets and physical activity, childhood obesity has reached epidemic proportions, with rapid increases in low- and middle-income countries. Many interventions to reduce obesity and promote rights, including bans on advertising to children and packaging and labelling requirements, interfere with individual or commercial rights. Traditionally, industry actors have monopolized rights-based arguments to oppose public health interventions. Increasingly, in both tobacco and diet-related litigation, governments and public health advocates are

---

[144] Amended Complaint for Declaratory and Injunctive Relief and Demand for Jury Trial in the matter of *Pastor William H. Lamar IV, et al. v. the Coca-Cola Company et al.*, No. 2017 CA 004801 B (D.C. Sup. Ct. filed, Nov. 14, 2019, by Order dated Oct. 1, 2019).

[145] C King and M Siegel, 'The Master Settlement Agreement with the Tobacco Industry and Cigarette Advertising in Magazines' (2001) 345 *N. Engl. J. Med.* 504.

[146] C Rodríguez-Garavito, 'Beyond the Courtroom: The Impact of Judicial Activism on Socioeconomic Rights in Latin America' (2010) 89 *Tex. L. Rev.* 1669, 1676.

harnessing the power of rights-based advocacy in supportive of public health measures.

The rights to health, food, and children's rights oblige governments to reshape food systems and societies that ensure all children have access to nutritious diets and opportunities for play and recreation. Rights-based advocacy, including litigation, can help hold governments and corporations accountable, driving the fulfilment of these fundamental rights.

3. The child's right to health as a tool to end childhood obesity

Katharina Ó Cathaoir and Mette Hartlev[1]

1. INTRODUCTION

Childhood obesity rates have soared worldwide in recent years. The causes are multifaceted and complex, spanning genetics, environment and behaviour. What is clear, however, is that governments can do more through law and policy to create an environment where children and their families enjoy good health. Yet, political momentum is sluggish and stilted, likely hindered by lack of will, the perceived complexity of the task and opposition from powerful business interests. Therefore, experts and advocates concerned about childhood obesity must persuade governments of their responsibilities in this area.

In light thereof, this chapter interprets and analyses States' obligations to prevent childhood obesity with reference to children's right to health under the Convention on the Rights of the Child (CRC).[2] We posit that through undertaking to ensure the right to the highest standard of attainable health, States have obligations to address childhood obesity. Further, we argue that international human rights and international public health can be mutually reinforcing: the World Health Organization (WHO) provides vital technical guidance, while the CRC offers moral and legal weight. By studying the WHO's technical recommendations, States' rather vague obligations under the right to health can be elaborated, and children's enjoyment of their rights correlatively strengthened.

Accordingly, this contribution asks, what are States' obligations in relation to childhood obesity under the right to health? Further, to what extent do the recommendations of human rights bodies complement those of the WHO

---

[1] The work is carried out as a part of the research programme 'Governing Obesity' funded by the University of Copenhagen Excellence Programme for Interdisciplinary Research (www.go.ku.dk). This contribution was last updated in August 2018.
[2] Convention on the Rights of the Child (adopted 20 November 1989, entry into force 2 September 1990) 1577 UNTS 3.

Commission on Ending Childhood Obesity (ECHO)?[3] Can the two systems reinforce each other to end childhood obesity?

In section 2, States' duties under international public health and the global development agenda are introduced as complementary responsibilities, with the work of ECHO and the Sustainable Development Goals (SDGs) in focus. In section 3, our approach to interpreting the right to health – a children's rights approach that is guided by the work of the Committee of the Rights of the Child (CRC Committee) – is introduced. The right to an open future is also advanced as a theoretical underpinning. Section 4 analyses the right to health in the context of childhood obesity, assessing States' obligations through the CRC Committee's general comments and concluding observations, as well as recommendations of other human rights bodies. In Section 5, the scope of States' obligations is outlined considering parents' interconnected responsibilities. Finally, section 6 recommends how States can pursue their responsibilities to children's health in a manner that avoids stigma and discrimination.

2. ENDING CHILDHOOD OBESITY: ECHO AND THE SDGs

Before delving into the right to health, this section outlines States' interconnected responsibilities under international public health and the SDGs – the most high-profile development standard agreed upon by States. While the WHO has issued a variety of technical documents and resolutions with recommendations relevant to ending childhood obesity, we focus on the recent framework recommended by ECHO and endorsed by the World Health Assembly (WHA).[4] The reason for zeroing in on the former is that the ECHO recommendations are the most up-to-date and comprehensive concerning children. They can be further clarified through reference to more detailed WHO standards, such as the WHO set of recommendations on the marketing of foods and non-alcoholic beverages to children.[5]

---

[3] WHO, *Report of the Commission on Ending Childhood Obesity* (2016); WHA69(12) Report of the Commission on Ending Childhood Obesity (2016).

[4] Ibid.

[5] WHO, *Set of Recommendations on the Marketing of Foods and Non-Alcoholic Beverages to Children* (WHO 2010) – Resolution WHA 63.14. See also, WHO, *Fiscal Policies for Diet and Prevention of Noncommunicable Diseases Technical Report* (WHO 2016).

2.1 WHO – ECHO Ending Childhood Obesity

In contrast to tobacco control (an area in which the WHO has negotiated an international treaty – the Framework Convention on Tobacco Control[6] - FCTC), the WHO has not used its law-making powers in obesity prevention. Instead, it has acted as a technical agency, a role with which the WHO, primarily comprised of medical professionals, is more comfortable. While the WHO has been criticized for its approach towards obesity, it is not surprising given that the Organization has limited funding, with little earmarked for non-communicable diseases. Despite growing recognition that legislation has an important role to play, encouraged in part by the success of the FCTC, the WHO is predominately a technical agency, not experienced with legislation as a public health tool.[7]

That being said, the WHO's technical role is important in childhood obesity prevention. It offers all States guidance on measures that are most likely to be feasible and successful in ending childhood obesity. The Organization is also developing its ability to support States in building capacity to use law as a tool to reduce the burden of NCDs.[8] Indeed, the WHO has been more progressive in relation to childhood obesity than obesity affecting adults.[9] It is likely that the WHO's approach is influenced by theories of responsibility. Children are generally viewed as blameless, with greater support for measures to protect them, whereas adults are expected to behave 'responsibly', with less protection from the State.

This chapter considers that ECHO's recommendations can offer concrete indicators for States to draw on in fulfilling their obligations under the right to health. International public health governance can support the realization of the right to health, and vice versa. The recommendations can guide the interpretation of State obligations for the right to health in relation to obesity prevention.

---

[6] WHO, Framework Convention on Tobacco Control (adopted 21 May 2003, entered into force 27 February 2005) 2302 UNTS 166. The WHO FCTC was adopted unanimously by the WHA in May 2003 in Resolution WHA 56.1, 2003.

[7] See, e.g., A Taylor, 'Global Governance, International Health Law and WHO: Looking towards the Future' (2002) 80 *Bulletin of the World Health Organization* 975.

[8] See, e.g., WHO European Office for the Prevention and Control of Noncommunicable Diseases, *Key Considerations for the Use of Law to Prevent Noncommunicable Diseases in The Region* (WHO 2017).

[9] For the WHO's approach to obesity in adults, see, e.g., WHA Resolution 'Global Strategy for the Prevention and Control of Noncommunicable Diseases' (22 March 2000) A53/14; WHO, *Global Strategy on Diet Physical Activity and Health* (WHO 2004), endorsed by the WHA resolution 57.17 at the 57th Assembly (22 May 2004).

After all, WHO's Constitution recognizes the right to health.[10] Further, ECHO calls on States, and other duty bearers, to end childhood obesity based on their moral and legal responsibilities under the CRC. ECHO's implementation plan highlights governments' 'ultimate responsibility for ensuring their citizens have a healthy start to life'.[11] Further, the WHO's unique role as the international health agency means that it has vital influence on realizing the broader right to health at a global level. At the same time, WHO is not a human rights agency; its recommendations should provide technical guidance, but not limit the scope of States' obligations under the right to health.

Mindful of the differing but complementary competences of the respective bodies, ECHO's recommendations can guide the CRC Committee's and other human rights actors' interpretations of the right to health and childhood obesity. In the context of food, ECHO calls on States to undertake a range of responsibilities, from informing the population on a healthy diet, including labelling and front-of-pack interpretative symbols, to bolder measures like implementing taxes on sugar-sweetened beverages, implementing the WHO recommendations on marketing to children, and developing nutrient profiles. (see Figure 3.1 below). States should develop guidance on physical activity and ensure that children have adequate spaces and opportunities to do so. Governments should promote and protect breastfeeding, including through implementing the WHO International Code of marketing of breastmilk substitutes and subsequent WHA resolutions.[12] Guidance for NCD prevention should be integrated in current guidance for preconception and antenatal care. ECHO places special emphasis on protecting and promoting healthy diets and physical activity in childcare settings. Children with obesity should be treated and their weight managed. Finally, interventions should be monitored and measured for effectiveness. The interplay between these recommendations and those of public health bodies will be discussed in greater detail in section 4.

2.2 The SDGs

The goal of ending childhood obesity is further underscored by the global development agenda.[13] Through the SDGs, States have committed to relevant

---

[10] Preamble, Constitution of the World Health Organization (adopted 22 July 1946, entry into force 4 July 1948) 14 UNTS 185.
[11] ECHO report, n3, para 13.
[12] World Health Assembly Resolutions of the executive board at its 67th session and of the 34th on the international code of marketing of breast-milk substitutes 1981 Geneva - WHO Resolution EB67.R12.
[13] General Assembly Resolution, Transforming Our World: The 2030 Agenda for Sustainable Development, UN Doc A/RES/70/1, 25 September 2015. See also, Note

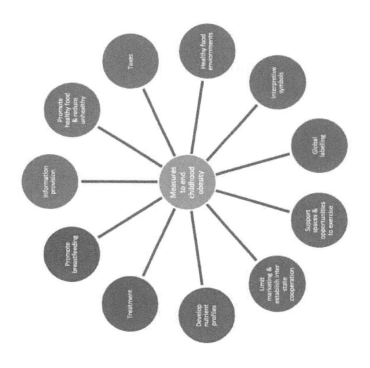

Figure 3.1　Key ECHO Recommendations to States on Ending Childhood Obesity

goals and targets: access to safe and nutritious food, an end to malnutrition in all its forms (target 2.1 and 2.2), and a reduction in premature mortality from NCDs (target 3.4). By eliminating childhood obesity, States may also contribute to the realization of other closely related goals and targets: universal health coverage (target 3.8), quality education (Goal 4), reduced inequalities (Goal 10) and sustainable consumption (Goal 12). While the SDGs are not legally binding, they are subject to broad political agreement and carry important moral weight. Again, these separate but interconnected targets underscore States' responsibilities to act and thereby support the common goal of ending childhood obesity. In fulfilling these important goals, States must draw on specific recommendations, such as evidence-based recommendations coming from ECHO.

3. INTERPRETING CHILDREN'S RIGHTS

The CRC is the primary international legal instrument that enshrines children's rights, including the right to health. The CRC is ratified by all UN Member States, apart from the United States of America. It ensures that children are recognized as holders of an impressive spectrum of rights, from civil and political, to economic, social and cultural rights. It preserves both legal entitlements to the enjoyment of rights, and principles which governments should honour when taking actions to respect, protect and fulfil children's rights.[14] According to the CRC Committee, the following four 'general principles' should be considered when interpreting children's rights: children's *best interests* should be the *primary* consideration in all actions concerning the child,[15] the child's *right to be heard and participate* in all matters affecting him/ her,[16] the *right to non-discrimination*[17] and the *right to life*.[18] This provides a unique normative framework for the interpretation of the convention.

As an international treaty, the rights and the corresponding obligations contained in the CRC are phrased broadly. On the one hand, this enables our understanding of rights to develop organically over time, in line with societal developments. It means that the manner in which the drafters understood

---

by the Secretary-General transmitting the report of the Special Rapporteur on the right of everyone to the enjoyment of the highest attainable standard of physical and mental health, UN Doc A/71/304, 5 August 2016.

[14] Under CRC, Art 4, States Parties must take 'all appropriate legislative, administrative, and other measures for the implementation' of all rights.
[15] Ibid., Art 3.
[16] Ibid., Art 12.
[17] Ibid., Art 2.
[18] Ibid., Art 6.

rights in the late 1980s is not definitive and is instead subject to evolution. On the other hand, it can allow for unprincipled and impractical interpretations based on the interpreter's subjective understanding of the text. This can prove unhelpful as, it is submitted, treaty interpretations must be sufficiently persuasive for governments to consider them valid and the State thereby bound.

A major obstacle to accurately interpreting the CRC (and other UN human rights treaties) is that compliance is not monitored by an international court that can issue binding judgments or compel a party to the treaty to comply. The CRC, as with complementary human rights treaties, such as the International Covenant on Civil and Political Rights, is monitored by a body of independent experts, in this instance, the Committee on the Rights of the Child. This contrasts with regimes like international trade law, which ensure State compliance with treaties through the establishment of dispute resolution processes and the threat of economic sanctions in cases of non-compliance.[19] The relative weakness of compliance mechanisms in international human rights law has led commentators to question the scope of the obligations imposed, i.e. whether States should implement obligations immediately or in stages.[20]

The CRC Committee is composed of 18 experts 'of high moral standing and recognized competence in the field' who monitor the progress made by the States Parties in realizing rights under the CRC and provide guidance on the steps necessary to fulfil their obligations.[21] Although the Committee's interpretations are not strictly binding, having been tasked with monitoring the CRC, they are persuasive. First, the Committee makes 'authoritative'[22] recommendations to States, called concluding observations, on the actions they should take to comply with the treaty. These recommendations respond to the reports that the States Parties to the CRC are required to submit every fifth year. Secondly, the Committee drafts general comments – detailed analyses of specific rights and obligations under the treaty.[23] They are widely viewed as an authoritative

---

[19] The European Convention on Human Rights, on the other hand, is enforced by a court that renders binding decisions. However, the Court's jurisdiction is limited to its States parties (Council of Europe Member States). Further, the Convention primarily protects civil and political rights, not economic and social rights. For this reason, its contributions are not considered here. Council of Europe, European Convention for the Protection of Human Rights and Fundamental Freedoms, as amended by Protocols Nos. 11 and 14, 4 November 1950, ETS 5.

[20] See, e.g., A Boyle, 'Some Reflections on the Relationship of Treaties and Soft Law,' (1999) 48 *ICLQ* 907.

[21] CRC, Art 43.

[22] CRC Committee, 'Report on the Second Session' adopted by the Committee at its 46th Meeting, UN Doc CRC/C/10, 9 October 1992, para 42.

[23] CRC, Art 45(d).

interpretation of obligations that carry 'political and moral weight'.[24] General comments have legal significance: international courts, both the International Court of Justice and European Court of Human Rights have cited them in their decisions.[25] Furthermore, some domestic courts refer to general comments when interpreting national and international law.[26] Finally, where States have ratified the third optional protocol to the CRC, the Committee can issue non-binding views/ decisions on concrete cases.[27]

Yet, as the Committee has no powers to impose sanctions on States, it must rely primarily on its persuasive ability to induce States to comply, an ability significantly strengthened when complemented by external pressure from domestic and regional courts, national human rights bodies, civil society and other UN mechanisms, including the Universal Periodic Review.

This contribution focuses on the approach of the CRC Committee to the interpretation the CRC. Considering the above, States should take the Committee's recommendations seriously when implementing their duties under the CRC. Civil society can further use the Committee's recommendations to press for reform. In the next section, we introduce rights-based

---

[24] D Otto, 'Gender Comment: Why Does the UN Committee on Economic, Social and Cultural Rights Need a General Comment on Women?' (2002) 14 *Canadian Journal of Women & Law* 11; N Ando, 'General Comments/ Recommendations' in *Max Planck Encyclopedia of Public International Law* (OUP 2010).

[25] The International Court of Justice has referred to general comments in two advisory opinions (Legal Consequences of the Construction of a Wall in the Occupied Palestinian Territory, Advisory Opinion, ICJ Reports 2004, p 193; Judgment No 2867 of the Administrative Tribunal of the International Labour Organization upon a Complaint Filed against the International Fund for Agricultural Development, Advisory Opinion, ICJ Reports 2012, p 10, para 39) and one judgment (*Ahmadou Sadio Diallo (Republic of Guinea v Democratic Republic of the Congo)*, Merits, Judgment, ICJ Reports 2010, p 639, see paras 66–67).

[26] The UK Supreme Court has referred to the CRC Committee's General Comments, see *In re JR* 1 July 2015 [2015] UKSC 42 [2016] AC 1131; *ZH (Tanzania) v Secretary of State for the Home Department*, Supreme Court 1 February 2011 [2011] UKSC 4 [2011] 2 AC 16. In contrast, a search of Irish judgments for references to general comments yielded only two results: the Irish District Court referred to General Comment No 10 of the Committee on the Rights of the Child without pronouncing on the weight it attributed to the source (*see Director of Public Prosecutions v TC* [2017] IEDC 07, para 22); and the Irish High Court referred to a general comment of the UN Committee on Economic, Social and Cultural Rights (*NHV v Minister for Justice & Equality and Ors* [2017] IESC 35, para 16).

[27] Optional Protocol to the Convention on the Rights of the Child on a communications procedure Adopted and opened for signature, ratification and accession by General Assembly resolution A/RES/66/138 of 19 December 2011 entered into force on 14 April 2014. As the CRC Committee has not issued any views on childhood obesity, these are not discussed here.

approaches as a means of articulating children's rights and States' obligations under the CRC.

3.1 Rights-based Approaches

Rights-based approaches originated in the context of development from a desire to move beyond addressing needs, towards focusing on individuals' rights and entitlements.[28] Since 1997 the UN General Assembly has called upon all its agencies and programmes to mainstream human rights into their programmes and activities.[29] A common understanding of a human rights-based approach was developed in 2003, which outlined three elements of a human rights based approach to development.[30] First, all policies, programmes and actions should *further the realization of human rights*. Secondly, *human rights standards and principles should guide* all actions, cooperation and programming in all sectors and in all phases of the process.[31] Finally, all policies, programmes and actions should *contribute to the development of capacities* of the duty bearers to meet their obligations and/or the rights holders to claim their rights.

Based on this common understanding, UN agencies and others have accommodated the definition of such an approach in their mandate. For example, according to the WHO:

> A human rights-based approach to health specifically aims at realizing the right to health and other health-related human rights. Health policy making and programming are to be guided by human rights standards and principles and aim at developing the capacity of duty bearers to meet their obligations and empowering rights-holders to effectively claim their health rights.[32]

Therefore, the WHO clearly recognizes the potential for health and human rights to complement each other. While the extent to which UN agencies have

---

[28] M Robinson, 'Introduction' in M Santos-Pais, *A Human Rights Conceptual Framework for UNICEF* (Innocenti Essay no 9 1999) iv.

[29] UN General Assembly, 'Renewing the United Nations: A Programme for Reform', UN Doc A/51/950, 17 July 1997.

[30] 'The Human Rights Based Approach to Development Cooperation - Towards a Common Understanding among the United Nations Agencies' (Second Inter-Agency Workshop, May 2003).

[31] The common understanding lists human rights *standards* and *principles* including universality and inalienability; indivisibility; inter-dependence and inter-relatedness; non-discrimination and equality; participation and inclusion; accountability and the rule of law (ibid).

[32] WHO, 'A Human Rights-Based Approach to Health', www.who.int/hhr/news/hrba_to_health2.pdf (accessed 12 February 2018).

successfully implemented rights-based approaches is questioned, the latter have become common parlance among UN agencies' mandates.[33]

To shape a human rights-based approach to children's rights, we rely on the work of the CRC Committee, as although rights-based approaches are increasingly adopted in the field of children's rights, their precise contours are not always clear. Inter-governmental and non-governmental organizations, as well as academics, often adopt their own conception of a child rights-based approach.[34] Reflecting this fluidity, unprincipled rights-based approaches have been criticized as 'vague generalizations'.[35]

From its earliest general comments, the CRC Committee recommended that States adopt child-centred, child-friendly or child rights-based approaches.[36] The Committee's description of a rights based approach – clearly influenced by the UN common understanding – encompasses four central elements: (1) further the realization of children's rights; (2) by developing duty bearers' capacity to do so; and (3) supporting rights holders' capacity to claim their rights; (4) while guided by general principles.[37] These elements are very close to the definition of a rights-based approach in the 'common understanding'. Yet, this broad outline does not articulate how States should fulfil these responsibilities.

Therefore, the general comments of the CRC Committee were systematically analysed through content analysis. The aim was to provide a method of interpreting children's rights under the CRC through a detailed, traceable interpretation of what the Committee means by a children's rights approach.[38] The

---

[33] See further, B Meier and W Onzivu, 'The Evolution of Human Rights in World Health Organization Policy and the Future of Human Rights Through Global Health Governance' (2014) 128(2) *Public Health* 179.

[34] For an account of rights-based approaches see S Gruskin, D Bogecho and L Ferguson, 'Rights-based Approaches to Health Policies and Programs: Articulations, Ambiguities, and Assessment' (2010) 31 *J Public Health Policy* 129.

[35] J Tobin, 'Beyond the Supermarket Shelf: Using a Rights Based Approach to Address Children's Health Needs' (2006) 14 *International Journal of Children's Rights* 275, 276.

[36] See, e.g.: CRC Committee, General Comment No 1: The aims of education, UN Doc CRC/GC/2001/1, 17 April 2001, para 2; CRC Committee, 'General Comment No 3: HIV/AIDS and the right of the child, UN Doc CRC/GC/2003/3, 17 March 2003, para 20.

[37] CRC Committee, General Comment No 13: The Right of the Child to Freedom from all forms of Violence, UN Doc CRC/C/GC/13 18 April 2011, para 59.

[38] Every general comment of the CRC Committee (18 at the time) was analysed. The texts were read several times and then analysed paragraph by paragraph. After the initial readings, paragraphs were coded by reducing the topic sentence to a shorter summary line and finally to one or two words to capture the central ethos of the paragraph. After this initial coding, themes were built. The codes were then rechecked in

results of the content analysis assert that a children's rights approach should build the capacities of rights holders and duty bearers, and fulfil children's rights, through crafting an enabling environment, pursuing empowerment through societal and legal transformation, and ensuring accountability.[39]

First, following the Committee's approach, an *enabling environment* requires that duty bearers develop a setting that avoids rights' infringements and supports rights' fulfilment.[40] At a macro level, this requires States to develop policies, such as information campaigns to tackle harmful attitudes and discrimination. In the case of childhood obesity prevention, this could encompass measures suggested by ECHO, like developing a healthy food environment and opportunities to engage in physical activity. Further, States should use law to ensure a regulatory framework that protects the rights enshrined in the CRC.[41] An enabling environment includes an obligation to protect children from harm by non-State actors.[42] This may require protective regulation that limits drivers of obesity, like unhealthy food marketing, and empowering legislation that promotes the population's understanding of nutrition, like food labelling.

Through *empowerment*, children are supported in enjoying their rights, while duty bearers are buttressed in fulfilling their obligations. The content analysis, like ECHO, emphasizes that while States have duties to prevent childhood obesity, other actors have responsibilities too. The CRC Committee identifies several duty bearers, such as States, parents and families, schools, the

---

light of the developed codes and some were rephrased. Infrequent codes were excluded as without multiple references (4+), they could not be indicative of an 'approach'. Thematic content analysis was used to establish patterns or themes within data. After the themes had been designed, the codes were searched again to ensure coherence and accuracy (See, Katharina Ó Cathaoir, 'A Children's Rights Perspective on Obesogenic Food Marketing to Children' (PhD thesis, University of Copenhagen, 2017).

[39] CRC Committee, General Comment No 5: General Measures of Implementation of the Convention on the Rights of the Child, UN Doc CRC/GC/2003/5, 27 November 2003, para 11.

[40] General Comment No 3, n36, para 42; CRC Committee, General Comment No 4: Adolescent health and Development in the context of the Convention on the Rights of the Child UN Doc CRC/GC/2003/4, 1 July 2003, para 8.

[41] CRC Committee, Joint General Recommendation No 31 of the Committee on the Elimination of Discrimination against Women/General Comment No 18 of the CRC Committee on Harmful Practices, UN Doc CEDAW/C/GC/31/CRC/C/GC/18, 14 Nov 2014, para 30.

[42] CRC Committee, General comment No 17: The Right of the Child to Rest, Leisure, Play, Recreational Activities, Cultural Life and the Arts, UN Doc CRC/C/GC/17, 17 April 2013, para 14.

media and businesses.⁴³ The State has an important role in empowering both rights holders and duty bearers through awareness raising, education, information, training, the provision of adequate resources and dissemination of the provisions and principles of the CRC.⁴⁴ Further, children should be recognized and respected as rights holders, and members of communities, cultures and religions.⁴⁵ Children must not only be protected but also empowered to access their entitlements. This can be achieved through information dissemination and raised awareness, but it also requires the creation of an environment where healthy choices are supported, not one where unhealthy options are the norm.

Lastly, *accountability* represents a 'sub-theme' of empowerment and the enabling environment. Duty bearers should be held accountable through monitoring, evaluation and review of their duties and the measures taken to fulfil their responsibilities. Further, duty bearers must provide an accessible right of redress and remedy where rights are breached.⁴⁶ For example, if a company fails to honour its human rights commitments to children, for example, by breaching marketing standards, children should have a right of redress and access to some form of compensation. While companies' responsibilities are non-binding, States retain the primary duty and must ensure adequate reparation for infringements of children's rights.⁴⁷

Additionally, besides the general principles listed above, the CRC Committee also frequently draws on further subsidiary principles, which can be applied when interpreting the scope of rights and obligations, and the correct balance between rights and responsibilities. *Indivisibility, interdependency, interconnectedness and equality* require that individual rights are not analysed in a vacuum. Instead, the full spectrum of rights should be considered.⁴⁸ Therefore, a State's obligations to prevent childhood obesity are not limited to

---

⁴³ General Comment No 1, n36, para 21; General Comment No 4, n40, para 7; General Comment No 5, n39, para 56.

⁴⁴ CRC Committee, General Comment No 16: State Obligations regarding the Impact of the Business Sector on Children's Rights, UN Doc CRC/C/GC/16, 17 April 2013, para 56; CRC Committee, General Comment No 15: The Right of the Child to the Enjoyment of the Highest Attainable Standard of Health, UN Doc CRC/C/GC/15, 17 April 2013, para 91; CRC Committee, General Comment No 13, n37, paras 44, 73.

⁴⁵ CRC Committee, General Comment No 6: Treatment of Unaccompanied and Separated Children Outside their Country of Origin, UN Doc CRC/GC/2005/6, 1 September 2005, para 42.

⁴⁶ CRC Committee, General Comment No 5, n39, para 24; CRC Committee, General Comment No 10: Children's Rights in Juvenile Justice UN Doc CRC/C/GC/10, 25 April 2007, para 98; CRC Committee, General Comment No 9, The Rights of Children with Disabilities, UN Doc CRC/C/GC/9, 27 February 2007, para 26.

⁴⁷ The issue of accountability is pursued in further detail in subsequent chapters by Bartlett and Curtis in this volume.

⁴⁸ General Comment No 15, n44, para 96.

the right to health, and rights, such as the right to adequate food and freedom of expression, must also be weighted in analysing States' duties. In addition, the CRC Committee advocates a *gender perspective*.[49] In the case of childhood obesity, laws and policies should analyse whether gender creates barriers to, for example, physical exercise or access to nutritious food, leading to differential impacts. Further, the principle of *human dignity*[50] underlines that laws and policies on childhood obesity must respect children as rights holders. At the same time, *vulnerability* underscores the need for special attention to be paid to children: childhood is a state of evolution during which children, as individuals and groups, are particularly vulnerable to rights' violations.[51] Therefore, policies should recognize children's susceptibility to certain drivers of obesity, such as marketing, and the differential impact of obesity on children. Finally, *family unity* underscores the dependence of children on their parents, and the need to preserve this relationship where possible.[52] Accordingly, the State should approach childhood obesity prevention from the perspective of supporting the family in realizing children's rights, not as antagonistic.

While this approach is influenced by the building blocks of the UN common understanding and the CRC Committee's description, it provides a more normative approach that makes use of the detailed guidance set out by the Committee. It focuses on the specifics of the CRC and childhood, viewing States as owing special duties to children.

3.2   The Right to an Open Future

Building on this approach, we adopt the children's 'right to an open future' as an underlying theory guiding the interpretation of rights. Without a theory of what serves children best, rights-based approaches can be rendered empty or lack transparency. Instead, we need a conception of 'best', i.e., what is the optimal outcome for the child?

While the right to an open future was originally advanced in the context of parents' rights and duties, we apply this underpinning to the role of the State. The right to an open future – as we conceive of it – implies that if children's rights are violated, certain options will be closed before children can exercise them.[53] The State should therefore preserve this autonomy-like right so

---

[49]   General Comment No 4, n40, para 28.
[50]   General Comment No 1, n36, para 8.
[51]   General Comment No 3, n36, para 5.
[52]   General Comment No 7: Implementing Child Rights in Early Childhood, UN Doc CRC/C/GC/7/Rev.1, 20 September 2006, para 7.
[53]   J Feinberg, 'The Child's Right to an Open Future' in H LaFollette and W Aiken (eds), *Whose Child? Children's Rights, Parental Authority and State Power* (Littlefield, Adams & Co 1980) 126.

that children can make their own choices when they have the capacity to do so.[54] Where there is a conflict between children's rights, and other rights and interests, the State should adopt an approach that ensures an open future for every child. Within reason, children and parents' autonomy may be limited to prevent irreparable harm to the child's rights, with a view to safeguarding the prospect of future autonomy. Thus, protecting children's future autonomy may require limiting current choices in a manner that would not be possible with adults who already exercise full autonomy.[55]

This approach is applicable to obesity prevention, as often the harms that laws and policies seek to mitigate do not appear until later in life. For instance, children with obesity are more likely to be obese as adults and experience health concerns such as diabetes and cardiovascular disease.[56] Further, children often do not have the same capacity as adults to envision long-term consequences of short-term dietary behaviour, such as the formation of entrenched habits, preferences or perceived needs.[57] Indeed, behavioural research claims that adults also often act irrationally and do not make healthy food choices despite having the needed information.[58] Accordingly, both current and future impacts should be considered in policymaking.

In light of the foregoing, in obesity prevention, we submit that the focus of the State should be on protecting children's open future through avoiding their health being compromised before they have decision-making capacity. Still, in pursuing a rights-based approach, States should also avoid stigmatization and normative assumptions on personal appearance and instead concentrate on promoting health (discussed further in section 6). As Feinberg warns, the child's future should be interpreted in a neutral manner and courts (or the State) should not impose their conception of the 'good life'.[59] Accordingly, limitations on freedoms must be proportionate. In other words, children cannot be protected from every potential harm and risk, and the harms posed by actions and inactions must be balanced. Therefore, while banning the sale

---

[54] Ibid., 125.
[55] Ibid., 127.
[56] M Simmonds et al., 'Predicting Adult Obesity from Childhood Obesity: A Systematic Review and Meta-Analysis' (2016) 17 *Obes Rev* 95.
[57] Cognitive development and understanding of nutrition/ healthy eating is linked: see, T Xu and I Jones, 'An Investigation of Children's Understanding of Food and Nutrition' (2016) 44(4) *Early Childhood Education Journal* 289; GG Zeinstra et al., 'Cognitive Development and Children's Perceptions of Fruit And Vegetables: A Qualitative Study' (2007) 4 *International Journal of Behavioral Nutrition and Physical Activity* 30.
[58] See, e.g., MP Kelly and M Barker, 'Why is Changing Health-Related Behaviour so Difficult?' (2016) 136 *Public Health* 109.
[59] 'The Child's Right to an Open Future', n53, 139.

of sugar sweetened beverages in schools could be justified with reference to children's rights, blanket bans in all retail outlets with a view to protecting children would likely stretch the scope of States' duties. In the next section, children's right to health in the context of obesity prevention is interpreted using the foregoing approach.

4. THE RIGHT TO HEALTH AND CHILDHOOD OBESITY

The right to the highest attainable standard of health is a universal human right recognized in numerous human rights treaties, spanning the International Bill of Rights (the Universal Declaration on Human Rights (UDHR) and the International Covenant on Economic, Social and Cultural Rights (ICESCR)), and the CRC.[60] While the right to health is not the only right of importance to childhood obesity, there is an undeniably strong link between its aims and childhood obesity.[61] Although UN committees have been slow to define health, the broad definition of health enshrined in the preamble to the WHO Constitution can guide the human rights framework – 'a state of complete physical, mental and social wellbeing'.[62] Clearly, States Parties have undertaken an important mission to respect, protect and fulfil the right to health that includes preventing childhood obesity.

The scope of the obligation undertaken by States under the CRC is phrased broadly:

> States Parties recognize the right of the child to the enjoyment of the highest attainable standard of health and to facilities for the treatment of illness and rehabilitation of health. States Parties shall strive to ensure that no child is deprived of his or her right of access to such health care services. (article 24.1)

The right to health is thus not limited to access to health care but also includes health promotion and disease prevention. The CRC Committee has recognized the right to health as:

> ... an inclusive right, extending not only to timely and appropriate prevention, health promotion, curative, rehabilitative and palliative services, but also to a right

---

[60] UN General Assembly, International Covenant on Economic, Social and Cultural Rights, 16 December 1966, United Nations, Treaty Series, vol. 993, p 3, Art 12; UN General Assembly, Universal Declaration of Human Rights, 10 December 1948, UNGA Res 217 A (III) (UDHR) Art 25.

[61] The full spectrum of rights are considered in the chapter by Roache and Cabrera in this volume.

[62] Constitution of the World Health Organization, n10.

to grow and develop to their full potential and live in conditions that enable them to attain the highest standard of health through the implementation of programmes that address the underlying determinants of health…[63]

Drawing on this interpretation, it is reasonable to consider obesity prevention and treatment as within the scope of States' obligations under the right to health. After all, obesity is a cause of various diseases, such as cardiovascular disease, insulin resistance, diabetes and psychological conditions. Overweight and obesity in childhood portend a higher likelihood of adult obesity and premature death, thus preventing children from developing to their full potential and attaining the highest standard of health. Therefore, a common-sense understanding suggests that States Parties are under an obligation to respond to increasing obesity rates and strive to end childhood obesity through both health promotion and disease prevention. However, acknowledging that States have a responsibility goes only so far.

Instead, it is necessary to develop a clear interpretation of States' obligations. As a starting point, considering the rights-based approach analysed above, it is submitted that States should promote an environment that enables and empowers children to attain the highest attainable standard of health. To fulfil this obligation, States could adopt various measures as suggested by ECHO. The State could create a healthy environment through informing children and families on healthy diets and exercise, and advising schools, the media and businesses of their responsibilities to create a healthy environment for children.

However, information and education alone are insufficient. The State is uniquely mandated to use regulatory tools as a means of protecting children from the drivers of ill health and promoting healthful behaviour. Law is a powerful means of holding duty bearers to account through monitoring, evaluation and review of their duties and the measures taken to fulfil their obligations. Law can also outline duty bearers' (such as parents) responsibilities to fulfil their obligations. Furthermore, legislation can enshrine a right to redress and remedies where children's rights are violated, such as where companies promote unhealthy food in contradiction to their responsibilities to children. This approach largely aligns with that of ECHO, introduced above. But, is there coherence between the public health and human rights approaches in practice?

---

[63] General Comment No 15, n44, para 2.

4.1 Recommendations from Human Rights Bodies

Clearly, ECHO has issued several important recommendations (section 2.1) but are these reflected in the recommendations of human rights bodies?[64] The CRC Committee has made recommendations on childhood obesity in three general comments.[65] Yet, there is scope for its approach to be strengthened. For instance, between 2000 and 2017, the CRC Committee issued 34 concluding observations to 33 countries relating to childhood obesity.[66] Most of these recommendations are general, merely calling on the State to take an obscure form of action to address childhood obesity. These recommendations can serve to highlight obesity as a human rights issue, but clearer guidance is of greater assistance to States and advocates alike. Besides the CRC Committee, in 2012, the UN High Commissioner for Human Rights made recommendations on obesity prevention in the context of children's right to health. Similarly, in

---

[64] Parts of this analysis is derived from KÓ Cathaoir, 'Childhood Obesity and the Right to Health' (2016) 18 *Health and Human Rights Journal* 249; KÓ Cathaoir, 'Child Rights as a Basis for the Regulation of Food Marketing: The Role of the UN Convention on the Rights of the Child' in T Liefaard and J Sloth-Nielsen (eds), *The United Nations Convention on the Rights of the Child* (Brill Nijhoff 2017).

[65] CRC Committee, General Comments Nos 15, 16, 17, n42 and n44.

[66] CRC Committee Concluding Observations (up to 2017): Georgia (UN Doc CRC/C/GEO/CO/4, 9 March 2017), Saint Vincent and the Grenadines (UN Doc CRC/C/VCT/CO/2-3, 13 March 2017), Nauru (UN Doc CRC/C/NRU/CO/1, 28 October 2016), Suriname (UN Doc CRC/C/SUR/CO/3-4, 9 November 2016), UK (UN Doc CRC/C/GBR/CO/5, 12 July 2016), Brunei Darussalam (UN Doc CRC/C/BRN/CO/2-3, 24 February 2016), United Arab Emirates (UN Doc CRC/C/ARE/CO/2, 2015), Brazil (UN Doc CRC/C/OPAC/BRA/CO/1, 2015), Jamaica (UN Doc CRC/C/JAM/CO/3-4, 10 March 2015), Switzerland (UN Doc CRC/C/CHE/CO/2-4, 26 February 2015), Hungary (UN Doc CRC/C/HUN/CO/3-5, 14 October 2014), Poland (UN Doc CRC/C/POL/CO/3-4, 30 October 2015), Mexico (UN Doc CRC/C/MEX/CO/4-5, 3 July 2015), Saint Lucia (UN Doc CRC/C/VCT/CO/2-3, 13 June 2014), Netherlands (UN Doc CRC/C/NLD/CO/4, 8 June 2015), Armenia (UN Doc CRC/C/ARM/CO/3-4, 8 July 2013), Slovenia (UN Doc CRC/C/SVN/CO/3-4, 8 July 2013), Malta (UN Doc CRC/C/MLT/CO/2, 18 June 2013), Tuvalu (UN Doc CRC/C/TUV/CO/1, 29 October 2013), Austria (UN Doc CRC/C/AUT/CO/3-4, 3 December 2012), Canada (UN Doc CRC/C/CAN/CO/3-4, 2 February 2012), Iceland (UN Doc CRC/C/ISL/CO/3-4, 23 January 2012), Cook Islands (UN Doc CRC/C/COK/CO/1, 22 February 2012), Republic of Korea (UN Doc CRC/C/KOR/CO/3-4, 2 February 2012), Seychelles (UN Doc CRC/C/SYC/CO/2-4, 23 January 2012), Italy (UN Doc CRC/C/ITA/CO/3-4, 31 October 2012), Finland (UN Doc CRC/C/FIN/CO/4, 3 August 2011), Cuba (UN Doc CRC/C/CUB/CO/2, 3 August 2011), Denmark (UN Doc CRC/C/DNK/CO/4, 7 April 2011), Spain (UN Doc CRC/C/ESP/CO/3-4, 3 November 2010), Belgium (UN Doc CRC/C/BEL/CO/3-4, 18 June 2010), Sweden (UN Doc CRC/C/SWE/CO/4, 26 June 2009), Chile (UN Doc CRC/C/CHL/CO/3, 23 April 2007), (UN Doc CRC/C/CHL/CO/4-5, 30 October 2015).

2014, the Special Rapporteur on the Right to Health drew attention to States' obligations to prevent obesity, while in 2016, the Special Rapporteur outlined obligations regarding sport and healthy lifestyles.

Below, the concrete guidance of these human rights bodies is categorized under two headings: recommendations relating to a healthy diet and those on physical activity. Subsequently, it is suggested that through systematically drawing on ECHO's plan, the CRC Committee's approach could be strengthened to offer more concrete and effective guidance to both States Parties and civil society.

4.1.1   A healthy diet

Human rights bodies call on States to promote a healthy diet, particularly through information provision. For instance, the CRC Committee advises States to limit exposure to 'fast foods', while simultaneously promoting more healthful options.[67] In its concluding observations, the CRC Committee has recommended that States 'develop policies to ensure that healthy food choices are available and affordable, and strengthen awareness campaigns to promote the benefits of healthy eating for children'.[68] States should 'address issues of malnutrition, anaemia and other micronutrient deficiencies, as well as obesity through, inter alia, education and the promotion of healthy feeding practices'.[69] Similarly, according to the Committee on Economic, Social and Cultural Rights (CESCR) that monitors ICESCR, access to nutritionally adequate food is a core obligation.[70] The CESCR stresses the importance of taking measures to prevent, treat and control epidemic and endemic diseases and to provide 'education and access to information concerning the main health problems in the community, including methods of preventing and controlling them'.[71]

In General Comment No 15 on the right to health, the CRC Committee made more specific recommendations: calling on States to regulate unhealthy food marketing and limit unhealthy food in schools and other places.[72] In its concluding observations, the Committee has reinforced regulation of marketing. For instance, it suggested that Brazil 'establish a regulatory framework for

---

[67] General Comment No 15 (n44) para 47.
[68] CRC Committee, Concluding Observations Nauru, UN Doc CRC/C/NRU/CO/1, 28 October 2016, para 43(e).
[69] CRC Committee, Concluding Observations Georgia, UN Doc CRC/C/GEO/CO/4, 9 March 2017, para 32(d).
[70] Committee on Economic, Social and Cultural Rights (CESCR), General Comment No 14, The Right to the Highest Attainable Standard of Health (Art 12), UN Doc E/C12/2000/4, 11 August 2000, para 43.
[71] Ibid., para. 44.
[72] General Comment No 15, n44, para 47.

advertisements, with a view to protecting children from misleading advertising'.[73] Other recommendations in General Comment No 15 include, advising States to ensure access to adequate, appropriate and safe food,[74] to promote breastfeeding[75] and ensure access to clean drinking water.[76] The Committee has offered further targeted observations, calling on Poland and the United Kingdom to systematically gather data on nutrition, including overweight and obesity, and monitor and assess the effectiveness of existing policies.[77]

Other human rights bodies have made more detailed recommendations. The UN High Commissioner for Human Rights focused on children's access to adequate nutrition, with parental education, regulation of advertising, and the promotion of healthful foods recommended.[78] Similarly, the Special Rapporteur on the Right to Health emphasized that States should ensure available and accessible food in the necessary quantity and quality,[79] including by regulating the conduct of the food industry.[80] A number of measures were suggested, such as access to sufficient information through nutrition guidelines and labelling,[81] taxation of unhealthful foods and price reduction of healthful foods,[82] provision of healthful food in child-centred institutions, limiting access to fast food and drinks, and regulating advertising and marketing of 'unhealthy food and beverages'.[83]

Human rights bodies further highlight the impact of the business sector on children's rights in the context of obesity.[84] In line with States' obligations to protect, 'States must take all necessary, appropriate and reasonable measures to prevent business enterprises from causing or contributing to abuses of chil-

---

[73] CRC Committee, Concluding Observations Brazil, UN Doc CRC/C/BRA/CO/2–4, 30 October 2015.
[74] General Comment No 15, n44, para 43.
[75] Ibid., para 44.
[76] Ibid., para 48.
[77] CRC Committee, Concluding Observations United Kingdom of Great Britain and Northern Ireland, UN Doc CRC/C/GBR/CO/5, 12 July 2016, para 67; Concluding Observations Poland, CRC/C/POL/CO/3-4, 30 October 2015, para 37.
[78] UN Human Rights Council, Report of the United Nations High Commissioner for Human Rights on the Right of the Child to the Enjoyment of the Highest Attainable Standard of Health, UN Doc A/HRC/22/31, 4 December 2012, para 44.
[79] UN General Assembly, Report of the Special Rapporteur on the right of everyone to the enjoyment of the highest attainable standard of physical and mental health, UN Doc A/HRC/26/31, 1 April 2014, para 12.
[80] Ibid., para 25.
[81] Ibid., paras 17–19.
[82] Ibid., paras 19–21.
[83] Ibid., para 38.
[84] General Comment No 16, n44, para 19.

dren's rights'.[85] Furthermore, States are advised to engage with mass media to support healthy lifestyles.[86] States should ensure that marketing and advertising does not negatively affect children's rights through adopting regulations and encouraging businesses to adopt codes.[87] This includes implementing and enforcing international standards, although the Committee has not drawn States' attention to the WHO marketing recommendations. Given that the Committee has recognized other non-binding WHO documents, it is likely to be an oversight, not a rejection of the marketing recommendations.[88]

While States are the primary duty bearers, food and beverage companies are also recognized as holding responsibilities in relation to obesity. For instance, the High Commissioner called on companies to comply with the UN Guiding Principles on Business and Human Rights and 'limit the advertisement of food and drinks detrimental to children's health and development'.[89] The Special Rapporteur also encouraged private industry to adopt standards to improve nutrition quality, and increase product labelling and information.[90] Still, the CRC primarily obligates States, meaning that its ability to persuade companies is more limited.[91]

4.1.2 Physical activity

Physical activity is encouraged by the CRC Committee, with detailed guidance coming from the Special Rapporteur.[92] In its concluding observations to Sweden, the CRC Committee recommended the country 'strengthen measures to inter alia address overweight and obesity, and promote a healthy lifestyle among adolescents, including physical activity'.[93] The CRC Committee called on Iceland to 'promote healthy lifestyle among children and their parents',[94] including through public education.[95] In regard to Denmark, the CRC Committee suggested the State develop opportunities to take part in physical

---

[85] Ibid., paras 28, 21.
[86] Ibid., para 58.
[87] Ibid., para 59.
[88] General Comment No 15, n44, para 66, General Comment No 16, n44, para 57.
[89] Report of the UN High Commissioner, n78, para 107.
[90] Special Rapporteur, n79, paras 28–32.
[91] Companies responsibilities in relation to obesity are discussed further here: KÓ Cathaoir, 'Children's Rights to Freedom from Obesity: Responsibilities of the Food Industry' (2018) 36 *Nordic Journal of Human Rights* 109.
[92] The High Commissioner called on States to promote physical exercise in the school curriculum. Report of the UN High Commissioner, n78, para 102.
[93] Concluding Observations Sweden, n66, para 45(b).
[94] Concluding Observations Iceland, n66, para 37.
[95] Concluding Observations Saudi Arabia UN Doc CRC/C/SAU/CO/2 (CRC 17 March 2006) para 56.

activity.[96] In contrast, the Special Rapporteur articulated States' obligations to respect, protect and fulfil, such as through promoting exercise in national planning, active commuting and schools.[97] The CRC Committee should draw on this report and develop detailed targets.

4.2   Assessment

Human rights bodies have made several recommendations to States Parties on ending childhood obesity. In culmination, they mirror most of those made by ECHO (see Table 3.1 below). However, there is little interaction between public health and human rights. Further, the CRC Committee generally fails to make specific recommendations in its concluding observations to States. Instead, the Committee often expresses concern and makes general recommendations to the State party to 'manage', 'take measures' or strengthen efforts to address obesity in children. Obesity is typically mentioned alongside other 'lifestyle' vices, such as tobacco or alcohol use.[98] The CRC Committee's recommendations emphasize education and sometimes marketing regulation. Unlike the Special Rapporteur, the Committee has not made recommendations on taxation or labelling.

A more effective approach would be for the Committee to draw up a list of specific recommendations on childhood obesity, citing WHO documents, such as the ECHO reports. These recommendations could be made to States during the dialogue between the Committee and the State party. Where civil society expresses concern regarding childhood obesity, the Committee could question whether the list of measures have been considered. This would not require the Committee to diverge from existing practice in human rights. As noted above, many of these recommendations have already been highlighted in general comments or other human rights reports.

The Committee's current approach to childhood obesity offers little guidance as to the specifics of a child rights approach to obesity. The CRC Committee should highlight the value added by a rights-based approach through, inter alia, highlighting children's rights principles, such as, empowerment, best interests and participation. This way, both human rights and public health can draw on each other's strengths and cooperate to end childhood obesity.

---

[96]   Concluding Observations Denmark, n66, para 50.
[97]   Report of the Special Rapporteur on the right of everyone to the enjoyment of the highest attainable standard of physical and mental health A/HRC/32/33, 4 April 2016, paras 25, 99.
[98]   Concluding Observations Austria, n66, para 51.

Table 3.1   *Comparison of ECHO and Human Rights' Bodies Recommendations*

	ECHO	Human rights bodies
Information	✓	✓
Taxes	✓	✓
Limiting marketing	✓	✓
Front of pack symbols	✓	
Labelling	✓	✓
Nutrient profiles	✓	
Guidance and spaces for exercise	✓	✓
Promote and protect breastfeeding	✓	✓
Preconception and antenatal guidance	✓	
Emphasis on childcare settings	✓	✓
Treat and manage weight	✓	✓
Monitor and measures interventions	✓	Concluding observations
Access to clean water	✓	✓
Focus on healthy childcare environment	✓	✓

5. SHARED RESPONSIBILITY: STATE AND PARENTS

Having analysed States' duties, it must be asked, what is the scope of parental responsibility and how does it affect States' obligations? First, under the CRC, States' obligations must be interpreted with due respect for parental responsibilities. Therefore, the latter limit the State's discretion: when undertaking appropriate measures States must consider the rights and duties of parents, legal guardians, etc.[99] The family's important role is recognized in the preamble to the CRC, which refers to the family as 'the fundamental group of society and the natural environment for the growth and wellbeing of all its members and particularly children'. Accordingly, under Article 18.1 CRC, parents and guardians have the 'primary responsibility for the upbringing and development

---

[99] CRC, Art 3.2.

of the child'. Therefore, the State should not usurp the role of parents. The CRC Committee in turn recognizes that parents play a crucial role in fulfilling children's rights.[100]

Secondly, States owe obligations not only to children, but also to families. This means empowering parents through information and advice, as well as putting structures in place that support parents in fulfilling their obligations. This is clear from the text of the CRC, whereby States should provide the family with appropriate assistance, for example through the provision of information, as well as the development of 'institutions, facilities and services for the care of the children'.[101] This has been interpreted by the Committee to include a responsibility on the State to 'provide an environment that facilitates the discharge of all duty bearers' obligations and responsibilities ... and a regulatory framework'.[102] Furthermore, parents should be empowered by training in the necessary skills,[103] and parenting education and counselling.[104] This education should include aspects on positive child-rearing for parents and caregivers, and provision of accurate and accessible information on specific risks.[105]

Finally, parental rights are conditional, and subject to limitations.[106] Thus, the State must protect children from neglect and abuse, although children should only be separated from their parents where it is in their best interests.[107] As the CRC enshrines children's rights, parental responsibilities derive from their children's superior rights. The deciding factor for the legitimacy of State action or inaction should be the best interests of the child, in light of the object and purpose of the CRC.[108] The CRC Committee urges parents to recognize children as rights holders and listen to their views.[109]

However, while parents should carry out their responsibilities in the best interests of the child under Article 18 CRC, only States are under legal obligations. Parents' responsibilities under the CRC are moral in nature.[110] Accordingly, the CRC Committee has admitted that it is not its role to 'pre-

---

[100] General Comment No 7, n52, para 15.
[101] CRC, Arts 18.2, 24(e).
[102] General Comment No 15, n44, para 91.
[103] General Comment No 7, n52, para 14(c).
[104] Ibid., para 20(c), para 31.
[105] General Comment No 13, n37, para 44(c).
[106] CRC, Arts 18, 5.
[107] Ibid., Arts 19, 9.1.
[108] Ibid., Art 3.
[109] General Comment No 4, n40, para 7.
[110] Urban Jonsson, 'An Approach to Assess and Analyse the Health and Nutrition Situation of Children in the Perspective of the Convention on the Rights of the Child' (1997) 5 *International Journal of Children's Rights* 367, 374.

scribe in detail how parents should relate to or guide their children'.[111] Instead, the precise legal obligations of parents are left to domestic law.

In light of this, States should shape an environment that enables children to achieve good health and empowers both parents and children. Children should not only be protected but empowered to understand and access the determinants of health. In the case of obesity prevention, both parents and children have an interest in children's good health and wellbeing. States should avoid illegitimate restrictions on parental autonomy, and instead support parents and children in pursuing a healthy diet and exercise. States can pursue this through guidance and advice for parents on nutritious meals, but also through structural supports, like building and maintaining safe and accessible places to play and investing in active commuting, and supporting access to affordable, age-appropriate food through limiting promotion and subsidies of unhealthy food, while promoting nutritious food.

Thus, while parents play an important role, they do not control the regulatory environment. For instance, some measures suggested by both ECHO and human rights bodies, such as taxation and marketing restrictions, are powers exercised by States. Generally, neither parents nor States are capable of upholding children's rights alone; instead each has separate but interconnected responsibilities. States are obligated to 'shape environments in ways that enable families to create living conditions that support their children'.[112] Parents are responsible for day-to-day care and guidance. Only in extreme cases where a child's open future is severely threatened, will removing an obese child from their parent's care be appropriate.[113]

---

[111] CRC Committee, General Comment No 8: The Right of the Child to Protection from Corporal Punishment and other cruel or degrading forms of Punishment, UN Doc CRC/C/GC/8, 2 March 2007, para 46.

[112] A Eide, *A Commentary on the United Nations Convention on the Rights of the Child, Article 27: The Right to an Adequate Standard of Living* (Nijhoff 2006) 14.

[113] Removal of children from their parents due to overweight appears to be rare and only justifiable in cases of imminent severe harm. In 2014, a British newspaper found 74 instances where a child had been removed from its family due to obesity, Martin Bagot, 'Seventy-four kids taken into care for their own protection as they are TOO FAT' (*The Mirror*, 27 February 2014) http://www.mirror.co.uk/news/uk-news/seventy-four-kids-taken-care-protection-3190690 (accessed 12 February 2018). In 2011, in the US, a severely obese child was removed from his mother on grounds of medical neglect. The case precipitated a debate on the role of the state and family. See, Janice D'Arcy, 'Ohio mom loses custody of obese son: Using government intervention for a childhood epidemic', *Washington Post*, 29 November 2011.

6. BALANCING HEALTH PROMOTION WITH STIGMA PREVENTION

It is important not only to stress the obligations of States to end childhood obesity, but also to raise awareness of how they can do so in a human rights sensitive manner. In light of the rights-based approach analysed above, States should promote an environment that *enables* and *empowers* children to enjoy the highest attainable standard of health instead of simply imposing their vision of the good life through public health strategies. Indeed, public health policies insensitive to human rights may lead to stigmatization and adverse health effects.

It is well documented that obese and overweight children are exposed to teasing, bullying, social exclusion and other kinds of victimization, both by other children, and by teachers and even family members.[114] This can be characterized as stigmatization as defined by Goffmann and further developed by Link and Phelan. According to Goffman, stigma can be understood as 'an attribute that is deeply discrediting', and stigmatization is seen as a process of dehumanizing, degrading, discrediting and devaluing people in certain population groups.[115] Following Link and Phelan's concept of stigmatization, stigma is a process linked to the exercise of power, and includes labelling, stereotyping, separation, status loss, and ultimately direct, structural, or insidious discrimination.[116] Apart from discrimination, stigma also has several health-related consequences for the stigmatized person. Stigma is documented to provoke, for example, depression, anxiety, adverse physical health behaviours and outcomes, such as binge eating, increased food intake, avoidance of physical activity, and increased weight gain, which ultimately reinforce obesity.[117] Consequently, stigma has a negative impact on the stigmatized person's physical and mental health and is an impediment to the realization of the human right to health.

Drivers of stigma can be found at different levels in society. They may be associated with power relations operating in the individual, social and cultural

---

[114] RM Puhl and JD Latner, 'Stigma, Obesity and the Health of the Nation's Children' (2007) 4(133) *Psychological Bulletin* 557; Lindelof et al., 'Obesity Stigma at Home: A Qualitative, Longitudinal Study of Obese Adolescents and Their Parents' (2011) 7 *Childhood Obesity* 462.

[115] E Goffman, *Stigma: Notes on the Management of Spoiled Identity* (Simon & Schuster 1963) 3–5.

[116] BG Link and JC Phelan, 'Conceptualizing Stigma' (2001) 27 *Annual Review of Sociology* 363.

[117] RM Puhl and CA Heuer, 'Obesity Stigma: Important Considerations for Public Health' (2010) 100(6) *American Journal of Public Health* 1019.

fields, and also manifest in institutional settings. Likewise, stigma also has its drivers at a societal level, where both public policies and the actions of public authorities and the media can create or sustain stereotypes and prejudices.[118] In this respect, it is important to recognize that well-meaning efforts to improve public health, through, for example, information campaigns and other societal interventions to prevent obesity, seem to worsen the stigmatization of obesity and obese people.[119] Stigma has also historically been used deliberately as a public health strategy, such as, in regards to smoking and tobacco consumption, where the denormalization and marginalization of smokers and smoking has been seen as an effective tool in reducing tobacco consumption.[120]

Therefore, it is important to pay attention to the potentially stigmatizing role of public health policies in this area. State Parties have a duty to balance their obligation to provide children with opportunities to live healthy lives, with their obligation not to expose children to stigma and its potentially severe negative impact on their health.[121] Obesity prevention programmes specifically directed at overweight and obese children will easily label children as having an undesirable condition, thus exposing them to stigma.[122] In this regard, the child rights based-approach outlined in section 3 should serve as guidance. A child rights-based obesity prevention program would, in contrast to an individually-focused approach targeting overweight and obese children, set out to create an *enabling environment*, where the focus is on all children's access to physical activity and healthy eating. In addition, it would emphasize the *empowerment* of children, for example, by promoting weight tolerance and body-esteem approaches.

Both the ECHO report and the CRC Committee show awareness of the risk of stigmatization. The ECHO report contains references to stigma as a concern in regard to overweight and obese children.[123] Recommendation 5.7 mentions

---

[118] Report of the Special Rapporteur on the human right to safe drinking water and sanitation, 'Stigma and the realization of the human rights to water and sanitation', UN Doc A/HRC/21/42, 2 July 2012, paras 18–21.

[119] RM Puhl, JL Peterson and J Luedicke, 'Fighting Obesity or Obese Persons? Public Reactions to Obesity Related Health Messages' (2012) 37 *International Journal of Obesity* 774; RM Puhl, JL Peterson and J Luedicke, 'Public Reactions to Obesity-Related Public Health Campaigns: A Randomized Trial' (2013) 45 *American Journal of Preventive Medicine* 36.

[120] R Bayer, 'Stigma and the Ethics of Public Health: Not Can We But Should We' (2008) 67 *Social Science and Medicine* 463.

[121] M Hartlev, 'Stigmatisation as a Public Health Tool to Fight Obesity – A Health and Human Rights Perspective' (2014) 21(4) *EJHL* 365.

[122] RM Puhl and JD Latner, 'Stigma, Obesity and the Health of the Nation's Children' (2007) 4(133) *Psychological Bulletin* 557.

[123] ECHO Report, n3, 7 and recommendations 5.7 and 6.

physical education as a means of challenging stigma and stereotypes,[124] while recommendation 6 notes that health workers and others sometimes discriminate against overweight and obese children.[125] The Report further stresses that all forms of discrimination are unacceptable, and that stigmatization and bullying need special attention. The CRC Committee is also aware of the risk of stigmatization by mass and social media. In General Comment no 15, the CRC Committee stresses that communication programmes and material should not be harmful to children and to general health, and that such strategies should not perpetuate health related-stigma.[126] This could, for example, be the case if obese children are problematized as contrary to society's expectations, as in a public health campaign by Children's Healthcare of Atlanta, where an image of young overweight girl was promoted with the tag line: 'It's hard to be a little girl if you're not'.[127]

It is positive that there seems to be an increasing awareness of the risk and consequences of stigmatisation. However, the impact public health policies (intentionally or unintentionally) could have on the stigma of obese children is not specifically addressed by ECHO or by the CRC Committee. This is a crucial issue that needs more attention when State Parties pursue their obligations to ensure the right to the highest attainable standard of health. As outlined above, a child rights-based approach could serve as guidance.

7. CONCLUSION

ECHO has documented that childhood obesity is a significant problem for children's health, and as such also for children's *human right* to enjoy the highest attainable standard of physical and mental health. Obesity is not only a problem during childhood, it affects children's future health as adults, and their ability to grow up and enjoy the full range of fundamental human rights. The ECHO report includes several recommendations to States on how to end childhood obesity. These recommendations reinforce existing WHO recommendations, including those on the marketing of foods and non-alcoholic beverages to children. But how can we ensure that these recommendations – which are not legally binding – are implemented and taken seriously by States?

Turning from the public health to the human rights framework, States have legal responsibilities under international human rights law to ensure that children live under conditions that enable and empower them to live a healthy life,

---

[124] Ibid., 31.
[125] Ibid., 32.
[126] General Comment No 15, n44, para 18.
[127] WA Bogart, 'Who Wants a Fat Child?: Care for Obese Children in Weight Obsessed Societies' (2015) 5(1) *Oñati Legal Series* 8.

and to grow and develop to their full potential. The CRC demands that States act to respect, protect and fulfil children's right to health. In doing so, States should apply a *child rights-based approach*. This implies that states' actions should be guided by children's rights principles, including the child's best interests, the right to be heard and participate, the right to non-discrimination and the right to life.

Although there clearly is a human rights obligation on States to act in relation to childhood obesity, there are also several challenges in ensuring compliance with the CRC. First of all, it is not obvious from the wording of the Convention how States precisely should act to fulfil their obligations. Furthermore, compliance with the CRC is not monitored by a court with judicial power to ensure that States comply with their obligations. Compliance relies on the CRC Committee issuing recommendations to States, either directly through concluding observations, or more generally in general comments. As demonstrated in this chapter, the CRC Committee and other human rights bodies have made a number of recommendations to State Parties in relation to childhood obesity. Some of the recommendations are rather vague, and the CRC Committee does not systematically address childhood obesity when it reviews State Parties' reports. The Committee could also be criticized for not taking the opportunity to highlight a clearer child rights-based approach to obesity.

We argue that international human rights and public health can be mutually reinforcing, and contribute to ending childhood obesity. The spirit of the recommendations issued by the human rights bodies complement those of the WHO and ECHO. Still, the CRC Committee and other human rights bodies could profit from drawing on WHO documents and the ECHO report, which provide comprehensive and evidence-based technical recommendations. Concluding observations generally fail to harness targeted recommendations. Similarly, the WHO could benefit from adopting a clearer human rights and child rights approach in its technical documents and by drawing on the moral and legal weight offered by the CRC.[128] It is encouraging that the ECHO final report recognizes the significance of children's right to health in ending childhood obesity. Engaging with children's rights could also raise awareness on how to ensure that public health policies do not stigmatize obese and overweight children and, as such, have negative impacts on their health. Furthermore, children's rights are binding law (unlike ECHO) and underscore

---

[128] See also, A Garde et al., 'For a Children's Rights Approach to Obesity Prevention: The Key Role of an Effective Implementation of the WHO Recommendations' (2017) 8(2) *EJRR* 327; A Garde et al., *A Child Rights-Based Approach to Food Marketing: A Guide for Policy Makers* (UNICEF 2018).

children's entitlements as rights holders, and the State's corresponding obligations to end childhood obesity. Finally, the child's best interests should always be the primary consideration in all government policies and actions.[129] Using this as a guiding principle to better integrate a human rights and public health approach to childhood obesity should ensure all children a right to an open future.

---

[129] See further, chapter by Garde and Byrne in this volume.

4. Human rights, childhood obesity and health inequalities

Marine Friant-Perrot[1] and Nikhil Gokani[2]

1. INTRODUCTION

The prevalence of childhood obesity, and its rapid increase, is not distributed equally across populations. Some groups of children are more likely to live with obesity than others, with childhood obesity being strongly associated with belonging to a socioeconomic position group consuming more energy-dense diets.[3] These health inequalities are largely systematic, and are mostly the result of the social, political and economic environment in which children live and play.[4] These unfair differences in health outcomes not only mean that children from such groups have a higher chance of developing obesity, they are also likely to suffer worse consequences of obesity, and such obesity-related inequalities are likely to continue over the course of a child's life[5] and thus

---

[1] Marine Friant-Perrot's contribution was translated from French by Anaëlle Chansay, PhD student at the University of Nantes.
[2] I would like to thank Professor Chris Willet for his comments on an earlier draft.
[3] Y Wang and H Lim, 'The Global Childhood Obesity Epidemic and the Association Between Socio-Economic Status and Childhood Obesity' (2012) 24(3) *International Review of Psychiatry* 176.
[4] For high income countries, see for instance: DM Zarnowiecki, J Dollman and N Parletta, 'Associations Between Predictors of Children's Dietary Intake and Socioeconomic Position: A Systematic Review of the Literature' (2014) 15(5) *Obesity Reviews* 375. For low- and middle-income countries, see for instance: BM Popkin and MM Slining, 'New Dynamics in Global Obesity Facing Low- and Middle-Income Countries' (2013) 14(2) *Obesity Reviews* 11; SJ Ulijaszek, 'Inequality and Childhood Overweight and Obesity: A Commentary' (2017) 12(3) *Pediatric Obesity* 195.
[5] A Palloni, 'Reproducing Inequalities: Luck, Wallets, and the Enduring Effects of Childhood Health' 43(4) (2006) *Demography* 587; A Case et al., 'The Lasting Impact of Childhood Health and Circumstance' (2005) 24 *Journal of Health Economics* 365; PM Connell et al., 'How Childhood Advertising Exposure Can Create Biased Product Evaluations That Persist into Adulthood' (2014) 41 *Journal of Consumer Research* 119.

also have harmful impacts on health, quality of life and life expectancy in their adult years.[6]

Despite the creation of a health-promoting environment for all children being recognized by the international community as a matter of societal responsibility,[7] inequalities in childhood obesity are growing.[8] Within legal frameworks, social, cultural and economic rights are well placed to help reduce the prevalence of obesity. These human rights are inspired by the principle of solidarity and, as they are conceived as instruments of social transformation, they aim to provide corrective measures to economic liberalization.[9] As their essence is to protect everyone equally, the reduction of health inequalities in childhood obesity can be articulated within this human rights discourse. In particular, through helping to restore a real capacity for choice in food consumption, and thereby supporting healthier diets for every child, the right to non-discrimination on the basis of socioeconomic status and the principle of equality can be thought of as a foundation for realizing social rights, in particular the right to health and the right to food.

Section 2 begins by demonstrating that the right to non-discrimination and the principle of equality are fundamental to the debates on reducing inequalities in childhood obesity. The section, first, argues that variations in socioeconomic factors, which lead to inequalities in childhood obesity, raise issues of discrimination; and should be seen as offending against the protections guaranteed by human rights instruments, and in particular the right to non-discrimina-

---

[6] JJ Reilly, 'Descriptive Epidemiology and Health Consequences of Childhood Obesity' (2005) 19(3) *Best Practice & Research Clinical Endocrinology & Metabolism* 327; JP Mackenbach, 'Socioeconomic Inequalities in Morbidity and Mortality in Western Europe' (1997) 349 *Lancet* 1655l; A Case, A Fertig and C Paxson, 'The Lasting Impact of Childhood Health and Circumstance (2005) 24 *Journal of Health Economics* 365.

[7] See, for instance: WHO Global Action Plan on the Prevention and Control of NCDs 2013-2020 (WHO 2013); Obesity and Inequities: Guidance for Addressing Inequities in Overweight and Obesity (WHO 2014); Final Report of the WHO Commission on Ending Childhood Obesity (WHO 2016).

[8] See for instance: LJ Johnson et al., 'Social Inequalities in Childhood Obesity: Trends, Determinants, and Interventions' in H Dele Davies et al. (eds), *Obesity in Childhood and Adolescence* (2nd edn, ABC-CLIO 2018); GK Singh, 'Trends and Contemporary Racial/Ethnic and Socioeconomic Disparities in US Childhood Obesity' in D Bagchi (ed.), *Global Perspectives on Childhood Obesity: Current Status, Consequences and Prevention* (2nd edn, Elsevier 2019); D Bann, 'Socioeconomic Inequalities in Childhood and Adolescent Body-Mass Index, Weight, and Height from 1953 to 2015: An Analysis of Four Longitudinal, Observational, British Birth Cohort Studies' (2018) 3(4) *The Lancet Public Health* PE194.

[9] See for instance: C Wellman, 'Solidarity, the Individual and Human Rights' (2000) 22(3) *Human Rights Quarterly* 639.

tion in the Convention on the Rights of the Child (CRC) as well as others rights which must be met without discrimination. The section, secondly, argues that the right to non-discrimination is inherently connected with the principle of equality; and that the right to non-discrimination should therefore be seen as seeking to promote equality of opportunity, and in particular the restoration of a genuine freedom for children to access nutritionally-balanced diets which can help prevent obesity.

Furthermore, as States must respect, protect and fulfil the rights of the child without discrimination on the basis of socioeconomic status, redirecting public policies towards greater emphasis on reducing inequalities in the process of preventing childhood obesity requires analysis of the available tools. Beyond the justiciability of protecting children from discrimination, there is a need to implement policies which transcend the simple procedural equality of the often-used method of providing all consumers with basic nutritional information, to acting more directly in limiting the harmful and inequitable effects of the food environment on children and their families.

Section 3, therefore, explores the implications of a human rights approach grounded in the right to non-discrimination on the basis of socioeconomic status and, more specifically, the opportunities in law for reducing health inequalities in childhood obesity prevention strategies.[10] The section, first, explores the scope of the State's duties to respect, protect and fulfil the right to non-discrimination and the other rights which must be met without discrimination. The section, secondly, discusses the existing legal mechanisms used to prevent obesity, and the legal tools available to help reduce inequalities in childhood obesity. To this end, it argues that the currently favoured intervention of providing nutritional information is insufficiently effective, promotes inequalities and exacerbates discrimination. It therefore calls for State implementation of restrictions on the marketing of unhealthy food to children as an evidence-based method to reduce inequalities and help better fulfil children's right to non-discrimination and protect them from unnecessary commercial influences.[11]

These issues have not been the subject of a comprehensive exploration in the literature.[12] Some academics have drawn connections between health inequali-

---

[10] *A Child Rights-Based Approach to Food Marketing: A Guide for Policy Makers* (UNICEF 2018).

[11] 'Unhealthy food' refers to nutritiously poor food and non-alcoholic beverages that are high in fats, sugar or salt. This follows the World Health Organization: 'Set of Recommendations on the Marketing of Foods and Non-Alcoholic Beverages to Children' (WHO 2010).

[12] But see shorter earlier work by one or both of the co-authors of this chapter: *A Child Rights-Based Approach to Food Marketing: A Guide for Policy Makers*

ties and human rights generally,[13] or between health inequalities and other specific rights, such as the right to health.[14] Others have sought to develop the right to non-discrimination generally,[15] or more specifically in relation to other concerns.[16] However, there have been few attempts to understand the link between health inequalities and the right to non-discrimination.[17] Moreover, within the literature which has begun to attempt this,[18] there has not been an attempt to look at childhood obesity, healthy diets, nutritional information and the CRC. This chapter, therefore, develops the literature in several respects. First, this chapter contributes to the understanding of the right to non-discrimination both generally and as expressed in the CRC. Secondly, it develops a deeper understanding of the link between the right to non-discrimination and health inequalities. Thirdly, it adds to the literature an understanding of the role of the right to non-discrimination and the principle of equality as they apply to inequalities in childhood obesity. Fourthly, it adds to the literature an exploration of the role of unhealthy food marketing restrictions as a tool in helping to move closer to fulfilling the child's right to non-discrimination. Fifthly, through the specific study on nutritional information, the chapter further develops

---

(Unicef 2018); A Garde, N Gokani and M Friant-Perrot 'Children's Rights, Childhood Obesity and Health Inequalities' (2018) 43 *UNSCN News* 65.

[13] See for instance: P Hunt and G Backman, 'Health Systems and the Right to the Highest Attainable Standard of Health' (2008) 10(1) *Health and Human Rights* 81; J Burns, 'Mental Health And Inequity: A Human Rights Approach to Inequality, Discrimination, and Mental Disability' (2009) 11(2) *Health and Human Rights* 19; R Atuguba, 'Equality, Non-Discrimination and Fair Distribution of the Benefits of Development' in *Realizing the Right to Development* (United Nations 2013).

[14] J Ruger, 'Toward a Theory of a Right to Health: Capability and Incompletely Theorized Agreements' (2006) 18(2) *Yale Journal of Law & The Humanities* 3.

[15] See for instance: B Abramson, *Article 2: The Right of Non-Discrimination* (Martinus Nijhoff Publishers 2008).

[16] See for instance: K Stronks et al., Social Justice and Human Rights as a Framework for Addressing Social Determinants of Health. Final Report of the Task Group on Equity, Equality and Human Rights Review of Social Determinants of Health and the Health Divide in the WHO European Region (WHO 2016).

[17] For the few non-legal papers trying to link discrimination with health inequalities see for instance: P Braveman and S Gruskin, 'Defining Equity in Health' (2003) 57 *Journal of Epidemiology and Community Health* 254.

[18] For the few attempts see: G MacNaughton, 'Untangling Equality and Non-Discrimination to Promote the Right to Health Care for All' (2009) 11(2) *Health and Human Rights* 47; P Braveman, 'Social Conditions, Health Equity, and Human Rights' (2010) 12(2) *Health and Human Rights* 31; A Chapman, 'The Social Determinants of Health, Health Equity, and Human Rights' (2010) 12(2) *Health and Human Rights* 17.

the broader literature on behavioural economics[19] and the limits of consumer empowerment by information.[20]

2. INEQUALITIES IN CHILDHOOD OBESITY AND SOCIAL JUSTICE

Health inequalities, sometimes known as health inequities,[21] are the differences in health between groups of individuals[22] which are systematic, socially produced (and therefore modifiable) and unfair.[23] At all geographical levels, both within and between countries, there is clear evidence that some groups of children live with worse health outcomes than other groups of children.[24]

More specifically, health inequalities in childhood obesity are strongly associated with belonging to a socioeconomic position[25] group consuming more

---

[19] See for instance: D Kahneman, P Slovic and A Tversky, *Judgment under Uncertainty: Heuristics and Biases* (CUP 1982); A Tversky and D Kahneman, 'Judgment under Uncertainty: Heuristics and Biases' (1974) 185(4157) *Research* 1124; M Rabin 'Psychology and Economics' (1998) 36(1) *Journal of Economic Literature* 11.

[20] See for instance: G Howells, 'The Potential and Limits of Consumer Empowerment by Information' (2005) 32 *Journal of Law and Society* 349; C Willett, 'Re-Theorising Consumer Law' (2018) 77(1) *Cambridge Law Journal* 179; G Hadfield, et al., 'Information-Based Principles for Rethinking Consumer Protection Policy' (1998) 21 *Journal of Consumer Policy* 131.

[21] It should be noted that, in a strict sense, inequalities refer to the generic differences in health; whereas inequities are those inequalities which are also systematic, socially produced and unfair. Whereas inequalities are factual statements, and inequities normative statements which demands regulatory action as a matter of social justice, this distinction is not always used. The terms are commonly used interchangeably to refer to the narrower definition of inequities. Following the wider literature, the remainder of this paper uses the phrase 'health inequalities' as synonymous with the more accurate 'health inequities'.

[22] I Kawachi, et al., 'A Glossary for Health Inequalities' (2002) 56 *Journal of Epidemiology & Community Health* 647, 647.

[23] M Whitehead and G Dahlgren, 'Concepts and Principles for Tackling Social Inequities in Health: Levelling Up Part 1' (WHO Regional Office for Europe 2007).

[24] See for instance: M Marmot, 'Social Determinants of Health Inequalities' (2005) 365 *Lancet* 1099.

[25] Socioeconomic position is a description of the social hierarchy or ranking of individuals or groups based on sociological and economic goods. It is used here to refer to social status in its widest sense, including factors which may not traditionally be considered to relate to socioeconomic status, such as gender, sexuality and ethnicity. There are many other definitions, and indeed the use of socioeconomic position is in itself not universal, but the concept aims 'to capture an individual's or group's access to the basic resources required to achieve and maintain good health': V Shavers, 'Measurement

energy-dense diets.[26] In high-income countries, there is an inverse association between the socioeconomic position of a child and his or her obesity status.[27] This is amplified in some groups, especially in relation to ethnicity,[28] sex[29] and other family circumstances.[30] In low- and middle-income countries, childhood obesity is linked with factors of both higher socioeconomic position, such as increased wealth, and lower socioeconomic position, such as lower levels of education and maternal malnutrition during gestation.[31]

While childhood obesity largely results from an energy imbalance, its development follows a complex, multifactorial pathway. This pathway largely begins with the child's exposure to an unhealthy environment, followed by the child's behavioural response to that environment and, in turn, the child's bio-

---

of Socioeconomic Status in Health Disparities Research' (2007) 99(9) *Journal of the National Medical Association* 1013, 1013.

[26] Y Wang and H Lim, 'The Global Childhood Obesity Epidemic and the Association between Socio-Economic Status and Childhood Obesity' (2012) 24(3) *International Review of Psychiatry* 176.

[27] D Zarnowiecki, et al., 'Associations Between Predictors of Children's Dietary Intake and Socioeconomic Position: A Systematic Review of the Literature' (2014) 15(5) *Obesity Reviews* 375.

[28] A El-Sayed et al., 'Ethnic Inequalities in Obesity Among Children and Adults in the UK: A Systematic Review of the Literature' (2011) *Obesity Reviews* e517; T Olds et al., 'Evidence That the Prevalence of Childhood Overweight is Plateauing: Data from Nine Countries' (2011) 6 *International Journal of Pediatric Obesity* 342; S Kumanyika, et al., 'Community Energy Balance: A Framework for Contextualizing Cultural Influences on High Risk of Obesity in Ethnic Minority Populations' (2012) 55 *Preventive Medicine* 371; J Brug et al., 'Differences in Weight Status and Energy-Balance Related Behaviours According to Ethnic Background among Adolescents in Seven Countries in Europe: The ENERGY-Project' (2012) 7 *Pediatric Obesity* 399; N Gupta et al., 'Childhood Obesity in Developing Countries: Epidemiology, Determinants and Prevention' (2012) 33 *Endocrine Reviews* 48.

[29] J Sobal and A Stunkard, 'Socioeconomic Status and Obesity: A Review of the Literature' *Psychological Bulletin* 105(2) (1989) 260; L McLaren, 'Socioeconomic Status and Obesity' (2007) 29 *Epidemiologic Reviews* 29; M Jodkowska et al., 'Overweight and Obesity Among Adolescents in Poland: Gender and Regional Differences' (2010) 13 *Public Health Nutrition* 1688.

[30] S Robinson et al., 'A Narrative Literature Review of the Development of Obesity in Infancy and Childhood' (2012) 16(4) *Journal of Child Health Care* 339; G Tabacchi et al., 'A Review of the Literature and a New Classification of the Early Determinants of Childhood Obesity: From Pregnancy to the First Years of Life' (2007) 27 *Nutrition Research* 587; S Garasky, 'Family Stressors and Child Obesity' (2009) 38 *Social Science Research* 755.

[31] B Popkin and M Slining, 'New Dynamics in Global Obesity Facing Low- and Middle-Income Countries' (2013) 14(2) *Obesity Reviews* 11; SJ Ulijaszek, 'Inequality and Childhood Overweight and Obesity: A Commentary' (2017) 12(3) *Pediatric Obesity* 195.

logical response. Differences in the environment – such as greater promotion and availability of cheaper, energy-dense, unhealthy food – lead to variations in behaviours and biological responses. These environmental factors are known as the social determinants of health[32] and are responsible for many of the differences in rates of obesity between groups.[33] Not only do members of socioeconomic groups consuming energy-dense diets have a higher chance of developing obesity, members of these groups are also likely to suffer worse consequences of obesity. Such obesity-related inequalities are likely to continue over the course of a child's life[34] and thus also have a harmful impact on health, quality of life and life expectancy in their adult years.[35] It follows that creating a health-promoting environment for all children is recognized by the international community as a matter of societal responsibility.[36]

This section seeks to show that the right to non-discrimination and the principle of equality are fundamental to the debates on reducing inequalities in childhood obesity. This section, first, argues that variations in socioeconomic factors offend the protections guaranteed by human rights instruments, and in particular the right to non-discrimination in the CRC as well as other rights which must be met without discrimination. While health inequalities have been linked with human rights generally[37] or linked with other specific rights,[38] this section goes beyond this work by developing the link between health inequalities and the right to non-discrimination.[39] It further adds to the literature an understanding of these issues in relation to the CRC, and in doing so also contributes to a better understanding of the right to non-discrimination

---

[32] Commission on Social Determinants of Health, 'Closing the Gap in a Generation: Health Equity through Action on the Social Determinants of Health' (WHO 2008), 1.

[33] M Campbell, 'Biological, Environmental, and Social Influences on Childhood Obesity' (2015) 79(1–2) *Pediatric Research* 205.

[34] A Palloni, 'Reproducing Inequalities: Luck, Wallets, and the Enduring Effects of Childhood Health' Demography 43(4) (2006) *Demography* 587; A Case et al., 'The Lasting Impact of Childhood Health and Circumstance' (2005) 24 *Journal of Health Economics* 365; PM Connell et al., 'How Childhood Advertising Exposure Can Create Biased Product Evaluations That Persist into Adulthood' (2014) 41 *Journal of Consumer Research* 119.

[35] J Reilly, 'Descriptive Epidemiology and Health Consequences of Childhood Obesity' (2005) 19(3) *Best Practice & Research Clinical Endocrinology & Metabolism* 327; J Mackenbach, 'Socioeconomic Inequalities in Morbidity and Mortality in Western Europe' (1997) 349 *Lancet* 1655l; A Case, et al., 'The Lasting Impact of Childhood Health and Circumstance (2005) 24 *Journal of Health Economics* 365.

[36] See n7.
[37] See n13.
[38] See n14.
[39] See n18.

more broadly.⁴⁰ This section, secondly, argues that the right to non-discrimination is inherently connected with the principle of equality; and that the right to non-discrimination therefore seeks to promote equality of opportunity, and in particular the restoration of a genuine freedom for children to access nutritionally-balanced diets which are not associated with obesity. In doing so, this section adds to the literature an understanding of the role of the right to non-discrimination and the principle of equality in relation to inequalities in childhood obesity, and in doing so also helps develops the existing literature on substantive equality.⁴¹

2.1 Inequalities and Non-discrimination

The social determinants of health, and therefore the variations in environments in which children live, raise issues of discrimination. The right to non-discrimination is granted in most national legal orders and is specifically recognized in almost all international human rights instruments. Its importance is seen through its inclusion in the second Article of the Universal Declaration of Human Rights (UDHR), the International Covenant on Civil and Political Rights (ICCPR), the International Covenant on Economic, Social and Cultural Rights (ICESCR), and the CRC. Article 26 ICCPR in particular recognizes the right to non-discrimination in conjunction with the right to health and the right to food.

The CRC, through its aim to protect children from behaviours and circumstances that 'offend the human dignity of the child',⁴² further acknowledges 'that children are born with fundamental freedoms and the inherent rights of all human beings and should not be discriminated against because they are children'.⁴³ The CRC does not itself provide a definition of discrimination, and neither is there a General Comment from the Committee on the Rights of the Child addressing discrimination specifically. Analysis of the General Comments of the Human Rights Committee, however, reveals that discrimination implies differentiation of similar situations, based on protected characteristics, which impairs the child's enjoyment of rights.⁴⁴ This notion of

---

⁴⁰ See n15.
⁴¹ See for instance: S Fredman, 'Substantive Equality Revisited' (2016) 14(3) International Journal of Constitutional Law 712.
⁴² Committee on the Rights of the Child, 'General Comment No. 1: The aims of education', CRC/GC/2001/1, United Nations, 17 April 2001, [10].
⁴³ F Sheahan, 'Translating the Right to Non-Discrimination into Reality' (Save the Children Sweden 2008), 9. See also: Art 2 in the UDHR, ICCPR and ICESCR.
⁴⁴ Human Rights Committee, 'General Comment No. 18: Non-Discrimination' (Thirty seventh session, 1989) HRI/GEN/1/Rev.9 (Vol. I) pp 195–8, [7]. But see [13],

discrimination is interpreted broadly. It includes circumstances and behaviours which are overtly discriminatory, and also policies which are discriminatory in a covert or hidden manner.[45] Discrimination also includes policies which have the purpose of discrimination, or the effect of discrimination. Moreover, discrimination can be the result of both laws or the result of systematic patterns of behaviours.

It is argued, therefore, that protecting children from discrimination that is caused by, and reinforced through, the social determinants of health falls within the duties of States. Under the right to non-discrimination enshrined in Article 2 ICESCR, as interpreted in General Comment 20 of the Committee on Economic, Social and Cultural Rights, States must contribute to the reduction of discrimination faced by vulnerable socioeconomic groups.[46] The list of grounds of discrimination listed in Article 2(2) ICESCR is very broad and the reference to 'any other characteristics' includes any form of differentiated treatment that does not have a reasonable and objective justification.[47] Paragraph 35 of General Comment 20, which interprets this provision, considers that '[i]ndividuals and groups of individuals must not be arbitrarily treated on account of belonging to a certain economic or social group or strata within society'.[48] Regarding children's vulnerability to malnutrition, the reference to Article 2 ICESCR must be combined with the rules laid down in the CRC which protects children from discrimination in three different ways.

First, Article 2(1) of the CRC provides protection as it recognizes non-discrimination as a guiding principle.[49] It prohibits discrimination against children in respect of each of the other specific rights provided under the CRC. Discrimination under Article 2(1) is prohibited if is based on the protected characteristics of the child or their parents, guardians or families. These characteristics include the many social determinants of health which childhood obesity is associated with, including race, sex, religion, social origin, disability and other status. 'Other status' here has been interpreted to include a child's

---

where the Committee noted that 'not every differentiation of treatment will constitute discrimination, if the criteria for such differentiation are reasonable and objective and if the aim is to achieve a purpose which is legitimate under the Covenant.', and which is a point repeated by the CRC Committee in General Comment 20, [21].

[45] See n42, [1].

[46] Committee on Economic, Social and Cultural Rights, 'General Comment No, 20, Non-discrimination in economic, social and cultural rights', E/C.12/GC/20, 2 July 2009.

[47] See n46, [27].

[48] Ibid.

[49] See: United Nations, 'Report of the Committee on the Rights of the Child', Supplement No. 41 (A/57/41) 2002, [38].

health status.⁵⁰ General Comment 20 further establishes that children cannot be discriminated against on the basis of socioeconomic position in the exercise of their right to health.⁵¹ Yet, disaggregated data reveal that children from lower socioeconomic groups live more with the major unhealthy risk factors of unhealthy diets and reduced physical activity.⁵²

It is submitted, therefore, that the child shall not be discriminated against in their right to the enjoyment of the highest attainable standard of health contained in Article 24 of the CRC, and to the right to a standard of living adequate for the child's physical, mental, spiritual, moral and social development set out in Article 27. The right to health in particular is almost universally recognized by all human rights texts, and is defined in the UDHR to include food, clothing, housing, medical care and necessary social services, with the special provision of assistance being required in childhood (Art 25). The right has evolved significantly, particularly with the general comments of the Committee on Economic, Social and Cultural Rights,⁵³ which, for instance, stated in General Comment No. 14 that the right to health includes access to nutritionally adequate food. Similarly, helped through the action of the UN

---

⁵⁰ 'Other' characteristics must be interpreted broadly so as to be sufficiently similar to the explicit characteristics. This would include the child's status of being overweight or obese: Committee on the Rights of the child, General Comment No. 3 (2003) HIV/AIDS and the rights of the child, CRC/GC/2003/1, [5] – where the Committee included HIV/AIDS status as being within 'other status' for the purposes of Art 2(1).

⁵¹ See n46.

⁵² Various studies and reviews have confirmed these findings. See for instance C Knai et al., 'Socioeconomic Patterning of Childhood Overweight Status in Europe' (2012) 9 *International Journal of Environmental Research and Public Health* 1472; G Tabacchi et al., 'A Review of the Literature and a New Classification of the Early Determinants of Childhood Obesity: From Pregnancy to the First Years of Life' (2007) 27 *Nutrition Research* 587; D Zarnowiecki et al., 'Associations Between Predictors of Children's Dietary Intake and Socioeconomic Position: A Systematic Review of the Literature' (2014) 15 *Obesity Reviews* 375; V Shrewsbury and J Wardle, 'Socioeconomic Status and Adiposity in Childhood: A Systematic Review of Cross-sectional Studies 1990–2005' (2008) 16(2) *Obesity* 275; S Weng, 'Systematic Review and Meta-Analyses of Risk Factors for Childhood Overweight Identifiable During Infancy' (2012) 97 *Archives of Disease in Childhood* 1019; Y Wang and H Lim, 'The Global Childhood Obesity Epidemic and the Association Between Socio-Economic Status and Childhood Obesity' (2012) 24(3) *International Review of Psychiatry* 176.

⁵³ M Trilsch, 'La Judiciarisation du Droit à la Santé: Quelles Perspectives pour la Procédure de Communications Individuelles devant le Comité des Droits eEconomiques, Sociaux et Culturels?' (2015) 57(1) *Revue de Droit International et de Croit Comparé* 43.

Special Rapporteur on the Right to Food,[54] the normative content of the right to an adequate standard of living is interpreted broadly to include:

> the right to have regular, permanent and free access, either directly or by means of financial purchases, to quantitatively and qualitatively adequate and sufficient food corresponding to the cultural traditions of the people to which the consumer belongs, and which ensures a physical and mental, individual and collective, fulfilling and dignified life free of fear.[55]

Secondly, Article 2(2) of the CRC prohibits unreasonable discrimination and punishment in all parts of the child's life, regardless of whether specific protection is afforded elsewhere in the CRC. Discrimination is prohibited in respect of the status, activities, and expressed opinions or beliefs of the child's parents, guardians or family. Therefore, inequalities resulting from discrimination on the basis of household income, education, access to economic goods and other similar factors should also be considered prohibited.

Thirdly, several articles in the CRC provide more specific protection. This includes the protection of children with disabilities. Not only are obese children more likely to face adverse consequences in life as a result of their health, including stigmatization,[56] in some circumstances obesity may be classified as a disability,[57] and thus, it is argued, requiring States to ensure that such a child enjoys 'a full and decent life, in conditions which ensure dignity, promote self-reliance and facilitate the child's active participation in the community' (Art 23).[58]

2.2 Non-discrimination and Equality

The right to non-discrimination gives rise to important obligations on the State. There is an obligation to eliminate discrimination on the basis of socio-

---

[54] W Barth Eide, 'From Food Security to the Right to Food' in W Barth Eide and U Kracht (eds), *Food and Human Rights in Development, Volume I: Legal and Institutional Dimensions and Selected Topics* (Intersentia 2005); J Ziegler et al., *The Fight for the Right to Food: Lessons Learned* (Palgrave Macmillan 2011).

[55] Commission on Human Rights, 'The Right to Food. Report by the Special Rapporteur on the Right to Food, Mr. Jean Ziegler', E/CN.4.2001.53, [14].

[56] M Hartlev, 'Stigmatisation as a Public Health Tool against Obesity: A Health and Human Rights Perspective' *European Journal of Health Law* (2014) 21(4) 365; I Janssen et al., 'Associations Between Overweight and Obesity with Bullying Behaviors in School-Aged Children' (2004) 113(5) *Pediatrics* 1187.

[57] See, e.g.: Court of Justice of the European Union, Case C-354/13, *Fag og Arbejde v Kommunernes Landsforening* ECLI:EU:C:2014:2463, [53].

[58] *A Child Rights-Based Approach to Food Marketing: A Guide for Policy Makers* (Unicef 2018).

economic position and eradicate discrimination in children's exercise of their rights to health and food on this basis.

Nevertheless, even if we consider these fundamental rights as potential levers to tackle inequalities in childhood obesity, it should be noted that they have so far been insufficiently mobilized. When litigated, these rights have been successful in reducing inequalities in terms of food security and the fight against undernutrition. In 2007, for instance, the right to food in the ICESCR was successfully argued as protecting indigenous people in Argentina to help create more equitable distribution of food and subsidies.[59] Similarly, in 2010 in Germany, in a case where the law resulted in a 14-year-old teenager receiving nutrition equivalent to a new-born and only 60 per cent of what an adult received, the right to health and the right to dignity proved meritorious arguments for vulnerable citizen to claim a higher minimum level of subsistence to ensure sufficient nutrition.[60]

Even in the relatively few examples of cases where inequalities have been successfully challenged, individual or collective actions such as litigation have been difficult to initiate, support and fund. With the justiciability of these rights not sufficiently established to make legal actions necessarily successful, these rights have not yet reached a level where they can universally be invoked in proceedings to reduce health inequalities. Moreover, the lack of clarity has sometimes resulted in outcomes which may actually increase gaps in health outcomes. For instance, in Brazil, the State was required to provide expensive medical surgery if it was necessary to preserve human health, even though this was likely to benefit only the most informed citizens of higher socioeconomic groups and therefore did not give sufficient regard to the equitable distribution of expenditure within the broader healthcare system.[61]

Part of this difficulty in making better use of the right to non-discrimination results from the right sometimes being conceptualized as a negative right leading to formal equality in law. Formal equality is rooted in consistency and rationality: comparable situations must not be treated differently, and different situations must not be treated in the same way. This seemingly fair construction, however, hides its limited utility in tackling the causes of inequality – there is an assumption that pre-existing norms are inherently neutral. This

---

[59] Supreme Court of Argentina, Case of *Defensor del Pueblo v Estado Nacional y otra* 18 September 2007, D.587, XLIII.

[60] Cour const., BVerfGE, 9 fév. 2010, Hartz IV, RDSS, 2010, p. 653, note Céline FERCOT.

[61] J Tobin, *The Right to Health in International Law* (OUP 2012); O Ferraz, 'The Right to Health in the Courts of Brazil: Worsening Health Inequities?' (2009) 11 *Health & Human Rights* 33.

incomprehension of context fails to lead to equality of opportunity and does not address the legacy of disadvantage.

Human rights law has traditionally made slow progress in moving away from viewing non-discrimination as a negative right to formal equality towards viewing it as a positive right to substantive equality.[62] Substantive equality, often captured through the principle of equality,[63] views non-discrimination, in part, by taking the focus away from individualistic factors towards more focus on the group collective experiences of inequality. This accepts that discrimination is not random but instead predominantly experienced by individuals sharing similar characteristics.[64] The principle of equality seeks to redress disadvantage, enhance participation, address stigma, accommodate difference and achieve structural change. Substantive equality, therefore, requires the adoption of measures intended to promote equality of opportunity when opportunities are significantly threatened.[65] It is posited that this implies equal access to a healthy diet. To ensure that children are empowered to control their own health to prevent obesity, they should be granted, on equal terms, genuine access to healthy food. Conversely, they must not be subjected to negative influences leading to an unhealthy diet. Granting equal access to healthy food implies a challenge to the food environment and the food environment's role in the development of nutrition-based diseases. Public health and nutrition policies should aim to improve not only individual determinants of eating habits but also act on environmental determinants.[66]

---

[62] See further: G MacNaughton, 'Untangling Equality and Non-discrimination to Promote the Right to Health Care for All' (2009) 11 *Health and Human Rights* 47; S Fredman, 'Combating Racism with Human Rights: The Right to Equality' in S Fredman (ed.), *Discrimination and Human Rights: The Case of Racism* (OUP 2001).

[63] It should be noted that some academics have argued that there is a right to equality. However, such a position is insufficiently developed and not universally accepted, and therefore this chapter maintains the distinction between the right to non-discrimination and the principle of equality.

[64] M Bell, *Racism and Equality in the European Union* (OUP 2008) ch 2.

[65] Fredman, n41.

[66] R Mc Gill et al., 'Are Interventions to Promote Healthy Eating Equally Effective for All? Systematic Review of Socioeconomic Inequalities in Impact' (2015) 15 *BMC Public Health* 457 ; M White et al., 'How and Why Do Interventions That Increase Health Overall Widen Inequalities Within Populations?' in SJ Babones (ed.), *Social Inequality and Public Health* (Policy Press, 2009), 64–81; N Larson and M Story, 'A Review of Environmental Influences on Food Choices' (2009) 38 (suppl 1) *Annals of Behavioral Medicine* S56. See further, e.g.: Final report of the WHO Commission on Ending Childhood Obesity (WHO, 2016); Obesity and Inequities: Guidance for Addressing Inequities in Overweight and Obesity (WHO Regional Office for Europe 2014); EU Action Plan on Childhood Obesity 2014–2020 (European Union 2014), 11.

Furthermore, to ensure that individuals can choose their diet on equal terms, it is necessary to restore genuine freedom of choice by ensuring a capacity or capability[67] for individuals to access a nutritionally-balanced diet. That is to say that one's choice of diet should not be purely theoretical but actually be achievable by all. Equal access to food for the entire population entails rethinking of freedom as the substantive empowerment of individuals, regardless of their environment and resources, to actually have access to healthy food. This would allow the preservation of a genuine capacity of choice for children and their families, and support healthier diets within economic resources and in accordance with their circumstances and backgrounds. Yet this must not lead to the standardization of diets. Between nature and culture, food does not simply boil down to a level of calories. The equation is complex because it is necessary to ensure equal access to food in sufficient nutritional quality and quantity while preserving cultural specificities. Inequalities should be reduced by law without limiting disparities: equality must exist in diversity – a point which has been upheld by the Human Rights Council.[68]

3. REALIZATION OF EQUALITY BY STATES

The right to non-discrimination and the principle of equality can both support the implementation of interventions to reduce health inequalities in childhood obesity. Tackling these inequalities requires, as a prerequisite, an understanding of the causes of the stratification of health outcomes across socioeconomic groups, as highlighted above. However, while some of the necessary and sufficient conditions involved in causation, and variation in patterning, of childhood obesity can be identified, this is largely based on correlation, not causation.[69] Without a complete model on behavioural risk in this patterning,[70] the options for prevention are for States to, most fundamentally, reduce inequalities in the distribution of socioeconomic factors and structural determinants, and then to tackle specific or intermediary determinants which

---

[67] A Sen, *The Idea of Justice* (Penguin Books 2009).

[68] Human Rights Council Thirty-third session Agenda item 5 Human rights bodies and mechanisms Right to health and indigenous peoples with a focus on children and youth Study by the Expert Mechanism on the Rights of Indigenous Peoples A/HRC/33/57, [48].

[69] J Bonnefoy et al., 'Constructing the evidence base on the social determinants of health: A guide' (NICE 2007), 14.

[70] On existing models see for instance G McCartney, C Collins and M Mackenzie, 'What (or Who) Causes Health Inequalities: Theories, Evidence and Implications?' (2013) 113 *Health Policy* 221; G Scambler, 'Health Inequalities' (2012) 34(1) *Sociology of Health & Illness* 130.

mediate the effect of socioeconomic position on health,[71] such as the marketing of unhealthy food to children.

This section seeks to demonstrate the implications of following a human rights approach grounded in the right to non-discrimination on the basis of socioeconomic status and, more specifically, the opportunities in law for reducing health inequalities in childhood obesity prevention strategies. First, we explore the scope of the State's duties to respect, protect and fulfil the right to non-discrimination and the other rights which must be met without discrimination. Second, we discuss the existing legal mechanisms used to prevent obesity, and the legal tools available to help reduce inequalities in childhood obesity. To this end, we argue that the currently favoured intervention of providing nutritional information is insufficiently effective, promotes inequalities and exacerbates discrimination. We therefore call for State implementation of restrictions on the marketing of unhealthy food to children as an evidence-based method to reduce inequalities and help better fulfil children's right to non-discrimination and protect them from unnecessary commercial influences. In doing so, this section adds to the literature an exploration of the role of unhealthy food marketing restrictions as a tool in helping to move closer to fulfilling the child's right to non-discrimination; which, in turn, also helps further develop the broader literature on behavioural economics[72] and the limits of consumer empowerment by information.[73]

3.1   Duties of the State

States are under an obligation to respect, protect, and fulfil[74] the rights of the child and to ensure non-discrimination on the basis of socioeconomic status in the exercise of these rights. These duties are not merely passive or negative: the State must also be proactive in tackling discrimination.[75] As the State cannot know the causes of discrimination without looking upstream in the

---

[71] H Graham, 'Social Determinants and Their Unequal Distribution: Clarifying Policy Understandings' (2004) 82(1) *Milbank Quarterly* 101; H Graham, 'Intellectual Disabilities and Socioeconomic Inequalities in Health: An Overview of Research' (2005) 18 *Journal of Applied Research in Intellectual Disabilities* 101. See also 'Closing the Gap in a Generation: Health Equity Through Action on the Social Determinants of Health' (WHO 2008).
[72] See n19.
[73] See n20.
[74] A Eide, 'Realization of Social and Economic Rights and the Minimum Threshold Approach' (1989) 10 *Human Rights Law Journal* 37.
[75] Committee on the Rights of the Child, 'General Comment No. 5 2003 CRC/GC/2003/5', [12].

causal chain to identify the factors which have contributed to discrimination,[76] States are under a specific duty to monitor situations as well as to collect and analyse both systematic and disaggregated data relating to the background and circumstances of children and their families.[77] Such duties may at times become obligations to take 'affirmative action in order to diminish or eliminate conditions which cause or help to perpetuate discrimination'.[78]

More specifically, to 'respect' means to refrain from undermining children's access to healthy food. This negative approach is more adept to under-nutrition, but it does help serve to address other forms of malnutrition. For instance, access to healthy food can be hampered in school catering, where social and geographic disparities could appear in the access to nutritionally-balanced canteen menus. In France, for example, a legislative amendment was presented to Parliament for a proposed bill on equality and citizenship, which sought to make access to healthy, locally grown produce compulsory in public catering. This was based on the right to health, with the aims of avoiding poor-quality, highly-processed school meals and to prevent local disparities in the diets of school children.[79] While the amendment was not adopted, it illustrates the application of the right to health and nutritional discrimination as reasoning to improve childhood diets.

To 'protect', beyond simple abstention, requires States to ensure that individuals, business actors and others do not interfere with access to adequate nutrition. This implies the adoption of measures to ensure the effectiveness of the rights of children to have access to a healthy diet, and not to be affected by negative influences. States should, therefore, adopt rules to ensure that industry actors do not infringe children's fundamental right to a healthy diet. In this regard, some conflicts may surface between children's rights and economic freedoms. In particular, there is a balance to be struck between industry's freedom of commercial speech and consumers' right to health and to a healthy diet.[80] In her interim report in 2016, Hilal Elver, the Special Rapporteur on

---

[76] See n15, 48.

[77] Committee on the Rights of the Child, 'General Comment No. 7 2005' CRC/C/GC/7.Rev1, [12].

[78] Human Rights Committee, 'General Comment No 18', 1989, HRI/GEN/1/Rev.8, [10]. See also P Alston, 'The Legal Framework of the Rights of the Child' 91(2) *Bulletin of Human Rights* 5. It should be noted that affirmative action must also be non-discriminatory.

[79] LOI no 2017-86 du 27 janvier 2017 relative à l'égalité et à la citoyenneté, JORF no 0024 du 28 janvier 2017.

[80] See further, chapters by Roache and Cabrera and Garde and Byrne in this volume.

Right to Food, underlined the responsibility that companies bear in order to avoid infringing human rights:

> Recognizing that industry self-regulation is ineffective, Governments should impose strong regulatory systems to ensure that the food industry does not violate citizens' human rights to adequate food and nutrition. It is recognized, however, that such efforts may face formidable resistance from a food industry seeking to protect its economic interests.[81]

The obligation to 'fulfil' implies that States should adopt appropriate legislative, administrative, budgetary, judicial and other measures to ensure the full realization of children's human rights. While childhood obesity is complicated, and its eradication complex, reducing inequalities in childhood obesity presents further challenges. First, and most fundamentally, tackling health inequalities requires a reduction in the inequalities in the distribution of socioeconomic factors, such as education and employment. Secondly, inequalities in health can be reduced by tackling intermediary determinants, such as the consumption of energy-dense diets, which mediate the effect of socioeconomic factors on health.[82] While such actions should benefit all in society universally, it should be at a scale and intensity that is proportionate to the level of disadvantage.[83] These actions require a comprehensive, multi-level, multi-sector, health-in-all policies approach with the backing of political will.[84]

3.2   Legal Tools

There are many interventions, of varying effectiveness, which can contribute to reducing levels of childhood obesity, including increasing physical activity, school-based education programmes or improving medical treatment.[85] Some interventions can even achieve a reduction in inequalities in childhood

---

[81] H Elver, 'UN Special Rapporteur on the Right to Food: Report', A/71/282 3 August 2016.
[82] Closing the Gap in a Generation: Health Equity Through Action on the Social Determinants of Health (WHO 2008).
[83] *'Fair Society, Healthy Lives: Strategic Review of Health Inequalities in England'* (The Marmot Review 2010), 16.
[84] 'A Conceptual Framework for Action on the Social Determinants of Health' (WHO 2010).
[85] E Waters et al., 'Interventions for Preventing Obesity in Children' (2011) *Cochrane Database Systematic Reviews*; C Summerbell et al., 'Evidence-Based Recommendations for the Development of Obesity Prevention Programs Targeted at Preschool Children' (2012) 13(1) *Obesity Reviews* 129.

obesity.[86] While no single intervention will prevent or reverse childhood obesity and its inequalities, of the options available to the State at individual, community and national levels, States have mostly opted for empowering consumers and parents through mandatory food information.[87] Consumer empowerment through information rests on the idea that if individuals are provided with sufficient, accurate information they will become well-informed; and well-informed consumers will make rational, healthy decisions in food purchasing and consumption decisions.[88]

Such policies transfer responsibility from the State, which decides the type and method of information consumers are given, to the consumer, who becomes responsible for making healthy food decisions. This is problematic as childhood obesity is heavily influenced by upstream factors which the child cannot influence. Influence over the environment in which the child lives, and the decisions he or she is able to take, are limited. Indeed, nutritional information is not an intervention aimed at all children due the child's limited cognitive capacity. This weak position of children in society has been reinforced by the CRC Committee.[89] Moreover, not only does this transfer of responsibility not take into account the wider context, it assumes that obesity is exclusively a matter of personal or family responsibility.[90]

This approach does have some economic and equitable advantages – such as correcting informational asymmetries which favour industry, and helping to fulfil the consumer's right to information.[91] However, it has been strongly criticized as an ineffective tool.[92] Moreover, not only are these policies insufficient

---

[86] C Bambra et al., 'How Effective are Interventions at Reducing Socioeconomic Inequalities in Obesity Among Children and Adults? Two Systematic Reviews' (2015) 3(1) *Public Health Research*; N Freudenberg, 'Commentary: Reducing Inequalities in Child Obesity in Developed Nations: What Do We Know? What Can We Do?' (2013) 31(1) *Revista Portugesa de Saude Publica* 115.

[87] A Alemanno and A Garde, 'The Emergence of An EU Lifestyle Policy: The Case of Alcohol, Tobacco and Unhealthy Diets' (2013) 50(6) *Common Market Law Review* 1745.

[88] M Friant-Perrot and A Garde, 'From BSE to Obesity: EFSA's Growing Role in the EU's Nutrition Policy' in A Alemanno and S Gabbi (eds), *Foundations of EU Food Law and Policy: Ten Years of the European Food Safety Authority* (Routledge 2014).

[89] See n77, [11(b)].

[90] See for instance: D Resnik, 'Responsibility for Health: Personal, Social, and Environmental' (2007) 33(8) *Journal of Medical Ethics* 444; C Newdick, 'Health Equality, Social Justice and the Poverty of Autonomy' (2017) 12 *Health Economics, Policy and Law* 411.

[91] I Ramsay, 'Framework for Regulation of the Consumer Marketplace' (1985) 8 *Journal of Consumer Policy* 353.

[92] Such critiques have been made many times in the broader consumer law and economics literature – see n20.

to reduce obesity in all groups of consumers, they are particularly ineffective for members of lower socioeconomic position groups and thus tend to promote inequalities.[93] This is for three reasons.

First, the assumption that consumers are given sufficient, accurate information which is not misleading is not always true. For instance, whereas many consumers would prefer to also receive nutritional information per portion of food, this is rarely mandatory. Similarly, a product labelled with a food claim, such as 'low in fat', may nonetheless have an overall unhealthy nutritional profile. Members of lower socioeconomic groups suffer worse from this assumption as, for instance, the most vulnerable consumers are often less able to understand nutritional information and health messages.[94]

Secondly, research in behavioural economics has brought to the fore the identification of two sets of systems of cognitive function.[95] Whereas most consumers make the vast majority of decisions relating to food using their brain's automatic system – which is effortless and fast but uncontrolled, emotional and engages superficially – information policies assume that consumers use their brain's reflective system – which is controlled, effortful and engages deeply, but is slow and has limited capacity.[96] This research reveals that consumers rarely act completely rationally, not least because consumers are subject to heuristics and biases. For instance, consumers do not always perceive nutritional information. Moreover, because of their circumstances, members of lower socioeconomic groups tend to be subject to greater limitations of both these types of cognitive systems. For instance, poverty causes psychological consequences, including stress and negative affective states, which lead to short-sighted and risk-averse decision-making, which reinforce habitual behaviours more strongly.[97] Similarly, poorer members of society will more often have to make decisions which require volition – this draws on finite psychological resources, so that earlier acts to maintain willpower for healthy decisions will have detrimental impacts on later attempts at volition.[98]

Thirdly, rationality is not the sole determinant of consumer behaviour, and the consumer's environment can result in purchasing decisions which are not

---

[93] N Gokani, 'Regulation for Health Inequalities and Non-Communicable Diseases: In Want of (Effective) Behavioural Insights' (2018) 24(6) *European Law Journal* 490.

[94] K Grunert and J Wills, 'A Review of European Research on Consumer Response to Nutrition Information on Food Labels' (2007) 15(5) *Journal of Public Health* 385; S Campos et al., 'Nutrition Labels on Pre-Packaged Foods: A Systematic Review' (2011) 14(8) *Public Health Nutrition* 1496.

[95] See n19.

[96] 'Mindspace' (Institute for Government 2010).

[97] J Haushofer and E Fehr, 'On the Psychology of Poverty' (2014) 344 *Science* 862.

[98] RE Baumeister et al., 'Ego Depletion: Is the Active Self a Limited Resource?' (1998) 74(5) *Journal of Personality and Social Psychology* 1252.

in the consumer's best health interests. Again, this becomes more difficult with members of lower socioeconomic groups. For instance, consumers may not be able to follow through with healthy decisions if their poverty means that purchasing is restricted by cost, as unhealthy energy-dense food is often cheaper.[99]

To overcome some of the limits in empowering consumers through information, these polices need to be placed within a broader strategy. To this end, restricting the marketing of unhealthy food to children offers an evidence-based intervention to reduce obesity for all children.[100] There is unequivocal evidence linking unhealthy food marketing to childhood obesity,[101] and increasing recognition that such marketing has a negative impact on children and the enjoyment of their rights. Moreover, as a group, children do not have the necessary cognitive capacity to identify the persuasive intent of advertising, and therefore marketing can manipulate behaviour through implicit persuasion, which may, in turn, explain why cognitive defences would not even protect older children.[102]

The WHO Set of Recommendations on the Marketing of Foods and Non-Alcoholic Beverages to Children[103] fleshes out the provisions that States should adopt to comply with their obligations under the CRC, which were unanimously adopted by the World Health Assembly in May 2010.[104] The WHO has published a framework implementation report[105] to provide technical support to States in implementing the Recommendations and in monitoring

---

[99] A Drewnowski and S Specter, 'Poverty and Obesity: The Role of Energy Density and Energy Costs' (2004) 79(1) *American Journal of Clinical Nutrition* 6; A Drewnowski, 'Obesity and the Food Environment: Dietary Energy Density and Diet Costs' (2004) 27(3) *American Journal of Preventative Medicine* 154.

[100] A Child Rights-Based Approach to Food Marketing: A Guide for Policy Makers (Unicef, 2018); A Garde, N Gokani and M Friant-Perrot 'Children's Rights, Childhood Obesity and Health Inequalities' (2018) 43 *UNSCN News* 65; A Garde, S Byrne, N Gokani and B Murphy, 'For A Children's Rights Approach to Obesity Prevention: The Key Role of Effective Implementation of the WHO Recommendations' (2017) 8(2) *European Journal of Risk Regulation* 327.

[101] E Boyland and M Tatlow-Golden, 'Exposure, Power and Impact of Food Marketing on Children: Evidence Supports Strong Restrictions' (2017) 8(2) *European Journal of Risk Regulation* 224.

[102] A Nairn and C Fine, 'Who's Messing With My Mind? The Implications of Dual-Process Models for the Ethics of Advertising to Children' (2008) 27(3) *International Journal of Advertising* 447; J Harris et al., 'The Food Marketing Defense Model: Integrating Psychological Research to Protect Youth and Inform Public Policy' (2009) 3(1) *Social Issues and Policy Review* 211.

[103] WHO Set of Recommendations on the Marketing of Foods and Non-Alcoholic Beverages to Children (WHO 2010).

[104] World Health Assembly, 'Resolution 63/14' (2010).

[105] A framework for implementing the set of recommendations on the marketing of foods and non-alcoholic beverages to children (WHO 2012).

and evaluating their implementation. Despite repeated calls on States,[106] they remain poorly implemented to date.[107] These Recommendations should be seen as a guide for actions that States should consider in order to end childhood obesity and empower children and their parents and families. As such, they have the potential to support a children's rights-based approach to obesity prevention, even though they do not specifically refer to children's rights.

Given that calorie consumption, rather than decrease in physical activity, appears to be the main driving force behind the growing obesity epidemic,[108] implementing the WHO Recommendations will reduce the preference, purchase requests and consumption of unhealthy food by all children. Yet it will have greater positive impacts on children from lower socioeconomic groups, and thus help towards reducing inequalities in childhood obesity. This is because the Recommendations call on States to adopt policies to tackle the two main components of marketing: the exposure (reach and frequency) and power (creative content, design and execution) of the marketing – both of which have a greater negative impact on children from socioeconomic groups associated with calorie-dense diets.

This is because children tend to be exposed to marketing more than adults.[109] Moreover, children from a lower socioeconomic status tend to be exposed to greater degrees of marketing,[110] as shown in relation to many media,

---

[106] Global Action Plan for the Prevention and Control of Noncommunicable Diseases 2013–2020 (WHO 2013); Final Report of the WHO Commission on Ending Childhood Obesity (WHO 2016).

[107] V Kraak et al., 'Progress Achieved in Restricting the Marketing of High-Fat, Sugary and Salty Food and Beverage Products to Children' (2016) 94(7) *WHO Bulletin* 540; A Garde and G Xuereb, 'The WHO Recommendations on the Marketing of Food and Non-Alcoholic Beverages to Children' (2017) 8 *European Journal of Risk Regulation* 211.

[108] B Swinburn et al., 'The Global Obesity Pandemic: Shaped by Global Drivers and Local Environments' (2011) 378(9793) *Lancet* 804; P Scarborough et al., 'Increased Energy Intake Entirely Accounts for Increase in Body Weight in Women But Not in Men in the UK between 1986 and 2000' (2011) 105(9) *British Journal of Nutrition* 1399.

[109] See, e.g.: M LoDolce et al., 'Sugar as Part of a Balanced Breakfast? What Cereal Advertisements Teach Children about Healthy Eating' (2013) 18(11) *Journal of Health Communication: International Perspectives* 1293.

[110] See, e.g.: SA Grier and S Kumanyika, 'Targeted Marketing and Public Health' (2012) 31(21) *Annual Review of Public Health* 349.

including television,[111] magazines,[112] outdoor advertising[113] and placement of fast-food outlets.[114] Such marketing is often specifically targeted towards these groups,[115] thereby amplifying their pre-existing vulnerabilities. This becomes even more of a concern because digital marketing methods can target children with precision.[116] Moreover, children are also more susceptible to unhealthy food marketing than adults. This inflated susceptibility to marketing is further amplified in children from lower socioeconomic groups.[117] It has been found, for example, that these children tend to make changes to their food preferences after only brief exposure to marketing.[118] Furthermore, obese children – who may already have been negatively impacted by unhealthy food marketing – are also more susceptible to such marketing than non-overweight children.[119] In the words of Anand Grover, then UN Special Rapporteur on the Right to Health: 'States have a positive duty to regulate unhealthy food advertising and the promotion strategies of food companies. Under the right to health, States are especially required to protect vulnerable groups such as children from violations of their right to health.'[120]

---

[111] J Adams et al., 'Socio-Economic Differences in Exposure to Television Food Advertisements in the UK: A cross-sectional study of advertisements broadcast in one television region' (2012) 15(3) *Public Health Nutrition* 487.

[112] See, e.g.: J Adams and M White, 'Socio-Economic and Gender Differences in Nutritional Content of Foods Advertised in Popular UK Weekly Magazines' (2009) 19(2) *European Journal of Public Health* 144.

[113] J Adams et al., 'Socio-Economic Differences in Outdoor Food Advertising in a City in Northern England' (2011) 14(6) *Public Health Nutrition* 945.

[114] K Smoyer-Tomic et al., 'The Association between Neighborhood Socioeconomic Status and Exposure to Supermarkets and Fast Food Outlets' (2008) 14(4) *Health & Place* 740.

[115] See n110.

[116] K Montgomery, 'Youth and Surveillance in the Facebook Era: Policy interventions and social implications' (2015) 39(9) *Telecommunications Policy* 771.

[117] G Cairns et al., 'Systematic Reviews of the Evidence on the Nature, Extent and Effects of Food Marketing to Children: A retrospective summary' (2013) 62(1) *Appetite* 209; S Lear et al., 'The Association Between Ownership of Common Household Devices and Obesity and Diabetes in High, Middle and Low Income Countries' (2014) 186(4) *Canadian Medical Association Journal* 258.

[118] S Kumanyika and S Grier, 'Targeting Interventions for Ethnic Minority and Low-Income Populations', (2006) 16(1) *The Future of Children* 187.

[119] J Halford et al., 'Beyond-Brand Effect of Television (TV) Food Advertisements/ Commercials on Caloric Intake and Food Choice of 5–7-Year-Old Children' (2007) 49 *Appetite* 263.

[120] A Grover, 'Unhealthy foods, non-communicable diseases and the right to health. Report of the Special Rapporteur on the right of everyone to the enjoyment of the highest attainable standard of physical and mental health', 2014, United Nations Document A/HRC/26/31. United Nations Human Rights Council, 11.

4. CONCLUSION

Despite efforts in tackling childhood obesity, benefits have not been experienced equally everywhere or by everyone. The widespread, entrenched inequalities in childhood obesity between and within societies reflect the differences in the conditions in which communities live. These health inequalities are systematic, socially produced and unfair: they are caused by the unequal distribution of socioeconomic resources. They are unnecessary and unjust, and they offend against the human rights of children and their families. Corrective action is required as a matter of social justice to restore children's autonomy, dignity and freedom in food choices.

These are not newly-discovered concerns. From the Alma-Ata Declaration of 1978[121] and the Vienna Declaration of 1993[122] to the Rome Declaration on Nutrition of 2014, [123] national and international actors have envisioned the eradication of inequalities in food provision and called for a global response to end all forms of malnourishment, including obesity. What is required is 'coordinated action among different actors, across all relevant sectors at international, regional, national and community levels...supported through cross-cutting and coherent policies, programmes and initiatives, including social protection, to address the multiple burdens of malnutrition and to promote sustainable food systems'[124] through reinforcing the idea that 'the progressive realization of the right to adequate food in the context of national food security is fostered through sustainable, equitable, accessible in all cases, and resilient and diverse food systems'.[125]

In order to provide greater attention to the under-researched issues of inequalities in childhood obesity, discrimination and equality – and to build on the normative impetus for more effective State intervention and to better understand the correct role of the State – this chapter has added depth to the theorization of inequalities in childhood obesity through the lens of human rights. An approach grounded in human rights increases accountability, by holding stakeholders to their commitments; increases legitimacy, as human rights derived from international treaties are universally recognised, inalien-

---

[121] Declaration of Alma-Ata International. Adopted by the Conference on Primary Health Care in Alma-Ata on 6–12 September 1978.
[122] Vienna Declaration and Programme of Action. Adopted by the World Conference on Human Rights in Vienna on 25 June 1993.
[123] Rome Declaration on Nutrition. Adopted by the Second International Conference on Nutrition in Rome on 19–21 November 2014.
[124] Ibid.
[125] See n123.

able international standards; and provides an advocacy tool to help galvanize political will.

While the existing literature has drawn connections between health inequalities and human rights generally[126] or other specific rights,[127] and developed the right to non-discrimination broadly[128] or in relation to other concerns,[129] this chapter has progressed the research by deepening the understanding of the link between health inequalities and the right to non-discrimination.[130] Moreover, it has provided a fresh view by seeking to demonstrate that the right to non-discrimination – and the rights to food and health, and to their exercise by children without discrimination on the basis of socioeconomic status – impose binding legal commitments on States to fulfil equality of opportunity in childhood nutrition. It has further argued that these duties place obligations on States to create environments which grant all children the capacity to choose healthy food and therefore reduce the prevalence of obesity.

Furthermore, as States continue to rely on ineffective policies which fail to sufficiently reduce childhood obesity and can even increase inequalities, this chapter has further argued that, in the exercise of rights to health and to adequate food, an approach grounded in the child's right to non-discrimination (as interpreted in this chapter) strengthens the capacities of children (as right-holders) to realize their rights and of States (as duty-bearers) to meet their legal obligations under the CRC and other binding human rights documents. It has, therefore, built on the broader literature on behavioural economics[131] and consumer information[132] to show that current mechanisms of obesity prevention, mainly nutritional declarations, are insufficiently effective and perpetuate inequalities; and introduced the idea that these measures therefore propagate discrimination. By demonstrating that the implementation of restrictions on unhealthy food marketing to children will help States move closer to fulfilling of the child's right to non-discrimination in the CRC, this chapter strengthens calls for such restrictions.[133] Of the many tools available to States, such restrictions are effective evidence-based opportunities to help

---

[126] See n13.
[127] See n14.
[128] See n15.
[129] See for instance: K Stronks et al., *'Social justice and human rights as a framework for addressing social determinants of health Final report of the Task Group on Equity, Equality and Human Rights Review of social determinants of health and the health divide in the WHO European Region'* (WHO, 2016) http://www.euro.who.int/__data/assets/pdf_file/0006/334356/HR-task-report.pdf (accessed 22 June 2019).
[130] See n18.
[131] See n19.
[132] See n20.
[133] See n12.

fulfil the State's obligations to improve nutrition, reduce obesity and other related non-communicable diseases and increase wellbeing for every child and particularly the most vulnerable children.

PART II

Utilising the space available for regulatory measures under international economic law

5. Sugar as commodity or health risk: The unmaking or remaking of international trade law?

Gregory Messenger

1. INTRODUCTION

Sugar is one of the world's most traded commodities: global production of sugar is at approximately 170 million tons, with world exports of 57.7 million tons.[1] As a widely traded commodity, over the course of its history sugar has served to stimulate both the normative and institutional framework of the world trade regime. In his ground-breaking monograph, *Sugar and the Making of International Trade Law*, Michael Fakhri traces the development of international trade law through the history of the sugar trade, identifying the key role that sugar has played in constituting the current world trade system,[2] from its substantive rules and principles, to the creation of multilateral institutions of trade.[3]

The resulting system, currently embodied in the World Trade Organization (WTO) is largely considered a success in international law circles: international trade law is one of the most effective regimes in international law, sporting comparatively detailed rules and a compliance system that outshines most others available to States.[4] Yet as obesity (in particular, childhood obesity) becomes a major health concern for both developed and developing States, sugar's place in the trade system takes on a more complex hue. As

---

[1] US Department of Agriculture, 'Sugar: World Markets and Trade' (May 2017) 4. For the purposes of this chapter, sugar is understood as both cane and beet sugar, its refined form, and other preparations for further use (such as syrups). In essence, sugar *as traded*, rather than products containing sugars (whether naturally occurring or added).
[2] M Fakhri, *Sugar and the Making of International Trade Law* (CUP 2014).
[3] See Section 2 below.
[4] On the WTO's (relative) strengths: G Messenger, *The Development of World Trade Law: Examining Change in International Law* (OUP 2016) 9–11.

governments' attempts to regulate the sugar industry become a global priority, their potential to come into conflict with international trade law increases, thus raising the question: might sugar be the unmaking of the trade system it did so much to inspire?

This chapter identifies key points of tension and opportunity between the global trade in sugar as a primary commodity and the regulation of sugar as an obesogenic consumer good. Public health objectives have often been portrayed as in direct conflict with the aims of trade law (and by extension private power).[5] If this situation were true it would present a crisis for the trade system, or a crisis for public health, either of which would be crippling for global development and wellbeing. Yet, in spite of the profound and fundamental challenges involved, this chapter suggests that the global obesity crisis and its relation to sugar need not be viewed in oppositional terms (that is, governments' health objectives conflicting with their trade obligations). Instead, the challenges raised by sugar and the desire to combat childhood obesity may serve not to unmake international trade law but, instead, to remake it, inspiring subtle but meaningful and long-lasting reforms within the international trade regime.

The chapter is structured as follows: Section 2 identifies the role of commodities, and in particular sugar, in the development of the international trade system; Section 3 sets out the transition from viewing the trade in sugar and sugar-based products as commodities to a public health concern; Section 4 examines the ways in which the international trade system has approached comparable situations previously, proposing that the WTO's Appellate Body has used the pressure from disputes arising over health or environmental issues to shape trade law in a more nuanced fashion than is often presented; Section 5 acknowledges the difficulties for trade law in responding to obesity prevention measures, though striking a hopeful note that such challenges can spur further evolution in international trade law to support governments in their public policy decision-making, without undermining the foundations of the trade system; Section 6 concludes.

---

[5] On the 'misunderstandings' involved see: WHO and WTO, *WTO Agreements and Public Health* (WTO/WHO 2002). Available at https://www.wto.org/english/res_e/booksp_e/who_wto_e.pdf (last accessed 24 September 2020).

2. SUGAR AND INTERNATIONAL TRADE LAW'S PAST

Commodities such as sugar have played a fundamental role in the development of the world trade system.[6] A number of recent studies have examined how international law, trade relations, or their nexus – trade law – have been forged through trade in commodities.[7]

The role of cotton, for example, has played a key role in determining the structure of the global economic system: global value chains where goods are manufactured across jurisdictions, the effect of specialization and mechanization on economies, these are all part of the cotton industry's history.[8] Economic historians note the important role the cotton industry played in the 'great divergence' – the point at which the economies of India, China and Turkey (inter alia) diverged from their comparable economic equivalence with States in Western Europe.[9] Levels of industrialization diverged as harvesting remained necessarily in the fields while spinning and weaving moved to the industrial heartland of England. Early industrialization in States such as India and Turkey was reversed as their economies specialized on growing, subsequently leading to a global economy characterized by the unequal structure with which it still struggles: developing economies dependent on specialization in cash-crops and primary goods production (and the attendant price fluctuations often entailed), coupled with an inability to benefit significantly from processes that add greater value to goods within global value chains.[10]

---

[6] For the purposes of this chapter 'commodities' are understood as primary goods which require little or no treatment to bring to market. Thus, raw cane sugar and refined sugar constitute commodities, while high-sugar beverages would not. There is some confusion as the term 'commodity' is often used in different circumstances, sometimes interchangeably with 'primary goods', other times not. For example, the term 'product' and 'commodity' were used interchangeably by the WTO panel in *Japan –Agricultural Products II* (WT/DS76/R, 27 October 1998, p 4 footnote 7) though in other agreements, the terms are used in the alternative: see, Art 6.3(d) of the WTO Agreement on Subsidies and Countervailing Measures: 'primary product *or* commodity' (emphasis added).

[7] For example: Fakhri, n2, S Beckert, *Empires of Cotton: A New History of Global Capitalism* (Random House 2014), K Miles, *The Origins of International Investment Law: Empire, Environment and the Safeguarding of Capital* (CUP 2013).

[8] See generally: Beckert, ibid.

[9] Ibid., 29–50. See also, K Pomeranz, *The Great Divergence: China, Europe, and the Making of the Modern World Economy* (Princeton University Press 2001).

[10] Further exacerbated by historically differential tariff treatment for manufactured goods and the effect of productivity gains globally: G Corea, *Taming Commodity Markets: The Integrated Programme and the Common Fund in UNCTAD* (Manchester University Press 1992) 5.

In the case of both sugar and cotton, as well as other commodities such as coffee and tobacco, the relationship between commodities and State-sponsored imperial projects was central.[11] The British Empire may have been 'built on a huge sugar, caffeine and nicotine rush'[12] but it was cotton that brought factories and centralized production.[13] Behind these processes were either the explicit or implicit use of military force by colonial powers.[14] Indeed, when the colonial powers sought to turn to law to resolve their increasing imperial trade conflicts, sugar was at the heart of the project.[15]

Fakhri draws attention to the manner in which the current institutional settlement in trade can be found in the history of sugar, which was the subject of the first truly multilateral international organization for trade.[16] The 1902 Brussels Convention created what to our eyes appears to be a very familiar institution: it regulated tariffs, it required national treatment (i.e., that imported goods be treated no less favourably than domestic goods), most-favoured nation provisions (restricting the ability to give trade preferences to one trading partner over another), and regulated the use of subsidies and countervailing duties (import duties levied to offset the effect of a trading partner's subsidization).[17] Although limited to sugar, and its historically contingent importance, the Brussels Convention provided a model for what would become the standard approach to coordinating international trade policy.[18]

Price fluctuations over the 1920s and 1930s in commodities like sugar were in the forefront of the minds of government officials when designing a new international trade regime after the Second World War. The parties negotiating the post-war economic settlement at Bretton Woods were sensitive to the impact that erratic prices had on the economic conditions leading up to war,[19] and thus, along with the creation of the International Monetary Fund (to monitor exchange rates and regulate competitive devaluations) and the

---

[11] European economic development as dependent upon overseas trade: Pomeranz n9, 4–7.
[12] N Ferguson, *Empire: How Britain Made the Modern World* (Penguin 2004) 15.
[13] Beckert, n7, xvii–xix and 56–7.
[14] See generally: E Hobsbawm, *Industry and Empire* (2nd edn, Penguin 1990), in particular: 28–32.
[15] On the intersection between international law and empire: A Anghie, *Imperialism, Sovereignty and the Making of International Law* (CUP 2005).
[16] Fakhri, n2, 21–9. Cf, P Mavroidis, *Trade in Goods* (2nd edn, OUP 2012) 326 arguing in favour of the 1927 International Convention for the Abolition of Import and Export Prohibitions and Restrictions.
[17] International Convention Relative to Bounties on Sugar (5 March 1902).
[18] Fakhri, n2, 21–9.
[19] For a recent history of the negotiations, see: B Steil, *The Battle of Bretton Woods* (Princeton University Press 2013).

International Bank of Reconstruction and Development ('the World Bank', to finance reconstruction efforts in war-torn territories), negotiators intended to create an International Trade Organization (ITO) to regulate global trade, and avoid the beggar-thy-neighbour protectionism of the pre-war period that had (in the eyes of many) contributed to the Second World War. The Havana Charter,[20] the ITO's constituent treaty, sought to regulate trade in commodities such as sugar comprehensively through the use of international commodity agreements.[21]

The ITO was not to be, however, as while the International Monetary Fund and World Bank became a reality, the US Congress refused to ratify the Havana Charter. While the ITO was stopped in its tracks, a remnant of the foreseen trade system, the General Agreement on Tariffs and Trade (GATT 1947) survived.[22] The GATT 1947 included a short set of rules to encourage non-discriminatory trade and the progressive reduction of trade barriers (principally tariffs until the 1960s).[23] By the time the Havana Charter failed in Congress, the GATT 1947 had already been applied provisionally, acting as the underlying rule set for trade amongst, at first mostly developed economies, and later the majority of trading States.[24]

The GATT 1947, being a mere fragment of the system envisaged as the ITO, did not contain specific provisions on the regulation of commodities. Instead the GATT 1947 carried only a handful of oblique provisions of importance to commodity trade: provisions on the use of quantitative restrictions (i.e., quotas) to relieve critical shortages of food stuffs or manage temporary surpluses in domestic production,[25] and limitations on the use of subsidies relating to the export of 'primary products'.[26]

---

[20] Final Act of the United Nations Conference on Trade and Employment (April 1948) UN Docs E/Conf. 2/78.
[21] See 'Proposals for Expansion of World Trade and Employment', State Department Publication No. 2411, December 1945, in Douglas Irwin et al., *The Genesis of the GATT* (CUP 2009) 244–61, at 249 (including a 'Release from Fear of Disorder in the Markets for Primary Commodities' as a core element in encouraging trade).
[22] General Agreement on Tariffs and Trade (30 October 1947) 55 UNTS 194.
[23] For an overview of this period see: M Matsushita et al., *The World Trade Organization: Law, Practice, and Policy* (3rd edn, OUP 2016) 1–9.
[24] The original Contracting Parties of the GATT 1947 were: Australia, Belgium, Brazil, Burma, Canada, Ceylon, Chile, China, Cuba, Czechoslovakia, France, India, Lebanon, Luxembourg, Netherlands, New Zealand, Norway, Pakistan, Southern Rhodesia, Syria, South Africa, United Kingdom, and the United States.
[25] Art XI.2(a) and XI.2(c)(ii) GATT 1947 respectively.
[26] Art XVI.3 GATT 1947.

In 1947 the GATT Contracting Parties were mostly developed economies, and in a number of cases, colonial powers.[27] As decolonization changed the structure of the international community, the consequences of centuries of 'war capitalism' became particularly prominent.[28] The place of commodities as part of this debate was central as many postcolonial States had economies heavily dependent on commodities, the direct result of colonial economic policies that sought to specialize production in the periphery to feed the manufacturing base in the centre. The expectation that greater trade by newly independent States would lead to convergence with the developed economies of the globe was disappointed, however, in large part because dependence on trade in commodities left postcolonial States subject to dramatic price fluctuations, bound to a system of agricultural or mineral production which did not encourage the production of high-value-added goods, and sensitive to the demands of large Western-owned private actors in the market.

Between the 1950s and 1970s, commodities increasingly became connected to development concerns, and as these concerns increased in importance, interest in them moved from the GATT to the United National Conference on Trade and Development (UNCTAD) and were further addressed in the wider movement for a New International Economic Order,[29] only nominally interacting with the GATT framework.[30] During this time, international commodity agreements were encouraged, attempting to limit price fluctuations through the creation of buffer stocks and supply management.[31]

By the 1980s, the international commodity agreements which sought to minimize price fluctuations had largely failed,[32] and their failure became linked to the wider division between development studies and neoliberal economics, between UNCTAD and the GATT, between import-substitution policies and

---

[27] See n23.

[28] The term used by Beckert, n7, chapters 2 and 3.

[29] See, inter alia, GA Res 3201 'Declaration on the Establishment of a New International Economic Order' 1 May 1974 (A/RES/S-6/3201).

[30] S Rolland, *Development at the WTO* (OUP 2012) 69. See also the UK's (amongst others) insistence that any new multilateral agreement on commodities be closely linked to the GATT system: Working Party on Commodity Problems, 'Brief Notes on the General Discussion at the Second and Third Meetings' (3 September 1955) Spec 274/55.

[31] On the structure and systems of such agreements: K Khan, *The Law and Organisation of International Commodity Agreements* (Martinus Nijhoff 1982).

[32] See, e.g., the acknowledgment that commodity agreements had been ineffective and that trade-distortive measures were at the root of the problem in agricultural trade: Note by the GATT Secretariat, 'Summary of Studies on Problems Affecting Trade in Agriculture and Their Causes' (31 March 1987) MTN.GNG/NG5/W/3.

the Washington Consensus.[33] The ascendance of market economics as a core element of a widely adopted political ideology in the 1980s led to a reformulation of how commodities were understood. Rather than being linked to fundamental postcolonial relationships or development challenges directly, commodities were instead to be treated like all other goods, but only insofar as this did not conflict with the economic interests of the West. Thus, while copper or guano were to be treated as any other good, agriculture was to have a separate regime that gave wide scope for wealthy economies such as the US and EU to subsidize domestic production and permit high tariffs.

The entry into force of the WTO in 1995 changed this settlement in a number of ways. It brought agricultural trade into the trade system more directly, seeking to reduce trade barriers through tariff reductions, commitments made on levels of agricultural subsidies, and a transparent system for the introduction of measures designed to protect human, animal, and plant life or health.[34] The commitment was to the development of a 'market-oriented agricultural trading system'.[35] Although this was ostensibly pictured as part of the 'development' dimensions of trade, no meaningful provision was made for concerns arising from price instability or over-specialization. Instead, liberalization of trade in agricultural goods was sold as a benefit to the developing economies of the world, working in part on the basis that the fluctuations of the past were a result of government intervention in the market, not a reason for it.[36] Meanwhile, large subsidies were allowed to be maintained to ensure that developed members were still able to subsidize were needed to protect their own large and influential domestic agricultural constituencies.[37] While there are a number of substantial benefits that accrue to developing economies from liberalization of agricultural goods, the special nature of their production

---

[33] On the ideological shift in the 1980s that went hand in hand with reduced commodity prices that benefited developed rather than developing States see: Corea, n10, 181. See also: M Trebilcock, 'Between Theories of Trade and Development: The Future of the World Trading System' (2015) *Journal of World Investment and Trade* 16, 122.

[34] Agreement on the Application of Sanitary and Phytosanitary Measures (SPS Agreement) (15 April 1994) LT/UR/A-1A/12. The balance between liberalization of trade in agricultural goods and measures to protect from dangers arising from such trade through introduction of an integrated agreement was previously used in the North American Free Trade Agreement (concluded 17 December 1992, entered into force 1 January 1994) 32 ILM 289, 605. On the motivations for the conclusion of the SPS Agreement see Messenger, n4, 121–7.

[35] Preamble (second recital), Agreement on Agriculture (15 April 1994) LT/UR/A-1A/2.

[36] See n31.

[37] See: Arts 6 and 7, Agreement on Agriculture.

and trade is not acknowledged under the GATT or the WTO Agreement on Agriculture. Indeed, it is notable that there are no commodity provisions under the General Agreement on Trade in Services (negotiated in the 1980s) comparable to the peripheral provisions under the GATT, as by the time of the advent of the WTO the shift away from seeing international commodity agreements as a solution for commodity price instability was nearly complete.[38]

As the promises of the Washington Consensus failed to deliver for many developing members, and paradoxically those for whom it had succeeded became a more powerful voice within the trade system, the WTO agreed to make development its focus by declaring the negotiating round launched in Doha in November 2001 a 'development round'.[39] While the Doha Development Round failed to make any substantial progress from its opening in November 2001 until Bali in 2013, the Bali Ministerial Conference (with further advances made at Nairobi in 2015) saw movement on a number of key issues of interest for the trade in commodities, including an Agreement on Trade Facilitation and a set of Ministerial Decisions on cotton, food security, and export subsidies.[40] Although the effectiveness of such decisions is yet to be seen, when contrasted with the generational and ideological shift from the GATT to the WTO, these advances seem timid by comparison. Yet, there is a sense in which they have marked a change in the atmosphere in multilateral trade negotiations and the institutions of global trade. This is echoed in the more recent advances in negotiations over the completion of the UN Sustainable Development Goals (SDGs) which have called on the WTO to act, in particular, with SDG 14.6 calling for the elimination of subsidies which contribute to illegal, unreported, and unregulated fishing.[41] Principally an environmental and development concern,[42] the focus on their regulation is squarely

---

[38] On the ideological context to the GATS negotiations, see: A Lang, *World Trade Law After Neoliberalism* (OUP 2011) 274ff.

[39] See: Doha Ministerial Declaration (14 November 2001) WT/MIN(01)/DEC/1.

[40] See: Bali Ministerial Declaration (11 December 2013) WT/MIN(13), Nairobi Ministerial Declaration (19 December 2015) WT/MIN(15)/DEC, Ministerial Conference, *Public Stockholding for Food Security Purposes*, Ministerial Decision of 7 December 2013, WT/MIN(i3)/38 WT/L/913 (2013); Ministerial Conference, *Export Competition*, Ministerial Decision of 19 December 2015, WT/MIN(15)/45 WT/L/980 (2015); Ministerial Conference, *Cotton*, Ministerial Decision of 19 December 2015, WT/MIN(15)/46 WT/L/981 (2015); Ministerial Conference, *Special Safeguard Mechanism for Developing Country Members*, Ministerial Decision of 19 December 2015, WT/MIN(15)/43 WT/L/978 (2015).

[41] 'Transforming our world: the 2030 Agenda for Sustainable Development', GA Res. 70/1, 25 September 2015 (2030 Agenda).

[42] On the overlap, see: G Messenger, 'Sustainable Development and the Commodities Challenge: The Eventual 'Greening' of the World Trade Organization?' (2017) *Trade, Law & Development* 1.

at the WTO where the Negotiating Group on Rules is actively attempting to draft a new set of rules to regulate their use.[43] This increased attention in trade spheres to the SDGs is of particular importance for public health policies, explicitly mentioned in SDGs 2 and 3, but of practical necessity for the completion of the vast majority of other Goals.

Commodities have always formed a fundamental part of the trade system, from the normative to the institutional level. Yet the focus on commodities has over time been principally on their effect on the economic conditions of members and their impact on development. In each instance, however, the aim is to produce a system whereby commodities may be traded freely and where their trade can benefit all participants in the trade system, to meet the promises of the WTO 'to secure a share in the growth in international trade commensurate with the needs of [developing members'] economic development'.[44] A consequence of the increased trade, however, is also increased availability, acceptability, and affordability. The reduction in sugar prices from increased trade (and government intervention through subsidies) augments its prevalence and the ease with which it can be used as an input in sugar-based products. It is at this point that the regulation of commodities, and in particular sugar, takes an extraordinary turn: from an economic concern over trade flows, to a health concern where the trade in sugar and sugar-based goods directly entails serious health concerns which also impact on development.

3. SUGAR: FROM COMMODITY TO PUBLIC HEALTH CONCERN

The story thus far has been of the central role that sugar and other commodities have had on the normative and institutional framework of the global economy, and the institutions of global trade (currently embodied in the WTO). Running in parallel, and often viewed in tension, has been the regulation of commodities' trade not only for economic reasons but also for health reasons. While economic concerns relate to the impact of trade on sugar price volatility, health concerns stress the need to regulate the ability of consumers to access products high in sugar. Regulation which seeks to discourage consumers from purchasing products or limiting their consumption (through higher taxes or restrictions in marketing, for example) have historically been a potential 'problem' for

---

[43] A compilation of the textual proposals put forward to the Negotiating Group on Rules (NGR) as at 27 July 2017 has been prepared by the Chair of the NGR: Negotiating Group on Rules, 'Fisheries Subsidies: Compilation Matrix of Textual Proposals Received to Date' (28 July 2017) TN/RL/W/232.

[44] Preamble (second recital), Agreement Establishing the World Trade Organization (WTO Agreement) (15 April 1994) 1867 UNTS 154.

trade law which views such measures as possible restrictions to trade. This need not be the case, however, as regulating to support public health objectives such as eliminating childhood obesity does not necessarily run counter to the aims of the trade system, although this is often the account given. Indeed, health concerns are a development concern, while the core objectives of trade law are based on the premise that economic liberalization leads to aggregate welfare gains which in turn promote development.[45]

The study of trade in commodities and their impact on development has tended to focus on more narrow questions of economic effects.[46] Yet, development is not only affected by the consequences of economic contraction in production industries or employment, but also by structural and intergenerational health concerns. That a commodity such as sugar presents health challenges directly impacts on the ability of States to develop economically, and its increased prevalence in the global economy as a consequence of increased liberalization has to be taken into account. This section tracks the parallel relevance of health concerns in trade and looks to the unique challenges of sugar as an obesogenic good in a liberalized global sugar market, drawing on contemporary and historical parallels.

Just as sugar played a fundamental role in the development of international trade law, so we might learn from the situation of another harmful yet prevalent commodity in the history of trade and international relations. During the 19th century, opium was a commodity like any other. It was traded first through monopolies granted by the Crown, and then later opened to what would now be considered a process of liberalization and deregulation. Increased productivity of opium farms in India saw increased supply, and the desirability of access to the lucrative Chinese market.[47] The consequence of British expansionism and French involvement in ensuring that the Chinese market accept these materials marked not only Chinese history but also debates within the empire over the appropriate limits of free trade.[48]

Palmerston's focus on Chinese measures to restrict the introduction and spread of narcotics was understood as a restriction on trade – something counterposed by Gladstone's insistence on acknowledging the evils of the opium

---

[45] See generally: J Bhagwati, *In Defense of Globalization* (OUP 2007).
[46] See n32 and corresponding text.
[47] For an introductory overview of the conflict in its context see: J Lovell, *The Opium War: Drugs, Dreams and the Making of China* (Picador 2012), also, B Inglis, *The Opium War* (Hodder and Stoughton 1976).
[48] See the account in: H Gelber, *Opium, Soldiers and Evangelicals: England's 1840–42 War with China and its Aftermath* (Palgrave Macmillan 2004) 19–39.

trade and its consequences, what he referred to as the 'infamous trade'.[49] At the time Palmerston's view dominated however, and here, in the conflict between 'free trade' and 'public health', the result was an aggressive expansion of 'war capitalism' and the prioritization of liberalized trade through any means, a result that shaped international trade law for a century.[50] This might not be considered an auspicious starting point, especially when one considers that in the case of sugar, the commodity in question is considerably more difficult to regulate due to its pervasive presence and status as a common staple of many diets. Regulation targeting the harmful effects of sugar is thus more varied and complex and does not lend itself to a resolution based on a simple ban, as was ultimately the case in the context of trade in opium.

We might also think of another more recent comparison: tobacco. As with sugar, trade in tobacco is also rooted in a colonial heritage of subjugation, slavery, and asymmetric power relations between international actors. Yet tobacco presents different challenges: its prevalence within society is partially constrained by its form of consumption (i.e., smoking or chewing) whereas one of the key problems faced with regulation of sugar is specifically that it is not always clear to consumers which goods are high in sugars and which are not.[51] Equally though, while the tobacco industry has historically had the support of connected sectors such as advertising in sporting affairs, the sugar industry is now more widespread.[52] Nonetheless, in the case of tobacco, after decades of concerted action by civil society and, more recently, health ministries, progress has been made on the international plane through the creation of a Framework Convention on Tobacco Control and more sensitive arbitral awards in investment litigation.[53]

In the case of both opium and tobacco, the commodity in question is harmful per se. In the case of sugar, the difficulty in part arises due to the nature of the risk involved, stemming from consumption over the small amounts recommended.[54] Thus, while tobacco and opium could be restricted by simple border measures or sales bans (should one wish), the same is not true for sugar. The

---

[49] See the debates 'On the War with China' Hansard, House of Commons (7–9 April 1840), Vol. 43, col. 673–948.

[50] This was also the case with international investment law and the law on the use of force, as 'gunboat diplomacy' was maintained for a further 60 years. See: M Sornorajah, *The International Law on Foreign Investment* (3rd edn, CUP 2010) 69.

[51] For example, note the challenges involved with formulating a definition for which drinks constitute a 'sugar sweetened beverage'.

[52] On the prevalence of advertising, in particular to children, see the chapters by Ó Cathaoir and Hartlev, Garde and Byrne, and Bartlett in this volume.

[53] Most notably, *Philip Morris v Uruguay* (8 July 2016) ARB/10/7.

[54] For guidelines on the acceptable level of sugar intake see: World Health Organization, *Sugar Intake for Adults and Children* (2015) available at http://www.who

ease with which sugar is traded and its prevalence in global markets is exactly one of the difficulties – cheaper and more widely available sugar and sugar products stimulates increased problems with obesity, particularly in nutritionally poor economies.

The challenge here is for trade bodies and trade law to respond effectively by balancing the desire to ensure that regulating for public health concerns does not undermine the benefits of a trade system which (at its best) improves economic conditions for populations. Yet, as has been identified, trade in sugar is not easily managed only by direct challenges on the basis of health. The increase in trade in sugar, the use of subsidies, and the introduction of trade barriers, all distort and shape the global sugar market which in turn impacts on prices within specific markets, increasing availability of cheap high-sugar goods.[55]

There have been seven disputes lodged at the WTO specifically on sugar (all of which relate to subsidies or import surge protections known as safeguards),[56] three over sugar syrups (and the appropriate classification of a sugar syrup product for the purposes of tariffs, as well as the use of anti-dumping duties, designed to combat predatory pricing),[57] and one on soft drinks (a dispute that drew attention primarily for its overlap with the dispute settlement system at NAFTA rather than its health implications).[58] Although seemingly technical and not raising public health issues in an explicit fashion, these disputes nonetheless have important consequences for health outcomes. Note, for example, the way in which changes to the EU sugar quotas and subsidies regime has engendered concern from civil society that the changes to the market will lead to an increase in cheap sugar or sugar-based products on the global market.[59]

.int/nutrition/publications/guidelines/sugars_intake/en/ (last accessed 24 September 2020).

[55] See further below at Section 6.

[56] *Thailand — Subsidies concerning Sugar* (DS507), *European Communities — Export Subsidies on Sugar* (DS283, 266, & 265), *Slovak Republic — Safeguard Measure on Imports of Sugar* (DS235), *Chile — Safeguard Measures and Modification of Schedules Regarding Sugar* (DS230), *Chile — Safeguard Measures on Sugar* (DS228).

[57] *Mexico — Anti-Dumping Investigation of High-Fructose Corn Syrup (HFCS) from the United States.* (DS101 & 132), *United States — Reclassification of Certain Sugar Syrups* (DS180). These duties are designed to combat the export of goods for below their normal value (a practice which damages industry by 'dumping' cheap imports into a market).

[58] *Mexico — Tax Measures on Soft Drinks and Other Beverages* (DS308).

[59] See the Commission note: 'Frequently Asked Questions: "The abolition of EU sugar production quotas"' (October 2016), available at https://ec.europa.eu/info/sites/info/files/food-farming-fisheries/plants_and_plant_products/documents/abolition-sugar-quota-faq_en.pdf (last accessed 24 September 2020).

In spite of the seeming challenges that sugar raises within the international trade system, or at least the desire to regulate sugar in the public interest, there are also a number of possibilities opened up by such challenges. The following section identifies how the trade system has adapted to similar pressures, and how rather than viewing the regulation of sugar as a 'problem', the trade system could instead maximize the opportunities presented to continue its transition to one concerned with balancing legitimate regulatory objectives of WTO members with the benefits that accrue from liberalized trade.

4. PUBLIC POLICY CONCERNS AS A DRIVER OF TRADE LAW

The WTO has long had a fraught relationship with other regimes in international law, in particular, the environmental, labour, public health, and human rights systems.[60] The WTO's entry into force in 1995 coincided with increased critical attention paid to the international trade system. While the GATT had largely existed in a diplomatic sphere unremarked by the population at large, increasingly civil society began to draw attention to the more formalized set of rules and dispute settlement that existed to ensure free(er) trade.[61]

4.1 The Regulatory Autonomy of WTO Members and the Role of Judicial Interpretation

The earliest sign of the increased attention paid to the relationship between trade law and the pursuit of non-trade objectives was the GATT-era dispute between the US and Mexico over dolphin-safe tuna.[62] The GATT panel examining this issue had sided with Mexico, considering that US restrictions on tuna that was not caught in a manner which did not catch dolphins as a by-product violated the GATT.[63] Nonetheless, it was at great pains to stress that the GATT placed few limitations on environmental protection policies.[64] The GATT panel might have imagined that taking the side of a developing

---

[60] See, e.g.: WTO & ILO, *Trade and Employment: Challenges for Policy Research* (WTO Secretariat 2007); O De Schutter, *Trade in the Service of Sustainable Development. Linking Trade to Labour Rights and Environmental Standards* (Hart 2015); E Bürgi Bonanomi, *Sustainable Development in International Law Making and Trade* (Edward Elgar 2015). See also further below at n67 and corresponding text.
[61] For the historical development from the GATT to the WTO, see J Jackson, *The World Trade System* (MIT Press 1997) 1–30.
[62] That is, tuna not caught in purse-seine nets. *United States — Restrictions on Imports of Tuna* (circulated 3 September 1991, unadopted) DS21/R.
[63] Ibid at paras 7.1–7.3. Specifically, Art XI:1 GATT 1947.
[64] *United States — Restrictions on Imports of Tuna*, para 6.1.

country that sought to access a large developed market and thus increase the wealth and prosperity of its fishing communities might have won it kudos. This was not how the decision was viewed by environmental groups, however, whose attention was now drawn to a shady neoliberal trade system that placed economic outcomes above living creatures (depicted in the literature as the then-commonplace TV dolphin Flipper, no less).[65]

As civil society grew more interested in the trade system's legal arrangements, so too did international lawyers in other fields. While other international institutions are hampered by deadlock (such as the UN Security Council with permanent members enjoying a veto) or weighted voting (such as the IMF where voting power reflects the relative financial weight of States), the WTO was negotiated as a new generation of post-Cold War institutions. It represented an extraordinary leap forward, with an institutional apparatus that was able to ensure compliance and effective dispute settlement, with consent to jurisdiction being a necessary precondition for membership of the Organization (unusual in international law terms).[66] It also carried with it a detailed set of rules, and perhaps most importantly, strong commitment from the major global economies, that might otherwise choose to 'go it alone'.[67]

By comparison, public health, human rights, labour rights, and environmental protection seemed to have been left out in the cold, without comparable institutional or normative frameworks to match the WTO. Which State then would prioritize public health, for example, if they came into conflict with the enforcement of a WTO obligation? Why would any member seek to protect dolphins, if the more effective system was interested in the economic effects of the protection, and not its objectives?

Together these two strands, attention from civil society and academics, resulted in what are termed the 'linkage' debates in trade law – that is, 'trade and ... labour/human rights/environment/etc.', with the debate revolving around the question of how trade was to relate to its various 'linked' partners.[68] Much of the discussion took place in oppositional terms. The opposition

---

[65] Note, e.g., 20 years later, commentators still using the image of Flipper: Global Trade Watch, 'Flipper Gets Axed' (15 September 2011) available at < http://citizen.typepad.com/eyesontrade/2011/09/flipper-again-on-the-wto-chopping-block.html>.

[66] See: Understanding on Rules and Procedures Governing the Settlement of Disputes (15 April 1994) LT/UR/A-2/DS/U/1 (DSU).

[67] An old concern that has returned since the change in US policy following the appointment of President Trump in the US.

[68] For example: P Alston, 'Resisting the Merger and Acquisition of Human Rights by Trade Law: A Reply to Petersmann' (2002) 13 *European Journal of International Law* 815; A Lang, 'Reflecting on Linkage: Cognitive and Institutional Change in the International Trading System' (2007) 70 *Modern Law Review* 523; T Cottier (et al. eds) *Human Rights and International Trade* (OUP 2005).

was sometimes ideological, whereby the underlying propositions of the two regimes are considered so distinct that to accommodate one is to inherently undermine the other. This was the concern of labour rights lawyers, for example, whose discipline was founded on a model of collective rights, not individualized conceptions of economic liberty.[69] Alternatively, the opposition was sometimes normative, as in the case of norm conflicts, where the question became either which norm was to take priority, which rule should apply (e.g., the more specific rule, or the later rule), or indeed whether a new systemic framework for understanding such different interactions was necessary.[70]

Yet, while the linkage debates stressed the dangers of trade's impact on other areas (or occasionally the reverse), the WTO itself, and in particular the Appellate Body (its *de facto* Court of Appeal) had already begun to move forward, responding to the concerns of the membership through a set of contentious decisions.[71] As members have been mostly unable to conclude new substantive rules at the WTO, its judicial arm (in particular, the Appellate Body) has had to find accommodation between members seeking to regulate for public policy objectives (such as combatting childhood obesity) while complying with their WTO obligations.

There are three examples which can be drawn upon, to see where trade law has responded to legitimate regulatory objectives of States and the heightened concerns of the public, producing an imperfect outcome that, nonetheless, moves away from the contrasting views often put forward: trade law not as a neoliberal trump against which no regulatory objective of the State may stand, but instead as a mediating force between legitimate national regulation and the expectations of gains from free(er) international trade. These three examples (one taken from environmental protection, and two from public health protection) each elucidate the WTO's accommodation of public policy concerns within trade law, principally through: (i) an expansive interpretation of exceptions; (ii) an expansive interpretation of what constitutes a 'like product'; and (iii) an expansive interpretation of whether a regulatory measure is discriminatory.

---

[69] E.g., Alston, ibid.

[70] Such debates continue today, see: A Gourgourinis, *Equity and Equitable Principles in the World Trade Organization: Addressing Conflicts and Overlaps between the WTO and Other Regimes* (Routledge 2015).

[71] Formally the Appellate Body is a quasi-judicial body as its decisions are subject to the adoption of the Dispute Settlement Body, a political body representing all members. That adoption is a formality does not alter the distinct nature of the relationship between the Appellate Body and the membership. See further: L Bartels, 'The Separation of Powers in the WTO: How to Avoid Judicial Activism' (2004) *International and Comparative Law Quarterly* 53, 861.

4.2 The Appellate Body's Expansive Interpretation of Exceptions under Art XX GATT

The *US – Tuna* dispute has already been mentioned, where a GATT panel was faced with the challenge of deciding on the permissibility of an environmentally worthy regulation that sought to protect dolphins incidentally caught during tuna fishing. Although, by finding in favour of Mexico, the Appellate Body's report supported a developing member who in the eyes of many was restricted from accessing the market of its largest trading partner, the public (particularly civil society) did not view the outcome positively.

Early in the life of the WTO, it faced a very similar dispute. The US introduced restrictions on the sale of shrimp which had not been caught with nets using turtle excluder devices (TEDs).[72] The concern at the time amongst environmentalists was that shrimp fishing was having a disastrous effect on the population of highly migratory turtles which were being caught up in the nets. From the perspective of some shrimp exporting nations (India, Malaysia, Pakistan, and Thailand) affected by the new regulations, the US was both protecting its own fishers (who were able to access government funding to adapt to the new requirements), and discriminating in favour of other trading partners (notably those in the Caribbean) who were also given access to US funding and granted extended transition periods to adapt to the new regulatory framework. In WTO terms, the measure was a clear violation of Article XI GATT which prohibits the use of quantitative restrictions. As with most legal obligations, exceptions exist to allow members flexibility in the performance of their obligations. In the case of the GATT, the main exceptions are the enumerated 'general exceptions' found under Article XX. These cover a range of topics, from public morals (Art XX(a)) to protecting human health (Art XX(b)). The principal question in this instance was the extent to which the relevant exception applies: that such a measure relates 'to the conservation of exhaustible natural resources' (Art XX(g) GATT).

In approaching the question as to whether turtles might constitute 'exhaustible natural resources', the Appellate Body took an expansive reading of the text.[73] While the negotiating texts from the original GATT (the GATT 1947) indicated that the sort of resources considered to be 'exhaustible' were not, in fact, living resources but mineral, the Appellate Body interpreted the text differently.

---

[72] Appellate Body Report, *US – Shrimp*, WT/DS58/AB/R (12 October 1998).
[73] Ibid., paras 127–134.

The Appellate Body, in a decision which is still considered to be of constitutional importance,[74] stated that it was important that the covered agreements (that is the treaties which form the corpus of WTO law) must be interpreted in light of changing understandings and conceptions of the international community. This was not a case of aggressive judicial activism: the rules in international law on interpretation of treaties require that a 'treaty shall be interpreted in good faith in accordance with the ordinary meaning to be given to the terms of the treaty in their context and in the light of its object and purpose'.[75] Acknowledging the changing nature of international concerns, and the importance of marrying environmental and trade objectives, the Appellate Body drew attention to the explicit reference made in the preamble to the WTO Agreement, encouraging liberalization:

> while allowing for the optimal use of the world's resources in accordance with the objective of sustainable development, seeking both to protect and preserve the environment and to enhance the means for doing so in a manner consistent with their respective needs and concerns at different levels of economic development.[76]

Thus, there was no special carve-out through the exception, rather a pre-existing right which had to be exercised within the limits consented to by members of the WTO. In the words of the Appellate Body, 'Members are free to adopt their own policies aimed at protecting the environment as long as, in so doing, they fulfil their obligations and respect the rights of other Members under the WTO Agreement.'[77]

---

[74] J Jackson, 'The Varied Policies of International Juridical Bodies—Reflections on Theory and Practice' (2004) *Michigan Journal of International Law* 25, 869.

[75] Art 31(1) Vienna Convention on the Law of Treaties (23 May 1969) 1155 UNTS 331. Further, per Art 31(3),

> There shall be taken into account, together with the context: (a) any subsequent agreement between the parties regarding the interpretation of the treaty or the application of its provisions; (b) any subsequent practice in the application of the treaty which establishes the agreement of the parties regarding its interpretation; (c) any relevant rules of international law applicable in the relations between the parties.

Articles 31 and 32 constitute rules of customary international law and are therefore binding on all States, irrespective of whether they are parties to the Vienna Convention. See: Appellate Body Report, *United States—Standards for Reformulated and Conventional Gasoline* (29 April 1996) WT/DS2/ AB/R, 17 and *Territorial Dispute Case* (Libyan Arab Jamahiriya/Chad) (Judgment) [1994] ICJ Rep 6, para 41.

[76] WTO Agreement, preamble, first recital. Appellate Body Report, *US – Shrimp*, para 131.

[77] Appellate Body Report, *US – Shrimp*, para 186.

The end result saw the US losing the dispute, not because of the environmental objectives, but because it had introduced the measures in a discriminatory manner (giving greater support to some trading partners over others, and preferring national fishermen over foreigners), thus violating the *chapeau* (the preambular paragraph of Article XX) which conditions the use of the general exceptions on 'the requirement that such measures are not applied in a manner which would constitute a means of arbitrary or unjustifiable discrimination between countries where the same conditions prevail, or a disguised restriction on international trade'.[78]

In doing so, and explicitly stressing the ability of WTO members to regulate to protect the environment, and the WTO's ability to accommodate such regulation, the Appellate Body drew attention to public concern over the need to acknowledge environmental issues at the WTO. At the same time, it explained its rationale, holding closely to the text of the agreements as consented to by the membership and interpreted in light of international law's customary rules on interpretation, thus shielding itself from accusations of activism. This approach has not only been applied to environmental protection under Article XX(b) but also public morals and the protection of human health.[79]

Nonetheless, although the *US – Shrimp* dispute explicitly recognised the right of members to regulate to protect the environment, the provision in question is an exception, allowing a measure that otherwise would constitute a violation. The member seeking to use the exception is both politically and legally, on the back foot. At the WTO, the:

> burden of proof rests upon the party, whether complaining or defending, who asserts the affirmative of a particular claim or defence. If that party adduces evidence sufficient to raise a presumption that what is claimed is true, the burden shifts to the other party, who will fail unless it adduces sufficient evidence to rebut the presumption.[80]

Thus, the regulating Member will need to make a prima facie case that it has met the requirements of the specific provision (in the case of obesity prevention, Article XX(b)) and the *chapeau*, that introduces the more specific clauses of Article XX, which in particular prohibits a use of the exception that could 'constitute a means of arbitrary or unjustifiable discrimination ... or a disguised restriction on international trade'.[81] After which, it is for the com-

---

[78] Ibid., para 184.
[79] For example, *China — Publications and Audiovisual Products* (DS363); *EC – Seal Products* (DS401); and *EC – Asbestos* (DS135).
[80] Appellate Body Report, *US—Wool Shirts and Blouses*, WT/DS33/AB/R, 14.
[81] Art XX GATT.

plaining member to identify where it considers that the requirements have not been met (e.g., that the measure is not necessary to achieve its aim).

It should be noted that members have rarely been successful in their use of Article XX at first blush, usually falling foul of the *chapeau*, and having to subsequently amend the measure in order to comply.[82] Although this does not give a good impression of the viability of the exceptions under the GATT, this has often been the result of discriminatory application of a measure protecting the public policy objective in question.[83] Further, this assumes that the only recourses to Article XX is through litigation. In practice, members will use such defences before claims are raised, setting off potential legal proceedings where the complaining member views that their claim has legs.[84]

Nonetheless, even where exceptions are considered viable, it is still preferable for the public policy objective pursued not to have violated an obligation in the first case. This was the question at stake in the *EC – Asbestos* dispute, where the EC sought to argue that its measure that prohibited asbestos products from Canada was not discriminatory as the two products in question where not alike, and thus between them there could be no discrimination.

4.3 The Appellate Body's Expansive Interpretation of 'likeness' under the GATT

In another highly commented case at the WTO, the Appellate Body again responded to public concerns over the scope of trade law's impact on the regulatory autonomy of the State in the field of public health. A French ban on the import and sale of asbestos products sparked a dispute between Canada (which was exporting the asbestos products) and the EU (which represents EU Member States at the WTO).[85]

A key element of the dispute revolved around the extent to which the EU was required to use Article XX(b) to justify the French ban on the asbestos products which would otherwise have violated the national treatment obligation under Article III.4 GATT which prohibits the use of internal regulation as a means to grant 'treatment less favourable' to an imported good over

---

[82] For example: *United States —Gasoline* (DS2 & 4); *United States — Shrimp* (DS58); *Argentina — Measures Affecting the Export of Bovine Hides and the Import of Finished Leather* (DS155); and *European Communities — Measures Prohibiting the Importation and Marketing of Seal Products* (DS400 & 401).

[83] Note, e.g., how in *US – Shrimp* the US did not extend support to all trading partners when introducing new regulations, only some.

[84] See P Van Den Bossche & W Zdouc, *Law and Policy of the World Trade Organization* (4th edn, CUP 2017) ch. 8.

[85] Appellate Body Report, *EC – Asbestos*, WT/DS135/AB/R (12 March 2001).

a national good.⁸⁶ As by this stage it was abundantly clear that asbestos posed serious health risks, it seemed perverse that a government should have to 'justify' its position when banning a product as detrimental to human health as asbestos. Instead, the EU argued that the products in question, the Canadian asbestos and other domestically available products (such as fibro-cement) that were apparently like asbestos, were in fact not alike and so the comparison in terms of treatment was not appropriate. The products available in the French market, although similar to the asbestos products in many ways, did not entail the same health risks. Thus, while Canada argued that the ban on its asbestos products was discriminatory, granting less favourable treatment to the imported Canadian product relative to the alternative domestic product, the EU maintained that such products could not be 'like products' as one set was harmful while the other was not.⁸⁷ If the products were not alike, there can have been no discrimination and thus no violation of Article III.4 GATT as argued by Canada.

At the first stage, the Panel conducted the customary tests to determine whether the products were alike: comparing physical characteristics, end-use, tariff classification, and consumer tastes and preferences.⁸⁸ Using these tests, the Panel found that the products were 'like', and therefore it was necessary to examine Article XX(b) and the extent to which this measure (the ban) was 'necessary to protect human, animal or plant life or health'.⁸⁹ Although the result was acceptable (Article XX was available to the EU in this instance), there was disquiet over the need to rely on an exception. Canada's appeal of the Panel's report would allow the Appellate Body to revisit this issue.

In its report, the Appellate Body returned to the likeness analysis that had been conducted by the Panel. It noted that while the Panel had identified the correct test, it had failed to take into account the health risks of the asbestos products as part of their physical characteristics.⁹⁰ In a subtle shift, the Appellate Body opened the likeness analysis under the prohibition on discrimination to a wider selection of factors that might otherwise have been considered. As with the *US – Shrimp* dispute, however, it did this in an overtly conservative manner, not adding another test or category but instead interpreting the existing tests to allow health effects to be taken into account in the analysis of likeness.⁹¹

---

⁸⁶ See further: H Hestermeyer, 'Article III' in R Wolfrum (et al. eds) *Max Planck Commentaries on World Trade Law: Vol 5* (Brill 2010).
⁸⁷ Appellate Body Report, *EC – Asbestos*, 11–15 for the respective arguments.
⁸⁸ Report of the Panel, *EC – Asbestos*, WT/DS135/R (18 September 2000) 153ff.
⁸⁹ Ibid., 423–31.
⁹⁰ Appellate Body Report, *EC – Asbestos*, 44.
⁹¹ Ibid., 46.

In these two examples, *US – Shrimp* and *EC – Asbestos,* the Appellate Body moved from avoiding a narrow interpretation of the otherwise limited general exceptions under Article XX GATT to a deeper understanding of likeness under Article III GATT. The shift was from acknowledging the right to regulate and an evolutionary approach to exceptions, to the earlier acknowledgment of health concerns in likeness (prior to any necessary resort to exceptions). This brought the ability of the State to regulate in public policy matters deeper into the framework of trade law. Finally, in a third example, the Appellate Body continued this responsive trend, embedding the concept of a legitimate regulatory distinction within disciplines on non-discrimination, not as an exception but as a part of the primary rule.

5. THE APPELLATE BODY'S EXPANSIVE INTERPRETATION OF DISCRIMINATION UNDER THE TBT AGREEMENT

The *US – Clove Cigarettes* dispute involved US restrictions on the sale of clove cigarettes.[92] Indonesia, as a large exporter of such cigarettes, raised a claim on the basis that while the US argued its restriction was designed to reduce the number of children smoking, in practice the continued acceptance of other flavoured cigarettes such as menthols (which the US *did* produce) undermined the aim of the measure.[93]

This dispute focussed on the Agreement on Technical Barriers to Trade (TBT) rather than the GATT.[94] The TBT Agreement sets out rules for the use of regulations, standards, and conformity assessment procedures. It accommodates a balance between the legitimate and desirable effects of regulation in ensuring product safety, protecting health, countering illicit practices, and so on, with the potential that such requirements might undermine trade. In this case, the Appellate Body focussed on the distinction between the TBT Agreement and the GATT. The TBT Agreement, the Appellate Body noted, did not have an equivalent set of explicit exceptions as are found in the GATT.[95] Thus, it was necessary to read into the disciplines under the TBT

---

[92] *US – Clove Cigarettes* (DS406).
[93] The factual background is available at: Report of the Panel, *US – Clove Cigarettes*, WT/DS406/R (2 September 2011), 1–5.
[94] Agreement on Technical Barriers to Trade, 15 April 1994, 1868 UNTS 120.
[95] Appellate Body Report, *US – Clove Cigarettes*, WT/DS406/AB/R (4 April 2012) para 175. See also Appellate Body Report, *US – COOL,* WT/DS384/AB/R (29 June 2012) para 272.

Agreement, equivalent protections for WTO members' regulatory autonomy to ensure balance. Note the Appellate Body's account:

> The balance set out in the preamble of the TBT Agreement between, on the one hand, the desire to avoid creating unnecessary obstacles to international trade and, on the other hand, the recognition of Members' right to regulate, is not, in principle, different from the balance set out in the GATT 1994, where obligations such as national treatment in Article III are qualified by the general exceptions provision of Article XX.[96]

In this instance, the Appellate Body focussed on whether a 'legitimate regulatory distinction' existed to explain the differential treatment between menthol cigarettes and clove cigarettes. The Appellate Body was able to do this, not only on the basis of the underlying balance within the TBT Agreement (as identified above) but also as a consequence of specific statements within the text of the agreement, in particular in the preamble which sets out its aims and objectives.[97] Further, by focussing this interpretation within the text of Article 2.1 TBT Agreement, and the existence of 'treatment no less favourable' the Appellate Body was able to square the circle: such treatment exists only where there can be no legitimate regulatory justification for it.[98]

Between *US – Clove Cigarettes*, and two other TBT cases litigated within short succession (*US – COOL* and *US – Tuna II*), the Appellate Body has entrenched the concept of the 'legitimate regulatory distinction' into WTO law.[99] Echoed in developments in investment law, international adjudicative bodies have acknowledged that governments may regulate in ways that not only might give rise to their use of an exception provision (in effect, a defence), but also that there are acts which, should a government pursue them in a legitimate matter, do not breach the obligation in question *ex ante*.

6. ACCOMMODATING GOVERNMENT MEASURES TO COMBAT CHILDHOOD OBESITY AT THE WTO

A clear lesson emerges from the three previous examples: when clarification has been required on matters of public policy concern, WTO law has responded to accommodate legitimate non-discriminatory measures. Acknowledgment of this pattern is key – it is essential to note that potential litigation at the WTO does not in and of itself constitute an impossible hurdle for regulating States –

---

[96] Appellate Body Report, *US – Clove Cigarettes*, para 96.
[97] Ibid., paras 89–96.
[98] Ibid., para 173.
[99] *US – Country of Origin Labelling* (DS384) and *US – Tuna II* (DS381) respectively.

a key observation in light of the critical need for urgent government action to respond to childhood obesity. As attention is increasingly placed on sugar, the concerns of sugar-exporting members or the host States of large sugar enterprises are more likely to be raised at the WTO. Such concerns may well be raised privately first, through correspondence from international law firms in Geneva or New York, then through the representations of diplomatic envoys, then at the relevant committees of the WTO, perhaps the TBT Committee or GATS Committee, and then finally, should it reach such a stage, to formal dispute settlement and a panel or the Appellate Body. The message that members have the policy space in which to regulate to protect public health sent by the Appellate Body permeates the system, signalling to members where they hold defensible positions or where their policies might require reconsideration. The role of the Appellate Body is to provide a corrective, clarifying what WTO law *is* rather than what some WTO members claim it to be. Members with influential industry lobbies will raise concerns in legal terms, but this does not mean that there is no space for the regulation of food markets to combat obesity.

7. THE COMPLEXITIES OF SUGAR'S RELATIONSHIP TO TRADE TODAY

Sugar has always been a driver in the trade system, pushing developments in the institutional and normative elements of the regime. The challenges, and thus opportunities, that sugar presents today, however, are greater than those of comparable commodities. The other public policy concerns examined here (tobacco, asbestos, tuna, and endangered turtles) could all be combatted through relatively simple regulatory measures. An import and sales ban on asbestos ensures that it will not be widely available on the open market. Combatting obesity, however, requires a far wider range of regulatory measures and approaches

In the first instance, sugar in small quantities is not harmful per se. It is the increasingly large amounts of sugar currently ingested by the average consumer (including through 'hidden' sugars that are not immediately obvious to the eater) that is the problem, a difference that makes quantitative restrictions less appealing from a regulator's point of view. Nonetheless, the very structure of the trade system, designed to encourage the progressive reduction of tariff and non-tariff barriers increases the prevalence of high sugar consumption across the globe. When accompanied by continued subsidization in many markets (not only the large developed economies of the EU but developing countries also), the consequence is sugar and sugar-based products at a low price, accessible at a historically rare level across the globe.

Second, many of the measures required to tackle childhood obesity relate not to goods but also services. For example, the prohibition of advertising of high-sugar beverages to children may have a goods dimension (a regulatory measure of the kind foreseen by Article III.4 GATT) but it will also entail a possible restriction on the provision of advertising services. Commitments to liberalise services at the WTO are limited, with members only opting in as they wish and the extent to which they wish under their GATS schedules (so-called positive listing). However, under free trade agreements such as the Comprehensive Economic and Trade Agreement between the EU and Canada, all services are subject to trade disciplines between those parties save where exceptions are made (negative listing).[100] When attempting to combat childhood obesity, affected services might include advertising services or wholesale distribution services involved in the import and export of the sugar itself.[101] The liberalization of services may also be regulated by obligations under bilateral or regional investment treaties, or other comprehensive trade agreements which include both trade and investment chapters. Similarly, an interference in the exercise of the intellectual property of the corporation which has invested heavily in building its brand will draw attention also, and these points are subject to WTO law which provides a forum for such challenges.[102]

Finally, where sugar taxes are proposed, trade law again will be of relevance. Nutrient profiling models such as those promoted by the World Health Organization are exceptionally helpful tools for members to encourage the use of a transparent and evidence-based system to distinguish between products that may attract a higher rate of tax due to their sugar (or fat, or salt) content, but it is essential nonetheless to ensure that any such measures comply with trade obligations such as Article III.2 GATT which prohibits the discriminatory application of tax regimes. This is not to suggest that these challenges would be successful, or that they ought to raise alarms in ministries, merely that the scope of the types of measures that are necessary to tackle childhood obesity will come into contact with a number of trade obligations which must be taken into account when formulating policy responses to the obesity epidemic.

---

[100] See the text of the Agreement: Council of the European Union, Interinstitutional File 2016/0206 (10973/16), 14 September 2016.

[101] The overlap between traded goods and their attendant services was explicitly litigated in the *EC – Bananas III*. Report of the Panel, *European Communities – Regime for the Importation, Sale and Distribution of Bananas*, WT/DS27/R/ECU (22 May 1997) para 7.282.

[102] Note the pending *Australia — Certain Measures Concerning Trademarks, Geographical Indications and Other Plain Packaging Requirements Applicable to Tobacco Products and Packaging* (DS467) dispute, which has yet to be published at time of writing but reportedly has found in favour of Australia (the regulating State).

One of the difficulties presented by combatting the health effects of sugar is that the policies required are varied and multi-sectoral. There is no magic bullet to combatting childhood obesity. Instead, what is required are a range of measures, many of which will have trade law implications. The key will be the extent to which the trade law system (as expressed through adjudicators of trade law disputes and the membership of trade institutions such as the WTO or regional trade agreements) respond to the underlying health concerns of each measure.

Indeed, this is exactly the possible advantage of sugar's role in developing trade law: the multi-faceted nature of regulation needed to combat obesity will require trade law not only to respond on one narrow ground relating to 'likeness' under Article III.4 GATT, or the appropriate scope of Article XX(b) GATT, but instead across the corpus of trade law identifying the fundamental underlying logic of the legal order as one that has to manage different public policy objectives, much as the Appellate Body showed it was capable of doing in *US – Clove Cigarettes*, more explicitly balancing trade liberalization and the regulatory autonomy of the State through its interpretative moves.[103]

8. CONCLUDING REMARKS

This chapter offers an account of trade law's interactions with public policy issues, and in particular health concerns, which demonstrates that the disciplines imposed by WTO agreements generally should not be seen as barriers to the adoption of regulatory measures associated with combatting child obesity. This is not intended to distort what is a complex picture,[104] or minimize the real concerns raised over the scope of trade law, but rather to offer a more hopeful account of how trade law has – and will continue – to adapt to pressure from the WTO membership and civil society on matters of critical importance. Nonetheless, it is important to recognise that international trade law (and in many cases the regional or bilateral obligations entered into by States through free trade agreements also) restrict the autonomy of governments in combatting the negative health effects of sugar and sugar-based products. This is not to return to the oppositional 'trade and …' debates but instead to reframe how trade law is depicted. It does not act as a straightjacket, trapping governments and halting any attempt to combat health crises such as childhood obesity. Rather, trade law can be better thought of as rules for traffic: restrictions that

---

[103] See R Howse, 'The World Trade Organization 20 Years On: Global Governance by Judiciary' (2016) 27(1) *European Journal of International Law* 9, at 48–66.

[104] For an illustrative account of the detailed legal analysis necessary for a comprehensive view see: B McGrady, *Trade and Public Health: The WTO, Tobacco, Alcohol, and Diet* (CUP 2011).

limit how one can go about one's business but still permitting destinations to be reached. The Appellate Body has been explicit about this, stating:

> it is within the authority of a WTO Member to set the public health or environmental objectives it seeks to achieve, as well as the level of protection that it wants to obtain, through the measure or the policy it chooses to adopt.[105]

International trade law has responded (albeit slowly and primarily through its quasi-judicial bodies) to the variegated needs of its membership, balancing competing interests but also – importantly – acknowledging the relationship between trade and the shared goals of sustainable development and the protection of human health and the environment.[106] International law develops through a process of claim and counterclaim, and trade law is not different in this regard, developing responsively.[107] In combatting childhood obesity, WTO Members will stimulate the development of trade law in new ways. Where sugar and obesity prevention play a particularly important role in this process is the multi-faceted nature of its regulation. As members pursue such regulatory approaches (which they must to meet their international commitments, not least those made at the World Health Organization and elsewhere), they will test the trade system as they seek to enforce their rights of regulation without undermining the rights of trading partners under WTO law.[108] Negotiations, consultations, and formal litigation will likely take place. This need not be a problem, indeed, drawing on the lessons of previous disputes arising from public policy measures, it may be that combatting obesity provides the trade system with the impetus it requires to continue to adapt to the regulatory needs of a membership still committed to liberal trade, but within a holistic model of development that understands health concerns as both economic and social in nature.

---

[105] Appellate Body Report, *Brazil – Measures Affecting Imports of Retreaded Tyres*, WT/DS322/AB/R (3 December 2007) para 140 (footnotes omitted). NB further also, at para 151, 'We recognize that certain complex public health or environmental problems may be tackled only with a comprehensive policy comprising a multiplicity of interacting measures.'

[106] See n42 and corresponding text.

[107] J Crawford, 'Chance, Order, Change: The Course of International Law' (2013) 365 *Recueil des Cours de l'Académie de Droit International* paras 1–2. On the responsive nature of international law: G Hernandez, *The International Court of Justice and the Judicial Function* (OUP 2014) 185.

[108] For detail on the nature of the obligations stemming from the World Health Organization see the Introduction and chapters in Part I of this volume.

6. Using food labelling laws to combat childhood obesity: Lessons from the EU, the WTO and Codex
Caoimhín MacMaoláin

1. INTRODUCTION

It is often difficult for individual States to adopt new food labelling laws that are designed to combat childhood, or any other type of, obesity. This is primarily due to the existence of international and/or regional obligations that these States have to promote free trade. For example, the Treaty on the Functioning of the European Union (TFEU) prohibition on national measures that inhibit trade between Member States and the harmonized provisions of the Food Information Regulation,[1] have significantly curtailed the potential for the use of legal remedies to tackle national health problems in those States which are members of the EU. There is also the possibility that World Trade Organization disciplines can have a similar, although probably less significant, impact on their attempts to deal with poor diet.

This chapter explores those attempts that have been made by the European Union, by EU Member States, by the UN Codex Alimentarius Commission,[2] and by individual WTO Members to introduce labelling requirements aimed at tackling poor diet and obesity. It first examines EU rules in this area, as these are the most restrictive in their effect on States' ability to establish new food labelling schemes. These alternative labels are deemed necessary because traditional formats for displaying nutrient information have been shown to be

---

[1] Regulation (EU) No 1169/2011 of the European Parliament and of the Council of 25 October 2011 on the provision of food information to consumers, [2011] OJ L 304/18.

[2] The Codex Alimentarius Commission (CAC), in operation since 1963, is a joint Food and Agriculture Organization of the United Nations (FAO) and World Health Organization (WHO) body which sets international food standards, codes and guidelines for its 188 member countries. For more on the work of the CAC see: www.fao.org (last accessed 22 September 2017).

confusing and difficult to understand.[3] The chapter sets out the ways in which some of the most high-profile national measures may conflict with EU free movement rules, while also identifying other alternative labelling formats that could be easier to reconcile with EU primary and secondary rules. It further assesses the EU rules themselves, noting that the Food Information Regulation, which was introduced primarily to address the recognized role for labelling in improving diet and nutrition, has failed to fully address shortcomings about the way in which nutrient declarations are presented.

The chapter also discusses several other international legal obligations in this field. While WTO disciplines do have an impact on the type of alternative labelling scheme that can be introduced by States, they are less interventionist than the similar rules which operate within the EU. In particular, the recognition in the updated Codex Guidelines on Nutrition Labelling assists States in showing how they can impose additional formats in a manner that is probably WTO-compliant.[4] There is a recognition that a serious public health problem exists and that more consumer-friendly labels are one part of a suite of measures that can be employed to help to address this.

Finally, the chapter concludes by drawing from all of the experiences presented to illustrate how additional or alternative nutrition labelling formats can be best developed to ensure that they are both consistent with the rules that relate to them and that they achieve the desired aim of assisting consumers in making healthier choices.

2. DEVELOPMENT OF NUTRITION LABELLING LAWS

2.1 EU Food Information Regulation

The first harmonized food labelling requirements for European Union Member States were introduced in December 1978,[5] setting out a series of compulsory indications that would have to be placed on all pre-packaged products, subject to some limited exceptions.[6] This included the product name, ingredients used,

---

[3] As set by the EU Food Information Regulation 1169/2011, n1.
[4] CAC/GL 2-1985, as amended.
[5] Directive 79/112/EEC of 18 December 1978 on the approximation of the laws of the Member States relating to the labelling, presentation and advertising of foodstuffs for sale to the ultimate consumer, [1979] OJ L 33/1.
[6] Ibid., Art 6 provided that ingredients would not have to be listed for fresh fruit and vegetables, carbonated water, vinegar, cheese, butter, fermented milk and cream and single-ingredient products, provided that they had not had other substances added to them in production. Art 9 of the Directive provided that no minimum durability date

quantity, durability, storage conditions or conditions of use, business operator details, origin details (but only where failure to disclose this could be misleading) and any instructions necessary for proper use.[7] There was also an undertaking in the Directive to introduce more specific labelling rules for alcoholic products, including ingredient listing requirements, within four years.[8]

The original framework food labelling directive was replaced in 2000.[9] The only significant additions to the list and format of the compulsory labelling indications that were made by this newer version of the Directive were the incorporation of quantitative ingredient declarations for those products which stated or suggested that certain foods had been included in production; the new durability category of 'use by' date for highly perishable foods; and the requirement to disclose alcohol content for beverages where this was more than 1.2 per cent by volume.[10]

Serious concerns about the links between poor diet and ill health, especially that arising out of obesity and related conditions, came to the fore soon after the introduction of this second framework food labelling directive. By 2005 the European Commission had officially recognised that unhealthy diets and a lack of physical activity were contributing to overweight rates, obesity and the development of disease. The Commission's Green Paper on promoting healthy diets and physical activity, which was published that year, commenced with the bold declaration that:

> [u]nhealthy diets and lack of physical activity are the leading causes of avoidable illness and premature death in Europe, and the rising prevalence of obesity across Europe is a major public health concern.[11]

---

would be required for fresh fruit and vegetables, vinegar, baked goods for immediate consumption, wines or beverages with an alcohol content of 10 per cent or more.

[7] Ibid., Art 3(1).

[8] Ibid., Art 6(3). Despite this, comprehensive labelling requirements for alcoholic products had still not been introduced by 2017. Alcoholic beverages are actually exempt from many of the food labelling requirements set out in the harmonising legislation. For more on this see n61 below.

[9] Directive 2000/13/EC of the European Parliament and of the Council of 20 March 2000 on the approximation of the laws of the Member States relating to the labelling, presentation and advertising of foodstuffs, [2000] OJ L 109/29.

[10] All inserted into Art 3(1) of Directive 2000/13. There was still, however, no inclusion of compulsory ingredient listing for alcoholic drinks, despite the original undertaking to address this matter by the mid-1980s.

[11] Para I.1. of the Commission Green Paper on 'Promoting healthy diets and physical activity: a European dimension for the prevention of overweight, obesity and chronic diseases', COM (2005) 637. This was later succeeded by the Commission White Paper on a Strategy for Europe on Nutrition, Overweight and Obesity Related Health Issues, COM (2007) 279.

This statement was backed-up in Annex 2 to the Green Paper, which detailed the direct relationship between diet, physical activity and health – identifying a significant increase in the prevalence of diabetes, as well as outlining the role of dietary factors in heart disease, cancers and osteoporosis.[12]

The Proposal for a Regulation on the provision of food information to consumers was then published by the Commission in January 2008.[13] It recognized that nutrition labelling was '[…] an established way for providing information to consumers to support health conscious food choices'.[14] Nutrition labelling had been harmonized at EU-level by the Nutrition Labelling Directive in 1990,[15] but its use had remained voluntary for all foods, except for those about which a health or a nutrition claim was being made.[16] One of the primary initiatives to come out of the proposal for a new food information regulation was to make nutrition labelling mandatory and to have much of this information compulsorily placed in the principal field of vision on the packaging.[17] This requirement has since mostly been set by including the nutrient declaration in the list of mandatory particulars that must be presented on all food labels covered by the Food Information Regulation,[18] with much further detail on the content and presentation provided by Articles 29–35 thereof. However, this information does not have to be presented in the 'principal field of vision', usually on the front of the packaging.[19] Instead, all of the compulsory nutrition

---

[12] The role that diet and nutrition play in the prevalence of these diseases was already clearly indicated by the World Health Organization (WHO) in its technical report on 'Diet, Nutrition and the Prevention of Chronic Diseases', (2003) WHO Technical Report Series 916, ISBN: 92-4-120916-X.

[13] Proposal for a Regulation of the European Parliament and of the Council on the provision of food information to consumers, COM (2008) 40.

[14] Explanatory Memorandum to the Proposal, ibid.

[15] Council Directive 90/496/EEC of 24 September 1990 on nutrition labelling for foodstuffs, [1990] OJ L 276/40.

[16] Nutrition labelling declarations were made compulsory for foods carrying nutrition claims by the terms of Directive 90/496, ibid. This was extended to include health claims by Art 7 of Regulation (EC) No 1924/2006 of the European Parliament and of the Council of 20 December 2006 on nutrition and health claims made on foods, [2006] OJ L 12/3.

[17] Art 34(1) of the 2008 Proposal, n13.

[18] Art 9(1)(l) of Regulation 1169/2011, n1. Annex V to the Regulation lists those foodstuffs which are exempted from the requirement to present a nutrient declaration, including most single-ingredient products, waters, salts, some teas and coffees, vinegars, chewing gum and all foods in small packages (largest surface area less than 25 cm^2) or those supplied directly by small-scale producers (usually of handcrafted products) to the final consumer.

[19] Art 34(3) of the Food Information Regulation provides that the only time that the nutrition information must appear on the front of the package is where it is a voluntary

information should be placed in the 'same field of vision'.[20] The key point to note, however, is that the Regulation makes the widespread inclusion of nutrition information on pre-packaged foods compulsory for the first time under EU law.

The inclusion of a nutrient declaration as one of the compulsory indications on food labels means that most pre-packaged foodstuffs must now therefore provide, in a prescribed manner, information about the product's energy value, fat and saturated fat content, carbohydrates, sugars, protein and salt.[21] This may be supplemented by additional information on monounsaturates, polyunsaturates, polyols, starch, fibre and vitamins and minerals.[22] The further requirements on this that are set by the Regulation provide detail on how energy values should be calculated,[23] how the nutrition information should be presented,[24] and what font sizes should be used in this presentation.[25]

More specifically, two of the provisions of the Regulation on nutrient declarations that are potentially very important for obesity prevention relate to (i) the possible use of additional alternative forms of expression and presentation by EU Member States; and (ii) the use of portion or unit sizes for the presentation of this nutritional content information.

2.2 Role of Alternative Labelling Formats in Preventing Obesity

The preparatory documents, such as the White Paper and the Regulation Proposal, that were published and considered in the creation of the Food Information Regulation, clearly recognize that obesity and being overweight is a problem and that compulsory nutrient declarations could be used as, at least part of, the remedy. These documents found that the previous '[...] three decades [had] seen the levels of overweight and obesity in the EU population rise dramatically, particularly among children',[26] and they acknowledged the

---

additional disclosure related to the energy value or to the energy value, fats, saturates, sugar and salt.

[20] Art 34(1) of the Regulation 1169/2011, n1.
[21] Ibid., Art 30(1) 1.
[22] Ibid., Art 30(2).
[23] Ibid., Art 31.
[24] Ibid., Art 34(3)(a).
[25] Ibid., Art 34(3)(b) in conjunction with Art 13(2) and Annex IV to the Regulation.
[26] Introduction to the Commission White Paper on Obesity, n11 above. The White Paper suggested that overweight rates amongst children were already at 30 per cent by 2006. The EU Action Plan on Childhood Obesity 2014–20 cites WHO European Childhood Obesity Surveillance Initiative 2010 figures which put the rate of overweight or obese six to nine year olds at closer to one-third, a rise from one in four according to the same study for 2008.

serious and sometimes chronic consequences of this for their health. It must now be questioned, however, as to whether merely making these disclosures obligatory is enough. While the 1990 Nutrition Labelling Directive did not make the presentation of this information compulsory for most pre-packaged products, most producers were carrying this information on the labelling of their wares regardless.[27] Including the nutrient declaration in the list of mandatory particulars is therefore unlikely to make much of a difference to usage rates. Studies suggest that it is not just the appearance of this information that is key to alerting consumers to the wholesomeness, or otherwise, of foodstuffs – but it is really the way that this information is presented that is of most significance.[28] These same studies show us that levels of understanding amongst consumers about how to interpret nutrient declarations is relatively low.[29] The changes made by the Food Information Regulation do relatively little to address this.

Several EU Member States have introduced their own alternative nutrition labelling formats in more recent years in an attempt to deal with this dislocation between the presenting of information in traditional tabular or list form and levels of consumer interest and understanding. If we want consumers to be put in a position where more informed choices on nutrient content can be and are made, as the Preamble to the Consumer Information Regulation suggests that we should, then these other formats, where they are shown to work in this regard, must be considered as a more viable alternative and a better way

---

[27] S Bonsmann, et al., 'Penetration of nutrition information on food labels across the EU-27 plus Turkey' (2010) 64 *Journal of Clinical Nutrition* 1379, where it was found that up to 97 per cent of products already carried nutrition information on the label, several years before this was made compulsory in the EU.

[28] There are a number of published studies which show that average consumers are generally unable to understand nutrient declarations in their prescribed linear or tabular formats. These studies include A Shine, et al., 'Consumer attitudes to nutrition labelling' (1997) *British Food Journal* 283; G Cowburn and L Stockley, 'Consumer understanding and use of nutrition labelling: a systematic review' (2005) *Public Health Nutrition* 21; and C Byrd-Bredbenner, et al., 'Consumer understanding of US and EU nutrition labels' (2000) 102 *British Food Journal* 615.

[29] Ibid. See also: K Grunert, et al., 'Use and understanding of nutrition information on food labels in six European countries' (2010) 18 *Journal of Public Health* 261, where it is contended that it is not just a failure amongst consumers to understand nutrition labels, but that there is also a lack of motivation in informing themselves about how to understand these declarations. Suitable alternative or additional labelling formats could help to address this apparent apathy.

of achieving the desired primary aim of food labelling. The Regulation does allow for this to some degree. Article 35 of the Regulation provides that:

> [i]n addition to the forms of expression referred to [above] the energy value and the amounts of nutrients [...] may be given by other forms of expression and/or presented using graphical forms or symbols in addition to words or numbers [...].

This allows Member States to adopt labelling formats that display the nutrient declaration in a more readily understandable format – such as colour-coded traffic-light or signpost labels. While this is a welcome development, the operation of these labelling schemes is somewhat restricted by the fact that they are subject to the prior satisfaction of a series of conditions. Article 35(2) of the 2011 Food Information Regulation provides that Member States may only recommend to food business operators the use of one or more additional forms of expression or presentation of the nutrient declaration. They can never prescribe use. Any additional format recommended at Member State level must be based on sound and scientifically valid consumer research. It can only be developed following consultation with a wide range of stakeholder groups. It must be designed to facilitate consumer understanding of the importance of the food to the energy and nutrient content of a diet. It must be based on harmonized reference intake levels or, where these do not exist, on generally accepted scientific advice on intake for certain nutrients or energy (calorie) levels. It must be objective and non-discriminatory.

All of these are, of course, perfectly legitimate considerations for the development of any additional labelling format. However, it is the final criterion set by this list that is potentially the most problematic for Member States seeking to employ a supplementary system for the presentation of nutrition information. This being that the application of any such scheme must not create an obstacle to the free movement of goods.

2.3   EU Treaty Obligations on the Free Movement of Food

During the negotiating process that preceded the introduction of the Food Information Regulation, the introduction of an EU-wide alternative labelling format was debated. However, it was ultimately rejected by the European Parliament's Environment, Public Health and Food Safety Committee, so none has therefore been prescribed or recommended by the Regulation or any other harmonizing legislation. Setting a clearer nutrition labelling format may have allayed the concerns of those EU Member States who have since decided that they need to put some alternative, clearer scheme in place. However, it can be difficult for those Member States looking to facilitate improved consumer understanding in this way to prove that a national nutrition label poses no impediment to free movement. Yet they are required to do so for any such scheme to be in compliance with the provisions of the Food Information Regulation.[30]

The TFEU may also have an impact upon the adoption or application of this type of national measure by Member States. Most significantly in this regard, Article 34 TFEU provides that: '[q]uantitative restrictions on imports and all measures having equivalent effect shall be prohibited between Member States'. While this provision is brief, its impact is considerable. There are several reasons for this. The first relates to the legal definition of a 'measure equivalent to a quantitative restriction'. The Court of Justice of the European Union (CJEU) in the *Dassonville* case stated that:

> [a]ll trading rules enacted by Member States which are capable of hindering, directly or indirectly, actually or potentially, intra-Community trade are to be considered as measures having an effect equivalent to quantitative restrictions.[31]

As can be seen from this, all national rules or requirements that have the potential to affect trade between EU Member States are deemed to be measures equivalent to actual quantitative restrictions. The volume of sales of non-national products need not necessarily have gone down by very much, or possibly even at all, as a result of the implementation of the measure.[32] There does not even have to be any real competition from non-national products for Article 34 TFEU to apply. There only has to be the potential for competition.[33] If a measure exists that obliges a non-national producer from another EU Member State to alter his product or packaging in some way then it is caught within this '*Dassonville* formula' and it may be deemed contrary to EU Treaty obligations. There are, however, exceptions to this. If it can be shown that a national measure serves a necessary purpose, that it is the most appropriate way of meeting this purpose, and that it is proportionate (i.e., that it does not go beyond what is necessary for the fulfilment of the purpose pursued) then it may be allowed.[34] Otherwise, the offending measure can no longer be applied.

---

[30] Regulation 1169/2011, Art 35(2).
[31] Para 5 of the judgment in Case 8/74, *Procureur du Roi v Benoît and Gustave Dassonville*, [1974] ECR 837.
[32] Case 249/81, *Commission v Ireland* (Buy Irish) [1982] ECR 4005. Discussed further in n41 below.
[33] Case 298/87, *Proceedings for compulsory reconstruction against Smanor SA*, [1988] ECR 4489.
[34] See, e.g., Case C-383/97, *Criminal proceedings against Arnoldus van der Laan* [1999] ECR I-731 where the Court of Justice was asked to rule on the compatibility of a German Code on meat products which was compelling producers and retailers to cease using trade names and instead move to more descriptive content on the

EU Member States can seek to validate a packaging or labelling requirement in one of two ways. Either, it must be shown that one of the Treaty-based exceptions, such as health protection, applies.[35] Or, a particularly persuasive 'rule of reason', such as consumer protection, must be shown to be sufficiently significant to endorse the maintenance of a trade-inhibiting measure.[36]

As stated at the outset of this chapter, it can be very difficult for EU Member States to justify the application of a national measure that is deemed to come within the broad definition of a 'measure equivalent to a quantitative restriction' on trade, despite the existence of the exceptions to this rule. This is the lesson that has emerged time and again from the cases that have been brought before the CJEU on the grounds that domestic measures, whatever form they may take, are often incompatible with Article 34 TFEU, and subsequently unjustifiable under Article 36 TFEU.[37] Of particular significance here is the fact that the Court has specifically stated that:

> [...] a Member State may not invoke public health grounds in order to prohibit the importation of a product by arguing that its nutritional value is lower or its fat content higher than another product already available on the market in question [because] the mere fact that an imported product has a lower nutritional value does not pose a real threat to human health.[38]

---

label. The Court found that a code such as this was within the scope of an Art 34 TFEU examination, that it was potentially justifiable on consumer protection grounds but ultimately that it was not justifiable in this instance as the consumer was already adequately informed by other information that appeared on the label. However, in Case C-366/2004, *Georg Schwarz v Bürgermeister Landeschauptstadt Salzburg* [2005] ECR I-11039 where the Court of Justice also initially found that an Austrian ban on the sale of unwrapped chewing gum from vending machines was an impediment to trade, and was therefore caught within the scope of the application of Art 34 TFEU, but also that it was justifiable in this case on health protection grounds.

[35] Art 36 TFEU provides that:
[t]he provisions of [Article 34 TFEU] shall not preclude prohibitions or restrictions on imports [that are] justified on grounds of public morality, public policy or public security; [or] the protection of health and life of humans, animals or plants [provided] such prohibitions or restrictions shall not [...] constitute a means of arbitrary discrimination or a disguised restriction on trade between Member States.

[36] As established by the Court of Justice of the European Union in Case 120/78, *Rewe-Zentral AG v Bundesmonopolverwaltung für Branntwein* (Cassis) [1979] ECR 649.

[37] Cases like *Schwarz*, n34, and *Scotch Whisky*, note 40 below, proving to be amongst the exceptions to this broader assertion.

[38] Para 15 of the judgment of the CJEU in Case 216/84, *Commission v France* (milk substitutes) [1988] ECR 793 and para 10 of the judgment of the CJEU in Case 274/87, *Commission v Germany* (meat substitutes) [1989] ECR 229.

While the CJEU has held that there are some circumstances where the marketing of foods can be restricted by health concerns, these are generally limited to those situations where there is scientific evidence indicating a real 'risk' to humans,[39] or where it can be clearly shown that the domestic court in a Member State is in a much better position to dictate what measures can be adopted to address a significant and specific public health concern.[40] In both circumstances, these exceptions are still fully accountable to free movement rules – so they will also only apply in very well-defined circumstances.

One of the key areas for potential conflict between national measures and TFEU rules on free movement relates to the fact that when a Member State introduces something like a traffic-light or signpost label for nutrient declarations there can be an automatic presumption that some domestic consumers, that is those who actively seek this information pre-purchase, will tend to favour those products that display this in the nationally-set format. The argument being presented is that produce that is sold displaying information in the additional voluntary format will see sales benefit amongst those consumers who are familiar with the national scheme. This is more likely to be the national produce of the State where the scheme is in operation. The level of preference for products carrying this type of labelling may be small, but its existence, actual or even potential, is sufficient to give the domestic product an advantage over those which have been imported from other EU Member States where the

---

[39] Such as it did in Case 174/82, *Criminal proceedings against Sandoz BV* [1983] ECR 2445, where it stated, in para 16 of the judgment, that:

> [where] there are uncertainties at the present state of scientific research it is for the Member States, in the absence of harmonization, to decide what degree of protection of the health and life of humans they intend to assure, having regard however for the requirements of the free movement of goods within the [Union].

[40] As determined in Case C-333/14, *Scotch Whisky Association and Others v The Lord Advocate and The Advocate General for Scotland* ECLI:EU:C:2015:845, para 49 of which states that:

> [[i]t is for the referring court, which alone has available to it all the matters of fact and law pertaining to the circumstances […] to determine whether a [less trade-restricting measure could be] capable of protecting human life and health as effectively as [in this case minimum pricing for alcohol].

To date, it could be stated that the 'risk' posed to human health arising out of the possibility of developing a non-communicable disease is not yet adequately accounted for in either food safety legislation, such as the General Food Law Regulation 178/02, [2002] OJ L 31/1, or food labelling legislation, such as the Food Information Regulation 1169/2011, n1. This is really one of the central themes of this chapter, that these diseases may be deemed a problem for the health of citizens, but that this is not yet considered as being a 'food safety risk' in some of the most significant pieces of relevant EU secondary legislation.

same, or a similar, scheme is not in use.[41] In addition to this, national produce is more likely to be reformulated to ensure, as far as it is possible to do so, that the food is presented with a more-favourable colour-coded reading (green or amber) than the non-national product that is not subject to a similar labelling scheme in its own State of production and therefore retains its less-favourable status (red). This is enough to render it potentially incompatible with both Article 34 TFEU and the last of the conditions for national schemes, as they appear in Article 35 of the Food Information Regulation.

Facilitating free movement therefore creates two general problems for Member States. The first is as outlined above – the difficulty in demonstrating that no preference will be shown by domestic consumers for products bearing nationally-organized voluntary labelling formats. The second is that general rules on the free movement of goods, coupled with the fact that the Food Information Regulation does not itself set any harmonized additional labelling format, means that all such schemes introduced by Member States must remain entirely voluntary. Food business operators from within the State are free to adopt, not adopt, or even modify any national template. Food business operators from other Member States cannot be prevented from marketing their products where they carry no such additional format, or where they have used an entirely different format, such as one that is more readily employed in their own State. The consumer can thus be met with a plethora of different nutrient declaration formats within the same State, or at a micro-level within the same retail establishment. This creates confusion.[42]

---

[41] Case law from the European Court of Justice has always provided that any sort of benefit to national produce, or detriment to non-national produce from other EU Member States, no matter how small or insignificant it may appear to be is, nonetheless, sufficient for it to be caught within the scope of TFEU rules on free movement, such as those set out in Art 34 TFEU. A good example of this can be seen in Case 249/81, *Commission v Ireland* [1982] ECR 4005 where, despite the fact that the sales of Irish produce on the domestic market actually fell during a State-backed advertising and labelling campaign, the Court held that its existence was enough to warrant an examination of the compatibility of the scheme with Art 34 TFEU. The Court ultimately found that the 'Buy Irish' campaign was contrary to these EU rules on the free movement of goods.

[42] A UK Food Standards Agency study has found that although the use of additional labelling formats, such as signposts, can aid consumer comprehension, the co-existence of a range of formats can instead lead to confusion. See: S Malam, et al., *Comprehension and Use of UK Nutrition Signpost Labelling Schemes* (FSA 2009).

2.4 Use of Traffic-light Nutrition Labels in the UK

One of the first EU Member States to introduce a national nutrition labelling scheme was the United Kingdom. The UK's Food Standards Agency (FSA) set a template for food business operators in 2006. Under the terms of the scheme, producers and retailers were free to follow the template, adapt the template, or to place no colour-coded or other alternative format for the nutrition information on the packaging of their products. The scheme had to be entirely voluntary in order to remain in compliance with EU free movement and labelling laws, as to make it compulsory would undoubtedly have led to immediate infringement proceedings being initiated by the European Commission. As a result, within months, a multitude of different versions of the colour-coded FSA template were in use in the UK 'with different visuals, colour and content making it hard for consumers to compare food'.[43] The scheme was clearly not working as intended. A new signpost labelling format was therefore launched in October 2012, soon after the introduction of the EU's own Food Information Regulation. The EU Regulation had by then made direct provision for the possibility of Member States introducing their own alternative nutrition labelling formats. The aim of the 2012 UK scheme was to set a more homogenized template that could, and hopefully would, be more rigorously followed by producers and retailers. This new model label was to be developed with input from stakeholders, the idea being that it would be more readily accepted and used by those retailers in particular who had been directly or indirectly involved in its creation. As already noted, the Food Information Regulation now specifically requires that a wide range of stakeholders are consulted before any additional format for the nutrient declaration can be introduced.

From a legal perspective, the single biggest stumbling block in the way of the success of any nationally backed signpost food label remains the fact that these schemes simply must remain voluntary. As discussed above, the Food Information Regulation makes it clear that these are additional labelling formats are subject to all free movement obligations. This, of course, means that retailers and producers remain free to use, adapt, or disregard any suggested signpost label. While some other EU Member States have developed or proposed their own additional labelling schemes, many more have objected to the UK version, which, as expected, has led to the commencement of infringement proceedings by the European Commission – which are still pending at

---

[43] By July 2006 there were at least 14 different signpost labels operating in the UK, none of which were identical to the FSA template, and none of which were the same as each other. See: C MacMaoláin, *EU Food Law: Protecting consumers and health in a common market* (Hart 2007) 235.

the time of writing. The primary concerns at EU and Member State level about the UK's, and similar other Member State, schemes are that they are overly simplistic. Objections have been expressed, for example, about the fact that potentially healthy products, such as some oils, could be stigmatised amongst consumers due to their high fat content, which would be displayed on signpost labels with a stark red indication, or that quality products, such as protected designations of origin and protected geographical indications would be disadvantaged as the possibility of product reformulation is usually not possible due to the legal requirements governing the operation of the schemes that have granted these products their protected status in the first place.[44] While this is the case, and the legal restrictions on the introduction of mandatory additional food labelling formats persist, signpost or traffic-light labels cannot operate with the desired level of success in their current format. Other possible label types and/or legal alterations must therefore be considered if food labelling can ever be properly used in the European Union and elsewhere as an important part of the fight against increasing rates of overweight and obesity. Alternative formats to the traffic-light label are considered later in this chapter.

2.5 Using Portion Sizes in Signpost Labels

Another difficulty arising out of the fact that national nutrition labelling schemes must be voluntary in order to remain in compliance with EU law relates to the inevitable flexibility that this provides the producer or retailer when determining how they are going to use the label on their product. If nothing can be prescribed, then everything is open to alteration. A potential safeguard against possible unscrupulous practice is set out in Article 7 of the Food Information Regulation, which provides that '[f]ood information should not be misleading, particularly as to the characteristics of the food'. Similar provisions existed in both of the Framework Food Labelling Directives,[45] the forerunners to this Regulation. Despite this, neither Article 7, nor these predecessors are used to tackle producers or retailers who present labelling information in a manner that is clearly designed to mislead. The deliberate use

---

[44] Art 7(1) of Regulation (EU) No 1151/2012 of the European Parliament and of the Council of 21 November 2012 on quality schemes for agricultural products and foodstuffs, [2012] OJ L 343/1, provides that all protected designations of origin and protected geographical indications must comply with a product specification which sets, amongst other things, details about the raw materials that are used in production. Producers that do not follow the product specification cannot use the protected food name.

[45] As set out in Art 2(1) of Directive 79/112, n5, and Art 2(1) of Directive 2000/13, n9.

of unrealistic portion sizes to express nutrient information is a good example of the type of practice that Article 7 could potentially be used to help prevent. Article 33(1) of the Food Information Regulation states that:

> [...] the energy value and the amounts of nutrients [...] may be expressed per portion and/or per consumption unit, easily recognisable by the consumer, provided that the portion or the unit used is quantified on the label and that the number of portions or units contained in the package is stated in addition to the form of expression per 100 g or per 100 ml.[46]

The portion or unit used for this expression should be indicated on the label in close proximity to the compulsory nutrient declaration.[47]

The use of portion sizes as the measure of nutrient content in a food product is, potentially, of great use to the consumer. Some products, for example, may only be used in very small amounts, such as a 'teaspoon' measurement of 5 ml, or as little as 15 ml or 10 g in any one serving. Expressions, therefore, on a per 100 ml or 100 g basis serve little useful purpose for these products as they would far exceed the actual quantities used. However, there is also a real difficulty with the way that portion sizes, which are often the primary point of reference for consumers when it comes to nutrient declarations, are determined. Presently, these portion sizes are generally set by the producer or retailer. They can be stated as being at almost any level. As a consequence, they are often misleading and unrealistic. For example, declarations about calorie content or sugar levels which are based on portions that are equivalent to a mere two squares of chocolate, or those about saturated fats which are based on one-fifth or less of a bag of crisps, can be very deceptive. Portion sizes like these are not based on normal consumer behaviour. The Food Information Regulation does seek to address this problem to some degree. Article 33(5) provides that:

> [i]n order to ensure the uniform implementation of the expression of the nutrition declaration per portion or per unit of consumption and to provide for a uniform basis of comparison for the consumer, the Commission shall, taking into account actual consumption behaviour of consumers as well as dietary recommendations, adopt, by means of implementing acts, rules on the expression per portion or per consumption unit for specific categories of foods.

---

[46] Art 32 of the Food Information Regulation, n1, provides that the energy value and the amount of nutrients must be expressed per 100 g or per 100 ml for liquids. Art 6(1) of the 1990 Nutrition Labelling Directive, n15, also provided for the possibility of expressing nutrient content on a 'per portion' basis, in addition to the more standard per 100 g or per 100 ml basis.

[47] Art 33(4) of the Food Information Regulation, ibid.

In other words, legislation can be introduced which sets guidelines, or possibly even more stringent measures, to ensure that portion sizes set out on food labels are both realistic and related to good dietary practice.[48]

It has been clear for some time that many producers who display nutrition information on the basis of a portion have been doing so in a misleading way.[49] There has, to date, been little regulatory control over this. By basing the colour-coded or other signpost information on lower portion sizes, the product can be represented as being less detrimental to health than it is in reality. Were portion sizes, or rules governing their use, to be introduced at EU level then the benefit is potentially twofold. The information would have to be based on more realistic consumer behaviour. The labels would also more clearly indicate to the consumer what the appropriate quantity of consumption is, in particular for foods that contain high levels of negative nutrients, such as added sugars or trans fats. While this has been tried elsewhere, perhaps most notably in the US and Canada,[50] a successful regulatory remedy has yet to be found for controlling unscrupulous behaviour in setting portion sizes. This is a complex and difficult issue, requiring a well-thought-out response.

3.   ALTERNATIVE HEALTH-PROMOTING LABELS

There is still some doubt and debate about whether the type of additional nutrition label for food that has been developed, and which continues to be introduced, in some Member States is really the best way of using labelling to tackle obesity. A number of factors must be considered when determin-

---

[48] Even where portion sizes are set on a more formal basis, such as the use of Reference Amounts Customarily Consumed (RACC), which were originally determined by the US Food and Drug Administration (FDA) in the 1980s, these were still found to be set at a substantially lower level than that which was more realistically being eaten by consumers. For further discussion on this see: C Roberto and N Khandpur, 'Improving the design of nutrition labels to promote healthier food choices and reasonable portion sizes' (2014) *International Journal of Obesity* 25.

[49] Canadian studies have shown that there is a tendency for products with a higher calorie level to list smaller serving sizes. See: J Chan, et al., 'Unregulated serving sizes on the Canadian nutrition facts table – an invitation for manufacturer manipulations', (2017) 17 *BMC Public Health* 418. A UK Food Standards Agency report has also suggested that the setting of portion sizes by manufacturers is varied, inconsistent and lacking in transparency. See: *Trends in portion sizes in the UK* (FSA, 2008). Similar findings have also been presented in T Lobstein, et al., 'Misconceptions and misinformation: the problems with guideline daily amounts. A review of GDAs and their use for signaling nutritional information on food and drink labels' (National Heart Forum 2007) and T Lobstein and S Davies, 'Defining and labelling "healthy" and "unhealthy" food' (2009) 12 *Public Health Nutrition* 331.

[50] See Chan et al., ibid.

ing the suitability of any type of labelling disclosure for this purpose.[51] The pre-conditions set out in the Food Information Regulation for the introduction of any signpost or similar types of format are helpful in ensuring that only those which are shown to be effective can ever be used by EU Member States in the first place. As was noted above, the Food Information Regulation prescribes that the use of any additional nutrient declaration can only take place after the production of sound evidence that consumers will actually benefit. They must be shown to clearly facilitate consumer understanding about the product and about the importance of a balanced diet more generally. As a consequence, additional alternative labelling formats, like the UK Food Standards Agency template, which can be overly simplistic, should encounter more difficulties from a legal perspective. The fact that some healthy and nutritional products would be subject to negative connotations by this simpler type of colour-coded set of distinctions also makes it more difficult for Member States to show that the scheme that they wish to introduce is both 'objective and non-discriminatory'. Despite these apparent difficulties, other States, such as France, have sought to trial the use of their own traffic-light food label, such as 'nutri-score'. Infringement proceedings against the UK in this regard have stalled on several occasions but, as outlined here, it is clear that these proceedings have foundation. The French scheme may ultimately be the subject of infringement proceedings as well as there may be similar concerns about aspects of its *modus operandi*. It is contended in this chapter that a different type of signpost label may thus now be required – one (or possibly more than one) that more readily passes the tests set out in Article 35 of the Food Information Regulation. There are several examples of good practice elsewhere that could be considered in attempts to establish a more suitable alternative to the 'simple' colour-coded traffic-light label that is generally advocated by consumer groups.

3.1   Need for Positive Labelling

The relationship between a food product and its impact on diet is, of course, only one factor that must be considered in addressing the obesity problem. Exercise and activity levels, genetics, psychology, age, medications and other elements that are beyond the scope of this chapter, all have the potential to impact upon human weight and poor health. Even within the category of nutritional and/or energy value, several complex factors must be considered

---

[51]   Lobstein and Davies, e.g., advocate the introduction of a labelling scheme based on 'nutrient profiling' in their work. While they see a range of disadvantages with the Nordic Keyhole Scheme, it is here contended that this latter scheme is more 'legally acceptable' in terms of the potential for compatibility with both European Union and WTO laws. This is discussed in more detail below.

when determining whether a product and the way in which it is expected to be consumed is likely to impact upon the health of the consumer. The Nordic Keyhole Nutrition Label, which was developed in Sweden in 1989, is a great example of how complicated information can be presented in an easily recognizable and simple format. A food product either carries the green and white keyhole symbol, or it does not – thus facilitating easy, yet informed, decision-making by the consumer.[52]

One of the European Commission's concerns about the use of traffic-light nutrition labels, apart from being based on an overly simplistic view of nutrients, is that they tend to be quite negative. The appearance of the Nordic Keyhole suggests that a product is at least healthier. However, the use of red colour-coding in the traffic-light system, and to a lesser extent (but still relevant) amber colour-coding, are seen as presenting negative connotations, suggesting that aspects of the product are unhealthy. The Keyhole label works on a very different basis. It is used as a method of easily identifying healthier food products, which are assessed on the basis of being in one of a number of food categories. Different food types, such as oils for example, can therefore have their assessment based on different standards in relation to fat content than other products which fall into a different food category, such as confectionary, biscuits or crackers. Each of the 25 product groups has different criteria for fats, sugars, salt and fibre. Products can then be assessed within these groups so that an olive oil, which may carry the keyhole symbol, can be easily distinguished from a less healthy vegetable oil. It is simple for consumers – yet it is based on more complex calculations and considerations than the traffic light label. It also portrays a positive, rather than a negative message, satisfying both EU Commission and industry concerns about the use of additional forms of nutrition labelling.

3.2 International Examples

Should it be felt that the use of a single symbol, like the Nordic Keyhole, as an additional type of nutrition label might not be sufficient to inform consumers about the values of a foodstuff, then other examples in operation elsewhere in the world may provide a suitable alternative template. The Australian Health

---

[52] Lobstein and Davies, n49, suggest that relatively 'unhealthy' products may still carry the keyhole symbol where the negative nutrient levels have merely been reduced, arguing that 'healthier does not necessarily mean healthy', underlining just how difficult it may be to produce an appropriate and acceptable format for alternative ways of presenting nutrition information. Dutch experiences with their 'vinkje' logo, which was ultimately abandoned after it was found to be misleading consumers, also support this latter point.

Star Rating, which was established in 2014, uses both an overall grading system and a set of more specific disclosures on the nutritional values of food products. The Health Star Rating is placed front-of-pack, assigning a product a score between half a star and five stars, depending on how healthy evaluations have shown the food in question to be. Nutrient declarations similar to those which must be presented under the terms of the EU Food Information Regulation must also be used, but the Star Rating provides the consumer with an additional format, one which it is hoped is easier to understand and upon which more informed choices can be made. Again, there was a high level of stakeholder involvement in the establishment of the Health Star system. The number of stars awarded is determined following calculations made about both the positive and negative nutrients in a food product. It is based on a calculator that was developed in consultation with Food Standards Australia New Zealand (FSANZ), known as the Health Star Rating Calculator. Again, however, the use of the health star ratings by manufacturers and retailers is entirely voluntary.

Health Star Ratings can appear in one of two possible ways. One is just to display the rating itself, presented using the established template and clearly indicating how highly the product is rated in terms of nutritional value. The second way is to list the star rating as well as additional information about the specific nutrient content of the product, including the energy in kilojoules, saturated fats, sugar and sodium, usually per 100 grams or per 100 millilitres, but also possibly for the entire pack where this constitutes a single portion. One positive nutrient can be included as well, such as fibre, protein, vitamins or minerals. Star ratings are awarded following an assessment of the entire nutrient profile based on energy, risk nutrients (saturated fat, sodium and sugars), and positive nutrients (such as fibre, protein, calcium, vitamins and minerals). The so-called 'risk nutrients' have been specifically chosen due to their apparent links with obesity and non-communicable disease.

Chile has taken a more negative approach in the introduction of its signpost nutrition labelling scheme. The first key difference between this label and those which have been introduced in the Nordic States and in Australia is that the Chilean requirements are legally binding rather than voluntary. The law targets the use of these stark signpost labels at products which are primarily intended for consumption by children.

Under the terms of Chile's new nutritional labelling law,[53] any product which exceeds set limits for calories, sodium, sugars or saturated fats per 100g must carry a black stop sign on the label which states that it is high in one or

---

[53] Law 20.606 on Food Labelling and Advertising.

more of these constituents.⁵⁴ Each high level of negative nutrient must carry its own individual stop sign – so some products will have to carry several, and possibly up to four, of these health warning labels. Any product which bears one of these stop signs is also subject to a number of marketing restrictions. They cannot be sold, marketed, promoted or advertised in any pre-third level educational establishment. They cannot be advertised in any form of media or communications that targets children under 14 years of age. They cannot be given for free to children under 14 years old. They cannot be sold with free gifts such as toys, stickers or other similar incentives aimed at children. There are some exceptions from the Chilean regulations. Foods without added sugars, sodium or saturated fats are exempt, as are those which are for special dietary uses, such as baby foods and dietary and athletic supplements.

While this scheme has been in operation since 2016, its compatibility with international legal obligations promoting free trade remains questionable, in much the same way that concerns have been raised at EU-level about the use of traffic-light nutrition labels there.

4. INTERNATIONAL OBLIGATIONS

Standards and obligations set by both the UN Codex Alimentarius Commission and the World Trade Organization have the potential to impact upon the types of nutrition labelling formats used in WTO Member States. The Codex Guidelines on Nutrition Labelling,⁵⁵ which were amended in 2016, and then again in 2017, are designed to ensure:

> [...] that nutrition labelling is effective in providing the consumer with information about a food so that a wise choice of food can be made; in providing a means for conveying information of a nutrient content of a food on the label; in encouraging the use of sound nutrition principles in the formulation of foods which would benefit public health; in providing the opportunity to include supplementary nutrition information on the label.

The inclusion of provisions on supplementary nutrition information is, of course, significant for States' attempts to tackle obesity. Principle B for

---

⁵⁴ The maximum permitted levels for these nutrients are set at 275 calories per 100 g; 400 mg of sodium per 100g; 10 g of sugar per 100 g; and 4 g of saturated fat per 100g for solid foods. These levels are reduced to 70 calories per 100 ml; 100 mg of sodium per 100 ml; 5 parts of sugar per 100 ml; and 3 parts of saturated fat per 100 ml for liquids. The black stop sign must be used to indicate any levels of these constituents in excess of this, introduced in a staggered way for the first 36 months after implementation.

⁵⁵ n4.

Nutrition Labelling is quite flexible in this regard, recognizing that the use of additional labelling formats may vary from State to State, and for good reasons. It states that:

> [t]he content of supplementary nutrition information will vary from one country to another and within any country from one target population group to another according to the educational policy of the country and the needs of the target groups.

Nutrition labelling is defined in the Codex Guidelines as being '[...] a description intended to inform the consumer of nutritional properties of a food' and as having two components, both the nutrient declaration and the use of supplementary nutrition information. There is a ready acceptance in the CAC Guidelines of the use of supplementary forms of nutrition labelling in addition to the more traditional tabular or linear format. The Codex guidelines set the same mandatory particulars as are used in the other nutrient declarations that have been assessed in this chapter – namely the inclusion, as a minimum, of details on energy value, protein, carbohydrate, fat sodium and sugars.[56]

Guideline 3.4. deals with how nutrient content details should be presented. While initial emphasis is on the presentation of nutrient content in numerical format, the use of additional means of presentation 'should not be excluded'.[57] Information should be expressed per 100 g or per 100 ml. Nutrient quantities per portion or serving are also recommended.[58] While Guideline 4.2. specifies that '[n]utrient content should be declared in a numerical, tabular [or sometimes linear] format', Guideline 5 goes on to provide some detail on the use by Members of supplementary nutrition information. It specifically states that: '[s]upplementary nutrition information is intended to increase the consumer's understanding of the nutritional value of their food and to assist in interpreting the nutrient declaration'.

As has been discussed throughout this chapter, it is also accepted in the Guidelines that there are a number of ways of presenting this information that may be suitable for use on food labels. While recognizing the value of these additional formats, the Guidelines do also provide that their use should (i) be optional; and (ii) should only be in addition to, and not in the place of, the more formal nutrient declaration. Perhaps most significantly, the Guidelines state that '[s]upplementary nutrition information on labels should be accompanied by consumer education programmes to increase consumer understanding and use of the information'.

---

[56] Guideline 3.2.1.
[57] Guideline 3.4.1.
[58] Guideline 3.4.4.

Food labelling requirements of any sort are also subject to World Trade Organization Agreements, most specifically the Agreement on Technical Barriers to Trade (TBT). Health labelling on food and drink products has been the subject of many of the specific trade concerns that have been brought by WTO Members to the TBT Committee. At least one-third of all concerns raised in this way since 2012 have concerned labelling measures introduced by States which are designed to promote nutrition and healthy diets.[59] The primary defence available to these States, where other Members are of the opinion that they may have created a technical barrier to trade by introducing an additional nutrition labelling format is that compliance with international standards, such as Codex, normally demonstrates compliance with TBT obligations. Having said that, there is clearly a potential issue for schemes, such as the Chilean stop signs, when it comes to compliance with the WTO Agreements. In particular, they may be vulnerable to the limitations put in place on such national measures by Article 2.2. of the TBT Agreement, which states that '[…] technical regulations shall not be more trade-restrictive than necessary to fulfil a legitimate objective'. While the protection of human health is listed as one such legitimate objective, any measure adopted must still be proportionate to the aim pursued, and no less trade-restrictive measure should be available in the circumstances. The burden of proof, however, would usually be on other States to show that Chile was acting in a manner beyond that which is permitted by the TBT Agreement.[60]

5. CONCLUDING REMARKS

The problems outlined in this chapter are part of a broader difficulty. They relate to the fact that it is often hard to process a clear policy objective, such as childhood obesity prevention, within a complicated legal environment. But it can, and sometimes does, work. Two examples suffice. First, the very sensible aim to reduce the amount of plastic waste by introducing a tax on plastic bags. Second, the equally sensible aim to prohibit tobacco poisoning in an enclosed public place by introducing smoking bans. Both of these laws are effective in

---

[59] WTO and FAO, 'Trade and food standards' (2017), ISBN: 978-92-870-4501-0. Also available at: www.wto.org (last accessed 22 September 2017).

[60] The Panel in DS 381, *US – Tuna II (Mexico)* noted that: 'the burden rests on Mexico, as the complainant, to demonstrate that the conditions are met, to conclude that a violation of Article 2.2. of the TBT Agreement exists'. This differs somewhat from the way in which infringement proceedings work at EU level, where it is generally up to the Member State that is the subject of the proceedings to justify taking the potentially offending measure. As noted earlier in this chapter, this can often be a difficult justification for the EU Member State to successfully make.

bringing about social change with important ameliorative effects. They are clear models for legislators. With regard to obesity, however, the various and often conflicting rules that relate to food labelling reflect an unhappy compromise between the obligations to free trade and the genuine desire to promote good health. There is little congruence between these rules and, even worse, there often seems to be insufficient or widespread political will to reconcile these problems. The result can be confused and conflicted, making lots of work for lawyers and compromising the health of citizens.

Despite these complications, an examination of the different types of additional signpost nutrition labels at least indicates several things about the way in which these schemes can best operate in a way that is both legally preferable and which most readily facilitates informed consumer choice. First, positive messages are preferable. Although not without its own complications, the award of stars, or the use of a symbol indicating wholesomeness has the added benefit of setting a standard that many within the food industry will seek to achieve so that their products can also carry these awards, giving them an obvious competitive advantage over rivals who are unable to do so. They can be a significant push factor in bringing about the reformulation of foodstuffs, positively altering the constituents, or levels of constituents, used in their production. Second, industry tends to favour such positive messages. This leads to fewer objections to the introduction of these labelling schemes. Related to this is the involvement of stakeholders in the creation of the labelling format and operations, which also inevitably leads to less disagreement about how they should function after their introduction. Third, the use of messages that are simple, but which also tend to be based on a complex set of variables are preferred. This negates the objections that can be raised from some operators within the food sector whose products may be highly nutritious but which by their nature have to carry negative connotations about one of the 'risk nutrients', such as sugar or certain types of fat. The more flexible approach of the Nordic Keyhole in particular offers a clear example of how products can be assessed on the basis of the food category that they belong to, rather than being compared to all food products, which can often be an unfair and misleading comparison to make. They also then provide the consumer with a quick and easy choice where the 'healthier' symbol is present. This is not the case for the traffic light label, which does not convey the same types of distinctions between different kinds of foods. The traffic light also compels the consumer to weigh up various, often conflicting, aspects of the nutrient profile to arrive at a decision. The latter must therefore overcome a series of legal restrictions that do not apply in the same way to other schemes operating in other European States.

Food labelling is, of course, only one aspect of the fight against obesity and related disease. Levels of overweight children continue to rise in most EU

Member States and in many other countries worldwide. Many of these States have responded by introducing legislative measures designed to assist better food choices. Public education campaigns, coupled with clear and understandable information, are key components in this. This is increasingly recognized, not just by the actions of States referred to throughout this chapter, but by the loosening of the regulatory reins by international and regional organizations as well. The value of alternative labelling formats is recognized by the United Nations through the Codex. This is also accepted as a potential way forward by the EU in the provisions of the Food Information Regulation discussed here, but also in the commitments undertaken to carry out impact assessments on the possibility of restricting the use of harmful substances, such as trans fats, in the production of food.[61] Any progress made in this regard would not just mark a significant departure from previous policy in this area, but possibly also a very significant addition to the range of measures that can be employed in more concerted attempts to reduce childhood obesity.

---

[61] As also set out in the Report from the Commission to the European Parliament and the Council regarding trans fats in foods and in the overall diet of the Union population, COM (2015) 619. A similar report was also presented on the important matter of alcohol labelling in the Report from the Commission to the European Parliament and the Council regarding the mandatory labelling of the list of ingredients and the nutrient declaration of alcoholic beverages, COM (2017) 58.

7. Investment protection agreements, regulatory chill, and national measures on childhood obesity prevention

Mavluda Sattorova

1. INTRODUCTION

As the editors emphasise in the introduction to this volume, the law can be harnessed as a powerful instrument to help transform food environments and promote healthier lifestyles. In pursuit of a childhood obesity prevention agenda, governments have a choice of regulatory instruments—from adopting rules on food labelling and other sources of food information and the regulation of food marketing to food subsidies and taxes aimed at changing consumer behaviour. While a growing number of countries have been adopting childhood obesity measures, questions remain as to whether and in what circumstances such measures might be disputed by industry interests. Investment arbitration claims mounted by Philip Morris against tobacco control measures implemented by Australia and Uruguay have shown that legislation enacted to protect public health can be contested by corporations invoking what used to be little known international investment agreements (IIAs) and the associated investor-State arbitration mechanism.[1] Although both tobacco claims ultimately failed,[2] concerns remain about the implications of investment treaty law for the future of public health regulations, including those aimed at preventing childhood obesity. In particular, critics of the investment treaty regime have

---

[1] J Hepburn and L Nottage, 'A Procedural Win for Public Health Measures' (2017) 18 *Journal of World Investment & Trade* 307, 308.

[2] See respectively *Philip Morris Asia Ltd v. Commonwealth of Australia*, PCA Case No. 2012–12, Award on Jurisdiction and Admissibility, 17 December 2015 (the case was dismissed on jurisdictional grounds), and *Philip Morris Brands Sàrl, Philip Morris Products SA and Abal Hermanos SA v. Oriental Republic of Uruguay*, ICSID Case No. ARB/10/7, Award, 8 July 2016 (the majority upheld the legality of the disputed tobacco measures).

long cautioned about its potentially chilling effect on progressive national policy-making in the public interest.

Regulatory measures that impose stricter public health standards, including by prohibiting or restricting the marketing and consumption of certain food products or ban their production, will likely affect commercial interests. The need to comply with new regulatory standards may entail additional costs for the affected businesses. Some might be forced to withdraw certain product lines or significantly modify them. Recent investment arbitration practice shows that, rather than internalising such costs, the industry is likely to resort to international investment law to recover them (or to pressure governments to withdraw the offending measures). In particular, foreign investors involved in the production and marketing of obesogenic foods may claim that, by creating additional costs in compliance, obesity prevention measures violate investment protection standards such as the protection against regulatory expropriation and the obligation to accord fair and equitable treatment to foreign investments.

This chapter will discuss the interplay between international investment law and national policies on childhood obesity prevention. The principal aim is to (1) elucidate why and in what circumstances international investment law may have a chilling effect on governmental policy-making in the area of childhood obesity prevention, and (2) examine how national policy-makers can avoid challenges from the affected industry interests when designing, adopting and implementing obesity prevention laws and regulations. The chapter will proceed with Section 2 outlining the meaning, manifestations and causes of a chilling effect of international investment law on national policy measures. Sections 3 and 4 will focus on the emerging empirical studies into regulatory chill with a view to identifying the factors that influence the interplay between national policy-making and international rules investment protections. Section 5 will discuss what I refer to as a chilling effect of investor behaviour on national policy-making. Section 6 will outline some recommendations as to how a possible chilling effect of investment treaties and investor conduct on the making and implementation of public health regulations could be countered through reforms of investment treaty provisions as well as national laws on foreign investment. Since childhood obesity prevention measures form part of an increasingly complex legal framework, Section 7 provides a toolkit for national policymakers. It outlines key issues that the regulator and those involved in devising and implementing national childhood obesity measures need to know in order to overcome any possible chilling factor and to ensure that new regulations are immune to a possible challenge from affected investors.

2. WHAT IS REGULATORY CHILL AND HOW MAY IT AFFECT CHILDHOOD OBESITY PREVENTION MEASURES?

Public health law and international investment law have traditionally been regarded as distinct fields of law, each guided by its own principles and pursuing its own objectives. Yet even before the emergence of investor-State disputes concerning public health measures, it was acknowledged that, in a drive to attract foreign investment, national governments—particularly in developing States—may compromise public health concerns. The need to promote economic growth, including through facilitation and protection of foreign investment, may stall regulatory innovation and at times encourage States to lower their regulatory standards protecting public health.[3] Such a regulatory race to the bottom can manifest itself in a so-called regulatory chill. To quote Tienhaara, '[f]undamentally, the notion of regulatory chill suggests that investment arbitration – as an institution – may influence the course of policy development'.[4] In a broad sense, regulatory chill can manifest itself in dampening across all areas of policy-making that may adversely affect foreign investors. Concerned about the risk of investor-State disputes being instigated by affected investors, national policy-makers could arguably prioritise the avoidance of such disputes even before they begin to consider new public policies that may be necessary to address social harms.[5] A narrower conception of regulatory chill envisages the chilling effect of investment law on specific regulations that have already been proposed or are in the process of being adopted by host States. This form of regulatory chill would manifest itself only after the respective government has been made aware of the risk of an investor-State dispute by foreign investors whose economic interests would be affected by the proposed or adopted regulatory measure.[6] Driven by fears over economic and other implications of investor-State arbitration, the respective government might respond to a threat of an arbitration claim by failing to adopt or implement public policy measures. The government might also modify the measures 'to such an extent that their original intent is undermined or their effectiveness is severely diminished'.[7]

---

[3] V Vadi, *Public Health in International Investment Law and Arbitration* (Routledge 2013) 9.

[4] K Tienhaara, 'Regulatory Chill and the Threat of Arbitration: A View from Political Science' in C Brown and K Miles (eds), *Evolution in Investment Treaty Law and Arbitration* (CUP 2011) 606.

[5] Ibid.

[6] Tienhaara, 'Regulatory Chill', n4, 607.

[7] Ibid.

Why the chilling effect? The contemporary investment treaty regime is represented by a vast network of bilateral and other international investment agreements which proliferated in 1980s onward. Currently there are over 3,000 IIAs in force. Recent studies show that an overwhelming number of States, in particular developing countries, have signed and ratified investment treaties without full knowledge of their actual and potential implications.[8] Although the bulk of investment treaties were signed between developing and developed countries, investment treaty protections are also being increasingly incorporated in bilateral and regional free trade agreements between developed States. The unique characteristics of the investment treaty regime are that it (1) offers investors extensive protections, such as a broad guarantee against regulatory expropriation (including national measures that have 'the effect of depriving the owner, in whole or in significant part, of the use or reasonably-to-be-expected economic benefit of property'[9]), (2) grants investors direct standing and right of action for damages against host States,[10] and (3) allows investors to bring their claims to international investor-State arbitration tribunals, thus sidestepping national remedies and national courts.[11] These characteristics of the investment treaty regime have a direct bearing on the pursuit by host States of various public policy objectives and may at times restrict the State's ability to adopt new childhood obesity prevention measures.

Recent investment arbitration cases involving corporate challenges to tobacco measures provide an ample illustration of how IIAs may affect national public health regulations. In *Philip Morris v Uruguay*, a multinational tobacco firm with corporate headquarters in Switzerland disputed tobacco control measures adopted by Uruguay. Philip Morris argued that the new policy detrimentally affected the corporation's investment comprising a tobacco manufacturing and marketing business in Uruguay, intellectual property rights as well as the goodwill associated with the affected tobacco brands.[12] Philip Morris argued that by precluding tobacco firms from marketing more than one variant of cigarette per brand family and mandating the increase in the size of graphic health warnings on packages, Uruguay's

---

[8] See e.g., L Poulsen, *Bounded Rationality and Economic Diplomacy: The Politics of Investment Treaties in Developing Countries* (CUP 2015).

[9] *Metalclad Corporation v. Mexico*, Award, 25 August 2000, (2001) 40 ILM 36, para 103.

[10] See M Sattorova, 'Investment Treaty Breach as Internationally Proscribed Conduct: Shifting Scope, Evolving Objectives, Recalibrated Remedies?' (2012) 4(2) *Trade, Law & Development* 315.

[11] See G Van Harten and M Loughlin, 'Investment Treaty Arbitration as a Species of Global Administrative Law' (2006) 17 *EJIL* 121, 332.

[12] *Philip Morris v. Uruguay*, n2, paras 63–73.

tobacco control laws breached investment protection obligations under the Uruguay-Switzerland IIA. It claimed that the disputed regulations amounted to an expropriation of the corporation's investment in Uruguay, as well as constituting an unreasonable impairment of use and enjoyment of investments, unfair and inequitable treatment and denial of justice.[13] Philip Morris requested that the tribunal order Uruguay to either withdraw the challenged regulations or refrain from applying them against their investments, or, in the alternative, award the firm damages of at least US$22.267 million, plus compound interest as well as the firm's fees and expenses, including attorney's fees, incurred in connection with the arbitration.[14]

As demonstrated by the recent attempts by corporations to use investment protections to thwart national public health measures, 'IIAs are legally binding instruments and not "harmless" political declarations.'[15] The breadth and elasticity of protections enshrined in IIAs enables investors to contest and claim compensation in cases concerning important national policy decisions, for instance in the area of environmental, energy and public health policies.[16] In 2009, the Special-Representative of the UN Secretary-General on the Issue of Human Rights and Transnational Corporations and Other Business Enterprises, Professor John Ruggie, reported to the United Nations Human Rights Council his concerns that 'some [investment] treaty guarantees and contract provisions may unduly constrain the host Government's ability to achieve its legitimate policy objectives, including its international human rights obligations. That is because under threat of binding international arbitration, a foreign investor may be able to insulate its business venture from new laws and regulations or seek compensation from the Government for the cost of compliance'.[17]

The dramatic rise in the number of claims brought by investors against host States over the past two decades has also prompted widespread concerns over the magnitude of financial consequences of investment arbitration for respondent States. Given the staggering amounts that have been awarded to investor-claimants and the high cost of the arbitration process, developing countries in particular have found themselves vulnerable due to the detrimental

---

[13] Ibid., para 12.
[14] Ibid.
[15] United Nations Conference on Trade and Development (UNCTAD), *World Investment Report 2015: Reforming International Investment Governance* (United Nations 2015) 125.
[16] Ibid.
[17] Report of the SRSG, Business and Human Rights: Towards Operationalizing the 'Protect, Respect and Remedy' Framework, A/HRC/11/13, para 30 (2009).

financial impact of the awards on a country's budget.[18] For instance, a recent UNCTAD study highlights that '[to] expedite payment of the awards, funds may be diverted from important development objectives, such as investment in infrastructure, education, health or other public goods'.[19] Critics also argue that concerns relating to the costs of defending claims in investment treaties in arbitration may also have a chilling effect on national regulatory innovation.[20] Indeed, even in cases where public health regulations were successfully defended in investment arbitration, the respective governments had to expend significant amounts in legal costs. For instance, in *Philip Morris v. Uruguay* the tribunal ordered the investor claimants to pay $7 million to Uruguay towards its legal costs which were estimated at approximately $10.3 million.[21]

Due to the heavy financial burdens investment arbitration cases often entail, government decision-makers in developing countries could arguably be more prone to avoiding investor-State disputes under investment treaties than decision-makers in developed countries.[22] These concerns are not unfounded: it has been reported that following threats of investor-State arbitration, the Indonesian and Costa Rican governments reversed their earlier decisions to refuse to grant mining permits.[23] Uruguay was also on the verge of watering down its tobacco control legislation after having learnt about the Philip Morris claim against Australia.[24]

Yet developed countries are not immune to the chilling effect of international investment law either. For example, a case-study conducted in the province of Ontario, Canada, found a link between investment treaties and the

---

[18] UNCTAD, *Best Practices in Investment for Development. How to prevent and manage investor-State disputes: Lessons from Peru* (United Nations 2011) 7.

[19] Ibid.

[20] J Bonnitcha, *Substantive Protection under Investment Treaties: A Legal and Economic Analysis* (OUP 2014) 117, also V Been and J Beauvais, 'The Global Fifth Amendment? The NAFTA's Investment Protections and the Misguided Quest for an International "Regulatory Takings" Doctrine' (2003) 78 *New York University Law Review* 30, 132.

[21] *Philip Morris v. Uruguay*, n2, para 583. See also 'Philip Morris fails in PCA arbitration against Australia over plain packaging laws', International Institute for Sustainable Development, 29 February 2016, available at https://www.iisd.org/itn/2016/02/29/philip-morris-fails-in-pca-arbitration-against-australia-over-plain-packaging-laws/ (accessed 30/09/2020) (reporting that the defence against the investment arbitration claim by Philip Morris cost Australia US$ 35 million).

[22] Bonnitcha, n20, 120.

[23] Ibid., also Tienhaara, n 4, 618; S Gross, 'Inordinate Chill: BITs, non-NAFTA MITs, and Host-State Regulatory Freedom: An Indonesian Case Study' (2003) 24 *Michigan Journal of International Law* 893.

[24] 'Uruguay bows to pressure over anti-smoking law amendments', *The Guardian*, 27 July 2010.

internal vetting of regulatory proposals.[25] New Zealand was also reported to have put its plain tobacco policy on hold while awaiting the outcome of investment arbitration between Philip Morris and Australia.[26] Other studies also suggest that 'in circumstances where a foreign investor opposes a preferred government policy on the basis of an investment treaty, and where that policy is at serious risk of non-compliance with the investment treaty, developed States ... have amended, delayed or withdrawn preferred policies'.[27] Similarly, in a somewhat different context it has been reported that the suggestions for a stronger articulation of environmental and sustainability requirements in the EU Renewable Energy Directive[28] failed to make their way into the final version of the directive because a compromise had to be made between the European Union's commitment to environment protection and sustainable development and its obligations under multilateral trade agreements.[29] The European Commission has acknowledged that the desire to prevent claims under WTO law was a motivating factor for not adopting stronger criteria.[30]

3. REGULATORY CHILL AND THE 'AWARENESS' THESIS

Both the supporters and critics of the investment treaty regime acknowledge that regulatory chill is very difficult to measure. Even despite the recent proliferation of investment disputes challenging various public policy measures, the existing pool of cases is not sufficient to allow for control of extraneous variables. As political scientists have long stressed, 'research on regulatory chill does not lend itself to statistical analysis'.[31] Although some argue that a detailed and comprehensive case-study approach can yield veritable results,[32]

---

[25] See G Van Harten and D Scott, 'Investment Treaties and the Internal Vetting of Regulatory Proposals: A Case Study from Canada' (2016) *Osgoode Legal Studies Research Paper Series*, No. 26.

[26] L Poulsen, J Bonnitcha and J Yackee, 'Transatlantic Investment Treaty Protection', Paper No 3 in the CEPS-CTR Project on TTIP in the Balance and CEPS Special Report No, 102, March 2015, 28. See also, S Boot, 'Tobacco Firm Ponders Challenge as Plain Packaging Bill Passes', *New Zealand Herald*, 10 September 2016.

[27] Poulsen et al., ibid.

[28] European Council Directive 2009/28/EC of the European Parliament and of the Council on the promotion of the use of energy from renewable sources and amending and subsequently repealing Directives 2001/77/EC and 2003/30/EC OJ 2009 L 140/16 (2009).

[29] See E Barrett Lydgate, 'Biofuels, Sustainability, and Trade-related Regulatory Chill' (2012) 15(1) *Journal of International Economic Law* 157, 164.

[30] Ibid., 160–164.

[31] Tienhaara, n4, 609.

[32] Ibid., 609–10.

others caution that '[e]ven with highly detailed case studies, past chilling effects are difficult to identify because they require counterfactual evidence about the regulations that would have existed in the absence of the purported chilling'.[33] As with other empirical methods, qualitative approaches have their own pitfalls— respondents in interviews and surveys may slant their portrayal of realities to fit their own individual preferences or institutional mandate.[34] The task of proving the existence of regulatory chill is also difficult because documents relating to government decision-making are extremely rarely in the public domain.[35]

The difficulties with proving the existence of a chilling effect are often deployed by the supporters of the investment treaty regime as a basis for dismissing the regulatory chill thesis in its entirety. However, as Tienhaara argues 'the repeated dismissals of the regulatory chill hypothesis by some practitioners and legal scholars are both premature and lacking in analytical rigour'.[36] Despite being open to charges of unreliability, recent qualitative studies of regulatory chill nevertheless offer very useful insights into the murky area of the interplay between investment treaty law and national policy-making in the public interest. Notwithstanding their methodological limitations, these case-studies provide a valuable empirical context for analysing the effect (chilling or otherwise) of investment treaty norms on national policy-making.

Those who dismiss regulatory chill argue that for investment treaties to have a chilling effect on public health regulations, government officials ought to be aware of international investment law and its liability implications. As Rubins and Coe argue, the regulatory chill thesis '[a]ssumes that regulators are aware of international law, but are they?'[37] Although 'regulators may be more conscious of the prospect of liability than ever before', the actions of many governments are 'clearly uninformed by the dictates of international law'.[38] In other words, since national policy-makers are by and large unaware about international investment law, their national policy-making is unlikely to be affected by the fear of pay-outs in a potential investor-State dispute. Lack of awareness about investment treaty law equals lack of fear of liability; hence no chilling effect on government decision-making.

---

[33] Bonnitcha, n20,115 (footnotes omitted).
[34] Poulsen, n8, 23.
[35] Bonnitcha, n20, 115-6.
[36] Tienhaara, n4, 627.
[37] J Coe Jr and N Rubins, 'Regulatory Expropriation and the Tecmed Case: Context and Contributions' in T Weiler (ed.), *International Investment Law and Arbitration: Leading Cases from the ICSID, NAFTA, Bilateral Treaties and Customary International Law* (Cameron May 2005) 597, 599.
[38] Ibid.

Indeed, recent empirical investigations of the impact of investment treaty law on government decision-making reveal a very limited awareness among government officials about the content and implications of investment treaty norms and practices. Of particular note is Côté's empirical investigation into the impact of international investment law on the exercise by host States of regulatory powers in the areas of public health, safety, and the environment protection.[39] Through her case study of Canada and a number of developing States, Côté explored trends in regulatory activities whilst also probing the level of awareness of investment treaties among government regulators. Her overall conclusion—drawing on evidence from interviews with government officials in Canada and developing States—is that there is a low level of awareness among national regulators both in Canada and developing States from Latin America and the Caribbean, Australasia, Europe, Africa and the Middle East.[40]

These findings are corroborated with those drawn from my empirical study of the impact of investment treaty law on government behaviour.[41] The study comprised small-scale interviews with government officials in developing countries, including Kazakhstan, Turkey, Ukraine and Uzbekistan (54 respondents). In addition to these country-specific case-studies, a number of encounter interviews were undertaken with government officials from Armenia, Azerbaijan, Belarus, Georgia, Kenya, Kyrgyzstan, Lebanon, Mongolia, Russia, Sri-Lanka, Tajikistan, and Jordan (15 respondents in total). These interviews, albeit limited in their quantity, offered interesting snapshots to inform the ongoing debate about investment treaties and their impact on public policy-making, in particular the making of public health policies. The overwhelming number of respondents showed no awareness about investment treaty law and investor- arbitration. Of the interviewed officials 19 respondents were directly or indirectly involved with the State in drafting or implementing public health policies—all of them reported no prior knowledge of investment treaty law.

Does the lack of awareness mean that concerns over the chilling effect of investment treaties on public health regulations can now be put to rest? As Tienhaara argued, the lack of awareness is largely irrelevant—'regulators can be made aware of the key aspects of international investment law by investors

---

[39] C Côté, 'A Chilling Effect? The Impact of International Investment Agreements on National Regulatory Autonomy in the Areas of Health, Safety and the Environment' (PhD Thesis, LSE, 2014).
[40] Ibid, 144–9 and 181–2.
[41] See M Sattorova, *The Impact of Investment Treaty Law on Host States: Enabling Good Governance?* (Hart 2018) 61–70.

and their lawyers when a conflict arises'.[42] Furthermore, 'a lack of knowledge about the specificities of investment law makes the threat of arbitration all the more potent, because regulators will be less likely to recognise when an investor is bluffing'.[43] Limited awareness among government officials, particularly in developing countries, may also increase the chances of their public health regulations being challenged by foreign investors on procedural grounds—the government that is aware of the meaning and implications of the investment treaty prescriptions of transparency, due process, and consistency is more likely to ensure that these requirements are complied with in the process of adopting a new public health policy.

Raising awareness about investment treaty law and its implications for host States is therefore of utmost importance to ensure that policy-makers draft their childhood obesity (and other public health) regulations in a manner that would bullet-proof them from potential investment claims by affected corporate actors. Of particular significance here is also capacity building training of government officials in developing States which often lack institutional and human capacity to address competing regulatory needs, international obligations and objectives. Recent political science studies show that decision-making in the investment treaty context varies with the extent of expertise in relevant government agencies and that developed countries with higher levels of administrative capacity may display different patterns of learning from their investment treaty experience than their developing country counterparts.[44] While developed countries will likely have sufficient in-house expertise, developing countries will generally not. Developed country officials are therefore more likely to be able to draft and implement their public policy measures in a way that would not violate investment treaty norms.[45]

4. DOES THE FEAR OF INVESTMENT ARBITRATION INFLUENCE NATIONAL POLICY-MAKERS?

Those who deny the chilling effect of investment treaties on national policy-making in the public interest also point out—correctly—that the regulatory chill thesis:

> assumes that the prospect of having to pay compensation will cause States to forbear from taking action, despite compelling regulatory objectives. While the apprehen-

---

[42] Tienhaara, n4, 611.
[43] Ibid.
[44] L Poulsen and E Aisbett, 'When the Claims Hit: Bilateral Investment Treaties and Bounded Rational Learning' (2013) 65 *World Politics* 273, 302.
[45] Tienhaara, n4, 612.

sion of international liability may prompt reflection and careful tailoring of means to ends, it seems less likely to cause abandonment of legislation at the heart of a government's mandate.[46]

In other words, the regulatory chill thesis presupposes that compliance with investment treaty obligations and the need to avoid future liabilities in investment arbitration is a predominant concern of host States, but is it?

Indeed, for investment treaties to have a chilling effect on national regulatory activities the host States must not only have the requisite level of awareness and understanding of international investment law but they must also be prepared to take measures to avoid investment claims by affected corporate interests. National governments must be committed to preventing the financial consequences of possible adverse rulings in investment arbitration cases where investors successfully challenge a new law or policy. Put differently, for regulatory chill to occur, host States must not only have signed and ratified investment treaties but also be internally committed to comply with their letter and spirit when designing and implementing national regulations, including policies aimed at preventing childhood obesity. The question is whether and to what extent national policy-makers are driven by the desire to abide by and prioritise the State's investment protection commitments.

The recent empirical studies suggest that even in cases where some government officials showed awareness of international investment treaties and their liability implications, investment treaties had only subtle if any influence on the design and adoption of new public policy measures.[47] Regulators, both in developed and developing States, appear to be driven primarily by factors such as concrete public policy needs, the recommendations of the international community, public opinion as well as domestic and regional constraints.[48] These findings resonate with those drawn from our case-studies.[49] When asked about the effect of investment treaties on national regulatory autonomy, our respondents pointed to a range of domestic and international factors that tend to bear on national policy-makers. As one respondent has put it:

> if the government wishes to adopt a new health and safety policy, the threat of an investment claim by a foreign corporation is unlikely to be the key factor in the government's calculations. Much will depend on where the impetus for a new policy comes from, on international and domestic pressures, and whether the adoption of the new policy is important for the government's prospects of being re-elected etc.[50]

---

[46] Coe and Rubins, n37, 599.
[47] Côté, n39, 195.
[48] Ibid.
[49] Sattorova, n41.
[50] Ibid.

These insights, together with findings from other recent empirical studies, support a conclusion that the impact of international investment law on public health policy-making is likely to be variously diffused, mitigated and mediated by a range of international and domestic factors, including States' obligations under international and regional conventions, treaties and guidelines, the actions of other countries, domestic political and economic constraints, and industry influence.[51] At present, the prospect of being drawn into investor-State arbitration alone does not seem to act as strong enough a factor to influence national policy-making in terms of encouraging host governments to prioritise foreign investors. Nor do investment treaties—and other international agreements—appear to act as an overwhelming force to discourage them from pursuing new public policy regulations.

A survey of awards in investment arbitration cases also supports the conclusion that host governments—in particular in developing countries—do not necessarily prioritise investment protection over public health and other public interest regulations. Cases involving an investor challenging a national public policy measure show that host States frequently opted to maintain disputed public policy measures notwithstanding the need to compensate the affected foreign investors.[52] In the words of Bonnitcha, 'the fact that States in these cases chose to pay out foreign investors ... serves to illustrate a simple point: States sometimes maintain measures that entail liability under investment treaty protections'.[53] The fact that host States often succeed in defending their public policy regulations in investment arbitration is frequently invoked by the opponents of the regulatory chill thesis in support for an argument that 'investment treaties do not impede efforts to raise regulatory standards'.[54]

5. REGULATORY CHILL AND INVESTOR BEHAVIOUR

Again, do the above findings suggest that the regulatory chill debate should be put to rest? As our interviews revealed, while investment treaties would be unlikely to discourage public policy-making there is still a likelihood of investment treaties being used as a pretext for scaling back or halting a new public

---

[51] Côté, n39, 171-3.
[52] See e.g., facts in *Metalclad Corpn v. Mexico*, Award, 25 August 2000, ICSID Case No ARB (AF)/97/1 (2001) 40 ILM 36; *Técnicas Medioambientales Tecmed SA v. Mexico*, Award, 29 May 2003, 10 ICSID Rep 130; and *Glamis Gold Ltd v. United States*, UNCITRAL, Award, 14 May 2009.
[53] Bonnitcha, n20, 121.
[54] Ibid, see also K Vandevelde, *Bilateral Investment Treaties: History, Policy, and Interpretation* (OUP 2010) 107.

policy by the government that succumbed to direct pressure from the industry.[55] A rather worrying trend that emerges from our and other empirical case studies[56] is a concern about the effects of investor behaviour on government decision-making including public health policy-making. Some of the interviewed government officials expressed concerns over the efforts by foreign corporations to influence the shape of domestic regulations. For instance, in one developing country where we conducted interviews, the instances of collusion between foreign pharmaceutical corporations and government officials have become so widespread that a specific term has been coined—pharma mafia.[57]

In another country, a Central Asian State, there is evidence of a multinational tobacco company having actively resisted the adoption of a tobacco regulation. In 1994, the tobacco firm learnt that the ministry of health had drafted a potentially highly effective piece of tobacco control legislation that would have banned tobacco advertising and smoking in public places and introduced health warnings.[58] The tobacco firm responded by describing the policy as a '"deal stopper" that contravened its earlier agreement with the host government'.[59] It sought to halt the adoption of the policy by depicting it as jeopardising foreign investment in the country, and threatening the health ministry that it would lead to 'the immediate demise of the domestic cigarette industry'.[60] The proposed policy was decried as 'seriously interfering with ... commercial freedom'.[61] Consequently, the intended bans on advertising tobacco were replaced by a code drafted by the tobacco industry, and the scope of the ban on smoking in public space was scaled back.[62]

These reports resonate with our interviews where a number of respondents shared the view that host governments may not always be concerned about implications of investment treaties and their liability consequences in cases where new public health policies are being prepared for adoption. However, host governments may invoke investment treaties to water down public health policies when being pushed to do so by the relevant foreign investors. In other words, they may use investment treaties as a pretext for slacker and less effec-

---

[55] Sattorova, n41, 172.
[56] Côté, n39, 194, reporting national policy-makers' concerns about the influence of the tobacco industry on the regulatory development process.
[57] Sattorova, n41, 149.
[58] AB Gilmore, J Collin and M McKee, 'British American Tobacco's Erosion of Health Legislation in Uzbekistan' (2006) 332 *British Medical Journal* 355, 356.
[59] Ibid.
[60] Ibid.
[61] Ibid.
[62] Ibid.

tive public health policies. Scholars have long suspected that regulatory chill might be attributable not to the threat of liability under investment treaty but to some other cause—such as the fear of discouraging foreign investment.[63] A fear of capital flight and a loss of competitiveness in international markets might prevent national policy-makers from raising regulatory standards.[64] Although empirical evidence to support this conclusion is still limited, there are some concrete examples of environmental regulations being discouraged due to the fear of a loss of foreign investment. The reported instances include the European Union and the United States where industry warnings of capital flight and a loss of competitiveness had a chilling effect on the adoption of new environmental tax legislation.[65] Some argue that developing countries are generally more vulnerable to industry pressures to lower their regulatory standards— developing countries are said to be particularly prone to 'race to the bottom' to attract foreign investment.[66]

6. ADDRESSING THE NEGATIVE EFFECT OF INVESTMENT (AND INVESTMENT TREATIES) ON PUBLIC HEALTH MEASURES

6.1 Investment Treaty Reform: Enabling National Policy-Makers Through Regulatory Flexibility Provisions

Even a cursory overview of the literature dedicated to regulatory chill reveals that the focus of the debate primarily falls on the causal link between investment treaties and national policy-making. The emphasis is thus on how to adapt treaties and national regulations to avoid negatively affecting foreign investors. The bulk of literature dedicated to the effect of investment treaties on regulatory space focuses on solutions which envisage either adapting national policies to the prescriptions of investment treaty law,[67] or adapting international investment law to provide more room for national policies in the

---

[63] Bonnitcha, n20, 115, see also Tienhaara, n4, 263.
[64] K Miles, *The Origins of International Investment Law: Empire, Environment and the Safeguarding of Capital* (CUP 2013) 181.
[65] Ibid., see also E Neumayer, *Greening Trade and Investment: Environmental Protection Without Protectionism* (Routledge 2001) 69–71.
[66] See ibid., also Vadi, n3, 9; K Tienhaara, Mineral Investment and the Regulation of the Environment in Developing Countries: Lessons from Ghana' (2006) 6 *International Environmental Agreements: Politics, Law and Economics* 371.
[67] See e.g., S Schill, 'Do Investment Treaties Chill Unilateral State Regulation to Mitigate Climate Change?' (2007) 5 *Journal of International Arbitration* 469.

public interest.[68] For instance, some argue that greater effort should be made to delimit the scope of investor protections, scale back definitions of 'investor' and 'investment', and insert comprehensive treaty exceptions for public health and other public policy measures.[69] There are also arguments that governments should avoid entering into future investment agreements that overly constrain their regulatory autonomy with respect to public health—a proposal which is not always feasible due to the salience of foreign investment in economic growth plans of both developed and developing countries.

As the number of investment disputes where host States have to defend their public policy measures addressing threats to the health of the population continues to rise, some scholars seek to assuage the growing concerns by arguing that investment treaties are usually interpreted in a manner that favours national regulatory autonomy, and that the risk of regulatory chill can be avoided if investment treaties are redrafted to include regulatory flexibility provisions.[70] Indeed, as part of a move towards more balanced investment treaty-making, some of the new-generation investment treaties already nominate certain social policy objectives as a basis for limiting investment protection and promotion objectives. They do so by expressly acknowledging, in treaty preambles and stand-alone "right to regulate" clauses, the contracting State parties' intention to achieve their economic growth objectives in a manner that is compatible with other specified policy objectives, including in public health.[71] For instance, the 2005 India-Singapore FTA expressly provides for the States' 'right to pursue economic philosophies suited to their development goals and their right to regulate activities to realize their national policy objectives'.[72] Other treaty preambles contain references to the State parties' obligations under other bodies of international law.[73]

---

[68] See e.g., Vadi, n3, 114–15; Andreas Kulick, *Global Public Interest in International Investment Law* (CUP 2012) 168; J Kurtz, 'Building Legitimacy through Interpretation in Investor-State Arbitration' in Z Douglas, J Pauwelyn and J Viñuales (eds), *The Foundations of International Investment Law: Bringing Theory into Practice* (OUP 2014) 257.

[69] H El-Kady, 'Towards a New Conceptualization of International Investment Agreements' (2016) 3 *BCDR International Arbitration Review* 327.

[70] See e.g., S Spears, 'The Quest for Policy Space in a New Generation of International Investment Agreements' (2010) 13(4) *Journal of International Economic Law* 1037.

[71] Ibid., 1044.

[72] The full text is available at http://investmentpolicyhub.unctad.org/Download/TreatyFile/2707 (accessed 30/09/2020).

[73] UNCTAD suggests that in order to reconcile investment guarantees with public policy objectives, new investment treaties could incorporate references to global standards on health, labour rights and environmental protection: UNCTAD, *World Investment Report 2016* (UN 2016) 111.

Likewise, a growing number of investment treaties now feature carve-outs and general exceptions to ensure that States can derogate from their investment protection commitments in pursuit of public policy objectives. Carve-outs and comprehensive public policy exceptions are regarded as a principal means to help safeguard the State's right to regulate and to address concerns relating to regulatory chill. In defending its tobacco policy in an arbitration case brought by Philip Morris, Uruguay invoked a public health exception contained in Article 2(1) of the relevant treaty[74] stipulating that:

> [e]ach Contracting Party shall in its territory promote as far as possible investments by investors of the other Contracting Party and admit such investments in accordance with its law. The Contracting Parties recognize each other's right not to allow economic activities for reasons of public security and order, public health or morality.

Yet the negative effect of investment treaties on national policy-making for public health cannot be addressed through merely incorporating declaratory provisions in investment treaty preambles and introducing public policy exceptions. The fundamental drawback of exceptions clauses is that they do not place public policy measures on the same footing as investment protection standards. In other words, host States' entitlement to pursue public policy objectives is on a back foot because it is framed as an exception, placing host States under a greater evidentiary burden in proving that the relevant measures are necessary to protect public health or address other public policy concerns. Furthermore, even despite a move towards greater inclusion of regulatory flexibility provisions in new and revised investment treaties, as a whole the investment treaty landscape remains highly fragmented. It lacks a consistent and uniform approach to reconciling investment protection commitments with State obligations to legislate and regulate in pursuit of various public policy objectives.

6.2 Preventing Negative Effects of IIAs Through Investor Obligations and Responsibilities

The shortcomings of regulatory flexibility provisions in investment treaties, however, are not the only ground for concern over international investment law and its impact on public health policies. In particular, I argue that the potentially negative effect of investment treaties on national childhood obesity

---

[74] Agreement between the Swiss Confederation and the Oriental Republic of Uruguay on the Reciprocal Promotion and Protection of Investments (1988), available at https://investmentpolicy.unctad.org (accessed 30/09/2020).

and other public health issues needs to be addressed not just through better regulatory flexibility provisions in the new and revised treaties but also through revisiting another tired and long-debated issue: the asymmetry of treaties as far as investor rights and obligations are concerned. As mentioned earlier, legal discourse about regulatory chill primarily focuses on the clash between investment protection norms and national policy measures, not on the interplay between investor activities and national policy measures. As a consequence, the debate ignores the role investment treaties and international investment law as a whole can play in preventing the negative effects of investor activities on national policy-making in the public interest. Since it is investors rather than investment treaties that may have a tangible negative impact on national policy-making, it is submitted that investment treaty law should play a greater role in actively pre-empting investor misconduct and in particular pre-empting or otherwise tackling investor efforts to halt or influence the adoption of new public policies in host States.

The need to address negative impacts of foreign investment on host societies has been acknowledged in a recent UNCTAD report:

> Although (foreign) investment can create positive conditions for improving peoples' lives, it can also carry the risk of negatively impacting on the environment, peoples' health and the enjoyment of their human rights. These effects can be aggravated due to domestic regulatory lacunae. It is important, therefore, that while IIAs continue to provide a firm basis for investment protection, they should also begin to address more directly investor responsibilities.[75]

One priority of the ongoing investment treaty reform should therefore focus on ensuring responsible investor behaviour. According to the UNCTAD, investment treaties can be redesigned (1) to maximise the positive contribution that investors can bring to societies ('doing good') and (2) to avoid negative impacts of investment ('doing no harm').[76] As far as a negative effect on national childhood obesity measures and other public health policies is concerned, particular efforts should be made to incorporate investment treaty provisions expressly addressing investor misconduct, ranging from bribery and corruption to, importantly, the exercise of improper influence over government officials. Some of the new generation treaties already feature such provisions. Mention should be made, for instance, of the CARIFORUM-EU Economic Partnership Agreement.[77] This agreement expressly requires that the contract-

---

[75] UNCTAD, *World Investment Report 2015: Reforming International Investment Governance* (UN 2015) 126.
[76] Ibid., 128.
[77] Economic Partnership Agreement Between the CARIFORUM States and the European Community, 30 October 2008, [2008] OJ L 289/I/3. See further C Ononaiwu,

ing State parties cooperate and take any necessary domestic measures to ensure that investors are forbidden from and held liable for bribing public officials.[78]

However, the existing approaches to investor misconduct tend to focus on State obligations to prevent and sanction corruption, bribery and other forms of improper influence. The onus is therefore on contracting State parties, not investors. To mitigate a negative effect of investment activities on national policy-making investment treaties need to be redesigned to incorporate bolder obligations imposed directly on investors. Such provisions should go beyond mere signalling of 'a commitment by the contracting State parties to the normative guiding idea of corporate social responsibility'.[79] Furthermore, such provisions should be enforceable through the treaty-based dispute settlement mechanisms. While this would 'considerably modify the normative structure of investment agreements'[80] there is growing consensus that such modifications are warranted in order to redress the existing lack of provisions on investor responsibilities.[81] With a few very recent exceptions, however, the majority of States are still reluctant to incorporate substantive provisions on investor duties and responsibilities in IIAs.[82] This is partly due to 'a lack of political will, scepticism towards respective innovations and probably a so far quite successful resistance from the side of the business community'.[83]

The developing countries that lack sufficient bargaining power (and political will) to insist on the inclusion of investor obligations and responsibilities in investment treaties can still include such provisions in their national laws on investment protection and promotion. For instance, the 1998 Law of the Republic of Uzbekistan on Foreign Investments features provisions on investor duties and responsibilities.[84] According to Article 11, investors are under an obligation to abide by national legislation; to refrain from any forms of direct or indirect influence over their investment partners or government

---

'Regional Investment Treaty Arrangements in the Caribbean: Developments and Implications' in N Jansen Calamita and M Sattorova, *The Regionalization of International Investment Treaty Arrangements* (British Institute of International and Comparative Law 2015) 205.

[78] Art 72 CARIFORUM—EU EPA, n77.

[79] K Nowrot, 'How to Include Environmental Protection, Human Rights and Sustainability in International Investment Law (2014)15 *Journal of World Investment & Trade* 612, 639.

[80] Ibid., 638.

[81] For a discussion of recent proposals, see J Amado, J Kern and M Rodriguez (eds) *Arbitrating the Conduct of International Investors* (CUP 2017).

[82] Nowrot, n79, 637.

[83] Ibid.

[84] Law No. 609-I, April 30, 1998, available at http://cis-legislation.com/document.fwx?rgn=965 (last accessed 30/09/2020).

bodies with the view to obtaining additional concessions and advantages; and to comply with health and safety and environmental protection standards set by law.[85] Investment arbitration practice shows that such provisions may be of use in countering investor claims: some arbitration tribunals have denied investment treaty protection to business activities tainted by a failure to comply with national laws.[86] Cumulatively, national laws can help deflect industry efforts to influence national policy choices or dispute national measures in investment arbitration.

7. PRE-EMPTING THE NEGATIVE EFFECTS OF INVESTMENT (AND INVESTMENT TREATIES) ON CHILDHOOD OBESITY MEASURES: A TOOLKIT FOR NATIONAL REGULATORS

As noted by the editors in the introduction to this volume, States wishing to regulate the food industry with a view to tackling childhood obesity would need to understand precisely how such regulations should be designed and implemented within the constraints of existing international investment rules. The preceding discussion has focused on international rules on investment protection and on the ways in which governments can avoid and mitigate their negative impact on national childhood obesity prevention measures. When operating at the national level, what are the necessary issues that the regulator and those involved in devising and implementing national childhood obesity measures need to be aware of to overcome any possible chilling factor and to ensure that new regulations will most likely withstand a possible challenge from investors? While recent investment arbitration cases show that investment treaties may restrict national policy-making, they are also instructive in providing concrete examples of pitfalls that national regulators would need to avoid. The recommendations below focus on the key investment protection standards business actors rely upon when using investment treaties to challenge public policy measures: expropriation, the prohibition of arbitrary, unreasonable and discriminatory treatment, and the fair and equitable treatment standard. The aim of this subsection is to outline the emerging trends in investment arbitration practice and how these trends should inform national regulators in the area of public health.

---

[85] Ibid.
[86] See e.g., *Phoenix Action Ltd v. Czech Republic*, Award, 9 April 2009 (Case No ARB/06/5) para 134; *Inceysa v. El Salvador* (ICSID Case No. ARB/03126, Award, 2 August 2006). For an overview of investment arbitration practice see S Schill, 'Illegal Investments in Investment Treaty Arbitration' (2012) 11 *Law and Practice of International Courts and Tribunals* 281.

As noted earlier, national childhood obesity measures that impose higher regulatory standards, or prohibit or restrict the use, production and marketing of certain obesogenic products will most likely affect commercial interests by creating additional costs or reducing the market share. The key investment protection standard the industry actors are likely to invoke to contest new regulatory measures is expropriation. What can national regulators do to prevent successful investor-State claims by the affected industries alleging that the new regulations amount to regulatory expropriation entailing the State's obligation to compensate? Investment arbitration practice reveals a growing acknowledgement by arbitral tribunals of the need to afford host States sufficient policy space. As stated in *Methanex v. United States*:

> as a matter of general international law, a non-discriminatory regulation for a public purpose, which is enacted in accordance with due process and which affects, *inter alios*, a foreign investor or investment is not deemed expropriatory and compensable unless specific commitments had been given by the regulating government to the then putative foreign investor contemplating investment that the government would refrain from such regulation.[87]

A growing number of investment tribunals held that where disputed regulatory measures are bona fide, aimed at protecting public welfare, non-discriminatory and proportionate, such measures should be seen as constituting a valid exercise by the State of its police powers in pursuit of public policy objectives and could not constitute an expropriation of the claimant's investment. To escape the finding of expropriation, national policy measures must also be proportionate and free from arbitrariness.[88] A measure will not be arbitrary if it is reasonably related to a rational policy, and the impact of the measure on the investor is proportional to the policy objective sought.[89] Policy measures must also be applied equally and without discrimination, and must not intentionally target foreign investors.[90] Recent jurisprudence also stresses the role of specific commitments and representations made by the government to the investor: where no such commitment has been made, the investor cannot expect the government to refrain from adopting new laws and policies.[91]

The existence of specific commitments may also be decisive for the outcome of the investor's claim of breach of the fair and equitable treatment

---

[87] *Methanex Corporation v. United States*, Final Award on Jurisdiction and Merits, 3 August 2005 (2005) 44 ILM 1345, para 287.
[88] *Philip Morris v. Uruguay*, n2, para 305.
[89] *Electrabel v. Hungary* (ICSID Case No. ARB/07/19, Award 25 November 2015) para 179.
[90] *Philip Morris v. Uruguay*, n2, paras 441–442.
[91] See eg *Methanex v. United States*, n87, para 287.

standard—another key guarantee commonly invoked by investors in disputing regulatory measures negatively affecting their economic interests. In determining the merits of the investor's claim of a breach of fair and equitable treatment, an arbitral tribunal is likely to examine whether the State has made explicit or implicit promises to the particular investors to the effect that a legal and regulatory framework applicable to its investment would remain unchanged. In a number of investment arbitration cases, the absence of such specific commitments served as a basis for denying investor claims relating to regulatory changes. As noted by the tribunal in *EDF v Romania*:

> [e]xcept where specific promises or representations are made by the State to the investor, the latter may not rely on a bilateral investment treaty as a kind of insurance policy against the risk of any changes in the host State's legal and economic framework. Such expectation would be neither legitimate nor reasonable.[92]

The major difficulty with any attempt to pre-empt the possibility of investors invoking the fair and equitable treatment standard to dispute new policy measures is that the standard is rather vague and open-ended. The jurisprudence of investment tribunals on fair and equitable treatment, as well as the formulation of the standard in investment treaties, has been widely criticised for lack of clarity, consistency and predictability in arbitral practice.[93] A recent UNCTAD report has observed that such shortcomings within international investment law would present considerable challenges to host States and their agencies that interact with investors.[94]

> If the State and its subnational entities do not know in advance what type of conduct may be considered a breach of a treaty, then it cannot organize its regulatory and administrative decision-making processes and delegation in a way that ensures that its conduct will not incur liability under the [fair and equitable treatment] standard.[95]

Notwithstanding this lack of clarity and predictability, certain elements of the standard have crystallised in recent arbitral jurisprudence. As a baseline, national regulators should be mindful that fair and equitable treatment requires due process and includes the obligation not to deny justice in criminal, civil,

---

[92] *EDF (Services) Ltd v. Romania* (ICSID Case No RB/05/13, Award, 2 October 2009) para 217.
[93] See e.g., J Kalicki and S Medeiros, 'Fair, Equitable and Ambiguous: What is Fair and Equitable Treatment in International Investment Law?' (2008) 22 *ICSID Review* 24.
[94] UNCTAD, 'Fair and Equitable Treatment: A Sequel' (United Nations 2012) 12.
[95] Ibid.

or administrative adjudicatory proceedings.⁹⁶ In *Philip Morris v. Uruguay*, the majority of the tribunal held that '[f]or a denial of justice to exist under international law there must be "clear evidence of [...] an outrageous failure of the judicial system" or a demonstration of "systemic injustice"'.⁹⁷ Even though a number of 'procedural improprieties and a failure of form'⁹⁸ were found in the way Philip Morris was treated by national judicial and administrative bodies in Uruguay, the majority found that such irregularities did not constitute a denial of justice under international law.⁹⁹ The dissenting arbitrator disagreed and found that, in interpreting the disputed national law provisions, the domestic bodies issued contradictory decisions which did amount to a denial of justice.¹⁰⁰ The dissenting opinion sounds a note of caution for policy-makers: even though the majority held that establishing a denial of justice contrary to the fair and equitable treatment standard requires an elevated standard of proof,¹⁰¹ national authorities should strive to eliminate any significant inconsistencies in the manner by which childhood obesity measures are implemented and construed by various agencies at the national level. Lack of consistency and internal contradictions have led to the finding of a breach of fair and equitable treatment in a number of investment cases.¹⁰² National inter-agency dialogue, both prior to the adoption of policy measures and in the course of their implementation, will help reduce the risk of policy instruments being marred by internal inconsistencies and subsequently disputed by industry actors. As summarised in a recent WHO report, to pre-empt challenges from investors, greater cooperation between health experts, regulators and lawyers is needed from the outset.¹⁰³

---

⁹⁶ *Waste Management Inc v. Mexico*, Award, 30 April 2004 (2004) 43 ILM 967, para 98.
⁹⁷ *Philip Morris v. Uruguay*, n2, para 500.
⁹⁸ Ibid., para 578.
⁹⁹ Ibid., paras 578–579.
¹⁰⁰ Ibid., para 499.
¹⁰¹ *Philip Morris v. Uruguay*, Concurring and dissenting opinion of Mr Gary Born, 8 July 2016, paras 40–72. For commentary, see T Voon, 'Philip Morris v. Uruguay: Implications for Public Health' (2017) 18 *Journal of World Investment and Trade* 321, 330–331.
¹⁰² See e.g., arbitral cases where inconsistency in governmental action led to the finding of an investment treaty breach: *Lauder v. Czech Republic* (UNCITRAL, Final Award, 3 September 2001) paras 290–300, and *MTD Equity Sdn Bhd and MTD Chile SA v. Chile*, Award, 25 May 2004 (ICSID Case No ARB/01/7) (2005) 44 ILM 91, para 113.
¹⁰³ WHO, 'Key Considerations for the Use of Law to Prevent Noncommunicable Diseases in the WHO European Region' (2017) 21, available at
http://www.euro.who.int/__data/assets/pdf_file/0009/333954/Moscow-report.pdf (last accessed 30/09/2020).

To conclude, even though international investment agreements can 'bite' and affect national policy-making, there is an emerging consensus that public health regulations that are evidence-based, carefully (and inclusively) designed, consistently implemented and appropriately targeted are less likely to be contested under investment treaties. If contested, such measures are likely to withstand the challenge, as long as specific representations have not been made to investors encouraging a legitimate expectation that progressive regulation would not apply to them. The burgeoning trends in investment arbitration practice support the view that national regulators can successfully implement childhood obesity prevention measures as long as they ensure that such measures are non-discriminatory, evidence-based, consistent, and compliant with due process. Regulators are also advised to refrain from making specific commitments to the industry, or individual actors, that a legal and regulatory environment would remain unaltered.[104]

8. CONCLUSION

As the importance of childhood obesity prevention is gaining more attention around the globe and giving rise to new regulatory solutions, the interplay between such regulatory measures and international investment law becomes more and more crucial. While the evidence of investment treaties producing a chilling effect on national policies is inconclusive, the recent empirical studies highlight the importance of raising awareness among government officials about international investment law and its implications for States. There is also emerging consensus that although investment treaties may not necessarily act as a decisive factor influencing national policy choices, investors have on occasion sought to stall or reverse the adoption of new public health regulations. One way to militate against detrimental interference by foreign investors in national policy-making is to incorporate stronger, bolder and enforceable provisions on investor duties and responsibilities, as well as sanctions for misconduct, in new and revised international investment agreements. It is also vital to raise awareness among national regulators about how the international investment regime works and what lessons can be drawn from the existing investment arbitration practice to ensure that new health measures are immune to challenges from the affected industry interests. In the absence of specific commitments given to the industry actors, a non-discriminatory, evidence-based, proportionate, and consistently implemented regulatory measures are likely to withstand any challenges by affected investors. Ultimately, the interplay between investment treaties and national health regulators can

---

[104] Ibid.

be optimised by closer coordination and dialogue between various national agencies. National authorities are advised to facilitate such engagement and to encourage the involvement of public health officials in the processes leading to the drafting and negotiation of international investment treaties.

8. International trade and childhood obesity: A Caribbean perspective
Nicole Foster

1. INTRODUCTION

This chapter examines the problem of childhood obesity from a regional perspective using the experience of members of the Caribbean Community (CARICOM).[1] It explores whether CARICOM States' regional and multilateral trade commitments constitute significant legal obstacles to efforts to tackle childhood obesity in the region, and comments on the potential role of international human rights law in accelerating action in this area. The chapter commences with an overview of the extent and underlying causes of childhood obesity within CARICOM. It then analyses CARICOM States' relevant obligations under the World Trade Organization (WTO), the Revised Treaty of Chaguaramas and the CARIFORUM-EU Economic Partnership Agreement and comments on their legal implications, with special reference to selected case law from the WTO. The chapter then briefly highlights two specific initiatives, taxes on sugar sweetened beverages in Barbados and Dominica and regional work on front of package labelling, to illustrate how CARICOM States can pursue meaningful public health interventions without necessarily violating their international trade obligations. The chapter ultimately concludes that, while CARICOM States' international trade obligations undeniably constrain their choice of public health measures and how they implement them, there is still sufficient policy space for CARICOM governments to take meaningful action to prevent and control childhood obesity. The chapter further argues that in fact the main obstacle to real progress has been a lack of political will and it suggests leveraging international human rights and its enforcement mecha-

---

[1] The members of CARICOM are; Antigua and Barbuda, the Bahamas, Barbados, Belize, Dominica, Grenada, Guyana, Haiti, Jamaica, Montserrat, St Lucia, St Kitts and Nevis, St Vincent and the Grenadines, Suriname, Trinidad and Tobago. The associate members are: Anguilla, Bermuda, British Virgin Islands, Cayman Islands and Turks and Caicos.

nisms to push Caribbean governments to act more promptly and decisively, while still respecting their international trade obligations.

2. THE CARIBBEAN COMMUNITY PUBLIC HEALTH AND NUTRITIONAL CONTEXT

There has been an astounding increase in obesity and diet-related non-communicable disease (NCD) rates in the Caribbean over the last five decades. The Caribbean Public Health Agency (CARPHA) reports that more than 60 per cent of Caribbean adults are overweight or obese with prevalence rates exceeding 80 per cent in some territories.[2] CARPHA further reports that one-quarter of all Caribbean women are obese, a figure which is double the obesity rate for men, and that average waist circumference is above the healthy limit among women in all CARICOM member States[3] Not surprisingly, the region also has high rates of complications from diabetes with diabetes-related lower extremity amputations in Barbados being among the highest globally.[4]

In recent decades there has also been a particularly rapid rise in the rates of overweight and obesity in Caribbean children with between 7–12 per cent of preschool-aged children in the region estimated to be overweight or obese, and up to 14 per cent of adolescents in some CARICOM member States being obese.[5] The 2011 WHO Global School Health Survey for Barbados reported that of the 26 schools surveyed, 65.3 per cent of the student body had a sedentary lifestyle after school hours; 31.5 per cent was overweight, 14.4 per cent was obese and 70 per cent of the student body engaged in low levels of physical activity.[6] This picture is particularly alarming considering that overweight adolescents have a higher risk of becoming overweight adults and accordingly have a high risk of developing a NCD in their lifetime.

The main impact of the prevalence of obesity and NCDs in the Caribbean is seen in the region's rates of NCD-related mortality, which are the highest in the Americas. Available regional data shows that with the exception of Haiti, NCDs cause between 65 and over 80 per cent of all deaths, between 62 and

---

[2] CARPHA, 'Promoting Healthy Diets, Food Security and Sustainable Development in the Caribbean through Joint Policy Action' (CARICOM Technical Brief prepared for COTED 9–13 November 2015) (CARPHA Technical Brief) 1.
[3] Ibid., 1.
[4] A Hennis et al., 'Explanations for the High Risk of Diabetes Related Amputation in a Caribbean Population of Black African Descent and Potential for Prevention' (2004) 27 *Diabetes Care* 2636.
[5] CARPHA Technical Brief, n2, 1.
[6] WHO, 'Global School-Based Health Survey 2011'(ID Number BRB_2011_ GSHS_ v01_M, 12, December 2013) www.who.int/chp/gshs/2011_Barbados_GSHS _FS.pdf.

over 80 per cent of premature adult deaths (30 to < 70 years) (i.e., among the most productive population group) and that cardiovascular disease and diabetes cause the majority of premature deaths from NCDs, followed by cancers.[7] The Healthy Caribbean Coalition (HCC) has reported that rates of death from NCDs in men in CARICOM countries (excluding Haiti and Trinidad and Tobago) were lowest in Jamaica (498 per 100,000 per year) and highest in Grenada (722 per 100,000) and Guyana (735 per 100,000).[8] By comparison, NCD-related mortality in the USA is lower for both men (458 per 100,000) and women (325 per 100,000) than in all CARICOM member States; and the same is true for Canada (387 per 100,000 in men and 265 per 100,000 in women).[9]

The high incidence of NCDs within the Caribbean region carries with it high (direct and indirect) economic costs. This economic impact is not limited to the national level, but is also felt at the individual/household level and poses a significant threat to the region's attainment of the Sustainable Development Goals. Globally, UNDP estimates that cumulative economic losses from the four principal NCDs in low- and middle-income countries will surpass US$7 trillion from 2011–2025.[10] In Jamaica, the 2001 estimated cost (direct and indirect) for diabetes and hypertension alone was US$460, 442, 870 or 5.8 per cent of GPD.[11] One UNDP study found that Barbados was losing Bds$145 million/US$72.5 million annually, approximately 2.6 per cent of projected GDP in 2015, as a result of missed work days, low productivity, reduced workforce participation and the cost of replacing workers from cardiovascular disease and diabetes.[12] More recently, at a side event held on the margins of the 2017 United Nations General Assembly, Barbados' Foreign Minister Maxine McClean reported that 60 per cent of national health expenditure is currently NCDs related which approximates to 5–6 per cent of Barbados' GDP.[13] In

---

[7] Port of Spain Declaration Evaluation Research Group, 'Accelerating Action on NCDs' (Evaluation of the 2007 CARICOM Heads of Government Port of Spain NCD Summit Declaration, Report on behalf of PAHO/WHO and CARICOM, September 2016) (Port of Spain Evaluation Report) 22.

[8] Healthy Caribbean Coalition, 'Responses to NCDs in the Caribbean Community', A Civil Society Regional Status Report, March 2014, 10.

[9] Ibid.

[10] UNDP, 'Addressing the Social Determinants of Non-Communicable Diseases' (UNDP, October 2013) 13.

[11] Jamaica Ministry of Health, 'National Strategic and Action Plan for the Prevention and Control of Non-Communicable Diseases in Jamaica 2013–2018' (Ministry of Health 2013) 5.

[12] Ministry of Health Barbados, WHO and UNDP, 'Investment Case for NCD Prevention and Control in Barbados' (WHO 2017)) iv.

[13] The side event was held on 22 September 2017 on the theme 'Childhood Obesity – A Development Time-bomb: Learning from SIDS to Accelerate Multi-sectoral Action in Support of the 2025 NCDs Targets and the SDGs'. The full text of Minister

Trinidad and Tobago, the economic burden from diabetes, hypertension and cancer is estimated to be TT$8.7 billion/US$1.3 billion annually, approximately 5 per cent of GDP.[14] In addition, health care costs and productivity losses are TT$3.5 billion/US$518.9 million for diabetes and TT$3.3 billion/US$489.2 million for hypertension.[15]

Of the four principal modifiable NCD risk factors identified by the WHO, the region's NCD epidemic has been driven primarily by poor diet and lack of physical activity.[16] This is consistent with the region's nutrition transition over the past 30 years which has been characterized by decreased consumption of indigenous staples, local fruits and vegetables and increased consumption of processed foods and beverages, added sugars, fats/oils, sodium, and animal-source foods.[17] The Food and Agriculture Organization (FAO) estimates that, with the exception of Haiti, CARICOM countries exceed the recommended population food energy guidelines or Recommended Population Food Goals (RPFGs) for their entire population.[18] The FAO also estimates that total CARICOM food energy availability is about 19 per cent above RPFG with the availability of protein, fats/oils and sugars/sweeteners at 35 per cent, 29 per cent, and 168 per cent above RPFGs respectively.[19]

This picture is further complicated by the fact that, with the exception of Guyana and Belize, CARICOM countries are net food importers. Almost all CARICOM countries import more than 60 per cent of their food and for half of them that figure is a staggering 80 per cent.[20] Additionally, econometric analysis of Caribbean food import demand has shown that it is price, that is, increased prices do not result in an equivalent decrease in the quantity of imported food demanded, particularly in the case of items such as oils and stales.[21] In 1995 the region's average food import dependence ratio was 0.54 and this increased to

---

McClean's statement is available at www.healthycaribbean.org/wp-content/uploads/2017/09/Statement-by-Minister-McClean-on-behalf-of-PM-Stuart-NCDs-Side-Event.pdf (last visited 1 October 2017).

[14] Trinidad and Tobago Ministry of Health, 'National Strategic Plan for the Prevention and Control of Non Communicable Diseases: Trinidad and Tobago 2017–2021' (Ministry of Health 2017) 14.

[15] Ibid.

[16] The other risk factors are tobacco use and harmful use of alcohol.

[17] CARPHA Technical Brief, n2, 3.

[18] FAO, 'State of Food Insecurity in the CARICOM Caribbean - Meeting the 2015 Hunger Targets: Taking Stock of Uneven Progress' (Sub-regional Office for the Caribbean, 2015) (FAO Food Insecurity Report) 5.

[19] Ibid.

[20] Ibid., 5.

[21] Ibid., 11.

0.71 by 2011.[22] The region's increasing dependence on imported food is also reflected in CARICOM's average food import quantity index which increased by 9 per cent in 2012 compared to the 2004–06 base-year, whereas food import unit value, and the value of food imports, increased by 57 per cent and 69 per cent respectively, during the same period.[23] Based on 2011 data, the top five food imports were: (i) processed foods; (ii) wheat; (iii) rice; (iv) meat (beef, chicken, mutton, pork); and (v) maize.[24] Of these, food items high in calories, sugars and sodium accounted for US$756 million annually (18 per cent of total food imports) and food items high in fats/oils accounted for US$516 million annually (12 per cent of total food imports) and staple food items accounted for US$480 million annually (11 per cent of total food imports) with Jamaica, Trinidad and Tobago, Haiti, the Bahamas and Barbados being the top food importers.[25] While globalization and the liberalization of international trade undoubtedly have contributed to making these imports more readily available within CARICOM, the region's current high reliance on imported food is also a consequence of a decline in the relative contribution of the primary sector to GDP and an associated increase in the contributions of the secondary and tertiary sectors.[26] The decrease in agriculture's contribution to real GDP between 1990–2013 within the region ranges from -2.5 per cent in Jamaica to -78.9 per cent for Saint Lucia.[27]

This daunting outlook appears even bleaker when one considers that the majority of CARICOM countries are small island developing States, whose vulnerability to natural and economic shocks often undermines efforts to improve regional food and nutrition security, thus compounding their reliance on food imports. The FAO reports that between 1990–2014, 182 major natural disasters occurred in the region causing US$16.6 billion in damage. Most recently on 18 September 2017 Hurricane Maria, one of the strongest Atlantic storms in history, ravaged the island of Dominica. While there is still no official estimate of the damage sustained, Prime Minister Roosevelt Skerrit indicated that the island had been totally devastated and the once lush, green 'Nature Isle' was reportedly stripped bare of its forestry and vegetation.[28]

---

[22] Ibid., 10.
[23] Ibid.
[24] Ibid., 9.
[25] Ibid., 11.
[26] Ibid., 7.
[27] Ibid.
[28] J Sharman, 'Hurricane Maria: Dominica loses 'all what money can buy' as Category 5 storm batters Caribbean Island', *The Independent*, 19 September 2017.

2.1 The Port of Spain Declaration 2007

The CARICOM Heads of Government Summit on NCDs in 2007 (the Port of Spain Summit) marked a turning point in the region's awareness of and response to its burgeoning NCDs crisis. The Port of Spain Summit was also the first meeting of its kind globally and as such set the stage for later global meetings such as the 2011 United Nations High Level Meeting on NCDs. The Port of Spain Declaration, 'Uniting to Stop the Epidemic of Chronic Non-Communicable Diseases' issued at the conclusion of the Summit called for a 'whole of society' approach to tackling NCDs. It addressed both NCD prevention and control and contained 15 actionable mandates and 27 commitments; 16 of these commitments were later reflected in the political declaration emanating from the 2011 United Nations High Level Meeting and included:

- The promotion of programmes for healthy school meals and healthy eating in education sectors;
- The elimination of trans-fats from diets of Caribbean citizens;
- The pursuit of trade policies allowing for greater use of indigenous agricultural products and foods; and
- The mandatory labelling of foods (or other measures to indicate food nutritional content).

Building on the Port of Spain Declaration mandate, in September 2014 the CARICOM Council for Human and Social Development endorsed CARPHA's Plan of Action for Promoting Healthy Weights in the Caribbean: Prevention and Control of Childhood Obesity 2014–2019.[29] This document focuses on prevention and control of overweight and obesity in persons from birth to 25 years, but is expected to have broader positive spin off effects within the general population. Its objectives are to:

- Make the environments where Caribbean children live and learn more supportive of physical activity and healthy eating.
- Create incentives to discourage unhealthy consumption patterns and to encourage healthier dietary choices.
- Empower communities to embrace active living and healthy eating. Provide parents and children with accurate information about food, nutrition and exercise to enable informed decisions.

---

[29] CARPHA, 'Plan of Action for Promoting Healthy Weights in the Caribbean: Prevention and Control of Childhood Obesity 2014 – 2019' (CARPHA Plan of Action) 5 http://carpha.org/publications (last visited 1 October 2017).

- Provide children and families who are affected by overweight/obesity with the necessary care and support.
- Safeguard children who may be affected by overweight/obesity from the associated bias, stigmatization and bullying.
- Improve the capability of systems within the government, private and civil society sectors to mount effective and coordinated responses.
- Foster multi-sectoral cooperation in responding to the epidemic realizing the pre-dominant, defining and upstream nature of issues related to international trade.
- Provide core data for tracking the movement and determinants of the epidemic.
- Provide information for measuring and assessing results of the Plan of Action.[30]

CARPHA also singled out the following policies for priority action as part of a six-point core policy package: mandatory nutritional labelling of foods; regulation of the school feeding environment; reduction of marketing of unhealthy food to children; product reformulation to reduce fat, salt and sugar levels; fiscal and trade measures; and promotion of fruit and vegetable consumption.

Initially CARPHA's strong leadership on the issue of childhood obesity also seemed to be reflected at the highest political level with CARICOM Heads of Government at their July 2016 meeting pledging 'to address issues such as … banning advertisement of potentially harmful foods which specifically target children; and elevating taxes on foods high in sugar, salt and trans-fats'.[31] However, Heads of Government have repeatedly failed to act upon their promises. At their meeting in July 2017, the tenth anniversary of the Port of Spain Declaration, CARICOM Heads of Government again failed to commit to concrete, time-bound, appropriately financed action in critical areas such as childhood obesity.[32] In response, HCC accurately commented that:

> While the Communiqué acknowledged insufficient action since 2007, one would have expected in response pledges to accelerate action through specific policy

---

[30] Ibid., viii–x.
[31] The communiqué issued at the conclusion of the 37th CARICOM Heads of Government Meeting (7 July 2016) can be found at: http://caricom.org/media-center/communications/communiques/communique-issued-at-the-conclusion-of-the-thirty-seventh-regular-meeting-of-the-conference-of-heads-of-government-of-the-caribbean-community-caricom-4-6-july-2016-georgetown-guyana (last visited 1 October 2017).
[32] The communiqué issued at the conclusion of the 38th CARICOM Heads of Government Meeting (7 July 2017) can be found at: http://caricom.org/media-center/communications/communiques/communique-thirty-eighth-caricom-heads-of-government-meeting (last visited 1 October 2017).

implementation. This was not forthcoming. Heads simply 'noted' the urgent crisis of childhood obesity in the region.... Solutions were limited to the promotion of healthy food consumption and increased physical activity. No mention was made in the official communiqué of fiscal policies to make the healthier choice the affordable choice.... In arguably the strongest statement of the NCD section in the Communiqué, Heads 'urge[d] acceleration of the Public Education Programme on Healthy lifestyles'; which, in the absence of policy recommendations, lays the responsibility for the NCD epidemic and the exponential rises in NCD risk factors, solely at the feet of individual Caribbean citizens – essentially relieving States of their responsibility to create healthy, supportive environments.[33]

In sum, despite its promising beginning in 2007, the region's record on combating NCDs and by extension childhood obesity has been mixed and generally disappointing. In fact, a 2016 evaluation of implementation of the Port of Spain Declaration found that indicators concerning diet, schools and communications had the lowest levels of implementation in the region.[34]

CARICOM States' poor implementation record to date raises questions about whether this inaction is simply the result of lack of political will or whether there might be external factors at play. One such external factor that can have a potentially significant impact on governments' ability to act in the area of childhood obesity prevention and control is the regime of international trade rules to which CARICOM States are subject. It is therefore worth exploring whether CARICOM States' international trade commitments have unduly constrained their governments' ability to take meaningful action to prevent and control childhood obesity.

3. INTERNATIONAL TRADE AND CHILDHOOD OBESITY WITHIN THE CARIBBEAN COMMUNITY

The international trade regime is based on the following core rules; the Most Favoured Nation (MFN) treatment and national treatment obligations, a prohibition on the use of quantitative restrictions and binding limits on duties on imports. These rules can be found in the General Agreement on Tariffs and Trade 1994 and form the foundation of the more specialised rules within the WTO regime as well as within regional and extra-regional arrangements.[35]

---

[33] HCC, 'Caricom Leaders Fall Short of 2007 Predecessors' (Statement on CARICOM Heads of Government 7 July 2017 Communique, 21 July 2017) https://www.healthycaribbean.org/caricom-leaders-fall-short-of-2007-predecessors/ (last visited 1 October 2017).

[34] Port of Spain Evaluation Report, n7, 28.

[35] General Agreement on Tariffs and Trade 1994 (adopted 15 April 1994, entered into force 1 January 1995) 1867 UNTS 187 (GATT).

The next sub-section will look more closely at the operation of these rules first within the WTO regime, then within the CARIFORUM-EU Economic Partnership Agreement and finally within the Revised Treaty of Chaguaramas in order to explore their possible legal implications for CARICOM States' efforts to prevent and control childhood obesity.

3.1   World Trade Organization Agreements and Trade in Unhealthy Foods

The MFN obligation found in GATT Article I essentially prohibits a WTO member from giving more favourable treatment to one or more WTO members to the exclusion of other WTO members in respect of traded goods.[36] Similarly, the national treatment obligation under GATT Article III prohibits WTO members from giving more favourable treatment to domestically produced goods over imported goods. These two obligations together give expression to the principle of non-discrimination. It must be noted, however, that these obligations are only applicable if the goods in question are 'like' products. Since there is no definition of 'like products' within the GATT, over time GATT/WTO panels and the WTO Appellate Body have developed criteria for determining likeness. In the goods sector, likeness has been determined based on the criteria set out in the GATT *Report of the Working Party on Border Tax Adjustments*, namely, physical characteristics, end uses, tariff classification and consumer tastes and habits.[37] These criteria have been applied fairly consistently over the decades, but the WTO Appellate Body has been careful to stress that determinations of likeness are to be made on an individual, case-by-case basis.[38] Accordingly, the list of factors that can be considered in assessing likeness is not a closed one.[39] Importantly from a public health

---

[36]   All CARICOM Member States, with the exception of the Bahamas, are members of the WTO. Bahamas is currently negotiating its accession to the WTO.
[37]   GATT, *Working Party Report on Border Tax Adjustments* (adopted 20 November 1970) L/3464.
[38]   In *Japan - Taxes on Alcoholic Beverages* the Appellate Body noted:
   In applying the criteria cited in *Border Tax Adjustments* to the facts of any particular case, and in considering other criteria that may also be relevant in certain cases, panels can only apply their best judgement in determining whether in fact products are 'like'. This will always involve an unavoidable element of individual, discretionary judgement.
WTO, *Japan - Taxes on Alcoholic Beverages* (4 October 1996) WT/DS8/AB/R [20].
[39]   The WTO Appellate Body has indicated that:
   These general criteria, or groupings of potentially shared characteristics, provide a framework for analyzing the 'likeness' of particular products on a case-by-case basis. These criteria are, it is well to bear in mind, simply tools to assist in

perspective, in *EC – Asbestos*, the WTO Appellate Body rejected Canada's argument that a product's health risks are irrelevant in determining likeness.[40]

The prohibition on quantitative restrictions such as bans or quotas is set out in GATT 1994 Article XI. The scope of the provision is quite broad and covers import or export prohibitions or restrictions of any kind other than duties, taxes or other charges. In *Canada – Certain Measures Concerning Periodicals*, Canada was found to have violated Article XI by imposing a complete ban on importation of certain magazines.[41] Other examples of quantitative restrictions include India's requirement that automotive manufacturers balance out certain imports with exports of equal value and the US' prohibition on the use of US Department of Agriculture and the Food Safety Inspection Service funds from being used to allow imports of Chinese poultry products.[42]

Article II GATT 1994 imposes a legally binding obligation on WTO members not to apply a higher rate of duty to imported goods than the multilaterally negotiated and agreed rate of duty (the bound tariff). In this way, Article II allows for a secure and predictable basis on which international trade can be conducted. The various bound tariffs are recorded in each WTO member's Schedule of Concessions and form an integral part of the Marrakesh Agreement Establishing the World Trade Organisation 1994.[43]

The Agreement on Technical Barriers to Trade is a specialised WTO agreement that is also particularly relevant to efforts to regulate trade in unhealthy foods.[44] Under this agreement WTO members are required to ensure that technical regulations, such as food labelling requirements, are non-discriminatory and do not create unnecessary obstacles to trade. WTO members are also encouraged to base their technical regulations on internationally agreed standards and to provide adequate notice of regulatory changes.

---

the task of sorting and examining the relevant evidence. They are neither a treaty-mandated nor a closed list of criteria that will determine the legal characterization of products.

WTO, *European Communities – Measures Affecting Asbestos and Asbestos-Containing Products* (12 March 2001) WT/DS135/AB/R [102] (*EC – Asbestos*).

[40] Ibid., [113].
[41] WTO, *Canada – Certain Measures Concerning Periodicals* (30 June 1997) WT/DS31/AB/R.
[42] WTO, *India – Measures Affecting the Automotive Sector* (12 March 2002) WT/DS146/AB/R; *United States – Certain Measures Affecting Imports of Poultry from China* (29 September 2010) WT/DS392/R.
[43] Marrakesh Agreement Establishing the World Trade Organization (adopted 15 April 1994, entered into force 1 January 1995) 1867 UNTS 154.
[44] Agreement on Technical Barriers to Trade, Marrakesh Agreement Establishing the World Trade Organization, Annex 1A (concluded 15 April 1994, entered into force 1 January 1995) UNTS 1868 120 (TBT Agreement).

The above rules all combine to create a strong network protecting exporters from unnecessary and arbitrary barriers to trade and ensuring the free flow of goods across and within WTO members' borders. Measures to address childhood obesity can implicate these rules in so far as they involve the imposition of higher duties and/or taxes on unhealthy foods, the banning of unhealthy foods or introduction of food labelling schemes which can all negatively impact the free flow of trade in the products in question. However, there are a number of flexibilities built into the GATT which mean that their legal implications are not as daunting as it might first appear.

The first flexibility that WTO members can exploit in seeking to address the problem of childhood obesity is that related to the interpretation of likeness under GATT 1994. Since the MFN and national treatment obligations only apply in respect of 'like' goods, once WTO members are able to substantiate distinctions between healthy and unhealthy foods based on their respective health risks, any less favourable treatment that is afforded to unhealthy foods would not violate the WTO member's MFN or national treatment obligations. This proposition is supported by cases such as *EC – Asbestos* discussed above.[45]

Besides the flexibility that comes from how likeness is determined, there are additional flexibilities built into the GATT that CARICOM States can and should exploit to help control and prevent childhood obesity. Thus, WTO members are free to raise import duties up to their bound tariff levels if they are currently applying a lower rate of duty and the increase is done in a non-discriminatory manner. Accordingly, to the extent that they are not currently applying their maximum allowable levels of import duty on products high in salt, fat and/or sugar, CARICOM States could implement increases in import duties targeting these products. This type of action has already been taken by other WTO members such as Fiji which, in response to health concerns from its Ministry of Health, increased import duties on palm oil and monosodium glutamate to their maximum level of 32 per cent.[46] This product-differentiation approach could also be applied to internal taxes such as sales taxes and value added tax (VAT) on domestic and imported products within a given market, provided it is implemented in a non-discriminatory manner. For example, Barbados currently has a number of goods that are exempt from VAT and the National Social Responsibility Levy based, among other things, on their nutrient profile.[47] The reverse is also permissible, that is,

---

[45] *EC – Asbestos*, n39.
[46] W Snowden and A Thow, 'Trade Policy and Obesity Prevention: Challenges and Innovation in the Pacific Islands' (2013) 14 (Suppl. 2) *Obesity Reviews* 150, 154.
[47] Barbados Revenue Authority Policy Note PPG No. 003/2017 National Social Responsibility Levy (the Levy or NSRL) Budgetary Proposals 2017 advises that '17.

imposition of a higher tax based on the poor nutrient profile of a given product as has been the case with taxes on sugar sweetened beverages (SSBs). It is also worth noting here that while WTO members cannot impose a duty higher than their bound tariff on any given good, they retain full freedom to reduce or even completely remove duties for any imported product. Thus, Snowden and Thow report that in its 2012 and 2013 budgets, Fiji significantly lowered the import duty on fruits and vegetables in order to encourage increased consumption of these products.[48]

The Cook Islands 2013 budget introduced a new, increased tariff on SSBs. The budget statement of the minister for finance emphasized the scale of obesity in the country and the sugar content of SSBs (52). The import tariff was initially increased by 15 per cent, with a subsequent per annum increase of 2 per cent to maintain 'the real value of the levy' (52).

The general exceptions clause under GATT Article XX provides yet another level of flexibility. Specifically, pursuant to Article XX(b), a WTO Member can maintain a measure that violates GATT 1994 provided this measure is necessary to protect human health and does not constitute arbitrary or unjustifiable discrimination between countries where the same conditions prevail or a disguised restriction on international trade. In this regard, the WTO Appellate Body has consistently stressed that it is for individual WTO members to determine their desired level of health protection and health has also been acknowledged as one of the most important human interests.[49] Having said that, Article XX is by no means a blank cheque for all public health measures and in fact there is a fairly rigorous standard that must be met in order to fall within the paragraph's protection as is illustrated below.

The first step in meeting the requirements of GATT Article XX(b) is for the WTO member in question to prove that the particular measure they have implemented is necessary to protect human health, with the standard of necessity being the principal hurdle they will have to overcome. Initially GATT dispute settlement panels interpreted the term necessary very restrictively resulting in it being an almost impossible standard to meet. Thus in *Thailand*

No Levy is payable on the food items listed in paragraph 20 of the First Schedule of the Value Added Tax Act, Cap. 87. The last approved list of zero rated food items is attached.' http://gisbarbados.gov.bb/download/notice-social-responsibility-levy/ (last visited 5 February 2017). The zero- rated items referred to in this Policy Note are items which are considered essential based on, inter alia, health considerations and include items such as fresh fruits and vegetables including imported products such as strawberries and blueberries.

[48] Snowden and Thow, n46, 154.
[49] *EC – Asbestos*, n39, 168; WTO, *Brazil – Measures Affecting Imports of Retreaded Tyres* (12 June 2007) WT/DS332/R [7.108].

– *Restrictions on Importation of and Internal Taxes on Cigarettes*, the panel indicated that Thailand's measures could only be considered to be necessary within the meaning of Article XX(b) if 'there were no alternative measures consistent with the General Agreement, or less inconsistent with it, which Thailand could reasonably be expected to employ to achieve its health policy objectives'.[50] However, more recently, the WTO Appellate Body has adopted a much more nuanced interpretation of necessity, one which emphasises the need for alternatives to be reasonably available and to secure the level of protection desired by the respondent State, while weighing and balancing the importance of the interests or values at stake.[51] The Appellate Body has further clarified in *United States – Measures Affecting the Cross Border Supply of Gambling and Betting Services* that a measure cannot be said to be reasonably available if it is financially or technically beyond the capacity of the particular State to undertake.[52]

Once a WTO member has been able to prove that their measure is necessary for human health, they must then demonstrate that the measure has not been applied in a manner that amounts to arbitrary or unjustifiable discrimination between countries where the same conditions prevail or a disguised restriction on international trade. The two concepts of arbitrary or unjustifiable discrimination and disguised restriction on international trade are related and give meaning to each other with many of the same considerations being applicable to both. Discrimination here is analysed from a different perspective to when discrimination is established under the substantive GATT provision. Here one is trying to ascertain whether there is a causal connection between the discrimination and the particular Article XX objective that is being pursued.[53] Some of the features of the application of measures that have been found to involve arbitrary or unjustifiable discrimination or to amount to a disguised restriction on international trade include: imposition of rigid, inflexible requirements which involve a decision-making process that does not afford countries due process;[54] and the exemption of regional partners or domestic service suppliers from bans on given goods or services.[55]

---

[50] GATT, *Thailand – Restrictions on Importation of and Internal Taxes on Cigarettes* (7 November 1990) [75].

[51] *EC – Asbestos*, n39, [172].

[52] WTO, *United States – Measures Affecting the Cross Border Supply of Gambling and Betting Services* (7 April 2005) WT/DS285/AB/R [308] (*US – Gambling*).

[53] WTO, *Brazil – Measures Affecting Imports of Retreaded Tyres* (3 December 2007) WT/DS332/AB/R [227] (*Brazil – Retreaded Tyres*).

[54] WTO, *United States – Importation Prohibition of Certain Shrimp and Shrimp Products* (12 October 1998) WT/DS58/AB/R.

[55] *Brazil – Retreaded Tyres*, n53, and *US – Gambling*, n52.

Besides GATT Article XX, the TBT Agreement also incorporates useful flexibility that States can use to address public health concerns such as childhood obesity. Specifically, Article 2.2 provides that technical regulations are not to be 'more trade-restrictive than necessary to fulfil a legitimate objective taking account of the risks non-fulfilment would create' and then goes on to explicitly recognise protection of human health or safety as one such legitimate objective.[56] There is an important connection between the TBT Agreement 2.2 and GATT Article XX and WTO disputes involving Article 2.2 have drawn heavily on the pre-existing Article XX jurisprudence especially regarding interpretation of the necessity standard.[57] Thus in *United States – Certain Country of Origin Labelling (COOL) Requirements (Recourse to Article 21.5 of the DSU by Canada and Mexico)* the WTO Appellate Body explained that a measure's contribution to the legitimate objective, the trade restrictiveness of the measure and the nature of risks at issue as well as the seriousness of the consequences from non-fulfilment and whether it was reasonably available were all relevant in making determinations under Article 2.2.[58] In *United States – Measures Concerning the Importation, Marketing and Sale of Tuna and Tuna Products*, the WTO Appellate Body found that the US' 'dolphin-safe' labelling provisions were not more trade-restrictive than necessary since the alternative proposed by Mexico would not make a contribution to the US' legitimate objective that was equivalent to that of the challenged measure.[59] They also found that if a proposed alternative would involve greater 'risks of non-fulfilment' it could not be considered a valid alternative, even if it were less trade-restrictive.[60] In *US – COOL (Art.21.5)*), the Appellate Body also clarified that a measure does not have to meet the particular objective completely or to exceed some minimum level of fulfilment in order to satisfy Article 2.2 and ultimately described the process of determining whether a measure is more

---

[56] WTO, *European Communities – Trade Description of Sardines* (29 March 2002) WT/DS231/R [7.120].

[57] The panel in *United States – Measures Affecting the Production and Sale of Clove Cigarettes* did however caution against a wholesale adoption of Art XX(b) jurisprudence in respect of Art 2.2: *United States – Measures Affecting the Production and Sale of Clove Cigarettes* (4 April 2012) WT/DS406/AB/R [46] (*US – Clove Cigarettes*).

[58] WTO, *United States — Certain Country of Origin Labelling (COOL) Requirements (Recourse to Article 21.5 of the DSU by Canada and Mexico)* (18 May 2015) WT/DS384/AB/RW (*US – COOL (Art.21.5)*) [5.197].

[59] WTO, *United States – Measures Concerning the Importation, Marketing and Sale of Tuna and Tuna Products* (16 May 2012) WT/DS381/AB/R (*US – Tuna II*). The same approach was adopted by the Appellate Body in *US – Clove Cigarettes*, n57.

[60] *US – Tuna II*, n59, [46].

trade restrictive than necessary under Article 2.2 as involving 'the holistic weighing and balancing of the factors as set out above'.[61]

Recently there has been some discussion within the academic community whether, in drafting exception clauses in trade and investment agreements, it is desirable to replace the word 'necessary' with less exacting wording such as 'relating to'.[62] Whatever merit there may be to this argument, it is nonetheless true that there is no likelihood of the GATT Article XX being amended in this manner in the foreseeable future (if at all). Accordingly, WTO members have to be prepared to engage with the existing Article XX and Article 2.2 language as they currently stand and exploit the existing flexibility. In addition, it is submitted that the existing language in Article XX and Article 2.2 function as important safeguards against abuse – the ultimate goal here is to strike an appropriate balance between trade and non-trade concerns such as health, not to tip the scales so far in favour of the non-trade concerns that the integrity of the trade system itself is compromised. Moreover, and most importantly, it is not at all clear that the current language of either Article XX or Article 2.2. has seriously constrained WTO members who wish to pursue bona fide public policy goals such as protection of health. Indeed, cases such as *EC – Asbestos*; *Brazil – Retreaded Tyres*; *US – COOL Art 21.5*; *US – Tuna II*; and *US – Clove Cigarettes* discussed above seem to suggest otherwise. In all of these cases the public policy concerns in question were either vindicated or, if the challenged measure was struck down, this was done because the challenged measure was implemented in a discriminatory manner (which in turn raises questions as to whether it was a bona fide public policy measure). As Messenger notes earlier in this publication, when clarification has been required, on matters of public policy concern, the WTO has responded to accommodate legitimate non-discriminatory measures.

The message that members have the policy space in which to regulate to protect public health sent by the Appellate Body permeates the system, signalling to members where they hold defensible positions or where their policies might require reconsideration.[63]

A clear illustration of this interplay within the WTO between genuine non-trade measures (which the GATT/WTO system allows) and discriminatory measures (which the GATT/WTO system does not allow) is provided by the *United States - Import Prohibition of Certain Shrimp and Shrimp Products*

---

[61] *US – Cool (Art. 21.5)*, n58, [5.198]
[62] See, e.g., S Lester and B Mercurio, 'Safeguarding Policy Space in Investment Agreements' IIEL Issue Brief 12/2017, 10, http://iielaw.org/wp-content/uploads/2015/08/Simon-Lester-and-Bryan-Mercurio-General-Exceptions-in-IIAs-IIEL-Issue-Brief-December-2017.pdf (last visited 14 February 2017).
[63] See Messenger in this volume.

(Recourse to Article 21.5 of the DSU by Malaysia) WTO Appellate Body decision.[64] The public policy goal at issue in this dispute was an environmental one, protection of sea turtles. The US initially went about pursuing this environmental goal by banning all shrimp not harvested with turtle excluder devices. Malaysia was able to successfully challenge this measure as involving arbitrary or unjustifiable discrimination, inter alia, because the US had imposed a rigid, inflexible standard that made no allowance for alternative methods of meeting the desired level of protection. Following the ruling, the US amended its requirements to remove the specific turtle excluder device element while still requiring States to demonstrate that their shrimp had been harvested in a sea turtle friendly manner. Malaysia objected to still being required to protect sea turtles in order to gain market access to the US and initiated compliance proceedings alleging that the US had failed to comply with the original ruling. The WTO Appellate Body rejected Malaysia's argument indicating that '[a]s we see it, the Panel correctly reasoned and concluded that conditioning market access on the adoption of a programme comparable in effectiveness, allows for sufficient flexibility in the application of the measure so as to avoid "arbitrary or unjustifiable discrimination"…'.[65] Ultimately, the environmental policy goals won the day once they were pursued in an appropriate, non-discriminatory manner. The same would arguably be true in the case of health measures.

In sum, although they incorporate high standards, the GATT 1994 and the TBT Agreement contain a number of useful flexibilities that allow States, including those in CARICOM, sufficient policy space to address their legitimate public health objectives, including regulating trade in unhealthy foods, without violating their WTO obligations.

3.1 CARIFORUM – European Union Economic Partnership Agreement Provisions and Trade in Unhealthy Foods

The 2008 CARIFORUM – European Union Economic Partnership Agreement (EPA) transformed these States' traditional trading relationship from one based on preferential trading arrangements to one based on non-preferential WTO-compatible arrangements.[66] The EPA's regime for trade in goods

---

[64] WTO, *United States - Import Prohibition of Certain Shrimp and Shrimp Products (Recourse to Article 21.5 of the DSU by Malaysia)* (22 October 2001) WT/DS58/AB/RW.

[65] Ibid., [144].

[66] Economic Partnership Agreement between the CARIFOUM States, of the one part, and the European Community and its Members States, of the other part [2008] OJ L 289/I/8. All Members of CARICOM (except Montserrat) and the Dominican Republic are parties to the EPA. The EPA has been applied provisionally since 29

includes rules on liberalisation of customs duties; disciplines on non-tariff measures, provisions on quantitative restrictions and on internal taxation and regulation; and provisions on technical barriers to trade. Since many of these provisions mirror or simply reaffirm the corresponding WTO provisions, the extra impact of the EPA on CARICOM States' ability to regulate trade in unhealthy foods will be felt where provisions involve higher levels of commitment than under WTO rules.[67] The liberalisation of import duties is one such area where CARIFORUM States have undertaken higher levels of commitment than is the case in the WTO.

Under the EPA CARIFORUM States committed to provide duty-free access to 86.9 per cent of imports from the EU over a phased 25-year period (i.e., until 2033) with the remaining imports being excluded from liberalisation.[68] These liberalisation commitments are important because they involve the application of lower levels of import duties than those which can be obtained in the WTO, and therefore potentially greater market access within CARICOM markets for EU exports, including exports of unhealthy foods.[69] CARIFORUM States' principal exclusions from liberalisation commitments are in the areas of agricultural and processed agricultural products, chemical, furniture and other industrial products. To the extent that some of the unhealthy foods CARIFORUM States would wish to maintain existing or high tariffs on are included within these exceptions they would be protected from further liberalisation. However, if not, any such product would be subject to gradual liberalisation with duty free access in the particular good being in place by 2033. In reviewing the CARIFORUM list of exclusions, there does not seem to be a clear pattern that would give some indication of the factors that influenced the determinations of what to include in the exclusions list. It seems likely that these decisions were made from a purely business perspective rather than being premised on NCDs/health-related concerns. This contrasts with the experience of countries such as Nauru which, during its negotiations for an

---

December 2008. The EPA joint institutions have met regularly since 2010 with the Joint CARIFORUM-EU Council (Ministers) and the Trade and Development Committee (senior officials) holding their four and seventh meetings respectively in November 2017.

[67] For example, Art 44 of the EPA chapter on technical barriers to trade provides that the parties affirm their commitment to the rights and obligations provided for in the WTO TBT Agreement and Art 46 provides for the application of all of the definitions of the WTO TBT Agreement to the chapter.

[68] EPA Art 16.2.

[69] The EC reports that the main EU imports to the Caribbean are: boats and ships, cars, construction vehicles and engine parts; phone equipment; milk and cream and spirit drinks: http://ec.europa.eu/trade/policy/countries-and-regions/regions/caribbean/ (last visited 14 February 2017).

Economic Partnership Agreement with the EU, and consistent with its efforts to control consumption of sugar sweetened beverages for health reasons, excluded sugary products from its commitment list.[70] It should also be noted here that Article 17 of the EPA gives Antigua and Barbuda, Belize, Dominica, Grenada, Guyana, Haiti, St Kitts and Nevis, St Lucia and St Vincent and the Grenadines the ability to seek adjustment of their bound tariffs but once again this seems to be informed more from an economic perspective bearing on their level of development rather than for health reasons.

Like GATT, the EPA does make provision for general exceptions to its disciplines. Article 224 of the EPA is in fact modelled on GATT Article XX and permits otherwise inconsistent measures once they are, inter alia, 'necessary to protect human, animal or plant life or health' and do not constitute 'an arbitrary or unjustifiable discrimination between countries where like conditions prevail' or a 'disguised restriction on trade'. Based on the similarity of the language in both treaties, it is submitted that the WTO Article XX jurisprudence would be highly persuasive in terms of interpretation of these provisions within the EPA. As with the WTO system, the main challenge will be ensuring that measures are not considered to involve arbitrary or unjustifiable discrimination or to be disguised restrictions on international trade. CARICOM States should therefore think carefully before creating any exceptions to policies and ensure that the criteria for any such exceptions are clearly defined and non-discriminatory. For example, exemptions for CARICOM domestic producers of unhealthy foods, even if limited to small-scale producers or service suppliers, would pose some difficulties in terms of satisfying the general exceptions requirements.

A unique and potentially useful aspect of the EPA is its adoption of sustainable development as one of its key objectives and thus as an integral part of the agreement itself. Chantal Ononaiwu and Henning Grosse Ruse Khan have commented that:

> The CEPA's demand for a comprehensive implementation and application of the sustainable development objective can be of particular relevance for defining the scope of substantive obligations in the CEPA and may support arguments in favour of balancing economic interests with other social or environmental interests in the process of CEPA implementation.[71]

Much will of course turn on the particular interpretation applied in a given case, but it is not inconceivable that the 'sustainable development' argument could be used in support of actions targeted at childhood obesity prevention

---

[70] Snowden and Thow, n 46, 153.
[71] H Ruse-Khan and C Ononaiwu, 'The CARIFORUM-EU Economic Partnership Agreement' in S Lester (et al. eds), *Bilateral and Regional Trade Agreements - Case Studies* vol 2 (2nd edn, CUP 2016) 137.

and control. However, the actual interpretation to be given to these various provisions still remains to be seen as to date there have not been any disputes under the EPA regime.

3.2 Revised Treaty of Chaguaramas and Trade in Unhealthy Foods

Trade and trade relations, internal and external, lie at the heart of CARICOM. CARICOM is governed by the Revised Treaty of Chaguaramas Establishing the Caribbean Community (RTC) including the CARICOM Single Market and Economy 2001 and its stated objectives include 'expansion of trade and economic relations with third States', 'enhanced levels of international competitiveness' and 'the achievement of a greater measure of economic leverage and effectiveness of Member States in dealing with third States, groups of States and entities of any description'.[72] The central aim of the RTC is the creation of a fully integrated internal market within CARICOM.[73] Article 79 of the RTC makes provision for the establishment and maintenance of a regime for the free movement of goods and services and enjoins members to refrain from trade policies and practices which nullify or impair the benefits conferred by the RTC.[74] All CARICOM members, except the Bahamas and Montserrat, are parties to the RTC. As a customs union, CARICOM States also operate a Common External Tariff, that is, all CARICOM States apply the same level of import duty to extra-regionally produced goods (which level would be higher than that for the same product if produced within the region).

As with the EPA, the RTC is built on the WTO foundation and thus mirrors much of the provisions of the WTO agreements, particularly the GATT, albeit now expressed in the specific context of CARICOM member States. Thus the RTC Article 91 prohibits the imposition of quantitative restrictions on the importation of goods of Community origin. Similarly the RTC Article 87 provides that goods of Community origin are to be imported free of duty within the Community and Article 90 provides for national treatment for goods of Community origin and like domestic goods in relation to fiscal charges (i.e., internal taxes and other internal charges of equivalent effect). The RTC

---

[72] Revised Treaty of Chaguaramas Establishing the Caribbean Community including the CARICOM Single Market and Economy 2001 (adopted 7 May 2001, entered into force 4 February 2002) 2259 UNTS 293 Art 6 (RTC).
[73] Ibid., Art 78(2)(a).
[74] Ibid., Art 79(2).

also contains a general exception clause that largely mirrors the provisions of GATT 1994 Article XX. Thus RTC Article 226 provides that:

> Nothing in this Chapter shall be construed as preventing the adoption or enforcement by any Member State of measures ...
> (b) to protect human, animal or plant life or health;

But this applies only if such measures do not constitute arbitrary or unjustifiable discrimination between Member States where like conditions prevail, or a disguised restriction on trade within the Community.

An important difference between the RTC provision and that of GATT 1994 is that it has a lower threshold as Article 226(b) does not require that a challenged measure be 'necessary' for human health before it can be provisionally justified under the article. Moreover, this use of language appears to be a deliberate choice rather than an oversight as the word 'necessary' is used in relation to some other paragraphs in the RTC Article 226. The impact of this drafting difference is that it would be easier for a CARICOM State (i.e., require less evidence and analysis) to satisfy the Caribbean Court of Justice (CCJ) that a challenged measure falls within the scope of paragraph (b) than would be the case if the matter were being litigated within the WTO.[75] One must be careful, however, not to overestimate the ultimate impact of this drafting difference, as Article 226 does still retain the language from GATT 1994 Article XX calling for measures not to amount to arbitrary or unjustifiable discrimination or a disguised restriction on trade. It is also worth recalling here that it is this latter language, rather than the necessity requirements of GATT 1994 Article XX, that have posed the most difficulty in terms of justifying WTO inconsistent measures in the past.

While there have been no cases involving the RTC Article 226 or Article 90 to date, there is every reason to believe that the CCJ will adopt an interpretative approach similar to that of WTO dispute settlement system as it relates to determinations of 'likeness' as well as in relation to what amounts to arbitrary or unjustifiable discrimination or a disguised restriction on international trade.[76] This position is based both on the similarity of the language of the two

---

[75] The CCJ has exclusive and compulsory jurisdiction in respect of matters concerning the interpretation and application of the RTC: RTC Art 211.

[76] There equally have not been any cases to date necessitating the CCJ to analyse the scope and application of the RTC provisions regarding national treatment, the prohibition on quantitative restrictions, etc. The case that came closest to raising these issues was *Rudisa Beverages & Juices N.V and Caribbean International Distributors Ltd. v The State of Guyana* [2014] CCJ (OJ) which concerned Guyana's imposition of an environmental levy on importation of non-returnable beverage containers, including those imported from within CARCIOM, without a similar tax being imposed on local

treaties as well as on the CCJ's willingness in other matters to reference WTO jurisprudence as evidence of international practice.[77]

In sum, notwithstanding fairly wide-ranging trade commitments at the regional, extra-regional and multilateral levels, it is clear that CARICOM States have flexibility to allow them to undertake some of the key interventions highlighted by CARPHA for addressing the region's childhood obesity problem. This is not in any way to suggest that this flexibility is limitless and that CARICOM States are therefore free to adopt whatever health policies they wish without having due regard to their international trade commitments. Accordingly, when crafting their childhood obesity interventions, CARICOM States should bear in mind the following inter-related guiding principles if they wish to minimise the chance of legal challenges within the WTO or other trade forum such as the CCJ.

(i) Ensure that proposed measures are proportionate, reasonable and rational

This requirement can be met by, as far as possible, basing policies on a global practice or international standards such as Codex Alimentarius guidelines. The second element concerns the value of basing public health and related policies on a global practice or international standards. As mentioned previously, the TBT Agreement has a preference for technical regulations to be based on an international standard. It will be easier to convince a panel that such a requirement is proportionate rational and reasonable since it would reflect an international consensus or at least a consensus of a wide range of countries rather than just reflecting a given State's individual judgment. Where international standards do not exist, States will have to be prepared to furnish convincing evidence of the merits of their case.

---

producers of non-returnable beverage containers. Guyana conceded from the outset of the case that the level was discriminatory and in violation of the RTC Art 87 and the CCJ therefore did not have to discuss any of these issues.

[77] For example, in *Cabral Douglas and The Commonwealth of Dominica* [2017] CCJ 1 (OJ) [20] the CCJ drew an analogy between the RTC Art 36 and the WTO General Agreement on Trade in Services in determining what amounts to cross-border provision of services based on the similar language of the two treaties. In addition, in *Maurice Tomlinson and The State Of Belize* [2016] CCJ 1 (OJ) [26]–[28] the CCJ referred to *India – Patent Protection for Pharmaceutical and Agricultural Chemical Products*, *United States – Section 301 – 310 of the Trade Act 1974* and *United States – Anti-Dumping Measures on Certain Hot Rolled Steel Products from Japan* when dealing with the consistency of domestic law with international obligations.

(ii) **Ensure that any targeting of particular products for differential treatment such as higher/lower taxation is backed by sound scientific evidence and thus can be easily justified on health grounds**

This in turn raises issues as to the amount and level of evidence needed to substantiate a State's claims and by extension the amount of deference States can anticipate will be made to their determinations.[78] In this regard, it should be noted that there is no pre-established evidentiary threshold and clearly the amount of evidence available may be limited by the state of science at the time. States should try as far as possible to undertake empirical studies in advance or at the very least ensure that their measures are monitored and evaluated post implementation. It is also worth noting here that States are free to draw on evidence of studies undertaken in other countries regionally or even internationally to the extent that the local circumstances are similar to their situation. Accordingly, in the case of CARICOM States, the experiences of Mexico and Chile on both SSB taxation and front of pack labelling can be quite influential and the same would be true of Barbados and Dominica once evaluations of their SSB taxes are complete. In seeking to substantiate the proportionality, rationality and reasonableness of their chosen health intervention, States can also usefully leverage their relationships with recognised international authorities such as the Pan American Health Organization and WHO in support of their claims.

The recent arbitral ruling in *Philip Morris Brands Sárl (Switzerland) and others v Oriental Republic of Uruguay arbitration* in the area of tobacco control provides an excellent example of both these points.[79] In that dispute Uruguay's legal position was significantly strengthened by strong support and testimony from PAHO, WHO, and the FCTC Secretariat. The arbitral tribunal attached significant weight to their opinions that Uruguay's measures were reasonable, effective, evidence-based means of responding to the public health threat posed by tobacco. These and similar bodies can clearly be powerful and persuasive allies in justifying various public health interventions and

---

[78] Mitchell and Henckels argue that in determining the extent to which a measure must achieve its objective, 'WTO tribunals afford substantial deference to measures in performing suitability analysis, in particular where measures form part of a complex set of mutually supportive measures directed at achieving a particular objective.' A Mitchell and C Henckels, 'Variations on a Theme: Comparing the Concept of 'Necessity' in International Investment Law and WTO Law' (2013) 14 *Chicago Journal of International Law* 93, 162.

[79] *Philip Morris Brands Sárl (Switzerland) and others* v *Oriental Republic of Uruguay* ICSID Case No. ARB/10/7 8 July 2016 (*Philip Morris Brands Sárl (Switzerland)*).

CARICOM governments would be well served by ensuring they engage them fully in the formulation (and possible defense) of their public health measures.

An important and often overlooked factor that can significantly influence the amount and nature of evidence needed and ultimately the determination of whether a given measure is deemed to be too trade-restrictive or not necessary, is how a particular measure is framed. States need to refrain from articulating expansive, overly ambitious objectives for the measures they are seeking to implement as the more ambitious the stated objective, the more evidence, both quantitative and qualitative, that will be needed to justify their measure. For example, when framing front of pack schemes, rather than stating that the aim is to reduce the prevalence of NCDs or to reduce or control childhood obesity, a State might instead indicate that the aim is to provide consumers with accurate information about food nutrient content to enable them to make informed nutrition decisions.

(iii)   Ensure that the proposed measures are non-discriminatory

Here States want to be conscious of any exceptions that are created to ensure that they are legitimate and clearly defined. States also need to be conscious of the coverage of their measures to ensure that there is appropriate capture. For example, front of pack schemes cannot be limited solely to imported processed and ultra-processed foods. This will be a particularly important consideration for CARICOM States who have important regional players within the food and beverage industry. Moreover, as discussed above, broad exceptions as well as poorly defined exceptions criteria have been problematic in a WTO context. States equally may wish to ensure that measures form part of a broader NCDs/obesity plan so that the targeting of individual products can be better understood and rationalised.

(iv)   Ensure that due process is respected

The need for transparency and inclusiveness in the formulation and application of public health measures is also an important consideration. It is worth recalling in this regard that the TBT Agreement has built into it requirements regarding advance notification of WTO members and allowing for consultation and comment by members. More generally WTO members have an obligation to publish their laws and regulations. In a domestic context, due process considerations raises an interesting question regarding the extent to which governments should involve the food industry in the formulation of the standards which will be used to regulate them. It is submitted that the process of formulation of standards needs to be one where industry is excluded but then they should be consulted in terms of how the standards should be implemented.

4. CURRENT CHILDHOOD OBESITY REGIONAL RESPONSES: FRONT-OF-PACKAGE LABELLING AND TAXATION INITIATIVES

As was mentioned above, the region's work in the area of childhood obesity is being informed by CARPHA's six-point policy package for priority action.[80] Among these six areas, current work is focused on implementing front of package labelling and SSB taxes. This choice of initiatives was influenced by the following factors:

(i) the perception of front of pack labelling as key for making progress in other priority areas such as marketing to children and product reformulation, as well as being low hanging fruit particularly when compared to restrictions on marketing;

(ii) CARICOM has recently deepened its bilateral relations with Chile which provided a useful platform for exchange of information and experiences on the work on NCDs prevention and control, particularly in relation to taxation and front of pack labelling;

(iii) PAHO has identified SSB taxation as one of the best buys for NCDs prevention and control;

(iv) there is a growing body of evidence on the efficacy of SSB taxes;

(v) tax measures are relatively easy to implement and offer the bonus of generating additional revenue for the government; and

(vi) these areas are priority areas for civil society organisations and donors.

Implementing restrictions on marketing, by contrast, is seen as much more difficult politically and otherwise, and for now it has been left to be addressed on an ad hoc, limited basis rather than based on a comprehensive regional push.[81]

4.1 Proposed Mandatory Front-of-Package Labelling with Nutritional Values

The WHO Global Strategy on Diet, Physical Activity and Health notes that '[c]onsumers require accurate, standardized and comprehensible information on the content of food items in order to make healthy choices. Governments

---

[80] That is, mandatory nutritional labelling of foods; regulation of the school feeding environment; reduction of marketing of unhealthy food to children; product reformulation to reduce fat, salt, sugar levels; fiscal and trade measures; and promotion of fruit and vegetable consumption.

[81] Trinidad and Tobago announced the banning of sale of sodas in schools effective 1 April 2017 and the Jamaican government recently signaled a similar intent.

may require information to be provided on key nutritional aspects, as proposed in the Codex Guidelines on Nutrition Labelling'.[82] The 2017 World Health Assembly endorsed an updated set of policy options known as 'Appendix 3' for NCD prevention and control which has front of package labelling listed as one of the 'best buys' (for reduction of salt intake) and nutritional labelling more generally is also listed as a recommended intervention to assist with reduction of total energy intake, sugars, sodium and fats.[83] The WHO Commission on Ending Childhood Obesity has also endorsed these initiatives.[84]

Efforts are currently underway regionally to make some headway with implementation of front of pack labelling. The CARICOM Regional Organisation for Standards and Quality (CROSQ) is the CARICOM agency responsible for setting regional standards for the labelling of pre-packaged foods. Currently, CARICOM member States apply the Codex International Standard via the CRS 5: 2010 Standard Specification for Labelling of Pre-packaged Foods and thus only require nutrition labels if a health claim is made. However, the Codex Guidelines on Nutrition Labelling were recently amended and now call for mandatory nutrition labelling, including NCD Reference Values, for all pre-packaged foods (i.e., even in the absence of health claims), except where national circumstances would not support such declarations.[85] Accordingly, with the assistance of CROSQ, CARICOM member States hope to revisit their existing standards to provide for mandatory, uniform Nutrition Facts Panels (NFP) on all packaged retail grocery foods and beverages sold within the region as well as to establish regional guidelines for standardised, interpretive nutrition labels on all packaged retail grocery foods and beverages for use in conjunction with Nutrition Facts Panels.

Standards development within CROSQ is based on a documented process that starts with the submission of a New Work Item Proposal (NWIP) through a National Standards Body from a member State. Jamaica is leading this process but the NWIP has not been submitted as yet. Once a standard is agreed

---

[82] WHO, 'Global strategy on diet, physical activity and health' (May 2004) WHA57.17 para 40.

[83] WHO, 'Report by the Director General, Preparation for the third High-level Meeting of the General Assembly on the Prevention and Control of Non-communicable Diseases' (18 May 2017) UN Doc A/70/27.

[84] Commission on Ending Childhood Obesity, *Report of the Commission on Ending Childhood Obesity* (WHO 2016).

[85] CODEX, Guidelines on Nutrition Labelling CAC/GL 2-1985 (last amended 2017) para 3.1.2:
Nutrient declaration should be mandatory for all other prepackaged foods except where national circumstances would not support such declarations. Certain foods may be exempted for example, on the basis of nutritional or dietary insignificance or small packaging.

within CROSQ, on declaration of this standard CARICOM States are required to develop a technical regulation/compulsory standard, dependent on their legislation to give mandatory effect to the implementation of the standard. The intention is to have the development of these new standards use a fast track procedure which takes approximately 12 months maximum rather than the usual 26½ months for normal standard development process. At the time of writing these proposals are still under development and so the precise details not known. However, bearing in mind the current close cooperation between Chile and CARICOM on these matters, it is anticipated that there may be some similarities between the two approaches. Certainly one would wish to see CARICOM duplicate the mandatory and strict nutrition thresholds present in the Chilean scheme.

It is worth noting here that mandatory interpretive labelling systems such as those being contemplated by CARICOM States, and already in place in Chile, have been the subject of some debate and scrutiny in the WTO. In particular, WTO members have raised concerns regarding: (i) the scheme's mandatory nature; (ii) whether there was a sufficient evidentiary base to these schemes; (iii) the broad range of products covered; (iv) the lack of internationally agreed front of package labelling guidelines/standards; and (v) the use of 'high' warnings (felt that they were more trade restrictive than necessary and unfairly targeting a select food items which could be part of a healthy diet if eaten in moderation).[86] It is submitted, however, that these objections should not deter CARICOM States from proceeding with their planned policy action. The growing body of evidence of the positive impact of these schemes can in turn be used to substantiate their reasonableness and rationality.[87] Moreover,

---

[86] See, e.g., the concerns raised by Brazil, Guatemala, the EU and US in TBT Committee meetings as early as 2013: Committee on Technical Barriers to Trade, 'Minutes of the Meeting of 17, 19 and 20 June 2013 (Note by the Secretariat) G/TBT/M/60.

[87] See, e.g., UNICEF, *Review of Current Labelling Regulations and Practices for Food and Beverage Targeting Children and Adolescents in Latin America Countries (Mexico, Chile, Costa Rica and Argentina) and Recommendations for Facilitating Consumer Information* (UNICEF, 2016); PAHO, *Recommendations from a Pan American Health Organization Expert Consultation on the Marketing of Food and Non-Alcoholic Beverages to Children in the Americas* (PAHO, 2011); G Cowburn and L Stockley, 'Consumer Understanding and Use of Nutrition Labelling: A Systematic Review' (2005) 8 *Public Health Nutrition* 21; S Campos et al., 'Nutrition Labels on Pre-Packaged Foods: A Systematic Review' (2011) 14 *Public Health Nutrition* 1496; K Hawley et al., 'The Science on Front-of-Package Food Labels' (2013) 16 *Public Health Nutrition* 430; C Hawkes et al., 'Smart Food Policies for Obesity Prevention' (2015) 385 *Lancet* 2410; A Arrua et al., 'Impact of Front-of-Pack Nutrition Information and Label Design on Children's Choice of Two Snack Foods: Comparison of Warnings and The Traffic-Light System' (2017) 116 *Appetite* 139.

the link between energy dense, nutrient-poor, ultra-processed foods and NCDs prevalence has also been widely documented and thus efforts to regulate these types of foods can hardly be said to be discriminatory (provided it is done in an even-handed manner, applying across the board to like domestic and imported goods.)

A useful tool in this process which would also speak to the evidence-based approach that has been adopted to these issues, is the PAHO Nutrient Profile criteria for identifying processed and ultra-processed products excessive in sodium, free sugars, other sweeteners, saturated fat, total fat and trans-fat.[88] This nutrient profile is itself evidence-based and utilizes the WHO Population Nutrient Intake Goals (PNIGs) in establishing its respective nutrient thresholds. Under the Nutrient Profile, a food is classified as 'excessive' in a given nutrient if its relative nutrient content is higher than the corresponding maximum recommended WHO PNIGs level. This Nutrient Profile is to be used for processed and ultra-processed products only.[89] It should also be noted that, in recognition of the importance of this issue generally, at its 44th session in October 2017, the Codex Committee on Food Labelling agreed to begin work on developing guidelines on front of pack nutrition labelling. This work will address: (i) purpose and scope; (ii) definition; (iii) general principles; and (iv) aspects to consider in the development of front of pack systems.[90] While completion of this work is several years off, it hopefully will also lend support to the actions of countries such as Chile, Ecuador and CARICOM in the area.[91]

4.2 Sugar Sweetened Beverages Taxes – Barbados and Dominica

Global evidence indicates that taxes can be an effective public health tool and there is emerging evidence that excise taxes on SSBs are also effective.[92] Within the Americas, a 10 per cent tax on SSBs (including syrups, concentrates and powders) in Mexico had the effect of a 6 per cent reduction in all SSBs.[93]

---

[88] PAHO, 'Pan American Health Organisation Nutrient Profile Model', PAHO, 2016.

[89] That is, it is not intended to be applied to unprocessed or minimally processed foods such as vegetables, grains, fruits, meat, fish, milk, and eggs) or to freshly prepared dishes made with these foods.

[90] Codex Alimentarius Commission, Report of the 44th Session of the CODEX Committee on Food Labelling (Asuncion, Paraguay 16–20 October 2017) REP18/FL.

[91] Chile: Ley 20.606 Sobre Composición Nutricional de Los Alimentos y Su Publicidad; Ecuador: Ley 4522, El Reglamento de Etiquetado de Alimentos Procesados.

[92] That is, a flat tax applied before purchase to specific goods such as luxury goods or, in this case, goods linked to specific health issues.

[93] M Colchero et al., 'Beverage Purchases from Stores in Mexico under the Excise Tax on Sugar Sweetened Beverages: Observational Study' (2016) 352 *British Medical Journal* h6704.

In addition, a year after the introduction of the tax, households with the fewest resources reduced their purchases of sugary drinks by the largest percentage (up to 17 per cent).[94] Evidence also shows that a tax of 20 per cent on sugary drinks can lead to a reduction in consumption of around 20 per cent, thus preventing obesity and diabetes.[95] SSB taxes have also been recommended by WHO as a key fiscal policy for diet.[96] Besides decreasing consumption, excise taxes can also generate useful additional revenues that can be directed towards NCDs prevention and control.

The urgent need for the CARICOM countries to act in the area of SSB taxes is attested to by the fact that a 2015 study of global consumption of sugar-sweetened beverages found that the Caribbean has the highest intake of sugar-sweetened beverages worldwide (1.9 servings per day).[97] The urgency of the situation notwithstanding, use of excise taxation as a public health measure in the Caribbean continues to be limited and out of the 14 Caribbean PAHO/WHO member States, only Barbados and Dominica currently have excise taxes on SSBs.

Barbados' SSB tax was implemented from 1 August 2015. It takes the form of a 10 per cent excise tax on the cost of locally produced and imported sweetened beverages. Barbados chose an excise tax because of the simplicity of administration/low cost associated with its implementation. The SSB tax is applied to products such as carbonated soft drinks, juice drinks, sports drinks and fruit juices falling under tariff headings 20.09, 21.06 and 22.02.[98] It however does not apply to beverages with intrinsic sugars such as coconut water and 100 per cent natural fruit juice.[99] An identification of product types approach was chosen rather than one utilising a caloric threshold for ease of implementation and the flexibility it gave in defining the products to be captured (e.g., substitutes or competing products).

The SSB tax is levied on the value of the product before Value Added Tax (VAT) is applied and is collected through the VAT and Excise Tax Administration System. At a 2017 PAHO workshop on fiscal policies, it

---

[94] Ibid.
[95] L Powell et al., 'Assessing the Potential Effectiveness of Food and Beverage Taxes and Subsidies for Improving Public Health: A Systematic Review of Prices, Demand and Body Weight Outcomes' (2013) 14 *Obesity Reviews* 110.
[96] WHO, *Fiscal Policies for Diet and Prevention of Noncommunicable Diseases* (WHO 2016). WHO, "Best buys" and Other Recommended Interventions for the Prevention and Control of Noncommunicable Diseases (WHO/NMH/NVI/17.9 2016).
[97] M Gitanjali et al., 'Global, Regional, and National Consumption of Sugar-Sweetened Beverages, Fruit Juices, and Milk: A Systematic Assessment of Beverage Intake in 187 Countries'(2015) 10(8) *PLoS One* e0124845.
[98] Barbados Excise Amendment No. 3 Regulations 2017, S.I. No. 77 of 2017.
[99] Ibid.

was reported by the Barbados Revenue Authority that the SSB tax generated Bds$13 million/US$6.5 million during 2015–16 and just over Bds$12 million/US$6 million during 2016–17, which is significantly more than the government's initial projected Bds$10 million/US$5 million.[100] Unfortunately, the revenue generated from the tax is simply deposited into the Consolidated Fund for general use by government and has not been earmarked in any way for NCD prevention and control or even for broader health programmes.[101] It is submitted that Barbados can certainly benefit from following the example of Jamaica which designates a portion of the monies collected from taxes on tobacco and alcohol to the National Health Fund. Besides the obvious benefit of making more funding available for health care/promotion, such an action would also be able to be relied on in substantiating the connection between the SSB tax and health objectives and thus add to the evidence base in terms of its performance from a health/NCDs perspective.

An evaluation of the effect of the 2015 SSB tax on beverage prices and sales in Barbados is presently being conducted at the University of West Indies on behalf of the Barbados SSB Tax Evaluation Steering Committee. Recently published preliminary conclusions indicated that there was a 6.3 per cent increase in the price of sugar-sweetened beverages and no significant change in the price of non-sugar sweetened beverages.[102] It was also reported that companies appeared to have absorbed some of the tax, which meant there was not full pass through to the consumer in terms of the price increase, which could potentially affect the overall impact of the tax.[103] Among the changes being contemplated for the SSB tax is a possible increase in the rate of the tax. HCC has also recommended extension of the tax's coverage from just beverages to foods high in sugar content as well.[104]

Following in Barbados' footsteps, Dominica introduced its SSB tax on 1 September 2015. Unlike Barbados however, the 10 per cent excise tax was imposed on drinks and *food* with high sugar content including sweets, candy, chocolate bars, soft drinks and other sweetened drinks (including energy

---

[100] PAHO, 'Workshop Report Caribbean Subregional Workshop on Alcohol, Tobacco and Sugar-Sweetened Beverages Taxation' (16 – 17 May 2017 Barbados).

[101] The Consolidated Fund is created under the respective Constitutions of CARICOM States. All revenues received by the government are credited to it and government expenditure is made from it. Use of these funds is subject to Parliamentary approval.

[102] M Alvarado et al., 'Trends in Beverage Prices Following the Introduction of a Tax on Sugar-Sweetened Beverages in Barbados' (2017) 105 *Preventive Medicine* S23.

[103] Ibid.

[104] PAHO, 'Workshop Report Caribbean Subregional Workshop on Alcohol, Tobacco and Sugar-Sweetened Beverages Taxation' (16–17 May 2017 Barbados).

drinks). The details of the tax and the products covered are set out in the Dominica Excise Tax (Amendment) Act 2015 using specified tariff headings and includes items such as 'chewing gum, whether or not sugar-coated, chocolate in blocks, slabs or bars, soft drinks (Soda) and malt beverages'.[105] Revenues generated thus far from the implementation of taxes on SSBs, alcohol and tobacco are reported to be over EC$2 million/US$740,822.[106] These monies are also deposited directly into the Consolidated Fund but the government has indicated its intention to designate some of these funds for use in the national 'Get Healthy' campaign. Understandably, however, following the passage of Hurricane Maria progress is this area has slowed.

Both Barbados' and Dominica's use of legislation to set out the goods attracting the tax based on tariff headings allows for a level of clarity and predictability in the application of their respective taxes. However, both Barbados and Dominica still need to be prepared to explain the basis on which the various tariff headings were selected and whether these choices were informed by reliable evidence or relevant international guidelines. Both Barbados and Dominica also need to be prepared to explain that their fiscal policies targeting SSBs is not isolated, but rather, form part of a broader plan to address the risk factors associated with NCDs (such as the regional front of package labelling initiative discussed above).

4.3 Human Rights as a Tool for Exploiting Trade Flexibilities

CARICOM's lack of meaningful progress on fighting childhood obesity in spite of a plethora of global and regional commitments as well as flexibility within the international system to address these concerns challenges those involved in this fight to identify additional tools that can be used to accelerate action in this area. A key consideration here is identifying tools that can be used by individuals and civil society more broadly to hold CARICOM governments to account for their failure to act and pressure governments to improve their implementation record. Human rights is one such tool that could make a positive contribution here as well as offer a different and valuable perspective on the problem of childhood obesity which tends to be viewed primarily as a health issue rather than one of development or human rights. Employing a human-rights based approach to childhood obesity prevention and control anchored in the child's right to health and the principle of the best interests of the child offers the possibility of greater buy in by the wider public but, more importantly, action by the respective governments. Such an approach

---

[105] SR0 28/2015.
[106] PAHO, 'Workshop Report, n104.

to the problem of childhood obesity in CARICOM offers the possibility of framing governments' obligation to act, not as a matter of political good will, but rather, as a consequence of legally binding international obligations that implicates their responsibility should they fail to meet these obligations. This in turn can put pressure on governments to comply. A human rights-based approach to the problem of childhood obesity in CARICOM can also help advance the 'whole of society approach' first endorsed by CARICOM Heads of Government at the Port of Spain Summit, but which CARICOM States have struggled to meaningfully implement. It can advance this work based on its grounding in the indivisibility and inter-dependence of all rights, including the right to health, and its focus on the individual as a being with dignity and worth who is entitled to be consulted and included in decisions which impact on their life.

The international human rights system offers other important tools for accelerating progress on tackling childhood obesity in the form of the reporting processes of its treaty bodies and of the Human Rights Council itself, Special Procedures/Rapporteurs as well as the General Comments of the various treaty bodies. Reporting can be used to 'shine a light' on CARICOM governments' failure to be proactive on issues of childhood obesity to date and also encourage constructive engagement and dialogue on this issue with the international community as well as civil society. Unfortunately, to date there has been very limited engagement by Caribbean civil society in the various reporting processes of the UN human rights bodies and what little engagement there has been has not touched on issues of health and the epidemic of childhood obesity. This needs to change. This lack of engagement is primarily the result of a lack of a strong NGO culture generally but it is also due to the regional NGOs' lack of knowledge of the international human rights system and how they can leverage it to their benefit. This is a high priority area for technical assistance and capacity-building.

Within the Caribbean, not all CARICOM member States are State parties to the International Covenant on Economic, Social and Cultural Rights, however, all of them have ratified the Convention on the Rights of the Child and are therefore legally bound as a matter of international law to implement its provisions.[107] Accordingly, there is significant scope to call them to account in both the CRC reporting processes as well as those within the Human Rights Council (through the Universal Periodic Review) for their failure to

---

[107] International Covenant on Economic, Social and Cultural Rights (adopted 16 December 1966, entered into force 3 January 1976) 993 UNTS 3 (ICESCR); Convention on the Rights of the Child (adopted on 20 November 1989, entered into force 2 September 1990) 1577 UNTS 3 (CRC).

make greater progress in addressing childhood obesity. For example, in its 2017 Concluding Observations on Antigua and Barbuda, the Committee on the Rights of the Child encouraged the government to '[d]evelop policies to ensure that healthy food and lifestyle choices are available and affordable and strengthen awareness-raising campaigns to promote the benefits of healthy eating for children'.[108] Arguably if there had been civil society submissions challenging the government on the specifics of its failure to be proactive on the matter of childhood obesity, the Committee's Concluding Observations may have been even more specific and could have helped to give greater impetus to government action in this area.

There is equally a role for greater engagement by CARICOM governments themselves on these issues. CARICOM member States' participation in the various international human rights mechanisms is currently quite limited in part due to limited financial resources. However, increased engagement by CARICOM governments in international human rights bodies would allow for greater policy coherence and consistency in how issues such as NCDs, obesity and childhood obesity are dealt with. It would also allow for greater integration of these priorities across government policy and offer an additional front on which to engage the UN, other human rights entities as well as bilateral partners.

5. CONCLUSION

The discussion above aims to demonstrate that CARICOM States' international trade obligations do not unduly constrain these countries' efforts to combat childhood obesity. As argued here, these countries retain sufficient regulatory autonomy and policy space notwithstanding a wide network of international trade obligations. The substantive provisions of existing trade agreements include flexibilities that allow CARICOM States to take action targeting unhealthy foods in order to discourage their consumption if necessary by relying on the general exceptions clause allowing measures to be taken for the protection of public health, provided they are not discriminatory. What is still lacking, however, is the commitment and political will by leaders at the highest level to take firm (and expeditious) action and exploit the flexibilities that are already available to them within the various trade arrangements to which they are parties. It is here that one sees the intersection between international trade and human rights, with trade and international human rights

---

[108] Committee on the Rights of the Child, 'Concluding observations on the combined second to fourth periodic reports of Antigua and Barbuda', UN Doc CRC/C/ATG/CO/2-4, 30 June 2017, 40.

working together to achieve the goal of healthier food environments for children as well as the wider population. Human rights tools can be used to apply political pressure to get the commitment and leadership that is needed to move the agenda forward by exploiting the flexibilities available to States including those within CARICOM. In addition, human rights can also make an important contribution to transforming governance mechanisms within States to allow for meaningful implementation of the 'whole of society' approach to combating childhood obesity within CARICOM that was called for in the Port of Spain Declaration.

PART III

Additional tools available under human rights law

9. Can the United Nations system be mobilized to promote human rights-based approaches in preventing and ending childhood obesity?

Asbjørn Eide and Wenche Barth Eide

1. INTRODUCTION

This chapter treats ending childhood obesity through a human rights-based approach as an aspect of the more general concern to promote and protect the human right to adequate food and the right to health for all. The normative, institutional and procedural foundation for applying a human rights-based approach are provided in Part I of this volume. Here we discuss the rationale for and potential of the United Nations to address diet-related health and connected global concerns from a human rights perspective. The specific purpose is to explore whether and how the UN system can be further mobilized to help reduce childhood obesity as a public health concern through human rights-based efforts.

The timing is auspicious, yet uncertain. The Sustainable Development Goals 2015–30, adopted by the UN General Assembly in 2015,[1] deal with food and health in Goal 2 (towards zero hunger) and Goal 3 (good health and wellbeing), with specified targets relevant to the theme of this book. On 1 April 2016, the UN General Assembly proclaimed the UN Decade of Action on Nutrition 2016–25.[2] Its proposed work programme[3] provides a modest but promising

---

[1] UN, 'Transforming Our World: The 2030 Agenda for Sustainable Development', UN Doc. A/RES/70/1 (21 October 2015).

[2] UN, 'UN Decade of Action on Nutrition 2016-25', UN Doc. A/70/L. 42 (1 April 2016).

[3] UN Systems Standing Committee on Nutrition, 'Work Programme of 5 May 2017' https://www.unscn.org/uploads/web/news/Work-Programme_UN-Decade-of -Action-on-Nutrition-20170517.pdf. This website and all subsequent websites cited in this chapter were live as at 20 February 2020.

opening for developing human rights-based approaches to practical action. The following years have seen increasing efforts to consider nutrition-related health within the context of food systems and food environments with healthy diets as the chief mediator. This has increased the potential of linking meaningfully the two SDGs with a right to food and right to health perspective. However, resistance by many states to strengthening such a perspective is on the rise, in line with the presently low support for human rights as a moral and legal compass in general.

In section 2 we recall efforts of UN reform undertaken around the turn of the millennium, to consolidate and further develop the relationships between human rights and development, as called for in the UN Charter (Art 1.3). UN Member States have developed a broad-ranging body of international human rights law, but implementation remains uneven due to conflicting interests both domestically and in the international community. Approaches based on the right to health may conflict with trade and other economic interests, as discussed by others in this book. This can undermine effective approaches such as those called for under the SDGs and the work programme developed for the Nutrition Decade. Efforts to shape and pursue policies through a human rights-based approach thus risk meeting both political and professional barriers.

We take a special look at how two UN organizations have applied human rights principles in their development cooperation: The Food and Agriculture Organization (FAO) and the World Health Organization (WHO). They were given the responsibility of leading the Nutrition Decade and understanding some of their past histories in that light may be useful to trigger efforts to enhance constructive action in health and nutrition by the UN through a human rights-based approach.

In section 3 we discuss whether the normative foundation set for the UN Nutrition Decade is sufficient to address childhood obesity not only as a priority *public health issue*, but also as a *human rights issue*. Prevention of childhood obesity becomes a test case to examine whether the UN Decade of Action on Nutrition can contribute to the original aim of the UN to link development with human rights.

Section 4 explores current developments in and performance by WHO and FAO as well as key UN human rights institutions and practices, assessing whether these are conducive to a future emphasis on the prevention of childhood obesity and noncommunicable diseases (NCDs) as a human rights issue.[4]

---

[4] Our considerations are limited to selected formal UN structures and do not include complementary activities of other stakeholders in this context.

Section 5 provides some concluding reflections and visions on how pressure from civil society and academia, in cooperation with concerned governments and UN staff, could enhance the performance of the relevant entities of the UN and strengthen a human rights-based approach to preventing childhood obesity.

2. THE UN AND HUMAN RIGHTS-BASED DEVELOPMENT

2.1 Reviving the Promotion of Human Rights-Based Development as a Major Purpose of the UN: In Search of a Common Understanding

Soon after he took office as Secretary-General in late 1996, Kofi Annan started a reform process aimed at renewing the purposes of the United Nations. His comprehensive reform agenda, *Renewing the United Nations: A Programme for Reform*,[5] proposed to strengthen 'unity of purpose' within the UN, reviving the focus on human rights which should cut across the entire UN Programme of Work. Annan called on the Specialized (development) Agencies of the UN system to mainstream human rights into their various activities and programmes. It all converged at the Millennium Summit in 2000 with the establishment of the Millennium Declaration[6] and the Millennium Development Goals.[7]

As described by Hartlev and O'Cathaoir in this volume, in 2003 the UN Development Group (UNDG)[8] adopted the 'UN Statement of Common Understanding on Human Rights-Based Approaches to Development Cooperation and Programming' ('Common Understanding'). At a follow-up of the Millennium Summit in 2005, Kofi Annan presented his report 'In Larger Freedom: Towards Development, Security and Human Rights for All.'[9] It asserted that 'the world must advance the causes of security, development and

---

[5] UN, 'Renewing the United Nations: A Programme for Reform', UN Doc A/51/950 (14 July 1997).

[6] UN, 'United Nations Millennium Declaration', UN Doc. A/RES/55/2 (18 September 2000).

[7] UN, 'The Millennium Development Goals Report 2015', http://www.un.org/millenniumgoals/2015_MDG_Report/pdf/MDG%202015%20rev%20(July%201).pdf.

[8] The UNDG is a high-level forum for joint policy formation and decision-making by a large number of UN agencies and bodies (including FAO, WHO and the High Commissioner for Human Rights) which guides, supports, tracks and oversees the coordination of development operations in 165 countries and territories.

[9] Report of the Secretary-General, 'In Larger Freedom: towards development, security and human rights for all', UN Doc. A/59/2005 (21 March 2005).

human rights together, otherwise none will succeed. Humanity will not enjoy security without development, it will not enjoy development without security, and it will not enjoy either without respect for human rights'.[10]

The General Assembly invited the Secretary-General to further strengthen the management and coordination of UN operational activities and to make proposals for greater coordination in the field of development. Kofi Annan appointed a 'High-Level Panel on UN System-Wide Coherence in the Areas of Development, Humanitarian Assistance and the Environment', which delivered its report in 2006. It recommended that the UN system should 'deliver as one' at country level, with one leader, one programme, one budget and, where appropriate, one office,[11] furthermore that:

> All United Nations agencies and programmes must further support the development of policies, directives and guidelines to integrate human rights in all aspects of United Nations work. The United Nations common understanding on a human rights-based approach to programming ... should provide useful guidance in this.[12]

2.2 Shifting Institutional Approaches to Human Rights by FAO and WHO

The past and potential contributions of FAO and WHO as specialized development agencies to operationalizing the right to adequate food and the right to health are critical in view of their leading roles in the evolving Nutrition Decade.[13] However, given their intergovernmental nature, their approach to and use of human rights in their activities have over the years been influenced by shifting political circumstances and by changes in leadership and leaders' approach to their mandates. The following are some selected events.

2.2.1 FAO

In the 1960s the Director-General of FAO, B R Sen, was instrumental in getting the right to freedom from hunger included in the ICESCR. Under Edward Souma from 1976 to 1993, an understanding of food security going beyond world food supply was introduced at the FAO General Conference

---

[10] Ibid., 1.
[11] Secretary-General's High-Level Panel on System-wide Coherence, 'Delivering as One', Follow-up to the Outcome of the Millennium Summit', UN Doc A/61/583 (20 November 2006).
[12] Ibid., para 51.
[13] We recognize important contributions of other UN bodies to setting human rights on the UN agenda, especially UNICEF in promoting the rights of women and children in connection with nutrition improvements from the early 1990s, and UNDP in relating its work with good governance to human rights principles.

in 1983 together with a proposal for a Food Security Compact, which was adopted by the Conference in 1985.[14] It confirmed food security and nutrition as a human rights issue, recognizing hunger and undernutrition as due to context-specific lack of operational entitlements. This understanding could have made it possible to address situations and cases of food insecurity in a specific and constructive way, but the timing was not yet politically ripe.

The first International Conference on Nutrition, organized jointly by FAO and WHO in Rome in 1992, could have been a new opportunity to substantiate the right to adequate food as a new moral and legal vision for food security. However, influential states including the USA succeeded in limiting reference to human rights to an overall general statement in the final Rome Declaration.[15] The accompanying Plan of Action restricted further follow up to '[c]onsumers have the right to a good quality and safe food supply, and government and food industry actions are needed to ensure this',[16] and referred to the need, when caring for the socio-economically deprived and nutritionally vulnerable, to 'recognize the dignity and rights of vulnerable people.'[17]

Jacques Diouf succeeded Souma in 1994 and took the initiative to convene the first ever World Food Summit (WFS) hosted by FAO in 1996. This milestone event called on the UN High Commissioner on Human Rights, in cooperation with the Committee on Economic, Social and Cultural Rights (CESCR) and the specialized agencies, to clarify the content of the right to food as a means of achieving the commitments and objectives of the WFS.[18] Clarification was achieved in 1999 with the adoption by the CESCR of its General Comment No. 12,[19] pointing to the dual aspects of the right to adequate food: ensuring access for all to sufficient food that also meets the dietary needs of the individual.

The WFS also recommended the elaboration of voluntary guidelines on the right to adequate food in the context of national food security for all.

---

[14] Report of the Conference of FAO, Twenty-third session 1985, Section V. E: Adoption of the World Food Security Compact (9–28 November 1985), http://www.fao.org/docrep/x5562E/X5562e05.htm.

[15] FAO and WHO, 'Declaration and Plan of Action for Nutrition', International Conference on Nutrition, Rome, December 1992 http://apps.who.int/iris/bitstream/10665/61051/1/a34303.pdf?ua=1.

[16] Ibid., para 32.

[17] Ibid., para 36.

[18] World Food Summit, 'Rome Declaration and Plan of Action', Commitment Seven, para 61 Objective 7.4 (13 November 1966).

[19] CESCR, General Comment No.12: The Right to Adequate Food, UN Doc E/C/12/1999/5 (12 May 1999).

At the follow-up Summit,[20] Member States agreed to draft such guidelines through an open-ended inter-governmental working group serviced by the FAO Secretariat, drawing on General Comment No. 12. The group, supported by a strong civil society representation, worked for 18 months in a heated political atmosphere.[21] In November 2004 the FAO Council subsequently adopted the 'Voluntary Guidelines on the Right to Adequate Food',[22] laying the groundwork for further theoretical and practical developments in FAO. A committed team of staff members who had served as the secretariat of the working group, became a Right to Food Unit and placed in the Division of Social Policies and Rural Institutions (ESP). The unit produced a series of informative materials, a comprehensive methodological toolbox and practical handbooks on implementing the human right to adequate food; it also provided advice and direct technical support to governments on the realization of the right to food approach as part of national security. The unit made explicit use of the core human rights principles contained in the 'common understanding', as simplified under the acronym PANTHER: Participation, Accountability, Non-discrimination, Transparency, Human dignity, Empowerment, and respect for the Rule of law.

The UN Special Rapporteur on the right to food at the time, Olivier De Schutter, evaluated FAO's role regarding human rights in 2013.[23] While he praised the high-quality work done by the Right to Food Team, he noted that these were only time-bound projects funded by individual donors rather than being part of the general programme and budget. Since the promotion of the right to adequate food within FAO was insufficiently institutionalized, De Schutter proposed the promotion of the right to food across all FAO activities through dedicated right to food support staff who could serve as 'service providers' to other divisions. He also suggested a network of senior-level

---

[20] FAO, Report of the World Food Summit: *five years later*' (10–13 June 2002), Appendix: Declaration, op. para 10. (2002).

[21] A Oshaug, 'Developing Voluntary Guidelines for Implementing the Right to Adequate Food: Anatomy of an Intergovernmental Process' in W Barth Eide and U Kracht (eds) *Food and Human Rights in Development, Vol. I: Legal and Institutional Dimensions and Selected Topics* (Intersentia 2005); I Rae, et al., 'History and Implications for FAO of the Guidelines on the Right to Adequate Food' in W Barth Eide and U Kracht (eds) *Food and Human Rights in Development, Vol.II Evolving Issues and Emerging Applications* (Intersentia 2007).

[22] 'Voluntary Guidelines to Support the Progressive Realization of the Right to Adequate Food in the Context of National Food Security' (FAO 2005) (hereafter 'Right to Food Guidelines').

[23] UN, Report of the Special Rapporteur on the right to food, Olivier De Schutter, 'Mission to the Food and Agriculture Organization of the United Nations', UN Doc A/HRC/22/50/Add.3 (14 January 2013).

focal points who would promote the mainstreaming effort, and strengthen the Development Law Service of the Legal Office to enable it to inject the right to food normative framework in all the legal advice it provides.[24] The latter has successfully expanded, including with several earlier right-to-food staff members.

The overall reduction of human rights capacity in FAO may be one reason why the Second International Conference on Nutrition (ICN2) in 2014 did not raise as hoped for the potential power of a rights-based approach to food security and nutrition. ICN2 did refer to the calls and recommendations of three preceding food summits to advance the Right to Food Guidelines but failed to make explicit use of the extensive material developed by the FAO Right to Food Team.[25]

An updated review by Anthes and De Schutter in 2018 points to a series of inter-connected influential factors, both of a political and in-house nature in FAO:

> The period from 1996 until roughly 2010 was particularly propitious for human rights mainstreaming, as there was strong support for the right to food among member States and the FAO leadership; however, the more recent period is one of retrenchment. ... [T]he evolution of the right to food's trajectory within FAO reveals that far from showing a steady, unidirectional progress, this troubled path reflects the dynamics of the contentious human rights agenda itself.[26]

Leadership had clearly been lacking to push the human rights agenda forward in FAO in the second decade of the millennium. The successor of Diouff, Brazilian Jose Graziano da Silva (2011–19) who had been the former coordinator of President Lula's Zero Hunger Programme, was a new hope but he never actively promoted the right to food as a human right in FAO. The Right to Food Team continued to suffer from serious resource and priority limitations, and while a small and able team still exists at the time of writing, it has no permanent full staff member and the voluntary funds from external resources will dry up by the end of 2020.[27] One can only hope that the new DG from August 2019, Qu Dongyi of China, might regenerate FAO as a true pro-

---

[24] Ibid., para 39(a).
[25] See FAO's Right to Food home page for all publications including educational material, country information, Methodological Toolbox and Handbooks on implementation, at http://www.fao.org/right-to-food.
[26] O De Schutter and C Anthes, 'The FAO as a Human Rights Food and Agriculture Organization of the United Nations: Advancing the Right to Food to Protect Public Health' in Benjamin M Meier and L Gostin (eds), *Human Rights in Global Health* (OUP 2018) 13.
[27] Personal communication, FAO staff and diplomatic sources.

motor of economic, social and cultural rights including the right to adequate food on a permanent basis. Hope may also lie in other new developments in Rome towards the end of the decade and carried forward into 2020, to which we return in section 3.

2.2.2 WHO

The preamble of the WHO Constitution (1946) states: 'The enjoyment of the highest attainable standard of health is one of the fundamental rights of every human being without distinction of race, religion, political belief, economic or social condition.' Notwithstanding this explicit language, shifts in leadership and prevailing political circumstances have influenced the organization's approach to human rights over the years, with periods of outright rejection of a human rights-based focus contrasted with periods where human rights were given significant attention.

The drafters of the ICESCR used this preamble when formulating Article 12.1 on the right to health. Given WHO's constitutional commitment it could be expected that the Organization would incorporate human rights in its policies and programmes. Meier and Onzivu describe how in the early years under the directorship of Brock Chisholm, WHO did use human rights as a basis for its work, but from 1953, the WHO Secretariat 'intentionally neglected human rights discourse during crucial years in the development and implementation of health-related rights, projecting itself as a technical organization above "legal rights" and squandering opportunities for WHO leadership in the evolution of rights-based approaches to health'.[28]

Halfdan Mahler, the Director-General from 1973-1988, shifted the major emphasis of WHO from communicable diseases to the promotion of basic health services. He was responsible for the milestone declaration adopted at the health conference in Alma Ata in 1978, which reiterated the fundamental nature of the human right to health and adopted a global goal of 'health for all' by 2000. Human rights also became important in regard to the HIV/AIDS epidemic, first as regards civil rights to non-discrimination against excessive restrictions, and gradually through understanding social and economic factors as determinants, involving the realization of economic and social rights.[29]

While Mahler's successor Hiroshi Nakajima de-emphasized human rights after 1988, attention was revived under Gro Harlem Brundtland between 1998 and 2003. She made use of Kofi Annan's reform plan to promote human rights

---

[28] B Meier and W Onzivu, 'The Evolution of Human Rights in World Health Organization Policy and the Future of Human Rights through Global Health Governance' (2014) 128 *Public Health* 179, 180.

[29] D Tarantola, 'Global Justice and Human Rights: Health and Human Rights in Practice' (2007) *Global Justice: Theory Practice Rhetoric* 1, 11–26.

in global health and to re-establish WHO as 'the world's health conscience'.[30] Some years of rethinking and organizational restructuring resulted in the institution of a Health and Human Rights Team as a focal point and for mainstreaming human rights throughout WHO. The Team found internal support from human rights focal points within select program clusters and the collaboration between technical officers and the UN Special Rapporteur.

When Brundtland left, her successor (Lee Jong-wok) moved away from efforts to mainstream human rights. The Department of Ethics, Equity, Trade and Human Rights focused from 2004 to 2010 increasingly on human rights capacity building in various forms, and worked with the UN Office of the High Commissioner for Human Rights to develop an information sheet on 'A Human Rights-Based Approach to Health.'[31] This period coincided with the activities of the first appointed UN Special Rapporteur on the right to health, Professor Paul Hunt (2002–08), which influenced developments in WHO.

Under Margaret Chan from 2007–17, human rights came to the forefront in the context of women's and children's health. The implementation of the UN Secretary-General's Global Strategy on Women and Children's Health in 2010 was framed in a human rights perspective, as was the implementation platform in WHO's 'Partnership on Newborn, Children and Maternal Health (PNCMH)'. Chan argued that this could achieve 'a WHO in which each staff member has the core value of gender, equity and human rights in his/her DNA'.[32] This led to the creation of a small unit in the Cluster of Family, Women and Children – the Gender, Equity and Human Rights Team (GER).[33]

An important project initiated in 2011 by the former Assistant Director-General for the Cluster of Family, Women and Children, Flavia Bustreo, and led by Paul Hunt (now in his personal capacity), searched for evidence of impact of a human rights approach to women's and children's health, with a report published in 2013.[34] It demonstrated that there was 'plausible evidence' that 'human rights-based policies, programmes and other interventions are effective to improve women's and children's health, and that human

---

[30] Meier and Onzivu, n28, 182.
[31] WHO and OHCHR, 'A Human Rights Based Approach to Health', Information brochure (2009) http://www.who.int/hhr/news/hrba_to_health2.pdf.
[32] Cited in S Sridharan, et al., 'Incorporating Gender, Equity, and Human Rights into the Action Planning Process: Moving from Rhetoric to Action' (2016) 9 *Glob Health Action* 1, 1.
[33] Meier and Onzivu, n28, 184.
[34] F Bustreo and P Hunt (eds), *Women's and Children's Health: Evidence of Impact of Human Rights* (WHO 2013).

rights-based approaches contribute to more equitable health-related outcomes for women and children'.³⁵

While this project was not continued as such, it must have inspired the establishment by the UN Secretary-General in 2016 of a one-year High-Level Working Group on the Health and Human Rights of Women, Children and Adolescents, co-hosted by WHO with the Office of the High Commissioner for Human Rights. The group was tasked with securing political support for the implementation of the human rights-related measures contained in the Sustainable Development Goals and the Global Strategy for Women, Children and Adolescent's Health, and providing guidance on how human rights can be integrated into health programming and how the impact of human rights on health outcomes can be better measured. The Working Group's report, and the approach taken, is a landmark for the WHO regarding steps to realize health-related human rights for women, children, and adolescents. ³⁶ While it does not deal with the specific topic of childhood obesity – concentrating on women's, children's and adolescents' health and rights – its human rights approach might give direction for future work.

Other documents appearing in 2017 have likely helped create a stronger human rights climate for WHO's activities. WHO sponsored and joined with several academic and other institutions to prepare the ground-breaking report on health and the role of law.³⁷ Chapter 16 addressed legal responses to poor nutrition, undernutrition, overweight and obesity, suggesting that law and regulatory policies to reduce diet-related diseases can be grouped around the following domains:

- the food environment, including the food retail environment;
- the food production system, including the food supply chain and food content regulations;
- consumer behaviour.

The report argues that legislation must ensure appropriate regulation to prevent harmful consequences for the right to health and to adequate food resulting from contemporary trends and developments, such as urbanization, globalized trade liberalization, and foreign direct investments that transform food chains by supermarkets replacing local markets. Such legislation should also prevent the marketing of ultra-processed low-quality food.

---

[35] Ibid., 13.
[36] WHO, Leading the Realization of the Human Right to Health and Through Health – Report of the High-Level Working Group on the Health and Human Rights of Women, Children and Adolescents (WHO 2017).
[37] WHO, *Advancing the Right to Health: The Vital Role of Law* (WHO 2017).

The timing of the report coincided with the election of the current Director-General, Tedros Adhanom Ghebreyesus. Regarding human rights he stated in a pre-election interview:

> We need to make sure WHO staff take this core value of the organization to heart and truly believe in it. That is how I believe we will most effectively mainstream human rights in WHO's public health programming.[38]

Dr Ghebreyesus has strongly emphasized 'universal health coverage' and the mainstreaming of human rights throughout WHO.[39] In mainstreaming human rights, it will be important to avoid short-circuiting between the two aims. Universal health coverage is not by itself a guarantee for the realization of the right to health, which, however can be pursued in part through universal health coverage.[40] In this regard, WHO's 'Fact sheets' website offer a substantive 'Health and Human Rights' narrative, ending with a section called 'WHO Response':

> WHO has made a commitment to mainstream human rights into healthcare programmes and policies on national and regional levels by looking at underlying determinants of health as part of a comprehensive approach to health and human rights.
> In addition, WHO has been actively strengthening its role in providing technical, intellectual, and political leadership on the right to health including:
> - strengthening the capacity of WHO and its Member States to integrate a human rights-based approach to health;
> - advancing the right to health in international law and international development processes; and
> - advocating for health-related human rights, including the right to health.

Addressing the needs and rights of individuals at different stages across the life course requires taking a comprehensive approach within the broader context of promoting human rights, gender equality, and equity.

As such, WHO promotes a concise and unifying framework that builds on existing approaches in gender, equity, and human rights to generate more accurate and robust solutions to health inequities. The integrated nature of the framework is an opportunity to build on foundational strengths and com-

---

[38] B Meier, 'Human Rights in the World Health Organization: Views of the Director-General Candidates' (2017) 19(1) *Health. Hum. Rights* 293.
[39] Ibid., 295.
[40] WHO, *Anchoring Universal Health Coverage in the Right to Health: What Difference Would it Make?* Policy Brief (2015).

plementarities between these approaches to create a cohesive and efficient approach to promote health and well-being for all.[41]

It must be legitimate to regard this as a summary of WHO's programme platform regarding health as a human right, and Dr Tedros' human rights leadership must be judged in that light. One might therefore have hoped for a more elaborate development of this commitment in the WHO Global Action Plan for 2019,[42] especially as it calls for strengthened collaboration among multilateral organizations to accelerate country progress on the health-related SDGs. It recognizes the need for always promoting equity of women and human rights but does not specify what is meant by a human rights-based approach to health.[43]

3. THE UN DECADE OF ACTION ON NUTRITION – A TEST PERIOD FOR STRENGTHENING GOVERNANCE AND ACCOUNTABILITY FOR NUTRITION FROM A HUMAN RIGHTS PERSPECTIVE?

3.1 The Nutrition Decade Work Programme

This work programme is based on recommendations in the Framework for Action on Nutrition adopted by ICN2 in November 2014. It is structured in six cross-cutting, integrative action areas: (1) sustainable, resilient food systems for healthy diets; (2) aligned health systems providing universal coverage of essential nutrition actions; (3) social protection and nutrition education; (4) trade and investment for improved nutrition; (5) safe and supportive environments for nutrition at all ages; (6) strengthened governance and accountability for nutrition.[44]

These actions should be seen as standards to be achieved, fitted to given needs and circumstances. The work programme also provides a set of Guiding Principles to give direction to the work and refers to human rights by assuming that the Nutrition Decade will provide, 'an enabling environment such that national, regional and international policies and programmes respect, protect and fulfil the right of everyone to have access to safe, sufficient, and nutritious food consistent with the right to adequate food and the fundamental right of

---

[41] https://www.who.int/news-room/fact-sheets/detail/human-rights-and-health.

[42] WHO, Strengthening collaboration among multilateral organizations to accelerate country progress on the health-related Sustainable Development Goals (2019).

[43] See further, B Meier and L Gostin, *Human Rights in Global Health. Rights-Based Governance for a Globalizing World* (OUP 2018).

[44] UN Work Programme, n3, para 18.

everyone to be free from hunger', referring to the ICESCR 'and other relevant United Nations instruments'.[45]

A more direct reference point is found under action area 4:

> Coherence between trade and nutrition policies is vital. Trade policies and agreements should support implementation of nutrition policies and programmes and should not negatively impact the right to adequate food in other countries.[46]

Reference is given to a General Assembly resolution on the Right to Food from 2014 which '[s]tresses that all States should make all efforts to ensure that their international policies of a political and economic nature, including international trade agreements, do not have a negative impact on the right to food in other countries'.[47]

These are vague terms, which should be clarified in future updates of the work programme. A more direct human rights approach should be developed for each section of the work programme. Applying a human rights-based approach also means observing certain principles under the 'common understanding' of the UN Development Group referred to in section 2 of this chapter.[48] These principles should direct the processes of action and actively enable an environment conducive to implementing the recommendations and meeting the standards successfully.

Action area 6 of the Nutrition Decade work programme is on 'Strengthened governance and accountability for nutrition'. This invites reflections on how a human rights-based approach can support such an ambition in the Decade. It would require the framework to be extended from proposed standards for achievement to also accommodate explicit process criteria based on human rights principles. Governance and accountability must include that states hold corporations accountable for their impact on the food environment, but also that the relevant UN bodies develop clear policies on the practical implications of this for governments and food-related corporations.

While WHO and FAO have been entrusted with the overall leadership for action in the Nutrition Decade, in collaboration with WFP, IFAD and UNICEF, guidance on strengthening governance and accountability is expected from the two entities mandated to coordinate the contributions of all stakeholders to implement the decade: the UN Committee on World Food Security (CFS) and the interagency UN System Standing Committee on Nutrition (UNSCN). To what extent are these two contributing to strengthen a human rights approach

---

[45] Ibid., para 16.
[46] Ibid., para 40.
[47] UN, 'The Right to Food', UN Doc. A/RES/68/177 (28 January 2014).
[48] n8.

to food security and nutrition, so as to enable a human rights environment for more effective UN action on child obesity?

3.2 The UN Committee on World Food Security (CFS)

CFS was established in 1974 as one of several technical intergovernmental committees of FAO. A fundamental reform in 2009 transformed it into a broader UN forum which also ensured that the voices of other stakeholders be heard in the global debate on food security and nutrition, including other UN agencies, a special Civil Society and Indigenous Peoples Mechanism (CSM), and also a Private Sector Mechanism (PSM). The CFS is responsible to the UN General Assembly through the Economic and Social Council (ECOSOC) and to the FAO General Conference.[49] FAO shares responsibility for its secretariat with World Food Programme (WFP) and the International Fund for Agricultural Development (IFAD).

The CSF is led by its 'Global Strategic Framework on Food Security and Nutrition (GSF)', which is regularly updated and discussed for re-adoption by the Member states. The annotated outline for the GSF adopted by CFS in 2011 stated the following:

> The global food security crisis has revealed the extent to which people are unable to enjoy their right to food. Lessons learned from an increasing number of countries that use the right to food as a framework for the design, implementation and evaluation of national laws, policies and programmes should be effectively disseminated. Incorporating right to food principles in the design and implementation of food security strategies, policies and programmes is an important step in this direction.[50]

All editions of the GSF have reflected this general creed which the CFS is therefore expected to reflect in its work.[51] Of special interest are therefore the thematic studies coming out of CFS' own High Level Panel of Experts (HLPE) based on work by specially appointed project teams on a range of development activities and their relation to food security (from 2014: 'food security and nutrition') as requested by the CFS. Of these studies, Report No. 4 on Social Protection for Food Security[52] was based on an explicit human rights platform,

---

[49] CFS, About the Committee on World Food Security, http://www.fao.org/cfs/home/about/en/.
[50] FAO, Global Strategic Framework for Food Security and Nutrition: Annotated Outline, CFS: 2011 (June 2011), IV - Policy Options, para 10.
[51] For more details see: CFS, 'Global Strategic Framework for Food Security and Nutrition (GSF)', Doc. CFS 2017/44/10/Rev.1 (October 2017).
[52] CFS-HLPE, 'Social Protection for Food Security', Report No.4 (Rome, 2012).

while Nos 8, 12 and 14 make varying references and recommendations for linkages to human rights and the right to food.[53]

Report No. 12, on 'Nutrition and Food Systems', sees food systems in terms of three constituent elements: food supply chains, food environments and dietary behaviour. Each of these and their interrelationships should be analysed with emphasis on the role of diets as a core link between food systems and their health and nutrition outcomes.[54] This framework is promising for analytically tracing relationships between a prevailing food environment and food choices that contribute to overweight and obesity.[55] The fact that the three elements mirror those applied in the simultaneous WHO report already referred to,[56] makes the two mutually supportive but with the WHO report based on a stronger understanding of the vital role of law in underpinning policy. However, the HLPE Report No. 12 does reflect, without being specific, a fair understanding of and attention to human rights, and holds that 'better results can be achieved if the determinants of the problems and the consequences of the decisions made are properly analysed, and if the principles of human rights inform the decisions made'.[57]

At the 45th CFS Session in October 2018, two themes were significant: a review and discussion about the extent to which, and how, the FAO Right to Food Guidelines of 2004 had been used by Member States and with what results; furthermore a discussion and endorsement of the terms of reference for a set of new 'Voluntary Guidelines on Policy Guidance for Food Systems and Nutrition' (VGFSN). The 46th CFS Session in 2019 saw the launch of the FAO booklet 'Fifteen years of implementing the Right the Food Guidelines'.[58] Meanwhile the preparation of a preliminary draft of the new guidelines started in early 2019 and the final draft should be ready for negotiation and adoption by the CFS at its 47th session in October 2020. Substantive support from Member States for a solid anchoring of the analyses and recommendations in human rights/the right to food has been limited, while the civil society mechanism together with a few states continue to promote it.

In parallel the CFS-HLPE is preparing Report No.15, 'Food security and nutrition: building a global narrative towards 2030'. It recognizes all forms of malnutrition and also the vulnerability of young children and youth to risks of overweight and obesity. An early draft for global electronic consultation in

---

[53] CFS-HLPE, Reports 2011- :, http://www.fao.org/cfs/cfs-hlpe/reports/en/.
[54] HLPE, 'Nutrition and Food Systems', Report No.12 (Rome, 2017).
[55] Ibid., 47, Box 5.
[56] n39.
[57] Ibid., 111.
[58] FAO, Fifteen years implementing the right to food guidelines (Rome, 2019).

February 2020 made human rights a priority; the final result is expected for the CFS 47 in October.

3.3 UN System Standing Committee on Nutrition (UNSCN)

The UNSCN was established in 1977. UNSCN reviews the overall directions, coherence, scale and impact of the UN systems response to the nutritional problems in the world. It is a point of convergence in harmonizing the policies and activities of the UN system and it develops policies and programmes in the UN systems in response to countries' nutrition needs.[59]

UNSCN acts as a catalyst for sharing knowledge, best practice and cutting-edge information. It is thus a forum where the member agencies can – in principle – develop joint global approaches and align positions and actions when addressing the complex nutrition challenges as they evolve; how far they are prepared to do so in practice is another matter.

According to the UNSCN Coordinator Stineke Oenema, the 'UNSCN, as a UN committee, is and will continue to be dedicated to advocating for human rights as one of the underlying principles of its work, as it has always been'.[60] Its earlier experience in this traces back to the work of the SCN Working Group on Nutrition, Ethics and Human Rights, established to spread information among and inspire members to explicitly appreciate the call on them by the UN Charter to bring human rights into their activities.[61] The reformed UNSCN is a valid arrangement for its general purpose but without thematic working groups. Hence there is structurally no particular aptitude to actively catalyse human rights understanding and approaches among members, although one must expect a readiness to harmonize if and when members strengthen their own initiatives. Thus, for the UNSCN the remainder of the Nutrition Decade will be crucial for how it might re-catalyse the interest across the UN family in living up to the Charter in their interaction with Member States.

---

[59] UNSCN, 'By 2030, end all forms of malnutrition and leave no one behind' (2017) Discussion Paper.

[60] UNSCN News 'A Spotlight on the Nutrition Decade', 42 (Summer 2017), https://www.unscn.org/en/Unscn-news?idnews=1682.

[61] U Kracht, et al., 'Human Rights in the United Nations System Standing Committee on Nutrition (SCN)', in WB Eide and U Kracht (eds), n21.

4. OPENINGS FOR RIGHTS-BASED PREVENTION OF CHILDHOOD OBESITY AND NCDS BY KEY UN DEVELOPMENT AND HUMAN RIGHTS BODIES

4.1 Towards Freedom from Obesity by Freedom from an Obesogenic Environment

The concept of 'the right to be free from obesity and related diseases', as a sub-category of the right to adequate food and the right to health, was coined and adopted by the UNSCN in 2007.[62] During the 1990s awareness of the 'nutrition transition'[63] and growing epidemiological evidence led to the concept of 'the double burden of malnutrition'.[64] The International Conference on Nutrition (ICN) in Rome in 1992 jointly organized by FAO and WHO mentioned obesity as a risk of NCDs but did not put the causes of this risk high on the agenda. At ICN2 in 2014 Member States committed themselves to 'reverse the rising trends in overweight and obesity and reduce the burden of diet-related noncommunicable diseases in all age groups'.[65] It also reaffirmed that improving diets and nutrition requires 'improving information for consumers, while avoiding inappropriate marketing and publicity of foods and non-alcoholic beverages to children'.[66]

While the human right to be free from obesity semantically mirrors the 'right to be free from hunger' in ICESCR, a better phrasing would be 'the human right to be free from obesogenic food environments'. This feeds directly into the mounting debates on dysfunctional food systems or food environments in contributing to different forms of malnutrition, and points to obligations of states to protect vulnerable groups from such environments.[67] Thus it touches upon the balance between state regulations and interests of

---

[62] Statement prepared by the then UN SCN Working Groups on 'Nutrition throughout the Life Cycle" and "Nutrition, Ethics and Human Rights', adopted at the 33rd Session of the UNSCN in Geneva in 2006 and reiterated at the 34th Session in Rome in 2007, https://www.unscn.org/files/Statements/Joint_statement_lifecycle_nehr_The_human_right_of_children_and_adolescents_to_adequate_food_and_bee_free_from_obesity.pdf.
[63] B Popkin and A Drewnovski, 'The Nutrition Transition: New Trends in the Global Diet' (1997) 55 *Nutrition Review* 31–43.
[64] WHO, 'The Double Burden of Malnutrition' (2017) Policy Brief, WHO/NMH/NHD/17.3.
[65] Second International Conference on Nutrition (ICN2), 'Rome Declaration on Nutrition', Doc.ICN2 2014/2 (November 2014), para 15.
[66] Ibid., para 13 f.
[67] This can be compared with obligations to protect from unhygienic and contaminating environments to prevent communicable diseases which contribute to and are aggravated by undernutrition.

business, advertising companies and retailers' presentation of goods in ways that may have implications for consumers' food behaviour.

In the following subsections we consider some relevant experiences and openings relevant to the prevention of child obesity and related NCDs, first by WHO and FAO as the lead agencies of the Nutrition Decade, and subsequently some critical human rights institutions and procedures. The recent years' revival of UNICEF as a child rights-based UN actor, including in fighting obesity and NCDs, concludes the overview.

4.2   WHO in the Forefront

WHO is in the forefront among standard setters tackling childhood obesity as a co-determinant of NCDs. WHO has long been concerned with the role played by food corporations in food processing and marketing that may create obesogenic environments. WHO's 'nutrition profiling' engagement is part of this, as is the 'Set of recommendations on the marketing of foods and non-alcoholic beverages to children' adopted by the World Health Assembly,[68] the 'Framework for implementation of the WHO set of recommendations on marketing of foods and non-alcoholic beverages to children',[69] and the report of the WHO Commission on Ending Childhood Obesity (ECHO).[70]

Yet, to what extent has WHO furthered a human rights perspective and approaches in applying these sources? The Framework on marketing refers repeatedly to the Convention on the Rights of the Child without going further into a rights-based approach; the same is true for the ECHO report. Together they constitute a useful collection of standards of achievement that could serve in operationalizing a human rights-based approach, when combined with human rights principles of conduct as under the 'Common Understanding'.

A particular site for such developments is the UN Interagency Task Force on NCD (UNIATF) led by WHO. A seminar in 2017 in Geneva[71] made a start by exploring how human rights are relevant to the response to NCDs, including across the six key pillars of the 'WHO Global Action Plan for the Prevention

---

[68]   WHO, 'Set of Recommendations on the Marketing of Foods and Non-Alcoholic Beverages to Children' (WHO 2010).

[69]   WHO, 'Framework for implementation of the WHO set of recommendations on marketing of foods and non-alcoholic beverages to children' (WHO 2012).

[70]   WHO, 'Ending Childhood Obesity: Securing the Future for our Children', Report of the Commission on Ending Childhood Obesity (ECHO) (25 January 2016).

[71]   UNIATF, Seminar on Noncommunicable Diseases and Human Rights held in Geneva on 20 February 2017, hosted by the secretariat of the WHO Inter-Agency Task force on NCDs and the WHO Global Coordinating Mechanism on NCDs, http://apps.who.int/iris/bitstream/handle/10665/260111/WHO-NMH-NMA-17.61-eng.pdf?sequence=.

and Control of Noncommunicable Diseases 2013–2020' (GAP).[72] The report from the seminar submitted to the UNIATF contains promising steps and prospects for a follow-up.[73] It recognizes that the extent to which human rights are realized has a definitive impact on the success of efforts to prevent and treat the four major NCDs and tackle their four main risk factors. Therefore, human rights represent much more than mere policy options.[74] Participants agreed on the duty of states to provide healthy environments by transforming obesogenic environments and creating policies to empower individuals to exercise autonomy over their health. Participants further recognized that the policy and legal environment in which people exercise their rights is not necessarily neutral and that effective policies will empower and motivate, besides having a focus on marginalized populations.[75] The engagement of all stakeholders from civil society and health care professionals to UN agencies was seen as imperative in order to build the capacity of front line workers. The training of health care professionals must cover human rights, professional standards and advocacy, while it is important to capitalize on synergies.[76]

Among next steps agreed was the development of further tools to articulate the role and relevance of human rights and to provide guidance on their concrete applications,[77] and a menu of indicators that could be included in the GAP.[78] In this connection we draw attention to and commend efforts by the OHCHR to define some of the human rights principles in measurable terms for assessment and monitoring.[79]

While the work within the UN family in these matters thus seems on a stable path anchored in the UNIATF in collaboration with the relevant technical divisions of the UN bodies concerned, hopefully a similar evolution will be reflected in the intergovernmental GCM/NCD[80] which 'will build on country

---

[72] WHO, 'Global Action Plan for the Prevention and Control of Noncommunicable Diseases 2013-2020' (GAP), (WHO 2013).

[73] The report was presented to the Ninth Meeting of the UNIATF on 9–10 November 2017 held at WHO in Geneva. No further action seems to have been taken at the time of writing.

[74] Ibid., para 6.

[75] Ibid., para 4.

[76] Ibid., para 11.

[77] Ibid., para 17.

[78] Ibid., para 18 ii.

[79] Office of the High Commissioner for Human Rights (OHCHR), 'A Human Rights-Based Approach to Data. Leaving no one Behind in the 2030 Development Agenda: Guidance Note to Data Collection and Disaggregation' (October 2015).

[80] Global Coordination Mechanism on the Prevention and Control of NCDs, see website at www.who.int/global-coordination-mechanism/about/en/.

needs and will ultimately aim at supporting country efforts across sectors to implement the Global NCD Action Plan'.[81]

Further normative guidance on addressing NCDs was expected from the 'WHO Independent Global High-level Commission on Noncommunicable Diseases' established by Dr Tedros in 2017.[82] The Commission was to advise the Director-General on 'bold and at the same time practical recommendations on how to transform new opportunities to enable countries to accelerate progress towards SDG target 3.4 on NCD'.[83] Some hoped that childhood obesity as a key factor in the NCD-epidemic would be given special attention by the Commission and that it would anchor its work on NCDs in a solid human right to health framework while explicitly appreciating 'the vital role of law' as endorsed by WHO.[84] With the UNIATF having made a kick-start through the seminar in 2017,[85] would the new High-level Commission take the next steps to encourage WHO as an organization approaching NCDs in a human rights context?

In its first report in June 2018,[86] the Commission recommends that 'all activities be framed within existing principles, including human rights- and equity-based approaches (including non-discrimination, gender equality, participation)…'.[87] However, the final report delivered in December 2019[88] is totally void of references to human rights or the right to health. Its Recommendation 6 calls on WHO 'to increase its engagement with the private sector to promote their effective and meaningful contribution to global NCDs targets and goals, and to provide technical support to Member States to increase the capacity needed for such engagements to national NCD responses'.[89] If this would mean getting industry to really respect the right to adequate food and health and act accordingly in their processing and marketing practice, it would perhaps have legitimacy. However, it is significant that one

---

[81] GCM/NCD, Terms of Reference, UN Doc A67/14 Add.1 (8 May 2014), para 3.
[82] WHO Update, 1 February 2018, http://www.who.int/global-coordination-mechanism/about/en.
[83] WHO, 'Terms of Reference for the WHO Independent High-level Commission on NCDs' (WHO 2018).
[84] WHO, n41.
[85] WHO, n72.
[86] WHO, 'Time to Deliver', Report of the WHO Independent High-level Commission on Noncommunicable Diseases (WHO June 2018).
[87] Ibid., p. 13 (under 'Rationale for the Recommendations').
[88] WHO, 'It's time to walk the talk', Final Report of the WHO Independent High-level Commission on Noncommunicable Diseases (WHO December 2019).
[89] Ibid., p. 21.

Commission member, Katie Dain, found reason to dissociate herself from this recommendation:

> While I fully support the need to engage relevant private sector in the response to prevent and control NCDs, I don't believe a platform is the best way to achieve this. ... These platforms have often provided a vehicle for the food, beverage and alcohol industries to promote ineffective voluntary approaches such as self-regulation, over and above the evidence-based policy, legislative, fiscal and regulatory measures ... that we know work. The composition and power balance of such platforms are often heavily weighted towards industry representation, therefore the potential for conflict of interest is rife.[90]

Dain rightfully points to the fact that when states seek to enhance public health through regulatory policies, they sometimes come into conflict with international trade and investment law. Individual states may risk being faced with legal challenges by powerful corporations.[91] Dain encourages WHO to:

> ... conduct a comprehensive analysis of the impact and lessons learnt of similar existing or previous platforms ... develop rules of engagement to manage conflict of interest and other risks of engagement, establish a robust monitoring and evaluation framework to measure the impact of the platform, introduce an annual independent review of the platform, and avoid duplication with the existing global architecture of NCDs, such as the WHO Global Coordination Mechanism on NCDs and UN Inter-Agency Task Force on NCDs.

WHO's Department of Nutrition for Health and Development (NHD) had already made transparent the conflicts of interest in nutrition policies and programmes at country level and provided guidance for how to manage them. A draft approach for the prevention and management of such risks in nutrition was presented at the 71st World Health Assembly in 2018 as a report to the Director-General.[92] The approach was announced to be piloted at country level in the six WHO regions and the document exposed to further consultations as a living document.

---

[90] NCD Alliance, Release of the second WHO Independent High-Level Commission report on NCDs, Statement by Commissioner Katie Dain, CEO of the NCD Alliance, 11 December 2019.

[91] See, e.g., Andrew Jacobs Andmatt Richtel, 'How Big Business got Brazil Hooked on to Junk Foods', *New York Times*, 16 September 2017, https://www.nytimes.com/interactive/2017/09/16/health/brazil-obesity-nestle.html?emc=etal.

[92] WHO, 'Safeguarding Against Possible Conflicts of Interest in Nutrition Programmes, Draft Approach for the Prevention and Management of Conflicts of Interest in the Development and Implementation of Nutrition Programmes at Country Level', WHO Doc. A71/23 (22 March 2018).

4.3 FAO and the Links Between Food Systems and Obesity

Undernutrition and hunger were initially the main priorities of FAO. Gradually, overweight and obesity have come to the organization's attention, duly addressed in several annual reports.[93] FAO could expand the links between obesity and food systems from a human rights perspective, given the organization already has shown such extensive expertise in the case of the right to adequate food. The Right to Food Guidelines in 2004[94] opened an active period of developing further the meaning and measurements for addressing food security and nutrition in human rights terms (section 2). Guideline 10.2 says: 'States are encouraged to take steps, in particular through education, information and labelling regulations, to prevent overconsumption and unbalanced diets that may lead to malnutrition, obesity and degenerative diseases.' FAO's strengthened interest in linking obesity to wider food systems is promising, also for demonstrating why undernutrition and obesity can exists side by side even within the same household. This parallels FAO's gradual shift in focus towards systems thinking around sustainable sources and resources for a sustainable food supply, and access through local food environments towards healthy diets.

Unhealthy food marketing to children was not yet in the picture when drafting the Right to Food Guidelines, beyond mentioning the International Code of Marketing of Breast-milk Substitutes in Guideline 10.5. 16 years later and with the global recognition of the responsibility of the food industry in line with the UN Guiding Principles on Business and Human Rights, FAO should draw on its broad experience with the right to food to elaborate on what it means to be free from an obesogenic environment in human rights terms. FAO's comprehensive Methodological Toolbox for the implementation of the right to adequate food[95] should be expanded to add new rights-based tools for actions in the interface between food systems and childhood obesity in collaboration with WHO and UNICEF. Such tools demand a high sensitivity to the role of law and new legislation within specific sectors of relevance.

Good working relationships between FAO and WHO in the rest of the Nutrition Decade is not only desirable but imperative given their joint leadership. Collaboration on human rights-based approaches should be specifically followed up when developing the human rights dimensions of the Decade's work programme. A possible mediator might be the informal 'Friends of the

---

[93] From 2017 co-authored with IFAD (International Fund for Agricultural Development), UNICEF, World Food Program and WHO; See, e.g., *State of Food Security and Nutrition in the World* (FAO 2019).
[94] See, n22.
[95] http://www.fao.org/right-to-food/resources/rtf-methodological-toolbox/en/.

Right to Food' group set up to strategize and make proposals towards greater human rights coherence in policy making.[96] The group works closely with the Civil Society Mechanism of the CFS in arranging discussions and strategizing. Jointly they should press the need for the CFS to revive FAO's latent potential in the field of operationalising the right to adequate food – but now within the global picture of malnutrition in all its forms as an overall UN system concern.

4.4 The UN Human Rights Council (HRC)

As the intergovernmental political body for human rights in the UN, can the Human Rights Council play a role in the fight against childhood obesity and NCDs? What mechanisms would the Council have for addressing childhood obesity? There are indeed several entry points of interest. We explore contributions of the Council-appointed UN Special Rapporteurs on the right to food and the right to health[97] and the Council's Working Group on Business and Human Rights.

4.4.1 The function of UN Special Rapporteurs on the right to food and on the right to health

The Special Rapporteurs constitute an important procedure by which the UN can increase awareness of human rights problems in specific countries or regarding thematic human rights. They can address issues at high political levels during their country missions on invitation; these opportunities should be further explored. Recent thematic Special Rapporteurs on the right to food and on the right to health have provided penetrating analyses relevant to obesity and NCDs and have presented useful recommendations to Member States and international organizations. All have underlined the problematic impact of corporate-driven economic globalization, including the intensification of industrial agriculture, with extensive foreign direct investments combined with a growing concentration among retailers and major suppliers, leading to widespread disappearance of local markets resulting in an entirely different food environment.

Olivier De Schutter, Special Rapporteur on the right to food between 2008 and 2014, dealt specifically with the problematic direction pursued by modern

---

[96] The informal "Friends of the Right to Food in Rome" was established in 2018 by delegates accredited to the Rome-based UN food agencies with the objective of advocating for positioning the Right to Adequate Food in the decision-making processes in these Rome-based UN agencies and to help disseminate the Right to Food,

[97] These belong to the set of thematic rapporteurs as contrasted to country-focused rapporteurs under the Special Procedures of the Council.

agri-food systems,⁹⁸ which focus mostly on increasing food production while neglecting the dietary consequences of the resulting food environment. Anand Grover, the Special Rapporteur on the right to health between 2008 and 2014, also describes how the process of globalization has resulted in the growing presence of ultra-processed food with negative consequences for obesity and NCDs.⁹⁹

Both rapporteurs call for national strategies for the realization of the right to adequate food towards adequate diets for all, making full use of the three main levels of state obligations for human rights – respect, protect, and fulfil.¹⁰⁰ They recognize however that prospects are limited: governments will face strong resistance not only by organized corporate networks, but also within their own societies.

Specifically, Grover emphasizes that 'States should formulate and implement a national public health strategy and plan of action to address diet-related NCDs, which should be widely disseminated'.¹⁰¹ De Schutter recommends adoption of 'a national strategy for the realization of the right to adequate food which integrates the objective of guaranteeing the right to adequate diets for all and sets specific targets and time frames for action'.¹⁰² Hilal Elver, the Special Rapporteur on the right to food between 2014 and 2020 is concerned with the responsibility of corporations:

> The [UN] Guiding Principles on Business and Human Rights ... formally recognize the responsibility of enterprises to avoid infringing on the human rights of others and to address adverse human rights impacts with which they are involved. Logically, this responsibility includes the adverse impacts of the food industry with respect to the right to adequate food ... Recent initiatives ... indicate the need for stronger accountability mechanisms at the national level, considering that voluntary corporate initiatives are proving ineffective.¹⁰³

---

⁹⁸ Report of the Special Rapporteur on the right to food to the Human Rights Council, UN Doc A/HRC/19/59 (26 December 2011).

⁹⁹ Report of the Special Rapporteur on the right to health, 'Unhealthy foods, non-communicable diseases and the right to health', UN Doc A/HRC/26/31 (1 April 2014).

¹⁰⁰ For an explanation of these categories see A Eide, 'State Obligations Revisited', chapter 6 in WB Eide and U Kracht (eds), n21.

¹⁰¹ See, n98, para 63.

¹⁰² See, n97, para 50(a).

¹⁰³ Interim Report of the Special Rapporteur on the Right to Food, UN Doc A/71/282 (3 August 2016), paras 68 and 73.

4.4.2 HRC Working Group on Business and Human Rights and the UN Forum on Business and Human Rights

The impact of major corporations on public life has massively increased during the last three decades of corporate-driven economic globalization. Corporations can indeed make and have made important positive contributions to development, but they can also cause serious harm to the realization of human rights, including the right to food and the right to health. The UN has been preoccupied with the need to ensure that corporations recognize their responsibility to respect these and other human rights in the societies in which they operate. After active, but failed efforts in the late 1990s and early 2000s, the UN Secretary-General appointed, in 2005, Harvard professor John Ruggie as Special Representative on the issue of human rights and transnational corporations and other business enterprises. Ruggie had been acting since 1997 as UN Assistant Secretary-General and as one of the main architects of the UN Global Compact (launched in 2000) which promotes voluntary corporate social responsibility. He was requested to clarify the roles and responsibilities of states, companies and other social actors in the human rights sphere.

Ruggie's final report sets out the Guiding Principles on Business and Human Rights (UNGP) built on three pillars: the obligations of states to protect human rights, the responsibility of corporations to respect human rights (carefully avoiding the term 'obligation'!), and a joint responsibility of the (host) state and the business enterprises to ensure the availability of remedies in case there have been violations of human rights during the activity of the business entity.[104] While states are bound by the human rights conventions to which they are parties, for the corporations these guidelines are voluntary. To enhance the pressure on business enterprises to respect human rights during their operations, the Council established a Working Group on Business and Human Rights. Among its activities is the organization of an annual UN Forum on Business and Human Rights at UN headquarters in Geneva, open to all stakeholders interested. The Forum has attracted wide interest and extensive participation by more than 2,000 participants and the lively debates have significantly increased the transparency of corporate activities in regard to human rights. The Forum could be an important arena for initiatives in the Nutrition Decade to discuss the responsibility of food-relevant businesses to respect the right of children to adequate food and to be free from an obesogenic environment.[105]

---

[104] UN, 'Guiding Principles on Business and Human Rights: Implementing the United Nations "Protect, Respect and Remedy" Framework', HR/PUB/11/04 (UN 2011).

[105] See further on this in section 5 of this chapter.

4.5 The Committee on the Rights of the Child and the Committee on Economic, Social and Cultural Rights

The Committee on the Rights of the Child (CRC) and the Committee on Economic, Social and Cultural Rights (CESCR) have both repeatedly examined the impact of business activities on the enjoyment of the rights. In its General Comment No. 15, the CRC spelled out the general obligations of states parties regarding the right to health. It has clear language on the responsibilities in relation to the International Code of Marketing of Breastmilk Substitutes, and the elimination of inappropriate marketing practices. In 2013, the CRC adopted its General Comment No. 16 regarding the impact of the business sector on children's rights,[106] which spells out a framework for implementation, including legislative, regulatory and enforcement measures, remedial measures, policy measures and coordination and monitoring measures, ending by spelling out possible collaborative and awareness-raising measures.

The CESCR's 'General Comment No. 24 on State Obligations under the ICESCR in the context of Business Activities'[107] reminds states parties, in paragraph 19, that the obligation to protect sometimes necessitates direct regulation and intervention, giving as examples measures restricting marketing and advertising of certain goods and services in order to protect public health, such as of tobacco products, and of breast-milk substitutes.[108] Producing and marketing unhealthy foods and beverages directed to children would be other examples that need similar protective measures in the future.

4.6 UNICEF

UNICEF deserves special recognition as a promotor of children's rights – in general and with specific regard to food and nutrition from a human rights perspective. This originated with UNICEF being the organizer of the World Summit for Children in 1990 following the formal adoption in 1989 of the UN Convention on the Rights of the Child. The Summit helped to quickly raise the number of states parties to the Convention, which is today ratified by all UN Member States but one (USA). At the same time UNICEF proclaimed its work with nutrition for women and children to be fully rooted in the CRC, under the active leadership of the then Chief of Nutrition in UNICEF, the late Urban Jonsson. His personal engagement contributed strongly to the momentum in

---

[106] CRC, 'General Comment No. 16 on State obligations regarding the impact of the business sector on children's rights, UN Doc. CRC/C/GC/16, (17 April 2013).
[107] CESCR, UN Doc. E/C.12/GC/24 (10 August 2017).
[108] By February 2020, 170 States had ratified this Covenant.

the UN for linking nutrition in general with human rights during the 1990s and into the first decade of the millennium. UNICEF has recently been especially active in exposing unhealthy food marketing to children and youth from a child rights perspective, both regarding breastmilk substitutes and junk foods directed to older children and their role in childhood obesity.[109] Hopefully, UNICEF will sustain and further cultivate its stance on human rights vis-à-vis malnutrition in all its forms.

5. VISIONS OF POSSIBLE FUTURE STEPS AND SOME CONCLUDING REFLECTIONS

5.1 Obstacles and Scope

The focus of this chapter has been the role of the UN system in the realization of the human rights to adequate food and the right to health. Is there a scope for mobilizing the UN system further towards ending childhood obesity? We recognize the obstacles. In the evaluation in 2012 of the proposal to 'deliver as one', it was soberly pointed out that 'delivering as one' could be more accurately described as 'delivering as if one', given the fact that each UN entity has its own governance structure, mandate and culture.[110] Voluntary coordination at country level among very diverse existing agencies and other UN bodies requires strong leadership and is made even more difficult by global organizations that are part of the UN system yet independent of its Charter, such as WTO. However, following the adoption, in 2015, of the UN Sustainable Development Goals, the importance of efforts to deliver as one has become even more pressing and has received renewed attention,[111] and led the UN to begin outlining a reform plan for the United Nations Development System in 2017.[112]

---

[109] UNICEF, A Child Rights-Based Approach to Food Marketing: A Guide for Policy Makers. 2018; UNICEF and UN Special Rapporteur on the Right to Food, 'Protecting Children's Right to a Healthy Food Environment', UNICEF, 2019.

[110] UN, 'Independent Evaluation of Delivering as One', Summary Report 2012, Section VII: Lessons learned. The full report was made available to Member States with the cover Note of the Secretary-General, UN Doc A/66/859 (26 June 2012).

[111] Sally Fegan-Wyles, 'Delivering as One: Could it Help the 2030 SDG Agenda?' (February 2016), Future United Nations Development System, Briefing 38.

[112] UN, 'Deputy Secretary-General Outlines Reform Plan for United Nations Development System, Urging Economic and Social Council to 'Stay Engaged', Press Release DSG/SM/1100-ECOSOC/6869 (6 October 2017) www.un.org/press/en/2017/dsgsm1100.doc.htm; UN General Assembly, Repositioning of the United Nations development system in the context of the quadrennial comprehensive policy review

Hopefully these evolving processes will also facilitate a stronger and more integrated focus on the double duty of states to reduce hunger and eliminate harmful food environments leading to obesity and NCDs, in line both with the SDGs and the aims of the UN Decade of Action on Nutrition.

5.2 Sources of Inspiration for Further Action

The following are some suggestions that could, if further pursued by relevant UN actors, strengthen human rights-based actions to reduce childhood obesity as a contributing factor to NCDs in the Nutrition Decade.

The High-Level Working Group on the Health and Human Rights of Women, Children and Adolescents and its report 'Leading the Realization of Human Rights to Health and Through Health' (section 2 above) focuses on women's, children's and adolescents' health and rights. It specifically addresses the International Code of Marketing on Breastmilk Substitutes with nine action points. Equally relevant is strengthening a human rights-based approach to childhood obesity. Another high-level working group should therefore be established to explore the human rights dimensions of obesity in childhood and adolescence as a factor in increasing NCDs. This group should consider the UN Guiding Principles on Business and Human Rights and elaborate the responsibility of food companies to respect human rights by reducing marketing pressure on children of unhealthy foods. Member States should be requested to regulate the nutrient content of processed foods as well as marketing practices in line with their protective obligations, drawing on both General Comment No. 16 of the Committee on the Rights of the Child and General Comment No. 24 of the CESCR. The recommendations of the group could feed directly into the UNIATF's normative guidance and technical tools addressed to Member States through the Global Coordinating Mechanism on NCDs.[113]

There is a need to stimulate efforts to bring these issues to the Human Rights Council (HRC). In 2013 The Council requested a technical guidance document on human rights-based approaches to policies and programmes to reduce preventable mortality and morbidity in newborns and children under five years of age, from the OHCHR and WHO for submission to the Council in 2014.[114] Inspired by that precedent, Council members might be encouraged to call for a similar technical guidance with focus on the application of a human

---

of operational activities for development of the United Nations system, UN Doc. A/RES/72/279, 2018.

[113] See: http://www.who.int/global-coordination-mechanism/about/en/.

[114] UN Human Rights Council, 'Technical guidance on the application of a human rights-based approach to the implementation of policies and programmes to reduce and

rights-based approach to policies and programmes to reduce preventable mortality and morbidity from all forms of malnutrition in childhood and adolescence. The new technical guidance should include all forms of malnutrition including those leading to overweight and obesity. To make it happen, lobbying from civil society and academia on Council delegates would be necessary.

In 2014 a parallel side event at the Third UN Forum for Business and Human Rights asked, 'Does the World Need a Human Rights Based Convention on Healthy Diets? Exploring the Role of Food Corporations towards the Rights to Adequate Food and Health'.[115] A more formal follow-up session should be proposed for a forthcoming Forum to address the responsibility of food companies to respect the right to adequate food and the right to health of children. It should be formed around the obligation of states to ensure protection against obesogenic environments by stronger regulatory legislation regarding ultra-processed foods and marketing practices to children.

Further inspiration can be taken from the long-standing focus of the Committee on the Rights of the Child on infant feeding and its request to states to report on frequency and length of breastfeeding in their countries. The International Baby Food Action Network (IBFAN) has no doubt had considerable influence on the Committee through its alternative country reports when states have their own reports discussed by the Committee. IBFAN has later expanded this to encompass studies of marketing of commercial infant and young children's foods in different countries with reference to CRC General Comment No. 16 on the impact of the business sector on children's rights.[116] The record of the CRC Committee in bringing up childhood obesity was reviewed by O'Cathaoir,[117] as regards its General Comment No.15 on the Right to Health,[118] which calls on states to also address obesity in children.[119] O'Cathaoir recommends that in light of the lack of clarity of state obligations, the committee on the CRC takes a leadership role in further elucidating and crystallizing the obligations of states parties.[120] We hold that a way to put this in motion can be through negotiations and adoption of an Optional Protocol

---

eliminate preventable mortality and morbidity of children under five years of age ', UN Doc. A/HRC/27/31 (30 June 2014), para 46.

[115] Report from the Parallel Side Events during the 3rd United Nations Forum on Business and Human Rights, Geneva 1–3 December 2014.

[116] See, n105.

[117] K O'Cathaoir, 'Childhood Obesity and the Right to Health' (2016) 18 *Health and Human Rights* 249.

[118] CRC, 'General Comment No. 15 on the right of the child to the enjoyment of the highest attainable standard of health (art. 24)', UN Doc CRC/C/GC/15 (17 April 2013).

[119] Ibid., para 47.

[120] See, n116, 257.

to the CRC, as suggested by a WHO/UNICEF/Lancet Commission, to protect children from harmful marketing.[121]

One triggering event for much of the above regarding child obesity in the context of food marketing practices, could be a joint statement by the two UN Special Rapporteurs on the right to food and the right to health together with the two specially relevant treaty bodies, CESCR and CRC, on the gravity of the issue of rising child obesity, NCDs and the role of business. This could build on a comparable statement in 2016 regarding promoting, supporting, and protecting breastfeeding.[122]

The potential power of organized requests from civil society/academia to the UN for special follow-up activities is also important. A notable case in point is the call in November 2019 from some 180 experts and practitioners (the present authors included) to the WHO and the Office of the UN High Commissioner of Human Rights, for a human rights approach to healthy diets and the need for guidelines, principles and processes for this to be laid out.[123] The list is open for new signatories and is growing.

Such guidelines could serve as one input into a general comment on the right to be free from malnutrition in all forms. The CESCR's General Comment 12 on the right to food focused on undernutrition and hunger and did not yet address malnutrition in the form of overweight and obesity. A new GC would be able to draw on other documents published in the interim, such as the CFS Voluntary Guidelines on Food Systems and Nutrition and the CFS-HLPE global narrative on food security towards 2030. Furthermore, the planned UN Summit on Food Systems in New York in 2021 will provide added inspiration. To be sure that it will treat equally relevant issues under ICESCR and the CRC, ideally such a general comment could be worked out jointly by the respective committees.

Finally, there is a dearth of transdisciplinary research that can align goals and policies in food systems, food security and nutrition with standards and principles of human rights, especially as related to SDGs 2 and 3 and the right to adequate food and to health. Higher education institutions are equally

---

[121] 'A Future for the World's Children? A WHO–UNICEF–Lancet Commission' (2020) 395 The Lancet 605.

[122] OHCRC, 2016, 'Joint statement by the UN Special Rapporteurs on the Right to Food, Right to Health, the Working Group on Discrimination against Women in law and in practice, and the Committee on the Rights of the Child in support of increased efforts to promote, support and protect breast-feeding', https://www.ohchr.org/en/NewsEvents/Pages/DisplayNews.aspx?NewsID=20871&LangID=E.

[123] K Buse, et al, 'Urgent Call for Human Rights Guidance on Diets and Food Systems', *British Medical Journal Blog*, 30 October 2019, https://blogs.bmj.com/bmj/2019/10/30/urgent-call-for-human-rights-guidance-on-diets-and-food-systems/.

slow in taking up food systems and nutrition from a human rights perspective. This hampers knowledge development and capacity building in critical parts of relevant ministries, public agencies as well as civil society. The UN High Commissioner and concerned development agencies should recommend to states that they encourage their own national universities and research institutions to undertake research on policy developments and contextual field actions from a human rights perspective, to heighten the understanding of how a human rights based approach can be operationalized to help accelerate the achievements in the upcoming 'Decade for action on the 2030 Agenda' and beyond.

5.3 New and Strengthened Alliances are Needed

A constructive interplay between academia in the borderline between human rights and public health, civil society, and supportive governments as well as UN staff open to professional external relations, is essential. Creative interaction may start at the national or international level. On the public health side, civil society including academia has already been instrumental in creating the necessary awareness of the seriousness of childhood obesity and its relations to NCDs. The challenge is to link public health-based nutrition standards with norms and principles for freedom from obesity and from an obesogenic environment. Several legally based public health-oriented academic groups are debating what this would mean in practice, while many leading public health circles hesitate to explore the human rights paradigm. Hopefully, this book can contribute to build further transdisciplinary alliances that combine research and informed activism vis-à-vis UN institutions and mechanisms. The UN Decade of Action on Nutrition should be used as much as possible to promote concerns with healthy diets under the human rights agenda and promote building the competence needed for this.

The hope lies in stronger alliances among food systems and public health scholars and activists on one hand and the promoters of recognized human rights on the other. Together they may be able to influence states and the UN specialized agencies to recognize the double-duty action required under human rights norms to counteract and prevent malnutrition in all forms: the duty to protect children from an obesogenic environment and protecting healthy diets, while promoting food security and good nutrition for all. Alliances of this kind may also serve as independent observatories of how human rights approaches are or will be applied in the Nutrition Decade. The possibilities are there to promote and encourage processes in assessments, analyses, policies and action based on human rights including the right to adequate food and diet-related health, for freedom from obesity and from an obesogenic environment.[124]

---

[124] An international seminar at the University of Oslo in April 2018 posed the question 'Can a human rights-based approach accelerate reduction of undernutrition and obesity?' See full programme and video-recording at, https://www.jus.uio.no/smr/english/research/projects/fohrc/.

10. Combatting obesogenic commercial practices through the implementation of the best interests of the child principle

Amandine Garde[1] and Seamus Byrne

1. INTRODUCTION

Part I of this book has established the value of a children's rights approach to the prevention of childhood obesity, discussing State obligations to respect, protect and fulfil the rights of children detrimentally affected by obesogenic food environments, fuelled in particular by the business models, operations and commercial practices of powerful multinational corporations. States have an obligation to prevent and remedy the infringement of children's rights caused or contributed to by third parties,[2] and legislation and regulation are essential instruments for ensuring that the activities and operations of business enterprises do not adversely impact on these rights. The provision of a clear and predictable legal and regulatory environment shapes business practices and should actively foster a culture that is respectful of these rights.[3] However, the more effective regulation may be, the more likely food business actors are to challenge its validity. Such actors invest heavily in opposing State regulation and argue that it is excessively restrictive of trade interests, as discussed in the second part of this book, and/or in breach of their commercial rights, including the right to (intellectual) property and the right to free (commercial) expression. The question therefore arises to what extent these trade interests

---

[1] We are extremely grateful to Dr Joshua Curtis for his insightful comments.
[2] See Unicef, *Obligations and Actions on Children's Rights and Business: A practical guide for sates on how to implement the United Nations Committee on the Rights of the Child's General Comment no. 16* (Unicef 2016).
[3] CRC Committee, General Comment No. 16, *State obligations regarding the impact of the business sector on children's rights*, UN Doc CRC/C/GC/16, 17 April 2013, Part VI.

and commercial rights may be legitimately invoked against the regulation of food business actors, and more specifically what principles should guide the establishment of a fair balance between commercial rights and human rights.

This chapter argues that the principle of the best interests of the child, which is enshrined in the Convention on the Rights of the Child (CRC), should be given its due weight in determining this balance and provides significant, untapped potential to support States in modifying food environments as part of the implementation of effective childhood obesity prevention policies. Under Article 3(1) CRC, '[i]n all actions concerning children, whether undertaken by public or private social welfare institutions, courts of law, administrative authorities or legislative bodies, the best interests of the child shall be a primary consideration'.

Described as the 'normative axis around which decisions relating to children revolve',[4] this provision lays down an obligation ('shall') of particularly broad scope, referring to all actions which directly or indirectly have an effect on an individual child, a group of children or all children defined as persons under the age of 18 within the jurisdiction of a State party. The Committee on the Rights of the Child (CRC Committee) has stated that the child's right to health and his or her health conditions, including nutrition, are central in assessing the child's best interests,[5] and that the best interests principle establishes a high threshold that should 'influence the development of policies to regulate actions that impede the physical and social environments in which children live, grow and develop'.[6]

States need to prioritize possible solutions which are in the child's best interests. This implies that States need, within the specific factual context of a given situation, to find what the relevant elements in a best interests assessment are, give them concrete content, and assign a weight to each in relation to one another (the best interests assessment). To do so, they need to follow a procedure that ensures legal guarantees and proper application of the right (the best interests determination).[7]

---

[4] H Stalford, 'The Broader Relevance of Features of Children's Rights Law: The 'Best Interests of the Child' Principle, in E Brems et al. (eds), *Children's Rights Law in the Global Human Rights Landscape* (Routledge 2017) 37.

[5] CRC Committee, General Comment No. 14 (2013) *The right of the child to have his or her best interests taken as a primary consideration,* UN Doc CRC/C/GC/14, 29 May 2013.

[6] CRC Committee, General comment No. 15, *The right of the child to the enjoyment of the highest attainable standard of health (art. 24)*, CRC/C/GC/15, 17 April 2013, para 13(c).

[7] CRC Committee, n5.

The Committee's threefold conceptual delineation of the best interests of the child principle provides a useful basis upon which to unpack its utility and potential application in regulating the activities of business actors, and the marketing practices of the food industry more specifically.[8] First, the best interests principle is *a substantive right* which subsumes the right of the child to have his or her best interests taken as a primary consideration. States have a legal obligation to ensure that it is upheld. Secondly, it is *a fundamental interpretative legal principle* which mandates the construction of legal provisions in a manner consistent with the child's best interests. States therefore need to consider where the best interests of the child lies when considering the different regulatory options available to them and choose the one that upholds the right of the child to have his or her best interests taken as a primary consideration. Thirdly, it is *a rule of procedure* requiring that any decision likely to impact upon the best interests of the child must include an evaluation as to the probable impact such a decision will have on the child's best interests. As such, it requires that all organs of the State justify each one of their decisions and demonstrate that it has upheld the best interests of the child as a primary consideration.

Bearing in mind this threefold conceptualization, this chapter first explores how State parties to the CRC should regulate the commercial practices of food business actors, and the marketing of unhealthy food to children specifically. It assesses why the best interests of the child requires the imposition of comprehensive restrictions, protecting all children from exposure to all such marketing (2). However, the make-up of Article 3(1) itself expressly recognizes the need to balance competing rights and interests. Its reference to 'a' (as opposed to 'the') primary consideration raises the question of the added value of Article 3 for determining how States can discharge their obligations to protect, respect and fulfil the rights of the child negatively affected by growing rates of childhood obesity. The second part of the chapter therefore reflects on the role that the best interests principle could assume in moderating legal confrontations between competing rights and interests, focusing on the arguments often invoked against regulation by food business actors, both in litigation before courts and tribunals and throughout the policy cycle before policy makers, as well as the mechanisms required to address these arguments and ensure that the best interests of the child are effectively upheld as a primary consideration (3).

---

[8] CRC Committee n6, para 13(c). See also J Zermatten, 'The Best Interests of the Child Principle: Literal Analysis and Function' (2010) 18 *International Journal of Children's Rights* 483–99, 485.

2. THE BEST INTERESTS OF THE CHILD AND THE IMPERATIVE TO PROTECT ALL CHILDREN FROM EXPOSURE TO UNHEALTHY FOOD MARKETING

In its recognition of the centrality of Article 3, the CRC Committee has highlighted that 'the best interests principle is aimed at ensuring both the full and effective enjoyment of all the rights recognised in the convention and the holistic development of the child'.[9] The actions of business actors are not immune or separate from the duty of States to uphold the best interests of the child which should be central to the development of legislation and policies, including general economic, trade or financial issues.[10] Given the prevalence of unhealthy food marketing and its harmful impact on child health, the Committee recognizes the necessity for appropriate regulation,[11] and has increasingly highlighted the urgency for such regulation in its concluding observations on State practice issued under the CRC's reporting process.[12] After providing a short summary of the evidence that food marketing is associated with child obesity, this section focuses on what constitutes 'appropriate regulation' in this policy area.

2.1 The Unequivocal Evidence that Food Marketing is Associated with Growing Rates of Child Obesity

Several systematic reviews have determined the extent, nature and impact of food marketing on children.[13] It is now 'unequivocal'[14] that the promotional strategies used by food companies contribute to the excess consumption of

---

[9] CRC Committee, n5, para 4.
[10] CRC Committee, n3, para 15.
[11] Ibid., para 59.
[12] For example, the CRC Committee urged Bahrain to '[I]ntensify their efforts to combat obesity ... and develop regulations regarding the marketing of unhealthy food that have a negative effect on children's health'. CRC Committee, UN Doc CRC/C/BHR/CO/4-6, 27 February 2019, para 37(b).
[13] G Hastings et al., *Review of Research on the Effects of Food Promotion to Children (final report)*, University of Strathclyde, Glasgow, 22 September 2003; J McGinnis et al., *Food Marketing to Children and Youth: Threat or opportunity?*, Institute of Medicine, National Academies Press, Washington, D.C., 2006; and G Cairns et al., *The Extent, Nature and Effects of Food Promotion to Children: A review of the evidence to December 2008*, WHO, December 2009.
[14] WHO, 'Report of the Commission on Ending Childhood Obesity', WHO, Geneva, January 2016, 18.

unhealthy food[15] and are a direct contributor to childhood obesity and related noncommunicable diseases (NCDs).[16]

Moreover, the advent of digital marketing, with its particularly engaging, immersive, invasive and personalized focus, has led to the emergence of an entirely new and insidious digital and marketing ecosystem[17] which presents acute challenges for regulating marketing practices in the best interests of the child. Digital marketing does not negate the impact of more 'traditional' media, such as television, cinema, outdoor and retail marketing. Instead, as the time children spend online, particularly on social media, is growing,[18] it becomes integrated with other channels, offering more opportunities for messages to be transmitted and for synergistic campaign effects to magnify their impact.[19]

Importantly, the effects of the creative marketing techniques used online are amplified by the ability in digital environments to hone content for specific audiences, drawing on the data of users, including their age, demographics, location, interests, moods and other personal characteristics. Specific audiences, not least children who are most vulnerable to their effects, receive direct, personalized 'micro-targeting' of marketing messages. Furthermore,

---

[15] B Swinburn et al., 'The Global Syndemic of Obesity, Undernutrition, and Climate Change: The Lancet Commission Report' (2019) 393 *Lancet* 802.

[16] For summaries of existing evidence, see G Cairns et al., 'Systematic Reviews of the Evidence on the Nature, Extent and Effects of Food Marketing to Children: A retrospective summary' (2013) 62 *Appetite* 209–15; and E Boyland and M Tatlow-Golden, 'Exposure, Power and Impact of Food Marketing on Children: Evidence Supports Strong Restrictions' (2017) 8(2) *European Journal of Risk Regulation* 224–36. See also F Folkvord (ed.), *The Psychology of Food Marketing and Overeating* (Routledge 2019).

[17] K Montgomery and J Chester, 'Interactive Food and Beverage Marketing: Targeting Adolescents in the Digital Age' (2009) 45 *Journal of Adolescent Health* S18–S29; B Kelly et al., 'New Media but Same Old Tricks: Food Marketing to Children in the Digital Age' (2015) 4 *Current Obesity Reports* 37–45; K Montgomery, 'Youth and Surveillance in the Facebook Era: Policy Interventions and Social Implications' (2015) 39(9) *Telecommunications Policy* 771–86; M Tatlow-Golden et al., 'Who's Feeding the Kids Online?', Irish Heart Foundation, Dublin, 2016; M Tatlow-Golden and A Garde, 'Digital Food Marketing to Children: Exploitation, Surveillance and Rights Violations' (2020 forthcoming) *Global Food Security*; WHO, 'Tackling Food Marketing to Children in a Digital World: Trans-disciplinary Perspectives: Children's Rights, Evidence of Impact, Methodological Challenges, Regulatory Options and Policy Implications for the WHO European Region', WHO, Copenhagen, 2016.

[18] WHO, 'Monitoring and Restricting Digital Marketing of Unhealthy Products to Children and Adolescents', WHO Regional Office for Europe, Copenhagen, 2019.

[19] WHO, 'Evaluating the Implementation of the WHO Set of Recommendations on the Marketing of Foods and Non-alcoholic Beverages to Children: Progress, Challenges and Guidance for Next Steps in the WHO European Region', Regional Office for Europe, Copenhagen, 2018; and WHO, 2016, n17.

data extraction allows advertisers to draw inferences and analyse responses instantaneously to craft their methods more precisely, increasing their persuasiveness.[20] Consequently, digital food marketing also raises privacy and data protection concerns, beyond the public health concerns on which this book primarily focuses.[21] The negative consequences of this 'predatory' food marketing system[22] are further exacerbated in the context of socio-economic health inequities.[23]

The WHO recommendations on the marketing of food to children

In May 2010, the 63rd World Health Assembly unanimously endorsed the WHO set of recommendations on the marketing of foods and non-alcoholic beverages to children (the Recommendations),[24] which urge Member States to protect children from the impact of unhealthy food marketing.

The 12 evidence-based recommendations reflect a global consensus to limit the negative impact which unhealthy food marketing has on children's overall health. To ensure a broad coverage and therefore a high level of public health protection, they adopt an extensive definition of the notion of 'marketing' as 'anything that acts to advertise or otherwise promote a product or service'.[25] They call on States to reduce both the exposure of children to, and power of, unhealthy food marketing as the two components of marketing impact,[26] and to set clear definitions to this effect, including: the age group for which restrictions shall apply; the communication channels, settings and marketing techniques to be covered; what constitutes marketing to children according to factors such as product, timing, viewing audience, placement and content of the marketing message; and what foods fall within the scope of marketing restrictions (i.e., what constitute unhealthy food[27]). In particular, Member States are specifically

---

[20] Tatlow-Golden and Garde, n17.
[21] On children's rights and privacy, see S Livingstone et al., 'Children's Data and Privacy Online: Growing up in a Digital Age: An evidence review', LSE, Media and Communications, 2018.
[22] E Mendell, and M Singer, 'The Global Syndemic of Obesity, Undernutrition, and Climate Change' (2019) 393 *Lancet* 741.
[23] On health inequities, see Friant-Perrot and Gokani's chapter in this volume.
[24] Resolution WHA63.14.
[25] Ibid., 7.
[26] Ibid., Recommendation 2.
[27] Unhealthy food is nutritiously poor and high in fat, sugar and salt. The distinction between healthy and unhealthy food is based on nutrition profiling, defined by WHO as the science of classifying or ranking food according to the composition of its nutrients, in the interests of preventing disease and promoting health: WHO, 'Nutrient Profiling': https://www.who.int/nutrition/topics/profiling/en/ (last accessed 15 May 2020). See also, Unicef, *A Child Rights-Based Approach to Food Marketing A Guide for Policy Makers; Technical Report* (Unicef 2018) 8.

requested to define settings where children gather and ensure that they are free from all forms of unhealthy food marketing,[28] and to recognize that comprehensive approaches covering all forms of unhealthy food marketing are more effective than stepwise approaches which, by definition, adopt a more selective, incremental approach to the limitation of the impact of unhealthy food marketing on children.[29] The Recommendations also acknowledge the central role which governments play in their implementation, highlighting their need to protect public health and avoid conflicts of interests.[30] Over the last decade, research has accumulated to demonstrate the ineffectiveness of industry-led, self-regulatory pledges to 'promote food responsibly to children'.[31] States must develop effective regulatory frameworks to uphold children's rights, not least their right to health[32] and their right to a healthy food environment.[33] Regrettably, however, progress towards the *effective* implementation of the Recommendations has been extremely slow in the last decade.[34]

---

[28] WHO Recommendations, n24, Recommendation 5.

[29] See the Guidance Notes to Recommendation 3, as well as the WHO report published in May 2012 to provide technical support to States in implementing, monitoring and evaluating their execution of the recommendations: WHO, 'A Framework for Implementing the Set of Recommendations on the Marketing of Foods and Non Alcoholic Beverages to Children', WHO, Geneva, 2012.

[30] WHO Recommendations, n24, Recommendation 6.

[31] For limited effectiveness of industry pledges and relevant literature, see WHO, 'Implementing the WHO Recommendations on the Marketing of Food and Non-alcoholic Beverages to Children in the Eastern Mediterranean Region', WHO, Cairo, 2018, section 4.1.

[32] Report of the Special Rapporteur on the right of everyone to the enjoyment of the highest attainable standard of physical and mental health, Anand Grover, UN Doc A/HRC/26/31, 1 April 2014.

[33] Unicef and UN Special Rapporteur on the Right to Food, 'Protecting Children's Right to a Healthy Food Environment', Unicef and United Nations Human Rights Council, Geneva, November 2019.

[34] A Garde (ed.), Special issue on the Implementation in Europe of the WHO Recommendations on Food Marketing to Children (2017) 8(2) *European Journal of Risk Regulation* 207–341; V Kraak et al., 'Progress Achieved in Restricting the Marketing of High-fat, Sugary and Salty Food and Beverage Products to Children' (2016) 94 *Bull World Health Organ* 540–48; R Magnusson et al., 'Legal Capacities Required for Prevention and Control of Noncommunicable Diseases' (2018) 97 *Bulletin of the World Health Organization* 108–17; Unicef, n27; WHO, 2019, n18; WHO, 2018, n31; WHO, 'Regional Action Framework on Protecting Children from the Harmful Impact of Food Marketing in the Western Pacific', Western Pacific Region, 2020.

2.2 The Best Interests of the Child and the Imperative to Protect All Children from Exposure to Unhealthy Food Marketing

It is increasingly apparent that the approaches traditionally used to implement the Recommendations have been far too limited to reduce the impact of unhealthy food marketing on children.[35] Reflecting on what a child rights-based approach entails in this policy area, including the best interests principle, helps to highlight these limitations and provides indications of the way forward. Without purporting to be exhaustive of all elements food marketing policies should consider, this section identifies two key recurring problems that States have insufficiently acknowledged when delineating the scope of their regulatory frameworks: the narrow definition of the group of children requiring protection from harmful marketing, which often excludes adolescents; and the narrow definition of what constitutes marketing to children, which fails to protect children from actual exposure to unhealthy food marketing.

For the inclusion of adolescents in the scope of protective regulatory frameworks

For the purposes of the CRC, a child means every human being below the age of 18 within the jurisdiction of a State party.[36] Nevertheless, defining the children who should be protected from the harmful impact of unhealthy food marketing has not been unproblematic. This stems from the assumption that older children possess the ability to recognize and resist marketing, which does not reflect the latest evidence on child development.[37]

Drawing on Jean Piaget's identification of 'milestones' in the cognitive development of children,[38] Deborah Roedder John distinguished three stages in her literature review on children's consumer socialization:

- the perceptual phase (aged three–seven), when children become capable of distinguishing an advert from a programme by its length and format;
- the analytical (aged seven–11), when children begin to understand the selling intent of advertising; and
- the reflective stage (aged 11–16), at the end of which children understand the persuasive intent of advertising on a par with adults.[39]

---

[35] See B Swinburn et al., n15.
[36] Convention on the Rights of the Child, 577 UNTS 3, 20 November 1989, Art 1.
[37] Tatlow-Golden and Garde, n17.
[38] J Piaget, *Origins of Intelligence in the Child* (Routledge 1936).
[39] D Roedder John, 'Consumer Socialization of Children: A Retrospective Look at Twenty-five Years of Research' (1999) 26 *Journal of Consumer Research* 183–213.

The research focusing on children's cognitive development has been used to support the argument that advertising to younger children, typically below 12, is inherently unfair and should be prohibited. It assumes that, once they reach the 'magic age',[40] children can protect themselves from the negative impact of advertising. However, more recent research suggests that older children, even if they may have the cognitive capacities to identify the persuasive intent of advertising, are not as resistant to (unhealthy food) marketing as adults.[41] Advertising can manipulate consumer behaviour via implicit persuasion, which may in turn explain why cognitive defence would not protect older children.[42] These findings are compounded by the fact that children's brains, including those of adolescents, are biased towards rewards and more likely to respond to cues in their environment, including marketing.[43] Moreover, the area of the brain that prompts inhibitory control is less developed in young children and adolescents than in adults.[44] Food selection is primarily a response of the human visual system, and food marketing promotes overconsumption,[45] particularly in overweight and obese children.[46] Marketing is persuasive even

---

[40] A Nairn and C Fine, 'Who's Messing with My Mind? The Implications of Dual-process Models for the Ethics of Advertising to Children' (2008) 27(3) *International Journal of Advertising* 447–70.

[41] G Murphy et al., 'See, Like, Share, Remember: Adolescents' Responses to Unhealthy-, Healthy- and Non-Food Advertising in Social Media' (2020) 17 *International Journal of Environmental Research and Public Health* 2181.

[42] See Nairn and Fine, n40. See also J Harris et al., 'The Food Marketing Defense Model: Integrating Psychological Research to Protect Youth and Inform Public Policy' (2009) 3(1) *Social Issues and Policy Review* 211–71.

[43] J Casey, 'Beyond Simple Models of Self-Control to Circuit-Based Accounts of Adolescent Behavior' (2005) 66(1) *Annual Review of Psychology* 295.

[44] F Van Meer et al., 'What You See is What You Eat: An ALE Meta-analysis of the Neural Correlates of Food Viewing in Children and Adolescents' (2015) 104 *Neuroimage* 35–43; and A Dagher, 'Functional Brain Imaging of Appetite' (2012) 23 *Trends in Endocrinology & Metabolism* 250–60.

[45] F Van Meer et al., 'Developmental Differences in the Brain Response to Unhealthy Food Cues: An fMRI Study of Children and Adults' (2016) 104(6) *American Journal of Clinical Nutrition* 1515.

[46] A Bruce et al., 'Obese Children Show Hyperactivation to Food Pictures in Brain Networks Linked to Motivation, Reward and Cognitive Control' (2010) 34 *International Journal of Obesity* 1494; E Stice et al, 'Relation of Reward from Food Intake and Anticipated Food Intake to Obesity: A Functional Magnetic Resonance Imaging Study' (2008) 117(4) *Journal of Abnormal Psychology* 924; S Yokum et al., 'Attentional Bias to Food Images Associated with Elevated Weight and Future Weight Gain: An fMRI study' (2011) 19 *Obesity* 1775; and S Davids, et al., 'Increased Dorsolateral Prefrontal Cortex Activation in Obese Children during Observation of Food Stimuli' (2010) 34 *International Journal of Obesity* 94.

when consumers pay little attention to marketing, which may be even more effective under these 'low involvement' conditions.[47]

These concerns crystallize when marketing is portrayed as entertainment, accentuating the difficulty for children of all ages to distinguish marketing from content. For example, online promotional games ('advergames') are highly immersive and rely on children playing for extended periods of time, with repeat visits. As advergames operate 'under the cognitive radar', children are unaware that they are the targets of unhealthy food marketing, even though advergames influence the dietary choices of both younger and older children, irrespective of their cognitive abilities,[48] relying on their impulsivity[49] and their 'attentional bias'.[50]

Furthermore, the CRC Committee has highlighted that adolescence is a life stage characterized by growing opportunities, capacities, aspirations, energy and creativity, but also significant 'vulnerability', particularly in 'our increasingly globalized and complex world'.[51] Importantly, the right of children to exercise more responsibility as their capacities evolve does not obviate States' obligations to guarantee protection to all persons up to 18 years from all forms of exploitation and abuse.[52] In seeking to provide an appropriate balance, States must consider the range of factors affecting decision-making, including: the level of risk involved; the potential for exploitation; understanding of adolescent development; recognition that competence and understanding do not necessarily develop equally across all fields at the same pace; and recognition of individual experience and capacity. In particular, the Committee

---

[47] A Dijksterhuis et al., 'The Unconscious Consumer: Effects of Environment on Consumer Behavior' (2005) 15(3) *Journal of Consumer Psychology* 193.

[48] See Nairn and Fine, n40. See also, J Harris et al., 'US Food Company Branded Advergames on the Internet: Children's Exposure and Effects on Snack Consumption' (2012) 6 *Journal of Child Media* 51; E Reijmersdal et al., 'Effects of Prominence, Involvement, and Persuasion Knowledge on Children's Cognitive and Affective Responses to Advergames' (2012) 26 *Journal of Interactive Marketing* 33; F Folkvord et al., 'Impulsivity, "Advergames," and Food Intake' (2014) 133 *Pediatrics* 1007; F Folkvord et al., 'The Role of Attentional Bias in the Effect of Food Advertising on Actual Food Intake among Children' (2015) 84 *Appetite* 251; F Folkvord and J van 't Riet, 'The Persuasive Effect of Advergames Promoting Unhealthy Foods among Children: A Meta-analysis' (2018) 129 *Appetite* 245.

[49] Folkvord et al., ibid.

[50] Ibid.

[51] CRC Committee, General comment No. 20, *On the implementation of the rights of the child during adolescence*, UN Doc CRC/C/GC/20, 6 December 2016, para 2. It also notes that adolescence 'is not easily defined, and that individual children reach maturity at different ages' and that the 'process of transitioning from childhood to adulthood is influenced by context and environment' (ibid., para 5).

[52] Ibid., para 40.

has emphasized that the right to health of adolescents is paramount and their health conditions are central considerations in assessing their best interests.[53] It has also noted the importance of recognizing adolescence as part of the life-course, with consequences for subsequent life stages, and the role that 'safe and healthy local environments'[54] play in promoting the resilience and healthy development of adolescents.

We argue that 'local environments' should be defined to include the digital environment where adolescents spend a significant proportion of their lives. All children should seize the opportunities the online environment provides for strengthening and expanding their engagement, their right to be heard, their right to information and their right to participation.[55] This reinforces the need to regulate harmful marketing practices effectively. As the CRC Committee has stated, 'the concept of the child's best interests is aimed at ensuring both the full and effective enjoyment of all the rights recognized in the Convention and the holistic development of the child.... and no right could be compromised by a negative interpretation of the child's best interests'.[56] The child's right to participation should not be sacrificed on the altar of commercial exploitation. Rather, the holistic development of the child requires that his or her right to participation be enhanced by the effective regulation of such marketing.[57] As the Committee has stated, the inherent risks associated with children's online participation can be mitigated 'through holistic strategies, including digital literacy, strengthened legislation and law enforcement mechanisms, and training parents and professionals'.[58] We hope that the imperative to protect the rights of all children from harmful marketing will feature prominently in the General Comment on children's rights in relation to the digital environment which is being drafted.[59]

For the inclusion of mixed audience programmes in the scope of protective regulatory frameworks
Even though the Recommendations define marketing broadly and explicitly acknowledge that States will protect children more effectively if they adopt a comprehensive approach to unhealthy food marketing, existing measures tend to focus on unhealthy food marketing that is 'targeted at', 'directed at'

---

[53] CRC Committee, n6, para 77.
[54] CRC Committee, n51, para 17.
[55] Ibid., para 47.
[56] CRC Committee, n5, para 4.
[57] WHO, 2016, n17, 20 and Unicef, 2018, n27, 31–47.
[58] CRC Committee, n51, para 48.
[59] https://www.ohchr.org/EN/HRBodies/CRC/Pages/GCChildrensRightsRelationDigitalEnvironment.aspx (last accessed 15 May 2020).

or 'appealing to' children, is 'child-directed', or is on 'children's programming' or 'children's media'. As a result, mixed content specifically designed to appeal to families, that is, both adults and children, rather than to children exclusively, is not considered to be children's content, notwithstanding the fact that children are exposed to it and therefore allowing marketing to children to continue unabated.[60] The best interests of the child require that 'child-directed marketing' be redefined so that children are protected from actual exposure to unhealthy food marketing in all programmes, media and settings where children gather.

In July 2010, the UK broadcast regulator Ofcom published an evaluation report assessing the effectiveness of the rules introduced between 2007 and 2009 to prohibit the marketing of unhealthy food on television 'in and around children's programmes'. The review concluded that, even though broadcasters were observing 'the letter and the spirit' of the scheduling restrictions, the volume of unhealthy food advertising aired throughout the day had increased.[61] Research goes even further, showing that children are exposed to more unhealthy food advertisements during programming which is not specifically aimed at them than they were before the restrictions were implemented.[62] The best interests principle requires that children who watch mixed audience programmes, in absolute numbers rather than as a proportion of the total audience, should not be left unprotected. One option would be to allow unhealthy food marketing on television only at specifically defined times where children can reasonably be expected not to watch television, for example, from 9pm to 5.30am as proposed in the UK.[63]

The regulation of digital marketing must also address mixed audience content. Unhealthy food is marketed extensively online, and the internet locations most visited by children are often those providing access to a wide range of content, including Google, Facebook, Instagram, YouTube and Snapchat.

---

[60] WHO, 2019, n18.

[61] Ofcom, *HFSS Advertising Restrictions: Final review*, Ofcom, 26 July 2010, 3.

[62] See, in particular, J Adams et al., 'Effect of Restrictions on Television Food Advertising to Children on Exposure to Advertisements for "Less Healthy" Foods: Repeat Cross-sectional Study' (2012) 7(2) *PLoS ONE* e31578; and E Boyland et al., 'The Extent of Food Advertising to Children on UK Television in 2008' (2011) 6 *International Journal of Paediatric Obesity* 455. For a more extensive discussion of the UK regulation of unhealthy food marketing, see A Garde et al., 'The UK Rules on Unhealthy Food Marketing to Children' (2017) 8(2) *European Journal of Risk Regulation* 270. For findings similar findings in Australia, see B Kelly et al., 'Trends in Food Advertising to Children on Free-to-Air Television in Australia' (2011) 35(2) *Australian and New Zealand Journal of Public Health* 131.

[63] *Introducing further advertising restrictions on TV and online for products high in fat, sugar and salt (HFSS)*, 18 March 2019.

As adults substantially outnumber children as overall users, these platforms cannot be considered 'children's media', despite their popularity with children.[64] Regulating digital unhealthy food marketing raises acute challenges, not least because large advertising and technology (ad tech) companies tend to operate behind 'walled gardens', preventing policy makers from fully understanding their *modus operandi*.[65] One could envisage a presumption whereby all unhealthy food marketing online should be prohibited, except when business actors involved in such marketing could demonstrate that the site used to promote unhealthy food is not supposed to be accessed by children below 18. In the absence of transparency on the part of food and ad tech companies regarding their online food marketing strategies, governments should act with caution and require that these food and advertising companies bear the burden of proving that children are not exposed to unhealthy food marketing.[66] Such an approach is also in keeping with the letter and spirit of the child's best interests principle in that it is the only one likely to protect children from actual exposure to harmful marketing without unduly restricting their right to participation.

A similar approach should apply to determine the 'settings where children gather', which should be free from all forms of unhealthy food marketing.[67] In particular, the UN Special Rapporteur on the Right to Health has urged governments to 'ban the advertising, promotion and sponsorship of all children's sporting events, and other sporting events which could be attended by children, by manufacturers of alcohol, tobacco and unhealthy foods'.[68] His specific ref-

---

[64] For an illustration of the limited effects of regulation focusing on children as a proportion of a total audience and/or on marketing 'targeted at' children, see ASA Ruling on Ferrero UK Ltd. Advertising Standards Authority, London, 4 July 2018, discussed in WHO, 2019, n18, 16–17.

[65] WHO, ibid. See also M Wlosik and M Sweeney, 'Walled Gardens vs Independent AdTech: The Fight for Ad Dollars and Survival', Clearcode, 8 May 2019: https://clearcode.cc/blog/walled-garden-vs-independent-adtech/ (last accessed 15 May 2020).

[66] The mechanisms which companies use to deliver targeted marketing in digital media are arguably the very mechanisms by which children could be identified and protected from digital marketing (e.g., profiling). See Tatlow-Golden and Garde, n17.

[67] See WHO, 2010, n24, Recommendation 5.

[68] Human Rights Council, 'Sport and Healthy Lifestyles and the Right to Health', Report of the Special Rapporteur on the right of everyone to the enjoyment of the highest attainable standard of physical and mental health, UN Doc A/HRC/32/33, 4 April 2016, paras 32 and 33. On sports sponsorship, see A Garde and N Rigby, 'Going for Gold – Should Responsible Governments Raise the Bar on Sponsorship of the Olympic Games and Other Sporting Events by Food and Beverage Companies?' (2012) 17 *Communications Law* 42; R Ireland et al., 'Commercial Determinants of Health: Advertising of Alcohol and Unhealthy Foods During Sporting Events' (2019) 97 *Bull World Health Organ* 290.

erence to the Recommendations[69] highlights how they promote a rights-based approach by requesting governments to restrict unhealthy food marketing to children, particularly in settings where they gather.[70] We argue that children's exposure to unhealthy food sponsorship can only be reduced effectively if such sponsorship is limited – assuming it is allowed at all – to only adult-only events.

The best interests principle is a dynamic concept that encompasses various issues which are continuously evolving. When assessing and determining children's best interests, States must ensure such protection and care as is necessary for their wellbeing,[71] considering what we know of any given situation at any given point in time. Despite the centrality of Article 3 within the CRC, some have criticized the principle for being too vague and indeterminate,[72] and for justifying paternalistic outcomes.[73] However, others have also argued that 'there is purpose to this lack of specificity – it allows for an appropriate balancing of considerations within a well-defined procedural framework'.[74] Based on the discussion above, we would go further and argue that the potency of the best interests principle resides in its inherent flexibility, thus enabling States to apply (and re-apply) the principle as the evidence base underpinning the impact of unhealthy food marketing to children evolves. As evidence stands, the distinction between direct and indirect food marketing to children is artificial, and the best interests of the child principle requires that States review their regulatory frameworks and adopt comprehensive restrictions protecting all children from exposure to unhealthy food marketing on all programmes and media which they engage with and in all settings where they gather.

---

[69] UN Special Rapporteur, ibid., para 32.
[70] Unicef, n27, 34.
[71] CRC, Art 3(2).
[72] R Mnookin, 'Child-Custody Adjudication: Judicial Functions in the Face of Indeterminacy' (1975) 39(3) *Law and Contemporary Problems* 226.
[73] N Peleg, 'International Children's Rights Law: General Principles' in U Kilkelly and T Liefaard (eds), *International Human Rights of Children* (Springer 2019) 141–3. See also A Daly, *Children, Autonomy and the Courts: Beyond the Right to be Heard* (Brill/Nijhoff 2018).
[74] Council of Europe, Commissioner for Human Rights, 2008 Janusz Korczak Lecture, 'The child's best interest: a generally applicable principle', delivered by Emily Logan.

3. THE BEST INTERESTS OF THE CHILD AS A PRIMARY CONSIDERATION: ENGAGING WITH THE OBJECTIONS TO FOOD MARKETING REGULATION

Several objections have been mounted against the regulation of unhealthy food marketing to children, and the more comprehensive the regulatory framework proposed, the fiercer industry opposition is likely to be. As children's right to health and related rights are not absolute, it is necessary to engage with these objections and determine what the imperative to uphold their best interests as a primary consideration entails for States.

The CRC Committee recognizes the need for a degree of flexibility in the application of the best interests of the child principle: once assessed and determined, these interests might conflict with other interests. Whilst Article 3(1) CRC does not mandate that States uphold the best interests of the child as *the* primary consideration in all actions concerning children,[75] it does require them to uphold these interests as '*a* primary consideration'. Therefore, 'high priority' must be given to the child's interests, which may not be considered on the same level as all other considerations.[76] Greater weight must be attached to what serves the child best. As the CRC Committee has stated: 'This strong position is justified by the special situation of the child: dependency, maturity, legal status and, often, voicelessness … If the interests of children are not specifically elevated, they tend to be overlooked.'[77]

> Viewing the best interests of the child as 'primary' requires a consciousness about the place that children's interests must occupy in all actions and a willingness to give priority to those interests in all circumstances, but especially when an action has an undeniable impact on the children concerned.[78]

The obligation to make the best interests of the child a primary consideration becomes crucial when States are engaging in weighing competing priorities. As a rule of procedure, the best interests of the child principle requires that States explain how the right to have the best interests of the child considered has been respected in decision-making, including how it has been weighted against other considerations.[79] Therefore, even if the Committee has stopped short of stating that short-term economic considerations should not be given

---

[75] M Freeman, *The Best Interests of the Child* (Martinus Nijhoff 2007) 25–74.
[76] CRC Committee, n5, para 37.
[77] Ibid.
[78] Ibid., para 40.
[79] Ibid.

priority over longer-term child development considerations, the requirement to 'explain' increases the burden on States to ensure that they move away from mere rhetoric and engage with actual evidence when balancing competing rights and interests.

After briefly identifying the rationale often advanced for the constitutional protection of advertising and other forms of promotion (3.1), this section discusses the potentialities of the best interests principle in litigation in the quest to promote fairer commercial practices, drawing a distinction between industry and public interest litigation, looking at the potential of the best interests of the child principle as a fundamental interpretative legal principle (3.2). It then engages with the role that regulatory child-rights impact assessments and child-rights impact evaluations can play throughout the policy process to ensure that the regulation of marketing practices are child-rights compliant and obesity prevention strategies more effective, looking at their role in ensuring that States discharge their obligation to explain how they have upheld the best interests of the child as a primary consideration (3.3).

3.1 The Constitutional Protection of Advertising as a Form of Expression: The Necessity of Balancing Competing Rights and Interests

As discussed in the introduction to this book, food business actors have largely benefited from trade liberalization, heavily investing in the marketing of their goods, services and brands to increase both their presence and their market share around the world. Moreover, they have relied – or threatened to rely – on various legal strategies to shield themselves from unwanted marketing regulation and therefore pursue their profitable trade expansion, largely unhindered by such regulation. Invoking arguments anchored in international trade and investment law, they have also invoked the right to free expression and other rights protected in national constitutions or regional charters of rights. These arguments are closely related and are often made together to convince governments that the marketing restrictions at stake are incompatible with higher norms and should not be adopted or, if already enshrined in law, should be annulled in a judicial review action.

In 1976, the US Supreme Court first ruled that commercial advertising was a form of expression worthy of the protection provided by the First Amendment to the US Constitution. After noting that 'the particular consumer's interest in the free flow of commercial information may be as keen, if not keener by far, than his interest in the day's most urgent political debate',[80] it declared:

> Advertising, however tasteless and excessive it sometimes may seem, is nonetheless dissemination of information as to who is producing and selling what product, for what reason, and at what price. So long as we preserve a predominantly free enterprise economy, the allocation of our resources in a large measure will be made through numerous private economic decisions. It is a matter of public interest that those decisions, in the aggregate, be intelligent and well informed. To this end, the free flow of commercial information is indispensable....[81]

In other words, it emphasized the paramount role of advertising in a free market economy not only for business actors, but also – and perhaps more importantly – for consumers and society. Paradoxically, however, this provision has been primarily invoked by aggrieved business actors, including tobacco manufacturers[82] and alcohol distributors,[83] and has proven remarkably effective in the US to stall the regulation of marketing practices intended to protect consumers from harm.[84] The rationale underpinning the reasoning of the US Supreme Court's case law has influenced other decision-making bodies including the European Court of Human Rights (ECtHR) who has also extended the scope of the right to free expression enshrined in Article 10(1) of the European Convention on Human Rights and Fundamental Freedoms (ECHR) to advertising and other forms of promotions.[85] Similarly, the Court of Justice of the European Union (CJEU) has adopted an expansive interpretation of the legal remit of free expression. When faced with challenges to advertising restrictions imposed either by the EU or by its Member States, the CJEU has often referred to ECtHR case law and opted for a broad reading of the notion of expression in both Article 10 ECHR and Article 11 of the EU Charter on

---

[80] *Virginia Pharmacy Board v Virginia Consumer Council* (1976) 425 US 748, 762, at 763.

[81] Ibid., 764 and 765.

[82] *Lorillard Tobacco Co et al. v Reilly, Attorney General of Massachusetts, et al.* (2001) 533 US 525.

[83] *44 Liquormart v Rhode Island* (1996) 517 US 484.

[84] No regulation of advertising has been upheld in the US since 2011. Granting constitutional protection to advertising is inherently problematic: it elevates advertising above other economic activities and increases the difficulties involved in its regulation. See in particular, S Mermin and S Graff, 'The First Amendment and Public Health, At Odds' (2013) 39 *American Journal of Law & Medicine* 298.

[85] See, in particular, *Markt Intern v Germany* Series A no 165 (1990) 12 EHRR 161; *Groppera v Switzerland* Series A no 173 (1990) 12 EHRR 321; in *Casado Coca v Spain* Series A no 285 (1994) 18 EHRR 1; *Krone Verlag GmbH & Co. KG v Austria* Series A no 9605/03 (14.11.08).

Fundamental Rights.[86] In highlighting the centrality of the role of advertising to the EU Internal Market, it has stated:

> A ban on advertising would tend to crystallize existing patterns of consumption, to ossify markets and to preserve the status quo [...] Such measures prevent the interpenetration of markets and are inimical to the very concept of a single market.[87]

The challenges mounted against Australian and UK tobacco plain packaging laws illustrate the multifaceted legal strategies that tobacco companies have used to delay, if not avoid, the implementation of restrictive tobacco control regulation. Similar strategies are used to challenge food marketing and labelling laws. For example, Chile has introduced extensive unhealthy food marketing restrictions to protect children below 14 years, as part of a suite of measures adopted to address escalating rates of childhood obesity.[88] In particular, it has banned the use of cartoon, equity brand and other child-attractive characters to promote unhealthy food, as well as the offer of unhealthy food with toys and gadgets, and similar marketing techniques aimed at children. In response to these wide-ranging measures food-exporting countries, including the US and the EU, challenged their lawfulness before the WTO's Technical Barriers to Trade Committee, whilst food companies Carozzi and Evercrip (PepsiCo's subsidiary in Chile) filed complaints before Chilean courts challenging their implementation.[89]

---

[86] This case law is discussed in A Garde, 'Freedom of Commercial Expression and Public Health Protection: The Principle of Proportionality as a Tool to Strike the Balance', in L Gormley and N Nic Shuibhne (eds), *From Single Market to Economic Union – Essays in Honour of John Usher* (OUP 2012) and, more recently, in D Doukas, 'Commercial Speech and Freedom of Expression in EU Law: A Paradigm of a Sliding Scale of Review for the European Court of Justice?' (2019) 44 *European Law Review* 739.

[87] AG Jacobs' Opinion in Case C-412/93 *Leclerc-Siplec* [1995], para 20.

[88] On the Chilean measures, see P Villalobos Dintrans et al., 'Implementing a Food Labelling and Marketing Law in Chile' (2020) 6(1) *Health Systems & Reform* 1.

[89] M Campbell, 'NCD Prevention and International Investment Law in Latin America: Chile's Experience in Preventing Obesity and Unhealthy Diets' (2020) 21 *Journal of World Investment & Trade* 781. If some States have started to restrict the use of marketing techniques which are used extensively to promote unhealthy food and are particularly popular with children, Chile is the first to have regulated the use of equity brand characters. This is a very welcome initiative, considering the developing evidence base that these characters influence children's food preferences: L McGale et al., 'The Influence of Brand Equity Characters on Children's Food Preferences and Choices' (2016) 177 *J Pediatr.* 33. On food packaging marketing more broadly, see also C Elliott and E Truman, 'The Power of Packaging: A Scoping Review and Assessment of Child-Targeted Food Packaging' (2020) 12 *Nutrients* 95.

As States come under growing pressure to improve food environments, one should expect food business actors to adopt similar strategies, at all levels, putting in sharp focus the question of how the best interests of the child can moderate legal confrontations between, on the one hand, the rights of business actors and, on the other, the rights of the child.

3.2 The Role of the Best Interests of the Child in Shifting the Paradigm: From Defensive to Strategic Litigation

If business actors have often invoked international and domestic human rights instruments to protect their interests from unwanted health-promoting regulatory frameworks, human rights law can, and should, also be invoked by public health actors to develop effective, evidence-based obesity and NCD prevention strategies which ensure a high level of public health protection in all policies. In this regard human rights should not only be used as a reactive shield to defend national rules when challenged on the basis that they unreasonably limit free expression and are unnecessarily trade restrictive. They should also be used as a sword to ensure that the commercial practices of food business actors do not promote obesogenic environments.[90] We argue that the best interests of the child principle provides a compelling legal basis upon which to assert the need for regulation to curtail the harmful effects of unhealthy food marketing and other similarly unfair commercial practices.

Defensive litigation: responding to free expression and trade challenges
Public health protection has long been recognized by courts as a legitimate public interest justifying the imposition of marketing restrictions including commercial expression rights. For example, Article 10(2) ECHR explicitly provides for public health derogations which are 'prescribed by law' and '*necessary*' in a democratic society'. Free trade is not unlimited either, and States retain a wide margin of discretion to protect public health under international and regional trade law.[91] In particular, recognizing advertising as a corollary to free trade does not mean that States are prevented from regulating advertising.[92] On the contrary, States can subject marketing practices to *reasonable* restrictions to achieve the legitimate objective of protecting human health. We argue that 'necessity' and 'reasonableness' assessments in all areas concerning

---

[90] A Garde, 'Law and Non-Communicable Diseases Prevention: Maximizing Opportunities by Understanding Constraints' in G Burci and B Toebes (eds), *Research Handbook on Global Health Law* (Edward Elgar 2018) chapter 13.
[91] See in particular Part II of this volume (in particular, chapters by Messenger and Foster).
[92] AG Jacobs, n87, para 22.

children should be determined on the basis that 'the best interests of the child shall be a primary consideration', and that such decisions must be justified and explained to demonstrate that this principle has been duly upheld. Legal reasoning is key. It is not sufficient for a court to state in general terms that other considerations override the best interests of the child: all considerations must be explicitly specified in relation to the case at hand, and the reason why they carry greater weight in the particular case explained. The reasoning must also demonstrate, in a credible way, why the best interests of the child might not be strong enough to outweigh the other considerations at stake.[93] This is how the procedural dimension to the best interests principle becomes operational which mandates that in any decision which affects children, the decision-making process itself 'must include an evaluation of the possible impact (positive or negative) of the decision on the child or children concerned'.[94]

Legislative and other regulatory authorities should be granted a broad margin of discretion to undertake the necessity or reasonableness assessments that the regulation of commercial practices requires. Advertising is indeed a complex and fluctuating field, and it is not for courts to substitute their assessment for that of the legislature.[95] This is particularly so as unhealthy diets and obesity are inherently multifactorial and can only be addressed through comprehensive, coordinated, multisectoral policies. However, a broad margin of discretion should not be a *carte blanche*.[96] If a strict proportionality review is inappropriate, courts should nonetheless explain how they have concluded that a regulatory measure is 'reasonable' or 'necessary'. To this effect, courts should engage with the best interests principle by determining, first, the relevant factors for consideration in the assessment and, secondly, the weight of each of these factors considering competing claims.

Explicitly engaging with the relevance of the best interests of the child principle in industry-led litigation should bring at least two particularly important elements to the fore that courts have not clearly articulated. First, it should highlight the low informative value of commercial expression for consumers. The use of powerful marketing techniques that are particularly popular with children, including equity brand and cartoon characters as well as tie-in and free-toy offers, has no informative value regarding the products, services or brands on offer; it merely indicates that the food business actors promoting them have invested massively in techniques intended to seduce children with a view to selling more of their products. One could further argue that such

---

[93] CRC Committee, n6, para 97.
[94] Ibid., para 6(c).
[95] Case C-71/02 *Karner* [2004] ECR I-3025, para 51.
[96] Garde, n86.

techniques not only fail to inform children and their parents on the products thus promoted, but they also actively detract their attention from their core attributes, not least their nutritional value. Advertising is primarily intended to persuade by appealing to our feelings and emotions, not our intellect. This is particularly so online where entertaining and immersive digital marketing techniques often operate beyond our 'cognitive radar', as discussed above. However, the rationale for protecting advertising as a source of product information presupposes that consumers use their cognitive decision-making abilities in the presence of commercial communications. The evolution of marketing strategies and related studies on how these strategies operate should lead courts to review the oversimplistic assumption that advertising informs rational choice: it is often specifically designed to create irrational desires, subvert cognitive intellectual engagement and compound the consumption impulse. This perspective unavoidably challenges the fundamental starting point for legal reasoning in such cases, which should not stem from the highly questionable assumption that advertising and other forms of commercial expression have intrinsic informative value but the humanistic and quasi universal value of protecting children's best interests.

Secondly, even if we accepted the rationale that advertising provided some (unavoidably partial[97]) information on which consumers could base their decisions, the evidence is unequivocal that the food industry disproportionately promotes the consumption of unhealthy food directly associated with growing rates of child obesity. In determining whether advertising restrictions are 'necessary' or 'reasonable', European courts have recognized that private economic interests should not be given the same weight as public health concerns.[98] It should arguably be even more so when children, who are particularly vulnerable consumers, are intended as direct beneficiaries of health-promoting measures. The obligation to uphold the best interests of the child as a primary consideration increases the need for courts and other adjudicating bodies to reflect the hierarchy of societal values[99] and ensure that harmful marketing

---

[97] It has been argued that food marketing to children is inherently misleading: see J Pomeranz, 'Television Food Marketing to Children Revisited: The Federal Trade Commission has the Constitutional and Statutory Authority to Regulate' (2010) 38(1) *J Law Med Ethics* 98.

[98] 'Human health protection will often prevail over the purely economic interest in the greatest possible competition, despite the significant role economic interests play in legal systems worldwide.' Case C-547/14 *Philip Morris,* ECLI:EU:C:2016:325, at paras 156 and 157 (see also para 193 of AG Kokott's Opinion). See also Case C-544/10 *Deutsches Weintor* [2012] ECLI:EU:C:2012:526 and Case C-157/14 *Neptune Distribution,* C-157/14 [2015] EU:C:2015:823.

[99] See S Wheeler, 'Global Production, CSR and Human Rights: The Courts of Public Opinion and the Social License to Operate' (2015) 19(6) *International Journal of Human Rights* 757.

practices are effectively regulated.¹⁰⁰ Such assessments should rest on existing evidence of the actual impact of unhealthy food marketing on children rather than assumptions on their abilities to resist marketing pressure in adolescence, the artificial classification of children's programmes/media/settings or the alleged informational value of advertising and similar forms of commercial expression. In the longer term the more explicitly a court decision relies on the best interests of the child principle, the more pressure business actors will have to ensure that their commercial practices effectively comply with children's rights.¹⁰¹ Effective legal reasoning is key to the extent that it clarifies the hierarchy of values, whilst ensuring that decisions are based on existing evidence rather than loud industry rhetoric. The case of *ZH (Tanzania) (FC) (Appellant) v Secretary of State for the Home Department (Respondent)*¹⁰² provides a useful frame against which to consider the judicial application of Article 3 CRC in practice. Although the case arose within an immigration context, the UK Supreme Court expounded the practical application of the principle, offering guidance regarding its wider deployment. In his analysis, Lord Kerr stated:

> It is a factor, however, that must rank higher than any other. It is not merely one consideration that weighs in the balance alongside other competing factors. Where the best interests of the child clearly favour a certain course, that course should be followed unless countervailing reasons of considerable force displace them.¹⁰³

The qualifications 'higher than any other' and 'considerable' clearly indicate how unlikely it is that the course of action identified as 'in the best interests of the child' could legitimately be set aside, particularly by uncompelling freedom of commercial expression or free trade arguments. Guided by the evidential correlation between food marketing and child obesity, courts can and should invoke 'the best interests principle' to mediate any legal tensions which prospective legal and regulatory restrictions may generate, and in particular provide a legally defensible, judicially permissible and methodologically rigorous way to dismiss the claims put forward by business actors that their right to free expression or their freedom to trade would be unduly limited when evidence-driven marketing restrictions are adopted. As discussed above, wide-ranging unhealthy food marketing restrictions are a necessary limitation to the food and ad tech industries' freedom to advertise or otherwise promote

---

¹⁰⁰ Even if we were to accept that advertising informed, Art 17 CRC mandates that States should ensure that the media are regulated appropriately to protect children from harmful information.
¹⁰¹ On the responsibility of business actors to respect human rights, see Bartlett's chapter in this volume.
¹⁰² [2011] UKSC 4.
¹⁰³ Ibid., para 46.

their goods, services and brands: they protect public health and uphold the best interests of the child as a primary consideration without constituting an unreasonable barrier to the trade in these goods, services and brands.

Strategic litigation: holding industry accountable when relying on unfair commercial practices
Similarly, the best interests of the child principle can support the protection of children from unhealthy food marketing and other harmful commercial practices in strategic public-interest litigation. Such litigation can alter existing practices and policies within a State, generate pressure points which stimulate responses from government, compel governments to formally respond to the specific policies and practices under consideration and ultimately, within a health context, shape public discourse around a particular issue.[104]

Litigation in Brazil exemplifies the potential of strategic litigation to protect children from unhealthy food marketing. In 2007, Alana, a non-profit organization, supported the Brazilian State in its legal challenge against Pandurata Alimentos Ltd for its *It's Shrek Time* advertising campaign in which children were encouraged to collect different wristwatches with the picture of Shrek and other licensed cartoon characters from the movie. In March 2016, the São Paulo Court of Justice held that the marketing strategies underpinning this campaign were illegal for two reasons. First, the campaign was deceptive because it took advantage of the naivety of children by marketing unhealthy food directly to them. In rejecting the claim that the campaign targeted parents, it held:

> Any marketing (advertisement or other actions that promote the sale of a product or a service) directed at children is deceptive. Decisions that involve purchasing food must be taken by the parents. As obesity is a matter of national concern, this issue is heightened. Therefore, prima facie, a marketing and advertising strategy directed at children must be deemed deceptive.

Secondly, the campaign involved an illegal tie-in agreement which manipulated the perception of children. To reach this conclusion, the court relied on three arguments:

- Brazilian law recognizes the vulnerability of the consumer in the consumer market;

---

[104] T Ezer and P Patel 'Strategic Litigation to Advance Public Health' (2018) 201(2) *Health Hum Rights* 149.

- children are especially vulnerable, and the Brazilian Constitution enshrines, as an absolute priority, their protection by the State, safeguarding them from any form of exploitation;
- the Constitution establishes consumer protection as a fundamental right, requiring that the State should defend consumer interests. Although the Constitution also grants freedom of expression to advertisers, invoked by the defence, restrictions are permissible.

The Brazilian court therefore concluded that marketing strategies were illegal if they exploited the poor discernment of children and conditioned the purchase of a thematic watch to the acquisition of a given quantity of food products.[105]

Even though its exact contours remain unclear, this decision raises three broader points of interest. First, no commercial business should have the legal constitutional right to impair parental authority. Although unhealthy food marketing restrictions are often presented by food business actors as an undue intrusion on parental authority or individual autonomy, such restrictions allow parents to decide more freely what food to purchase, thus restoring rather than impairing their authority.[106] Moreover, in the increasingly multifaceted media environment which children inhabit, it would be unrealistic to expect parents to be the only ones responsible for protecting their children from unhealthy food marketing. Under Article 18 CRC, parents or legal guardians have 'the primary responsibility for the upbringing and development of the child' and States are mandated to provide 'appropriate assistance' to them 'in the performance of their child-rearing responsibilities'. Child development is inextricably connected to the wider social and environmental factors that influence children's lives, and States have a duty to shape these factors and develop policies that support families and strengthen their parenting competencies so that all children can grow in healthy family environments. Far from marginalizing their role, the implementation of the Recommendations empowers parents by modifying obesogenic environments in their children's best interests, in line with the CRC.[107]

---

[105] We have used the translation of the decision provided by the Brazilian Institute for the Defense of Consumers in *Rights without Noise: The historic Superior Court of Justice of Court Superior ruling on food advertising directed at children*, 2017: https://criancaeconsumo.org.br/wp-content/uploads/2014/02/direitos-sem-ruido-eng1.pdf (last accessed 15 May 2020).

[106] L McDermott et al., 'International Food Advertising, Pester Power and Its Effects' (2006) 25(4) *International Journal of Advertising* 513.

[107] See section 3.3 of Unicef (2018), n (25) and Katharina Ó Cathaoir's PhD thesis *A children's rights approach to obesogenic marketing* (University of Copenhagen 2017), which discusses this point more extensively and refers to G Kent, 'Children's

Secondly, the notion of commercial 'exploitation', which is at the heart of this decision, warrants scrutiny. It is well established that consumer protection laws and policies recognize that child-consumers deserve specific protection from commercial practices that exploit their vulnerability and are therefore unfair.[108] Looking beyond the facts of the case, the argument that (unhealthy food) marketing exploits children takes yet another dimension in the age of digital media, as these media manipulate users, by means which they are not and cannot be aware of, thus affecting their autonomy and capacity to understand.[109] Such marketing arguably infringes not only their right to health, food and privacy, but also their right to be free from exploitation under Article 36 CRC. This provision requires that States 'shall' protect children from 'all other forms of exploitation', that is, all forms of exploitation which are not specifically covered by Articles 32–35 CRC, thus allowing the CRC to adapt to new forms of exploitative practices, and therefore cover many of the commercial practices employed by the digital media and adtech systems. For the purposes of this provision, child exploitation takes place when one person or persons take unfair advantage of a child by encouraging or coercing the child, by whatever means, to undertake an activity that provides that person and/or persons with a benefit, whether financial or otherwise, that is not commensurate with the benefit, if any, gained by the child.[110] In particular, social media networks encourage extensive peer transmission of marketing content through children's peer groups and beyond.[111] The use of hashtags and prompts to 'like', 'share' and 'tag' others in advertising posts facilitates the rapid, exponential spread of marketing through diverse networks.[112] This amounts to recruiting children to act as peer marketers. This is likely to be particularly powerful for unhealthy food as teens prefer to share unhealthy food marketing posts compared to healthy food marketing posts or marketing for non-food products; they also pay more attention to these posts and remember them more.[113] By capturing

---

Right to Adequate Nutrition' (1993) 1(2) *International Journal of Children's Rights* 133.

[108] For example, Art 5(3) of the EU Unfair Commercial Practices Directive specifically identifies age as a factor of vulnerability which needs to be duly acknowledged in determining the fairness of a commercial practice: Directive 2005/29/EU, OJ 2005 L 149/22.

[109] D Susser et al., 'Technology, Autonomy, and Manipulation' (2019) 8(2) *Internet Policy Review* DOI: 10.14763/2019.2.1410.

[110] J Tobin, *The UN Convention on the Rights of the Child – A Commentary* (OUP 2019) 1403.

[111] See earlier discussion at section 2.1 above.

[112] L Buchanan et al., 'The Effects of Digital Marketing of Unhealthy Commodities on Young People: A Systematic Review' (2018) 10(2) *Nutrients* 148.

[113] See Murphy et al., n41.

children's attention and engaging them directly in the transmission of harmful marketing through the use of peer-to-peer techniques, among others, the food and the adtech industries influence them, often beyond their awareness, and increase profits at hardly any costs to themselves, whilst capturing their attention for commercial gain and increasing their preference for unhealthy food.[114] Such practices cannot be in the child's best interests and should be prohibited. The requirement enshrined in Article 36 CRC that States 'shall take' appropriate measures is a term which leaves no leeway for the discretion of States parties. Accordingly, they are under strict obligation to undertake 'all appropriate measures' to fully implement this right for all children.[115]

Thirdly, this decision highlights the importance of promoting the role of NGOs and other bodies as watchdogs that can support States in their obligation to provide effective remedies and reparations for violations of the rights of the child, including by third parties such as business enterprises. States must ensure that effective enforcement measures are in place.[116] State agencies are often identified by the CRC Committee as important actors in the proactive investigation and monitoring of children's rights violations, not least as they may also have regulatory powers allowing them to impose administrative sanctions on businesses. States should also consider strengthening the capacity of civil society organizations, such as Alana, to engage in strategic litigation to hold the food industry accountable for its failure to act in conformity with children's rights and monitor State compliance with the CRC. This is even more important in light of the vast power imbalances between children/their families and food business actors, the litigation costs involved and the difficulties in securing legal representation.[117] The more strategic litigation is encouraged, the more harmful marketing practices can be exposed, and underpinning issues publicly debated and better understood. Anchoring food marketing cases in the CRC supports more effective advocacy and, ultimately, better compliance with the obligations it lays down, not least that the best interests of the child have been upheld as a primary consideration.

Children's rights violations often have a severe and long-lasting impact on child development.[118] One of the key contributions that a child-rights based approach to the prevention of obesity should make is to help to legitimize regulation intended to protect children from harmful commercial practices, whilst

---

[114] This is discussed more fully in Tatlow-Golden and Garde, n17.

[115] CRC Committee, General Comment No. 13: *The Right of the Child to Freedom from All Forms of Violence*, UN Doc CRC/C/GC/13, 18 April 2011, para 37.

[116] CRC Committee, n3. On the specific difficulties involved in obtaining a remedy for abuses that occur in the context of businesses' global operations, see Curtis' chapter.

[117] See B Swinburn et al., n15.

[118] CRC Committee, n3, para 24.

delegitimizing arguments invoked against such regulation by food business actors.[119] It is only then that courts can highlight the values that States have undertaken to promote over others and ensure that the best interests of the child are indeed upheld as a primary consideration.

3.3 Best interests, Child Rights Impact Assessment and Child Rights Impact Evaluation

The best interests of the child principle not only applies as a deliberative device to reconcile claims before national courts and tribunals, it also extends to all public authorities and organs of the State. Thus, the principle should become a central component underpinning all stages of the policy process, from development to implementation, monitoring and evaluation. States must ensure that all actors respect children's rights.[120] To this effect, all business-related policy, legislation or administrative acts and decision-making should be transparent, informed and include full and continuous consideration of their impact on the rights of the child.

Child Rights Impact Assessments (CRIAs) provide a method for anticipating the impact of policy on the rights of the child. A subdivision of broader human rights impact assessments,[121] they yield a number of benefits, including: increased compliance with human rights standards; greater integration of human rights within policy making; increased accountability by facilitating participation; and enabling empowerment by bringing rights-holders closer to policy development.[122] Child Rights Impact Evaluation's (CRIEs) complement CRIAs by monitoring and evaluating the actual impact of policy implementation on children's rights,[123] thus gauging the accuracy of CRIAs predictions and providing the basis for reforms where appropriate.[124]

At their core, CRIAs and CRIEs engage specifically with children's rights, using the framework of the CRC as their evaluative backdrop and placing the best interests of the child at their heart. As the CRC Committee has argued,

---

[119] See Unicef, 2018, n27.

[120] CRC Committee, n5.

[121] S Walker, 'Human Rights Impact Assessments: Emerging Practice and Challenges', in E Riedel et al. (eds), *Economic, Social and Cultural Rights in International Law: Contemporary Issues and Challenges* (OUP 2014).

[122] G de Beco, 'Human Rights Impact Assessments' (2009) 27(2) *Netherlands Quarterly of Human Rights* 139.

[123] CRC Committee, n3, paras 78–81.

[124] S Hoffman, 'Evaluation of the Welsh Government's Child Rights Impact Assessment procedure under the Children's Rights Scheme pursuant to the Rights of Children and Young Persons (Wales) Measure 2011', 2015, 11, who distinguishes ex ante and ex post CRIAs.

CRIAs provide a means of 'ensuring that the best interests of the child are a primary consideration in business-related legislation and policy development'.[125] In view of the necessity to balance competing interests, or the 'delicate choices' which 'have to be made about the priorities that the State seeks to pursue'[126] and given that the evidence base on the impact of unhealthy food marketing on diets and childhood obesity is both complex and evolving, the combined use of CRIAs and CRIEs can help ensure that such complexities are continuously addressed in policy and the best interests of the child are systematically upheld as a primary consideration, thus giving practical meaning to the CRC Committee's tripartite distillation of the principle.

However, children's rights rarely feature within the impact assessments which accompany proposed regulatory decisions regarding advertising and marketing practices. For example, Ofcom's 2006 Impact Assessment accompanying its consultation on UK television advertising of food and drink to children was silent on the issue of children's rights, let alone the best interests principle,[127] despite its status as a regulatory watchdog with legal responsibilities dispersed across a range of statutory frameworks. There are, to date, few exceptions to this rule.[128] So what difference could the adoption of CRIAs and CRIEs placing the best interests principle at their heart really make? There are at least two distinct, though closely related, contributions CRIAs and CRIEs could make to debates on food marketing regulation.

First, as stated above, Article 3(1) CRC is paramount when States weigh competing priorities, rights and interests, such as short-term economic considerations against longer-term child development decisions. We argue that CRIAs and CRIEs would more clearly identify regulatory tensions and conflicting interests, providing more transparency and therefore allowing for the best interests of the child to be explicitly recognized as a primary consideration, thus clarifying that these interests should be central throughout, and guide, the policy process rather than being overlooked as they have tended to be.

---

[125] CRC Committee, n3, para 78. See also Unicef 'Children's Rights in Impact Assessments', Unicef, Geneva, 2013.

[126] Report of the Special rapporteur on the right to food, 'Guiding principles on human rights impact assessments of trade and investment agreements', UN Doc A/HRC/19/59/Add.5, 19 December 2011, para 6.

[127] See https://www.ofcom.org.uk/__data/assets/pdf_file/0017/33353/Annex-7-Impact-Assessment.pdf (last accessed 25 June 2020).

[128] One is the parliamentary motion of the Peruvian Law 30021 which explicitly referred to several provisions of the CRC, including Art 3, as the normative basis for the proposal. The Peruvian parliamentary discussions also explicitly mentioned the principle of the best interests of the child as the basis for the new regulations. We thank Marcelo Campbell for this information.

In evaluating various regulatory options, CRIAs often engage in a costs-benefit analysis (CBA). In its most elemental manifestation, CBA ultimately enshrines an economic deductive assessment between the envisaged benefits and costs of a proposed measure.[129] Should the former outweigh the latter; such measures are deemed, in monetary terms, worthy of implementation. Therefore, with its inbuilt objective of providing a justificatory economic argument for the adoption of a particular course of action, CBA has become an inseparable component to decision-makers in pursuit of objectives which are economically prudent.[130] In its assessment of the aggregative costs and benefits associated with a specific measure, it possesses not only an economic and practical currency, but also an accessible political appeal and has, as such, become the instinctive 'go-to' evaluative mechanism upon which to determine a particular course of action.[131] Aside from its theoretical scaffolding, CBA often influences children's rights objectives in practice.[132] Properly deployed as part of CRIAs and CRIEs, CBA could provide the economic foundations for food marketing restrictions and other childhood obesity prevention measures, bearing in mind the consequential long-term economic impact of childhood obesity, itself a 'strong predictor of adult obesity, which has well-known health *and economic* consequences'.[133]

Secondly, by explicitly engaging with the arguments often put forward against food marketing regulation throughout the policy cycle, and in particular its alleged economic costs, CRIAs and CRIEs could also play an important role in raising awareness and minimizing the risks of industry-led litigation. As the history of tobacco control shows, litigation may not always be avoided: it is an integral part of the arsenal of tactics the tobacco industry has used over the years to delay the entry into force of unwanted legislation. CRIAs and CRIEs that use the CRC as their frame of reference will credibly engage with existing evidence, identify regulatory options, consider the impact of each option on children's interests and rights, and choose the one that best complies with

---

[129] See generally, M Snell, *Cost-Benefit Analysis: A Practical Guide* (Thomas Telford 2011).

[130] See, e.g., HM Treasury, *The Green Book, Central Government Guidance on Appraisal and Evaluation,* [2018] and HM Treasury, *Supporting public service transformation: cost benefit analysis guidance for local partnerships,* April 2014. See also, European Commission, *Guide to Cost-Benefit Analysis of Investment Projects, Economic appraisal tool for Cohesion policy 2014–2020,* December 2014.

[131] See, e.g., Independent Evaluation Group, *Cost-Benefit Analysis in World Bank Projects* (World Bank 2010) and OECD, *Cost-Benefit Analysis and the Environment: Further Developments and Policy Use* (OECD 2018).

[132] H Stalford, 'The Price is Rights! Cost Benefit Analysis and the Resourcing of Children's Services' (2019) 99 *Children and Youth Services Review* 395.

[133] WHO, 2016, n14, 7.

Article 3(1) CRC. Ultimately, such assessments will significantly strengthen the counter-arguments that comprehensive unhealthy food marketing restrictions are legitimate on public health and children's rights grounds, reasonable, necessary and not unduly restrictive of trade or so-called economic freedoms. This should in turn provide food for thought to industry actors who may hesitate before challenging evidence-based measures adopted to promote public health, prevent disease and uphold the rights of the child, and to policy actors who may more readily embrace such measures as a result of the lesser opposition they may encounter and their more systematic engagement with human rights frameworks.[134]

4. CONCLUSION

The CRC requires that States adopt preventive measures to regulate and monitor the food industry to promote the holistic development of the child. Unhealthy food marketing has a long-term negative impact on child health and is detrimental to the fulfilment of many rights protected under the CRC. To date, however, insufficient progress has been made around the world to regulate harmful business practices which promote unhealthy diets and therefore contribute to child obesity. If consciousness is growing regarding the place that children's rights must occupy in food marketing regulation, it has not yet translated into the acknowledgment by competent public authorities – courts and regulators alike – that the child's best interests should be upheld as a primary consideration. A tidal change is needed, and Article 3 CRC provides the legal framework against which all decisions concerning children, including the regulation of food business actors and the promotion of healthier food environments, must be taken.

If used effectively, the best interests of the child principle can become a powerful tool in the quest to end childhood obesity and protect children from obesogenic commercial practices. First, it should be more systematically invoked to remind State parties to the CRC, pursuant to their obligations thereunder, of the need to implement the Recommendations and regulate commercial practices in light of the evidence establishing the deleterious impact of unhealthy food marketing on children's health and rights. Secondly, it provides a methodology to address the claims of food business actors that regulation is either excessively trade restrictive or contrary to their commercial rights. Thirdly, it incentivizes strategic litigation from NGOs and other watchdogs entrusted with ensuring that business practices are not exploitative

---

[134] CRIAs and CRIEs should never become tokenistic or rhetorical devices which merely pay lip service to children's rights.

of children's vulnerability and conducive to poor health. Fourthly, the best interests of the child principle can become a robust evaluative hook upon which to frame child obesity strategies through its deployment throughout the policy process, particularly in CRIAs and CRIEs.

The impact of unhealthy food marketing on children's diets, health and rights is undeniable but remains 'dangerously underappreciated'.[135] 'Shared principles are needed on good governance of relationships with the commercial sector for protecting the rights and well-being of children.'[136] As this chapter has demonstrated, the application of the best interests of the child principle is an important one of these shared principles and provides a compelling foundation for States to take concrete steps to ensure that their rhetorical commitments to end childhood obesity effectively feed into policy and genuinely improve children's daily lives and promote their development.

---

[135] H Clark et al., 'A Future for the World's Children? A WHO-Unicef-Lancet Commission' (2020) 395 *Lancet* 605, 650.

[136] Ibid., 633.

11. Multinational food corporations and the right to health: Achieving accountability through mandatory human rights due diligence?

Oliver Bartlett[1]

1. INTRODUCTION

The responsibility of corporations to respect human rights is beyond dispute.[2] However, while there have been calls over the years from the international political community[3] and from scholars[4] for corporations to be directly accountable in law for promoting human rights, no such general obligation has been created. Multinational food corporations (MFCs) in particular have

---

[1] The author would like to thank the editors for their constructive and instructive feedback on this chapter. All errors and omissions are the sole responsibility of the author. All web links were last accessed on 3 March 2020.

[2] See, e.g.: P Alston (ed.), *Non-State Actors and Human Rights* (OUP 2006); D Kinley and J Tadaki, 'From Talk to Walk: The Emergence of Human Rights Responsibilities for Corporations at International Law' (2003) 44(4) *Virginia Journal of International Law* 931; J Nolan, 'Refining the Rules of the Game: The Corporate Responsibility to Respect Human Rights' (2014) 30(78) *Utrecht Journal of International and European Law* 7; D Arnold, 'Transnational Corporations and the Duty to Respect Basic Human Rights' (2010) 20(3) *Business Ethics Quarterly* 371; B Toebes and J Cernic, 'Corporate Human Rights Obligations under Economic, Social and Cultural Rights' in J Addicott et al. (eds), *Globalization, International Law, and Human Rights* (OUP 2012).

[3] Sub-Commission on the Promotion and Protection of Human Rights, Norms on the responsibilities of transnational corporations and other business enterprises with regard to human rights, UN Doc. E/CN.4/Sub.2/2003/12/Rev.2, 13 August 2003; Resolution on EU Standards for European Enterprises [1999] OJ C 104.

[4] See, e.g.: J Knox, 'Horizontal Human Rights Law' (2008) 102(1) *American Journal of International Law* 1; S Deva, 'Human Rights Violations by Multinational Corporations and International Law: Where From Here?' (2003) 19(1) *Connecticut Journal of International Law* 1.

consequently been able to place profits before the health of populations for decades with little prospect of being held to account.[5] Several practices of MFCs contribute to the creation of obesogenic environments[6] – environments in which the arrangement of social, political, economic, informational, infrastructural and other conditions collectively raise the likelihood of individuals becoming obese.[7] Children are particularly vulnerable to – and indeed actively manipulated by – obesogenic environments, in which unhealthy food and beverages are typically easily accessible, inexpensive, and attractive.[8] The right to health is undermined by any actor that contributes to creating or maintaining such an environment.

This chapter will explore how the food industry can be held to account for their role in creating obesogenic environments that undermine the right to health, particularly in relation to the marketing of unhealthy food to children. It will focus on the notion of human rights due diligence (HRDD) – one of the

---

[5] Considerable criticism has accumulated on this point, e.g.: S Narula, 'The Right to Food: Holding Global Actors Accountable Under International Law' (2006) 44 *Columbia Journal of Transnational Law* 691; J Richter, 'Public-Private Partnerships for Health: A Trend with No Alternatives?' (2004) 47(2) *Development* 43; K Leisinger, 'The Corporate Social Responsibility of the Pharmaceutical Industry: Idealism Without Illusion and Realism Without Resignation' (2005) 15(4) *Business Ethics Quarterly* 577; D Chirwa, 'The Right to Health in International Law: Its Implications for the Obligations of State and Non-State Actors in Ensuring Access to Essential Medicine' (2003) 19 *South African Journal of Human Rights* 541.

[6] Examples of such practices include: advertising unhealthy food and beverages to children to increase their appeal, E Boyland and R Whalen, 'Food Advertising to Children and its Effects on Diet: Review of Recent Prevalence and Impact Data' (2015) 16 *Pediatric Diabetes* 331; lobbying governments to prevent the adoption of effective obesity prevention interventions, D Miller and C Harkins 'Corporate Strategy, Corporate Capture: Food and Alcohol Industry Lobbying and Public Health' (2010) 30(4) *Critical Social Policy* 1; increasing the availability and affordability of their products by displacing local and traditional retailers and consolidating supply chains, E Igumbor, '"Big Food," the Consumer Food Environment, Health, and the Policy Response in South Africa' (2012) 9(7) *PLoS Med* e1001253; and even bribing children's rights advocates, M Nestle, 'Bribes: How Food Corporations Keep Opponents Quiet' (20 December 2010, *the atlantic.com*).

[7] The obesogenic environment has been defined in several other similar ways, e.g., 'the sum of influences that the surroundings, opportunities, or conditions of life have on promoting obesity in individuals or populations': B Swinburn, 'Dissecting Obesogenic Environments: The Development and Application of a Framework for Identifying and Prioritizing Environmental Interventions for Obesity' (1999) 29 *Preventive Medicine* 563.

[8] See, e.g.: M Nestle, *Food Politics: How the Food Industry Influences Nutrition and Health* (University of California Press 2013); R Moodie, 'Childhood Obesity – A Sign of Commercial Success, But a Market Failure' (2006) 1(3) *Pediatric Obesity* 133.

three pillars of the UN Guiding Principles on Business and Human Rights[9] (the UNGPs) – and explore the responsibility of MFCs to engage in right to health due diligence. It will also argue that, in addition to the legislative due diligence requirements that States have already begun to place upon multinational corporations, progressive courts might also rely on the horizontal effects of the right to health to place obligations of due diligence upon MFCs.

The first section of this chapter will briefly outline the current application of international human rights law to corporations. The second section will focus on HRDD and explore how MFCs might alter their current practices to better discharge their responsibilities under the UNGPs. The final section will examine how some States are already starting to give legal effect to the due diligence requirements advanced by the UNGPs, and how courts could build upon the acknowledged horizontal and indirect effects of the right to health to place obligations of due diligence directly upon MFCs.

2. MULTINATIONAL FOOD CORPORATIONS AND THE RIGHT TO HEALTH IN INTERNATIONAL LAW

The meaning and content of the right to health as set out in Article 12 of the International Covenant on Economic, Social and Cultural Rights,[10] has been extensively analysed in existing literature,[11] as has General Comment 14 of the Committee on Economic, Social and Cultural Rights (CESCR),[12] which clearly indicates that the right to health includes a right to social conditions

---

[9] United Nations Office of the High Commissioner for Human Rights, Guiding Principles on Business and Human Rights: Implementing the United Nations 'Protect, Respect and Remedy' Framework, UN Doc. A/HRC/17/31, 21 March 2011.

[10] International Covenant on Economic, Social and Cultural Rights (16 December 1977) United Nations Treaty Series, vol 993, p. 3.

[11] See, e.g.: S Jamar, 'The International Human Right to Health' (1994) 22 *Southern University Law Review* 1; J Tobin, *The Right to Health in International Law* (OUP 2012); L Gostin, *Global Health Law* (Harvard University Press 2014), see chapter 8 'Health and Human Rights'; E Kinney, 'The International Human Right to Health: What Does This Mean for our Nation and World?' (2001) 34 *Indiana Law Review* 1457; P Hunt, 'Interpreting the International Right to Health in a Human Rights-Based Approach to Health' (2016) 18(2) *Health and Human Rights Journal* 109; K Perehudoff and L Forman, 'What Constitutes "Reasonable" State Action on Core Obligations? Considering a Right to Health Framework to Provide Essential Medicines' (2019) 11 *Journal of Human Rights Practice* 1; C Lougarre, 'Clarifying the Right to Health through Supranational Monitoring: The Highest Standard of Health Attainable' (2018) 11(3) *Public Health Ethics* 251.

[12] CESCR, General Comment 14, The right to the highest attainable standard of health, UN Doc. E/C. 12/2000/4, 8 November 2000.

that facilitate the pursuit of the highest attainable standard of health.[13] With respect to children and obesity, such conditions might include protection from manipulative food marketing, the availability of reasonably priced nutritious foods, and clear, child-friendly information on the implications of various dietary choices – in other words the absence of an obesogenic environment.

General Comment 14 emphasizes that corporations, including MFCs, should accept responsibility for contributing to the realization of the right to health:

> While only States are parties to the Covenant and thus ultimately accountable for compliance with it, all members of society ... as well as the private business sector ... have responsibilities regarding the realization of the right to health.[14]

Furthermore, General Comment 14 states that:

> In order to create a favourable climate for the realization of the right, States parties should take appropriate steps to ensure that the private business sector and civil society are aware of, and consider the importance of, the right to health in pursuing their activities.[15]

General Comment 15 on the right to the child to enjoy the highest attainable standard of health, developed by the Committee on the Rights of the Child (CRC),[16] more clearly implicates MFCs in the realization of the right to health:

> Children's exposure to 'fast foods' that are high in fat, sugar or salt, energy-dense and micronutrient poor, and drinks containing high levels of caffeine or other potentially harmful substances should be limited. The marketing of these substances – especially when such marketing is focused on children – should be regulated and their availability in schools and other places controlled.[17]

Despite implicating MFCs in the realization of the right to health, international human rights law currently only addresses States directly.[18] States are expected

---

[13] See O'Cathaoir and Hartlev in this volume.
[14] General Comment 14, n12, para 42.
[15] Ibid., para 55.
[16] CRC, General Comment 15, The right of the child to the enjoyment of the highest attainable standard of health (art 24), UN Doc. CRC/C/GC/15, 17 April 2013; UN General Assembly, Convention on the Rights of the Child, 20 November 1989, United Nations Treaty Series, vol 1577, 3.
[17] Ibid, para 47.
[18] See: P Alston, 'The 'Not-a-Cat' Syndrome: Can the International Human Rights Regime Accommodate Non-State Actors?' in P Alston (ed.), *Non-State Actors and Human Rights* (OUP 2006); J Hessbruegge, 'Human Rights Violations Arising from Conduct of Non-State Actors' (2005) 11 *Buffalo Human Rights Law Review* 21.

to prevent human rights abuses by non-State actors,[19] but these actors do not directly hold human rights duties. This does not mean that it is impossible for international law to address non-State actors, who can be made the formal subjects of human rights treaties.[20] Indeed, several international treaties specifically concern human rights abuses by non-State actors,[21] and some supranational legal orders have even accepted that some duties based on fundamental rights owed by States to individuals can be interpreted as binding on non-State actors.[22] However, international law does not yet impose any direct legal duties upon corporations.

More recent proposals have sought to change this. In June 2014 the Human Rights Council (HRC) adopted a resolution tabled by Ecuador in September 2013 to establish an 'intergovernmental working group with the mandate to elaborate an international legally binding instrument on Transnational Corporations and Other Business Enterprises with respect to human rights'.[23] The first session of this intergovernmental working group took place in July 2015, and the most recent session, the fifth, took place in October 2019. This latest session considered a revised draft of the binding instrument,[24] and although broad support existed for the increased coverage provided by this draft, 'most delegations acknowledged there was still room for improvement',

---

[19] See, e.g.: R McCorquodale and P Simons, 'Responsibility Beyond Borders: State Responsibility for Extraterritorial Violations by Corporations of International Human Rights Law' (2007) 70(4) *Modern Law Review* 598; A Nolan, 'Addressing Economic and Social Rights Violations by Non-state Actors through the Role of the State: A Comparison of Regional Approaches to the "Obligation to Protect"' (2009) 9(2) *Human Rights Law Review* 225.

[20] S Ratner, 'Corporations and Human Rights: A Theory of Legal Responsibility' (2001) 111(3) *Yale Law Journal* 443.

[21] These include the 1948 Genocide Convention and the Geneva Conventions: C Jochnick, 'Confronting the Impunity of Non-State Actors: New Fields for the Promotion of Human Rights' (1999) 21(1) *Human Rights Quarterly* 56, 61–3.

[22] For example, the *Mangold* jurisprudence of the Court of Justice of the European Union, in which a general principle of EU law relating to employment rights protection was created and applied in a dispute between two private parties. This jurisprudence has not been universally well received – for discussion see: E Spaventa, 'The Horizontal Application of Fundamental Rights as General Principles of Union Law' in A Arnull et al. (eds), *A Constitutional Order of States – Essays in Honour of Alan Dashwood* (Hart 2011) 199.

[23] UN General Assembly Twenty-sixth session, Elaboration of an international legally binding instrument on transnational corporations and other business enterprises with respect to human rights, UN Doc. A/HRC/26/L.22/Rev.1, 25 June 2014.

[24] Legally Binding Instrument to Regulate, in International Human Rights Law, the Activities of Transnational Corporations and other Business Enterprises, OEIGWG Chairmanship Revised Draft 16.7.2019, available online at https://www.ohchr.org/Documents/HRBodies/HRCouncil/WGTransCorp/OEIGWG_RevisedDraft_LBI.pdf.

with many delegations calling for 'more precise language and more concrete measures throughout the draft',[25] resulting in the working group agreeing to consider revisions to the proposed text at its sixth session in 2020.[26] Thus, there remains an opening to place concrete legal duties on corporations, however this may be diminishing and would at least require significant further work.[27]

In the absence of a binding treaty on corporations and human rights, several soft law instruments have been developed in an effort to hold business actors to account for human rights violations,[28] of which the UNGPs are currently the most detailed.

The UNGPs formalize the most important *duties* of the State in ensuring that businesses can respect human rights, and the most important *responsibilities* that corporations have in doing so. The UNGPs are not to be 'read as creating new international law obligations',[29] but instead have the 'objective of enhancing standards and practices with regards to business and human rights so as to achieve tangible results for affected individuals and communities'.[30] The purpose of creating them was to recognize that '[w]hile corporations may be considered "organs of society", they are specialized economic organs, not democratic public interest institutions. As such, their responsibilities cannot and should not simply mirror the duties of States'.[31] Consequently, the UNGPs develop HRDD as a more appropriate process through which corporations can best discharge their responsibility to respect human rights.

The UNGPs were unanimously endorsed by the Human Rights Council,[32] but nevertheless attracted substantial criticism from NGOs and academic commentators on the basis that the approach taken was too weak, and that binding

---

[25] Report on the fifth session of the open-ended intergovernmental working group on transnational corporations and other business enterprises with respect to human rights, A/HRC/43/55, 9 January 2020, para 11.
[26] Ibid., see Recommendation (h) of the Chair-Rapporteur, on p. 18.
[27] For further commentary on this process, see: D Cassell and A Ramasastry, 'White Paper: Options For a Treaty on Business and Human Rights' (2016) 6(1) *Notre Dame Journal of International and Comparative Law* 1; O De Schutter, 'Towards a New Treaty on Business and Human Rights' (2015) 1(1) *Business and Human Rights Journal* 41; D Johnston, 'Human Rights Incorporated, Not Everyone Agrees' (2020) 13(1) *The Journal of Business, Entrepreneurship & the Law* 95.
[28] OECD Guidelines for Multinational Enterprises (OECD 2011) available online at http://www.oecd.org/daf/inv/mne/48004323.pdf; The UN Global Compact, https://www.unglobalcompact.org.
[29] UNGPs, n9, 1.
[30] Ibid.
[31] J Ruggie, 'Protect, Respect and Remedy: A Framework for Business and Human Rights', UN Doc. A/HRC/8/5, 7 April 2008, para 53.
[32] Human Rights Council Resolution 17/4, UN Doc. A/HRC/17/L.17/Rev.1, 15 June 2011.

human rights rules for corporations were needed.[33] Other commentators have criticized the vagueness of the UNGPs,[34] and their intentional avoidance of corporate human rights duties.[35] Nevertheless, what the UNGPs do achieve is a clear articulation of the proper societal division of responsibility for upholding human rights, in light of the fundamental nature of the various actors – the role of corporations should be to do everything reasonable to respect human rights, and the role of States should be to ensure that they achieve this.[36] They set out a clear route to achieving increased corporate respect for human rights, through a mechanism that operates in the realm of what is generally perceived as currently achievable, rather than what might be possible.[37] Consequently, it is feasible now for States to implement HRDD requirements within national policy on corporate human rights compliance, and even translate them into legal duties for corporations.[38]

---

[33] Human Rights Watch, 'UN Human Rights Council: Weak Stance on Business Standards' (*hrw.org*, 16 June 2011); United Nations: A Call for Action to Better Protect the Rights of those Affected by Business-Related Human Rights Abuses (Amnesty International Public Statement, 14 June 2011, IOR 40/009/2011); R Blitt, 'Beyond Ruggie's Guiding Principles on Business and Human Rights: Charting an Embracive Approach to Corporate Human Rights Compliance' (2012) 48(1) *Texas International Law Journal* 33; B Fasterling and G Demuijnck, 'Human Rights in the Void? Due Diligence in the UN Guiding Principles on Business and Human Rights' (2013) 116 *Journal of Business Ethics* 799.

[34] S Lagoutte, 'The UN Guiding Principles on Business and Human Rights: A Confusing "Smart Mix" of Soft and Hard International Human Rights Law' in S Lagoutte et al. (eds), *Tracing the Roles of Soft Law in Human Rights* (OUP 2016).

[35] N Jägers, 'UN Guiding Principles on Business and Human Rights: Making Headway Towards Real Corporate Accountability' (2011) 29(2) *Netherlands Quarterly of Human Rights* 159.

[36] A Ramasastry, 'Corporate Social Responsibility Versus Business and Human Rights: Bridging the Gap Between Responsibility and Accountability' (2015) 14(2) *Journal of Human Rights* 237, 246.

[37] This position of 'principled pragmatism' was a self-conscious stance adopted by John Ruggie in conceptualizing the UNGPs: Interim Report of the Special Representative of the Secretary-General on the Issue of Human Rights and Transnational Corporations and Other Business Enterprises, UN Doc. E/CN.4/2006/97, 22 February 2006, paras 70–81. On the limits of this stance see: G Dancy, 'Human Rights Pragmatism: Belief, Inquiry and Action' (2015) 22(3) *European Journal of International Relations*; L Catá Backer, 'Principled Pragmatism in the Elaboration of a Comprehensive Treaty on Business and Human Rights', in S Deva and D Bilchitz (eds), *Building a Treaty on Business and Human Rights: Context and Contours* (CUP 2017).

[38] However, the extent to which States have successfully implemented HRDD requirements through national action plans has been criticized by exerts: D Augenstein, 'Negotiating the Hard/Soft Law Divide in Business and Human Rights: The Implementation of the UNGPs in the European Union' (2018) 9(2) *Global Policy* 254;

The HRDD process set out in the UNGPs has also been more widely accepted by the business community than attempts to create formal legal obligations,[39] and a number of collaborations between food industry operators have been launched to advance the principles of HRDD.[40] Many companies understand that, in addition to the moral and legal imperatives for human rights compliance, transparent support for and promotion of human rights will be viewed positively by consumers of the company's brands.[41] Thus, the UNGPs are useful because they clarify practical ways in which corporations can proactively work to increase their human rights compliance to their own benefit. The next section examines the HRDD framework set out in the UNGPs and outlines the actions that this could require of MFCs.

3. MULTINATIONAL FOOD CORPORATIONS AND RIGHT TO HEALTH DUE DILIGENCE

A sizeable literature on the UNGP's HRDD framework already exists,[42] covering a number of broader issues relating to HRDD, including the style of impact

---

H Cantú Rivera, 'National Action Plans on Business and Human Rights: Progress or Mirage?' (2019) 4(2) *Business and Human Rights Journal* 213.

[39] Some proactive implementation of HRDD principles by businesses has taken place: R McCorquodale et al., 'Human Rights Due Diligence in Law and Practice: Good Practices and Challenges for Business Enterprises' (2017) 2(2) *Business and Human Rights Journal* 195. However, implementation of HRDD principles has proved to be variable across sectors: S Aaronson and I Higham, '"Re-righting Business": John Ruggie and the Struggle to Develop International Human Rights Standards for Transnational Firms' (2013) 36 *Human Rights Quarterly* 333.

[40] See the Global Compact's launch of the 'Food and Agriculture Business (FAB) Principles in 2014: https://www.unglobalcompact.org/library/2051. These have been endorsed by several MFCs: http://www.fstjournal.org/features/un-global-compact-targets-food-and-agriculture. See also the Food Network for Ethical Trade, established in 2016 by major UK food companies, which currently has 45 members: https://foodnetworkforethicaltrade.com

[41] B Freeman, 'Substance Sells: Aligning Corporate Reputation and Corporate Responsibility' (2006) 51(1) *Public Relations Quarterly* 12; D Aguirre, 'Multinational Corporations and the Realisation of Economic, Social and Cultural Rights' (2004) 35 *California Western International Law Journal* 53, 79.

[42] See, e.g.: Blitt, n33; Fasterling and Demuijnck, n33; D Kemp and F Vanclay, 'Human Rights and Impact Assessment: Clarifying the Connections in Practice' (2013) 31(2) *Impact Assessment and Project Appraisal* 86; R Hamann et al., 'Business and Human Rights in South Africa: An Analysis of Antecedents of Human Rights Due Diligence' (2009) 87(Suppl 2) *Journal of Business Ethics* 453; J Sherman and A Lehr, 'Human Rights Due Diligence: Is It Too Risky?' (2010) Corporate Social Responsibility Initiative Working Paper No 55; A Sanders, 'The Impact of the "Ruggie framework" and the United Nations Guiding Principles on Business and Human Rights

assessment to be employed in conducting due diligence,⁴³ or how the particular understandings of due diligence developed in corporate, tort, and other legal contexts should inform HRDD.⁴⁴

The purpose of HRDD is 'to identify and prevent certain deleterious human rights impacts that may arise in a given business venture, including those from associated business relationships or engagement with vulnerable minority groups or populations'.⁴⁵ While the corporate obligation to respect currently 'focuses on the negative formulation of companies doing no harm',⁴⁶ this does not mean that corporations should be passive in respecting human rights. Basing the obligation to respect upon HRDD reflects the fact that corporations should *actively* work to ensure they do no harm.⁴⁷

Accordingly, Prof. Ruggie's HRDD process comprises four parts:

[1] a statement of *policy* articulating the company's commitment to respect human rights; [2] periodic *assessment* of actual and potential human rights impacts of company activities and relationships; [3] *Integrating* these commitments and assessments into internal control and oversight systems; and [4] *Tracking* and reporting performance.⁴⁸

Principle 16 of the UNGPs accounts for part 1 and requires that 'business enterprises should express their commitment to meet this responsibility through a statement of policy'. Principle 17 accounts for parts 2, 3 and 4, and states that '(i)n order to identify, prevent, mitigate and account for how they address their adverse human rights impacts', business should carry out

---

on Transnational Human Rights Litigation' in J Martin and K Bravo, *The Business and Human Rights Landscape: Moving Forward, Looking Back* (CUP 2015); R Mares, 'Human Rights Due Diligence and the Root Causes of Harm in Business Operation: A Textual and Contextual Analysis of the Guiding Principles on Business and Human Rights' (2018) 10(1) *Northeastern University Law Review* 1; I Landau, 'Human Rights Due Diligence and the Risk of Cosmetic Compliance' (2019) 20 *Melbourne Journal of International Law* 1.

⁴³ J Harrison, 'Establishing a Meaningful Human Rights Due Diligence Process for Corporations: Learning From Experience of Human Rights Impact Assessment' (2013) 31(2) *Impact Assessment and Project Appraisal* 107; B Fasterling, 'Human Rights Due Diligence as Risk Management: Social Risk versus Human Rights Risk' (2017) 2(2) *Business and Human Rights Journal* 225.
⁴⁴ Sanders, n42.
⁴⁵ Blitt, n33, 48.
⁴⁶ Ramasastry, n36, 248.
⁴⁷ Ruggie, n31, para 61.
⁴⁸ J Ruggie, 'Engaging Business: Addressing Respect for Human Rights' (*Engaging Business: Addressing Respect for Human Rights*, Atlanta, 25 February 2010), available at https://sites.hks.harvard.edu/m-rcbg/CSRI/newsandstories/Ruggie_Atlanta.pdf.

a due diligence process that involves 'assessing actual and potential human rights impacts, integrating and acting upon the findings, tracking responses, and communicating how impacts are addressed'.[49] Practically speaking, the process should (a) cover adverse human rights impacts that a business may cause or be directly linked to, (b) vary in complexity depending on the size and nature of the business, and (c) be ongoing.[50] Principles 18, 19 and 20 then describe how businesses might assess, integrate, and track respectively.

Several observations could be made on the applicability of the HRDD framework to MFCs, the first of which concerns the human rights policy statement. Commentary on Guiding Principle 12 (corporations' responsibility to respect internationally recognised human rights) states that 'some human rights may be at greater risk than others in particular industries or contexts, and therefore will be the focus of heightened attention'. MFCs, certain of whose activities contribute to the creation of obesogenic environments, should therefore acknowledge their responsibility to respect the right to health. However, of the corporations operating in the food and agriculture sector that are examined by the Corporate Human Rights Benchmark[51] and KnowTheChain[52] organization, or identified on the Business and Human Rights Resource Centre database,[53] no company made specific reference to protecting the right to health in its human rights, sustainability, or ethics policy statements, with the sole exception of Arla Foods.[54]

Some MFCs do have policies on how they market their products to children, however none of these policies venture as far as declaring that children have a right to grow up in a health-promoting environment,[55] despite elaborating extensively on how children should not be the direct subjects of unhealthy food advertising, the need for increased healthy choice ranges for children, and the

---

[49] UNGPs, n9, 17.
[50] Ibid., 17–18.
[51] https://www.corporatebenchmark.org/agricultural-products-0.
[52] https://knowthechain.org/company-lists/.
[53] https://www.business-humanrights.org/en/company-policy-statements-on-human-rights. It should be noted that many of the links in this database appear to be out of date.
[54] 'Arla Foods Human Rights Policy', available at https://www.arla.com/globalassets/arla-global/company---overview/responsibility/human-rights/arla_foods_human_rights_policy_update.pdf.
[55] See the statements from McDonald's (http://corporate.mcdonalds.com/content/dam/AboutMcDonalds/2.0/pdfs/Global%20Guidelines%20for%20Childrens%20Marketing.pdf), Nestle (http://www.nestle.com/asset-library/documents/library/documents/corporate_social_responsibility/nestle-marketing-communication-children-policy.pdf), and Coca-Cola (http://www.coca-colacompany.com/content/dam/journey/us/en/private/fileassets/pdf/our-company/responsible-marketing-policy.pdf).

need for an active lifestyle for children, with even occasional references to WHO evidence on childhood obesity.[56] The reluctance of MFCs to admit that their consumers, especially children, have a right to health and that the corporation should be responsible for respecting it is particularly obvious in Nestle's policy statement – rather than acknowledging the potential impact of their business practices on the obesogenic environment, Nestle commits itself to 'responsible, reliable consumer communication that empowers consumers to *exercise their right to informed choice* and promotes healthier diets'.[57] A first suggestion might therefore be that MFCs should explicitly acknowledge their responsibility to respect the right to health, as part of more rigorous HRDD.

The second observation concerns the timing and subject matter of right to health risk assessment. Commentary on Guiding Principle 17 states that '[h]uman rights due diligence should be initiated as early as possible in the development of a new activity or relationship'. Furthermore, commentary on Guiding Principle 18 states that in the assessment process 'business enterprises should pay special attention to any particular human rights impacts on individuals from groups or populations that may be at heightened risk of vulnerability', and that they should 'seek to understand the concerns of potentially affected stakeholders by consulting them directly'. MFCs should therefore engage in right to health due diligence at the start of product or marketing development, to identify the contribution that products or marketing might make to the obesogenic environment (particularly for products targeted at children), and act to reduce this contribution. However, it is now clear that rather than engage openly with children, MFCs increasingly track their online activities and use this data to create sophisticated profiles of their consumption behaviour, from which digital and personalized marketing campaigns are designed.[58] The application of HRDD at the very beginning of the marketing process should arguably lead an MFC to question whether covert data collection from children to inform marketing strategies should be replaced with overt and transparent engagement, to understand all impacts that marketing campaigns have upon children and how children feel about being targeted with advertising messages for unhealthy foods. McDonald's even acknowledges that '[o]ur brand promise begins even before our customers enter our

---

[56] See in particular 'Nestle Marketing Communication to Children Policy' (http://www.nestle.com/asset-library/documents/library/documents/corporate_social_responsibility/nestle-marketing-communication-children-policy.pdf), at p. 1.

[57] Emphasis added. 'The Nestle Corporate Business Principles', available at http://www.nestle.com/asset-library/Documents/Library/Documents/Corporate_Governance/Corporate-Business-Principles-EN.pdf, at p. 6.

[58] *Tackling food marketing to children in a digital world: trans-disciplinary perspectives* (WHO Regional Office for Europe 2016).

restaurants',[59] and had the opportunity to honestly explore the effectiveness of their human rights due diligence procedures with respect to children in the 2014 'Report of the Sustainability and Corporate Responsibility Committee of the Board of Directors',[60] which was voluntarily released in response to shareholder demands for proof of human rights due diligence.[61] However, this report makes only one mention of children (in relation to child labour), of health (in relation to employee health and safety), and of participation (in relation to best practices in supplier accountability).

This was an opportunity for an MFC to publicly commit to effective right to health impact assessment, and to demonstrate that they conduct it at all stages of product and promotional development. Instead, the report states that '[m]anagement believes that its controls around human rights risk in its Company-operated restaurants and other Company facilities are robust'.[62] Furthermore, it indicates that the company's Global Compliance Office is responsible for monitoring changes in law that are relevant to the company's standards, coordinating investigations of violations of the standards, ensuring that appropriate actions are taken in response to violations, revising policies, and communicating with the Board of Directors – none of which appear to include a proactive role in advising product and marketing development teams on human rights responsibilities.

Other corporations also appear to have missed opportunities to implement right to health due diligence in line with the UNGPs framework. For example, Ferrero cite their 'Marketing to Children Road Test'[63] as an example of responsible practice. This title is suggestive of policy monitoring, but in fact the road test is a tool that allows Ferrero marketers to 'familiarize [themselves] with the concept of responsible advertising through real life examples', which appears to involve no actual engagement with consumers to understand their perspectives on responsible marketing. Mondelez have also developed a Mindful

---

[59] 'Standards of Business Conduct The Promise of the Golden Arches', available at http://corporate.mcdonalds.com/content/dam/gwscorp/scale-for-good/HUMAN%20RIGHTS_US_English_SBC.pdf, at p. 15.

[60] 'Describing the Duties of the Board of Directors and the Responsibilities of Management as Related to Sustainability and Corporate Social Responsibility Matters, including Matters Related to Human Rights' (9 January 2014) available at http://corporate.mcdonalds.com/content/dam/gwscorp/corporate-governance-content/board-and-committee-reports/Human_Rights.pdf.

[61] A Mehra and N Santiago, 'You Want Human Rights With That? McDonald's Serves Up Due Diligence on Human Rights' (*huffingtonpost.com*, 25 March 2014).

[62] 'Describing the Duties of the Board of Directors', n60, 3.

[63] 'Responsible Advertising: A Case Study of Company Compliance' https://ec.europa.eu/health/sites/health/files/nutrition_physical_activity/docs/ev_20160407_co06_en.pdf.

Snacking Guide, which seeks to help consumers 'build a healthier relationship with food' and 'have more balanced and healthy eating habits, but also remove any negative feelings or guilt that may be associated with snacking'.[64] This approach to consumer engagement trains consumers to function within the obesogenic environment, rather than establishing how the company's contribution to the obesogenic environment can be mitigated. A second suggestion might therefore be that MFCs should commit to assessing right to health impacts at the very earliest stages of product and marketing development, consult child consumers on their perception of the proposed activity, and feed the results back into the development process, in order to conduct more rigorous HRDD.

The third observation concerns the tracking of due diligence outcomes. Commentary on Guiding Principle 20 states that 'Business enterprises should make particular efforts to track the effectiveness of their responses to impacts on individuals from groups or populations that may be at heightened risk of vulnerability'. MFCs should therefore evaluate, for example, the extent to which their policies on marketing to children actually reduce children's exposure to unhealthy food marketing. However, MFCs do not effectively monitor such commitments. The most recent Annual Report of the EU Platform on Diet, Physical Activity and Health, produced in 2016 and covering activities in 2015, indicates that while MFCs[65] were getting better at reporting the activities they were undertaking as a result of self-regulatory commitments made as members of the Platform, they were getting worse at reporting the impact of those commitments upon public health. While 70 per cent of commitments reported outputs in clear detail in 2015, compared to 47 per cent in 2014, only 26 per cent reported clearly on outcomes in 2015, compared to 36 per cent in 2014. Moreover, only 48 per cent of commitments disseminated the results of their actions.[66] While Platform activities have continued, no further annual reports were produced after 2016. This likely coincided with the decreasing

---

[64] See https://www.mondelezinternational.com/-/media/Mondelez/Snacking-Made-Right/Mindful-Snacking/MindfulSnacking_ConsumerGuide_2017.pdf.

[65] The monitoring data can be taken to mostly represent the actions of MFCs, since they adopt the great majority of commitments within the Platform: O Bartlett and A Garde, 'The EU Platform and the EU Forum: New Modes of Governance or a Smokescreen for the Promotion of Conflicts of Interest?' in A Alemanno and A Garde, *Regulating Lifestyle Risks: The EU, Alcohol, Tobacco and Unhealthy Diets* (CUP 2015).

[66] Monitoring the activities of the EU Platform for Action on Diet, Physical Activity and Health: Annual Report 2016 (ICF Consulting Services, 2016), available online at https://ec.europa.eu/health/sites/health/files/nutrition_physical_activity/docs/2016_report_en.pdf, 3.

interest shown by the Commission in the Platform.[67] Indeed, the 'political turn against regulation and in favour of growth in Europe reduced the threat of legislation and regulation that makes self-regulation effective',[68] and this will likely have reduced the incentive that the MFC members had to monitor their commitments. This in turn appears to have been among the factors that prompted NGO members to revoke their membership of the Platform in July 2019.[69]

There are two possible reasons for the above deficiencies – either MFCs cannot show much evidence of the success of their commitments, or they are simply not interested in whether their commitments lead to greater respect for children's health. The latter may be true if one considers recent studies which indicate that MFC responsibility campaigns are often successful in promoting feelings of trust and support amongst parents and children for MFC brands.[70] MFCs may be more concerned to use responsibility initiatives to secure the respect of their young customers than to actually protect their health. Either way, MFCs do not effectively track and evaluate the effects of the right to health due diligence that they claim to conduct. According to the latest Annual Report for the Platform, 'within the monitoring reports [submitted for each commitment], the degree of detail varied significantly',[71] and according to consultancy firm ICF many commitments on marketing specifically may be ineffective because they 'lacked measureable information'.[72] A third suggestion might therefore be that MFCs should conduct genuine and critical evaluations of their responsibility commitments, engage seriously with independent evidence on the effectiveness of their initiatives,[73] and act upon any evidence

---

[67] S Greer et al., *Everything You Always Wanted to Know About European Union Health Policies but Were Afraid to Ask* (European Observatory on Health Systems and Policies 2019), 71.

[68] Ibid.

[69] 'NGOs leave EU Platform on Diet, Physical Activity & Health' (epha.org, 3 July 2019).

[70] Z Richards and L Phillipson, 'Are Big Food's Corporate Social Responsibility Strategies Valuable to Communities? A Quantitative Study with Parents and Children' (2017) 20(8) *Public Health Nutrition* 3372.

[71] Monitoring the activities of the EU Platform for Action on Diet, Physical Activity and Health, n66, 1.

[72] ICF Study Team, 'Overview of Commitments in the Areas of "Marketing and Advertising" and "Advocacy and information exchange"' (7 April 2016) available at https://ec.europa.eu/health/sites/health/files/nutrition_physical_activity/docs/ev_20160407_co04_en.pdf.

[73] A good example might be this study conducted on the marketing of ready to eat breakfast cereals to children, which found potential for success but with limitations: J Harris et al., 'Encouraging Big Food to do the Right Thing for Children's Health:

of consumers reacting negatively to responsibility initiatives,[74] in order to conduct more rigorous HRDD. In particular, MFCs should make a genuine effort to design products and marketing in line with the latest evidence on children's cognitive reactions to the modern food decision-making environment.[75]

Conducting right to health due diligence as suggested above may significantly increase the extent to which MFCs respect the right to health, particularly the health of children who, as a particularly vulnerable group of consumers, should be afforded specific protection from the obesogenic environment. To summarize the suggestions, MFCs should make further efforts to reflect in a sufficiently thorough and genuine manner upon the contributions that their current business practices make to the obesogenic environment (keeping in mind the relevant evidence and policy frameworks[76]) and then take effective action to neutralise or mitigate the effects of such contributions.

However, it must be acknowledged that the implementation of these suggestions would depend in large part upon the commitment and morals of an MFC's directors,[77] and the creation of a genuine culture of respect for the right to health.[78] Furthermore, and probably more crucially, it must also be acknowledged that an MFC's business model partly relies upon recruiting consumers at a young age and inducing them to build a relationship with the corporation's brands.[79] Given that obesity prevention policy is still heavily influenced by prevailing neoliberal ideals,[80] there are considerable economic

---

A Case Study on Using Research to Improve Marketing of Sugary Cereals' (2015) 25 *Critical Public Health* 320.

[74] See, e.g.: M Schröder and M McEachern, 'Fast Foods and Ethical Consumer Value: A Focus on McDonald's and KFC' (2005) 107(4) *British Food Journal* 212.

[75] *Tackling food marketing,* n58; E Boyland and M Tatlow-Golden, 'Exposure, Power and Impact of Food Marketing on Children: Evidence Supports Strong Restrictions' (2017) 8(2) *European Journal of Risk Regulation* 224; *Building momentum: Lessons on implementing robust restrictions of food and non-alcoholic beverage marketing to children* (World Cancer Research Fund International 2020).

[76] A Garde et al., *Food Marketing and Children's Rights* (Unicef 2018).

[77] Fasterling and Demuijnck, n33.

[78] Commentators have suggested that human rights education should become a core aspect of business school tuition. See, e.g.: W Stubbs and C Cocklin, 'Teaching Sustainability to Business Students: Shifting Mindsets' (2008) 9(3) *International Journal of Sustainability in Higher Education* 206.

[79] J Schor and M Ford, 'From Tastes Great to Cool: Children's Food Marketing and the Rise of the Symbolic' (2007) 35(1) *Journal of Law, Medicine and Ethics* 10; S Jones et al., '"Like Me, Want Me, Buy Me, Eat Me": Relationship-Building Marketing Communications in Children's Magazines' (2010) 13(12) *Public Health Nutrition* 2111; T Robinson et al., 'Effects of Fast Food Branding on Young Children's Taste Preferences' (2007) 161(8) *Archives of Pediatric and Adolescent Medicine* 792.

[80] J Henderson et al., 'Governing Childhood Obesity: Framing Regulation of Fast Food Advertising in the Australian Print Media' (2009) 69 *Social Science and Medicine* 1402.

incentives for MFCs to not implement the above suggestions, and to avoid full commitment to respecting the right to health. In fact, MFCs have developed a suite of tactics to divert attention from the fact that many of their core business practices neither live up to the normative standards of the right to health, nor comply with the responsibility to respect the right to health set out in the UNGPs.[81] Anand Grover acknowledged this in his role as Special Rapporteur on the right to health:

> under the guise of corporate social responsibility to meet their ethical obligations towards society at large, [MFCs] have attempted to shift the burden of the responsibility to make healthier choices onto consumers instead of addressing their role in creating an unhealthy food environment ... Such acts result in a negation of the right to health.[82]

The evidence gathered on MFC tactics demonstrates that they are determined to divert as much attention as possible away from the fact that being profitable at current levels, without fundamental product reformulation, depends upon business practices that undermine rather than respect the right to health.[83] MFCs arguably will not (and perhaps cannot) conduct effective right to health

---

[81] These tactics have been analysed in depth in the literature. On the use of corporate social responsibility initiatives see: Z Richards et al., 'Corporate Social Responsibility Programmes of Big Food in Australia: A Content Analysis of Industry Documents' (2015) 39(6) *Australian and New Zealand Journal of Public Health* 550, 555; A Garde and N Rigby, 'Going for Gold – Should Responsible Governments Raise the Bar on Sponsorship of the Olympic Games and Other Sporting Events by Food and Beverage Companies?' (2012) 17(2) *Communications Law* 42. On the use of self-regulation see: Bartlett and Garde, n65; A Garde et al., 'Implementing the WHO Recommendations whilst Avoiding Real, Perceived or Potential Conflicts of Interest' (2017) 8(2) *European Journal of Risk Regulation* 237. On the use of paternalist rhetoric see: G Jenkin et al., 'Framing Obesity: The Framing Contest Between Industry and Public Health at the New Zealand Inquiry into Obesity' (2011) 12(12) *Obesity Reviews* 1022; R Kersh, 'Of Nannies and Nudges: The Current State of U.S. Obesity Policymaking' (2015) 129(8) *Public Health* 1083. On the manipulation of the evidence base see: L Lesser et al., 'Relationship Between Funding Source and Conclusion Among Nutrition-Related Scientific Articles' (2007) 4(1) *PLoS Med* e5; K Brownell and K Warner, 'The Perils of Ignoring History: Big Tobacco Played Dirty and Millions Died. How Similar Is Big Food?' (2009) 87(1) *Millbank Quarterly* 259.

[82] Report of the Special Rapporteur Anand Grover on the Right of Everyone to the Enjoyment of the Highest Attainable Standard of Physical and Mental Health: Unhealthy Foods, Non-Communicable Diseases and the Right to Health, UN Doc. A/HRC/26/31, 1 April 2014, para 30.

[83] For a taxonomy of all of the various tactics employed by unhealthy consumption industries, including MFCs, see: R Moodie, 'What Public Health Practitioners Need to Know About Unhealthy Industry Tactics' (2017) 107 *American Journal of Public Health* 1047.

due diligence unless they are legally obliged to do so. The final section of this chapter therefore explores the options for creating such legal obligations.

4. IMPLEMENTING MANDATORY RIGHT TO HEALTH DUE DILIGENCE LEGISLATION

Legislation that places general due diligence obligations on corporations, and which imposes civil or criminal liability for non-compliance, is already relatively widespread.[84] Legislation specifically imposing HRDD obligations is novel, yet some States are now adopting such laws. On 21 February 2017, the French National Assembly adopted a bill that would become LOI n° 2017-399 du 27 Mars 2017, which requires that French companies with at least 5,000 French employees and 10,000 global employees 'must establish and implement an effective vigilance plan'.[85] The so-called duty of vigilance bill was challenged before the French Constitutional Council, but was upheld on 23 March 2017.[86] This legislation appears to significantly advance the objective of holding corporations responsible for identifying and mitigating the human rights impacts of their activities, but its first major test has been a disappointment so far. Six NGOs sent a formal demand to French oil company Total alleging that they had failed to produce a suitable vigilance plan to identify environmental and human rights impacts of its planned oil drilling activities in Uganda.[87] After Total denied the allegations, the NGOs filed a legal complaint under the vigilance law at the Nanterre High Court.[88] On 30 January 2020 the court declared that it did not have jurisdiction to hear the case, refused to examine the claims of the NGOs, and insisted that the case should be brought before the French Commercial Court.[89] Given that the Commercial Court was

---

[84] O de Schutter et al., *Human Rights Due Diligence: The Role of States* (International Corporate Accountability Roundtable, the European Coalition for Corporate Justice, and the Canadian Network on Corporate Accountability, 2012).

[85] English translation available at https://business-humanrights.org/en/french-duty-of-vigilance-bill-english-translation.

[86] Décision no. 2017-750 DC du 23 Mars 2017 du Conseil Constitutionnel.

[87] An English translation of the letter setting out the allegations of the NGOs can be found at http://blogs2.law.columbia.edu/climate-change-litigation/wp-content/uploads/sites/16/non-us-case-documents/2019/20190719_NA_na-1.pdf.

[88] A report (In French) produced by the NGOs to accompany the filing of their complaint can be found at http://blogs2.law.columbia.edu/climate-change-litigation/wp-content/uploads/sites/16/non-us-case-documents/2019/20191023_NA_na.pdf. An English language summary of the report can be found at https://notreaffaireatous.org/wp-content/uploads/2019/05/ResumeTOTAL_A4_ENGLISH.pdf.

[89] 'Total abuses in Uganda: French High Court of Justice declares itself incompetent in favour of the Commercial Court' (foei.org, 30 January 2020).

designed to settle disputes between corporations in a self-regulatory manner, the NGOs claimed that the ruling of the High Court sets the precedent that corporations will escape rigorous judicial human rights scrutiny under the vigilance law, and plan to appeal the ruling.[90]

In Switzerland, a Responsible Business Initiative was launched in April 2015[91] seeking the introduction of Article 101a on 'Responsibility of Business' to the Swiss constitution. Subparagraph (2) of the proposed new Article would read:

> (a) Companies must respect internationally recognized human rights and international environmental standards, also abroad … (b) Companies are required to carry out appropriate due diligence. This means in particular that they must: identify real and potential impacts on internationally recognized human rights and the environment; take appropriate measures to prevent the violation of inter- nationally recognized human rights and international environmental standards, cease existing violations, and account for the actions taken.[92]

The Federal Council (Swiss Government) recommended rejection of the Initiative.[93] However, the National Council (Swiss Parliament Lower House) formally adopted a counter-proposal to the initiative on 14 June 2018,[94] which struck a compromise position between the demands of civil society and the business sector, placing limited liability on corporations for damages caused by corporate human rights failings.[95] However, after substantial industry lobbying, the Council of States (Swiss Parliament Upper House) voted to reject the counter-proposal,[96] against the advice of its own Legal Affairs Committee.

---

[90] C Barbière, 'Oil giant Total's "corporate vigilance" in Uganda to be vetted by commercial peers' (euractiv.com, 31 January 2020).

[91] Under the Swiss Constitution, a federal popular initiative can be launched to change the constitution, if 100,000 signatures can be collected from the electorate within 18 months: https://www.ch.ch/en/demokratie/political-rights/popular-initiative/. The Responsible Business Initiative was launched by the Swiss Coalition for Corporate Justice: http://konzern-initiative.ch/?lang=en.

[92] The English translation (non-official) of the Responsible Business Initiative can be accessed here: http://konzern-initiative.ch/wp-content/uploads/2017/11/The-initiative-text-with-explanations.pdf.

[93] Message relatif à l'initiative populaire 'Entreprises responsables – pour protéger l'être humain et l'environnement' du 15 Septembre 2017, available at https://www.admin.ch/opc/fr/federal-gazette/2017/5999.pdf.

[94] The unofficial English translation can be accessed at http://www.bhrinlaw.org/180508-swiss-parliament-counter-proposal_unofficial_en-translation_updated.pdf.

[95] 'Another step towards the adoption of a mandatory HRDD bill in Switzerland' (corporatejustice.org, 16 July 2018).

[96] 'The compromise on a counter-proposal to the Swiss Responsible Business Initiative sinks in the Council of State' (corporatejustice.org, 13 March 2019).

A political stalemate has developed over the counter-proposal, with the National Council voting to reaffirm an amended version on 13 June 2019,[97] and the Council of State voting against it for a second time (again against the advice of its Legal Affairs Committee) on 18 December 2019.[98] In its second vote, the Council of States instead backed an alternative counter-proposal favoured by the Federal Council, which eliminates legal liability in favour of reporting requirements only, a position that has been criticised by UN experts.[99] This alternative counter-proposal was rejected by the Legal Affairs Committee of the National Council, which re-affirmed a further amended version of the original counter-proposal.[100] The two chambers of the Swiss Parliament must now agree on a legislative counter proposal to the Initiative – if no agreement is reached the proposal put forward by the Initiative itself, having received the necessary popular support, will be put before Swiss voters in a referendum.[101]

HRDD legislation does not have to be as broad as the French or Swiss examples. Legislation can mandate HRDD in relation to specific issues – a recent example is the UK's Modern Slavery Act 2015, section 54 of which requires that 'Every organisation carrying on a business in the UK with a total annual turnover of £36m or more will be required to produce a slavery and human trafficking statement for each financial year of the organisation.'[102] Another recent example is the Dutch Child Labour Due Diligence Act,[103] which requires Dutch corporations or those selling to Dutch consumers to establish if there is a reasonable suspicion that child labour has contributed to their supply chains, and if so to develop a plan of action on how to prevent it.[104] However, HRDD does not have to be the sole preserve of States. The European Union is currently considering a revision of its Non-Financial Reporting Directive,[105] following

---

[97] 'Parliament keeps Responsible Business counter-proposal alive' (swissinfo.ch, 13 June 2019).
[98] 'Responsible Business Initiative – Swiss Council of States adopts conservative counter-proposal' (swlegal.ch, 20 December 2019).
[99] 'UN experts raise concerns over Swiss 'responsible business' initiative' (swissinfo.ch, 1 October 2019).
[100] See https://www.business-humanrights.org/fr/node/203091.
[101] The latest updates to the process are detailed at https://www.business-humanrights.org/en/switzerland-ngo-coalition-launches-responsible-business-initiative#c203091.
[102] The UK Government issued the following guidance on the provision: https://www.gov.uk/government/uploads/system/uploads/attachment_data/file/649906/Transparency_in_Supply_Chains_A_Practical_Guide_2017.pdf.
[103] The text of the Act is available in Dutch at https://www.eerstekamer.nl/behandeling/20170207/gewijzigd_voorstel_van_wet.
[104] J Arvanitis and K Braine, 'Breaking Down the Dutch Child Labor Due Diligence Act' (kroll.com, 2 July 2019).
[105] The Directive, as implemented through national law, obliges large companies to publish annual reports detailing the impact of their activities on a range of

criticism from observers[106] and the findings of an independent report that the quality of companies' reporting pursuant to the Directive is generally not of a sufficient standard.[107] The European Commission recently published a study that contained a review of current business practices and existing national and EU due diligence legal frameworks, as well as an impact assessment of options for new EU level due diligence requirements – these ranged from reporting requirements to various configurations of due diligence as a legal duty of care for corporations.[108] These and other developments in HRDD legislation are now being analysed by an already fast-growing literature.[109]

Despite widespread civil society support,[110] the business community has predictably exerted considerable pressure upon law makers to avoid imposing mandatory HRDD.[111] Nevertheless, it is submitted that States should be con-

---

socio-economic issues: Directive 2014/95/EU of 22 October 2014 amending Directive 2013/34/EU as regards disclosure of non-financial and diversity information by certain large undertakings and groups, OJ L 330, 15.11.2014, 1–9.

[106] See, e.g.: K Buhmann, 'Neglecting the Proactive Aspect of Human Rights Due Diligence? A Critical Appraisal of the EU's Non-Financial Reporting Directive as a Pillar One Avenue for Promoting Pillar Two Action' (2018) 3 *Business and Human Rights Journal* 23; D Ahern, 'Turning Up the Heat? EU Sustainability Goals and the Role of Reporting under the Non-Financial Reporting Directive' (2016) 13(4) *European Company and Financial Law Review* 599; O Martin-Ortega and J Hoekstra, 'Reporting as a Means to Protect and Promote Human Rights? The EU Non-Financial Reporting Directive' (2019) 44(5) *European Law Review* 622.

[107] 'An analysis of the sustainability reports of 1,000 companies pursuant to the EU-non-Financial Reporting Directive' (Alliance for Corporate Transparency, 2019) available online at https://www.allianceforcorporatetransparency.org/assets/2019_Research_Report%20_Alliance_for_Corporate_Transparency-7d9802a0c18c9f13017d686481bd2d6c6886fea6d9e9c7a5c3cfafea8a48b1c7.pdf.

[108] L Smit et al., 'Study on Due Diligence Requirements through the Supply Chain', European Commission, 2020.

[109] See, e.g.: Z McKnight, 'Human Rights Due Diligence: Legislative Scan', Canadian Labour Congress Research Paper 53, August 2018; N Bueno, 'The Swiss Federal Initiative on Responsible Business – From Responsibility to Liability' in L Enneking et al. (eds), *Accountability, International Business Operations and the Law* (Routledge 2019); D Palombo, 'The Duty of Care of the Parent Company: A Comparison between French Law, UK Precedents and the Swiss Proposals' (2019) 4 *Business and Human Rights Journal* 265; S Rao, *Modern Slavery Legislation: Drafting History and Comparisons between Australia, UK and the USA* (Routledge 2019).

[110] See the Joint Statement of Support signed by 75 civil society organizations, trade unions, research organizations, law firms and academics, English version available at: http://corporatejustice.org/news/428-joint-statement-in-support-of-the-french-corporate-duty-of-vigilance-law.

[111] S Cossart et al., 'The French Law on Duty of Care: A Historic Step Towards Making Globalization Work for All' (2017) 2(2) *Business and Human Rights Journal* 317.

fident in adopting right to health due diligence legislation, since they can find sufficient legal grounding in the right to health itself.

It is widely acknowledged that States have a legal duty under the right to health to adopt suitable legislation to control corporations[112] – indeed, General Comment 14 states that States should 'take all necessary measures to safeguard persons from infringements of the right to health by third parties', including the measures that 'regulate the activities of individuals, groups or corporations so as to prevent them from violating the right to health of others'.[113] It has been suggested that this duty can be interpreted to mean that governments have a specific obligation to concretize HRDD in legislation, as part of their more general obligation to create conditions in which MFCs can effectively discharge their responsibility to respect the right to health.[114] Enacting HRDD legislation that applies to the food industry specifically and their contribution to the obesogenic environment could therefore be seen as part of the State's duty to protect the right to health. Certain case law from the field of tobacco control even points to the potential justiciability of this legal duty.

The right to health was relied upon by the Flemish Anti-Cancer League in *Vlaamse Liga tegen Kanker (Flemish Anti- Cancer League), et al. v Belgium Council of Ministers*[115] to argue that the State has an obligation to prohibit conduct contrary to the protection of health, which included ensuring that smoke free legislation did not exempt venues such as pubs. The court agreed that the right to health as enshrined in Article 23 of the Belgian Constitution must be considered relevant to the issue. It ruled that Belgium had an obligation to protect all its citizens from tobacco smoke, and consequently annulled sections of legislation that created exceptions in violation of this duty. Although not directed explicitly at the tobacco industry, this clearly indicates that the State's duty to protect the right to health can be relied on before courts to force stronger legislation in a non-communicable disease prevention context. Similarly, during the challenge to the EU's Tobacco Products Directive of 2014, which among other things banned tobacco companies from using characterizing flavours in cigarette manufacture, Advocate General Kokott unequivocally supported reliance on the right to health to control activities

---

[112] Nolan, n19; Chirwa, n5.

[113] General Comment 14, n12, para 51.

[114] 'Legally mandating and clarifying what is required of the due diligence component of the corporate responsibility to respect is one that should be taken by States as part of their duty to protect human rights': J Nolan, 'The Corporate Responsibility to Respect Rights: Soft Law or Not Law?' in S Deva and D Bilchitz (eds), *Human Rights Obligations of Businesses: Beyond the Corporate Responsibility to Respect?* (CUP 2013).

[115] Arrêt n° 37/2011 du 15 mars 2011.

of corporations whose practices are hazardous to health. Her Opinion stated that, 'the protection of human health has considerably greater importance in the value system under EU law than such essentially economic interests ... with the result that health protection may justify even substantial negative economic consequences for certain economic operators'.[116] The CJEU agreed, and held that a ban on characterizing tobacco flavours was proportionate because 'human health protection — in an area characterized by the proven harmfulness of tobacco consumption ... outweighs the interests put forward by the claimants'.[117] EU legislators had sufficiently balanced:

> the economic consequences of that prohibition and ... the requirement to ensure, in accordance with the second sentence of Article 35 of the Charter ... a high level of human health protection with regard to a product which is characterized by properties that are carcinogenic, mutagenic and toxic to reproduction.[118]

One possible counter argument is that the UNGPs are non-binding, and therefore a court should not rely upon them in creating binding legal obligations. In response to such an argument, it should be noted that in the field of NCD prevention, and again in the tobacco control field specifically, courts have shown an increasing willingness to interpret the right to health in light of non-binding advisory documents. In *Philip Morris Brands*, the CJEU had no qualms in relying on the non-binding Guidelines to the implementation of the Framework Convention on Tobacco Control (FCTC) in arriving at the conclusion that a ban on characterizing flavours was not only proportionate under EU law, but a requirement of the FCTC.[119] Furthermore, in *BAT v Secretary of State for Health*, which concerned the UK's tobacco plain packaging law, the UK Court of Appeal held that the trial judge 'was entitled to treat [the FCTC Guidelines] as telling in favour of subjecting the evidence of the tobacco companies to rigorous scrutiny',[120] and that it could not see 'any error of law in his reliance on the consensus underlying the guidelines ... the CJEU has in its consistent case law attached considerable weight to the view and opinions of the WHO on health issues'.[121]

If a court is willing, it is possible that it could go one step further than imposing legal obligations upon States to develop right to health due diligence

---

[116] Opinion of Advocate General Kokott in C-547/14 *Philip Morris Brands SARL and Others* [2015] ECLI:EU:C:2015:853, para 179.
[117] C-547/14 *Philip Morris Brands SARL and Others* [2015] ECLI:EU:C:2016:325, para 156.
[118] Ibid., para 190.
[119] Ibid., paras 110 and 119.
[120] *BAT v Secretary of State for Health* [2016] EWHC 1169 (Admin), para 205.
[121] Ibid., para 234.

legislation for MFCs. If rights to health in national constitutions are given horizontal effect, they could provide the basis for courts to place right to health due diligence obligations directly upon specific MFCs in appropriate circumstances.

Several jurisdictions around the world have a constitutional right to health that can be horizontally effective upon corporations. For example, Ecuador's 2008 Constitution contains a right to health provision alongside a provision for the horizontal effect of rights. Article 45 states that 'children and adolescents have the right to physical and psychological integrity ... to integral health and nutrition', and Article 88 states that:

> protection proceedings shall be aimed at ensuring the direct and efficient safeguard of the rights enshrined in the Constitution and can be filed whenever there is a breach of constitutional rights ... and when the violation proceeds from a particular person, if the violation of the right causes severe damage.

Argentina's Constitution gives constitutional status to Article 12 ICESCR. Article 75(22) makes clear that the provisions of the ICESCR 'have constitutional hierarchy, do no repeal any section of the First Part of this Constitution and are to be understood as complementing the rights and guarantees recognized herein'. Article 43 of the Argentine Constitution then provides a mechanism through which the right to health can be horizontally effective:

> Any person may file an expeditious and swift action of 'amparo' ... against any act or omission by public authorities or by private individuals, that presently or imminently harms, restricts, alters or threatens, in an arbitrary or manifestly illegal manner, the rights and guarantees recognized by this Constitution, by a treaty, or by a law.[122]

In other jurisdictions, such as India, the right to health has been interpreted to flow from other constitutional rights.[123] In 1981 the Indian Supreme Court held in *Francis Mullin* that the Article 21 right to life:

> includes the right to live with human dignity and all that goes along with it, namely, the bare necessaries of life such as adequate nutrition ... it must, in any view of the

---

[122] For a thorough analysis of the use of amparo actions to enforce constitutional rights, in Argentina and other Latin American states, see: A Brewer-Carias, *Constitutional Protection of Human Rights in Latin America: A Comparative Study of Amparo Proceedings* (CUP 2009).

[123] For further analysis, see: D Boyd, 'The Implicit Constitutional Right to Live in a Healthy Environment' (2011) 20(2) *Review of European Community and International Environmental Law* 171, 173.

matter, include the right ... to carry on such functions and activities as constitute the bare minimum expression of the human self.[124]

The Supreme Court held in later case law that the right to life 'must include protection of the health and strength of the workers, men and women, and of the tender age of children against abuse',[125] and by 1996 had settled the integral nature of the right to health to the right to life.[126] The right to health has since been extended to private parties – for example in *Kirloskar Brothers v Employees State Insurance*, the Supreme Court held that 'the Constitution enjoins not only the State and its instrumentalities but even private industries to ... provide facilities and opportunists for health and vigor of the workman',[127] arguably explicitly endorsing the horizontal effect of the right to health.

Certain evidence suggests that some progressive courts may be willing to use horizontally effective rights to health to place legal obligations directly upon corporations. For example, in the Argentine case of *Hospital Britanico*, the Supreme Court declared that 'the right to health ... inevitably penetrates private relations as much as it does semi-public ones',[128] and that 'the imposition of obligations on private health service providers constituted a valid means of fulfilling international obligations assumed by the state related to the right to health'.[129] In the Indian case of *Mehta*, the Supreme Court was called upon to decide whether the activities of a fully private company could be brought within the constitutional definition of the State, and thus be directly subject to right to health obligations. Although the Supreme Court refused to answer the question due to lack of time, they nevertheless declared that:

> [p]rima facie we are not inclined to accept the apprehensions ... that our including within the ambit of Article 12 ... those private corporations whose activities have the potential of affecting the life and health of the people, would deal a death blow to ... encouraging and permitting private entrepreneurial activity. Such apprehension expressed by those who may be affected by any new and innovative expansion of human rights need not deter the Court from widening the scope of human rights ... if otherwise it is possible to do so without doing violence to the language of the constitutional provision.[130]

---

[124] 1981 AIR 746.
[125] *Morcha*, 1984 AIR 802.
[126] *Punjab v MS Chawla*, CIVIL APPEAL NOS.16980-81 OF 1996.
[127] JT 1996 (2).
[128] Author translation from the original Spanish: *Hospital Británico de Buenos Aires c/ Estado Nacional (Ministerio de Salud y Acción Social)*, 13 March 2001, part VI, para 10.
[129] V Abramovich et al., 'Judicial Activism in the Argentine Health System: Recent Trends' (2008) 10(2) *Health and Human Rights* 53, 59.
[130] 1987 SCR (1) 819.

It could of course be argued that horizontal enforcement of the right to health through the courts has not been effective in generating actual corporate accountability. In Argentina, right to health actions claiming access to medical care that has been denied by private health insurers are common, yet compliance with court orders is not monitored and enforced particularly well.[131] In Colombia, where such litigation is even more common, the horizontal effect of the right to health has been manipulated by private insurers, who have the motivation to routinely deny services. This is because the Colombian Constitutional Court's decision in *T-760/08* attributed ultimate responsibility for deficiencies in private health care to the regulatory failings of the State, allowing private insurers to claim the costs of providing the services they had originally denied back from the government.[132] These experiences do not mean however that corporate accountability can never be secured through horizontal right to health litigation. Courts can consider the practical implications of their decisions, in order to ensure that any judgment on the right to health responsibilities of private companies are effective in practice. For example, heightened judicial supervision of any remedies granted could be mandated, or an independent third party could be appointed by the court to monitor the implementation of judgments.[133]

With these caveats in mind, an argument could be made that – against the background of the ongoing development of corporate human rights responsibilities under international law and in a growing number of national jurisdictions – courts could find that a MFC is obliged to perform right to health due diligence as a consequence of the horizontal effect of constitutional rights to health, in specific contexts. It is true that 'the courts have not been flooded with a huge volume of [due diligence] litigation based on human rights issues',[134]

---

[131] See research carried out by Paolo Bergallo on right to health 'amparo' claims in Argentina: P Bergallo, 'Argentina: Courts and the Right to Health: Achieving Fairness Despite "Routinization" in Individual Coverage Cases?' in A Yamin and S Gloppen (eds), *Litigating Health Rights: Can Courts Bring More Justice to Health?* (Harvard University Press 2011); P Bergallo, 'Courts and Social Change: Lessons from the Struggle to Universalize Access to HIV/AIDS Treatment in Argentina' (2010) 89 *Texas Law Review* 1611.

[132] Sentencia T-760/08 (Colom.), Sala Segunda de Revisión julio 31, 2008. For more detailed analysis, see: E Lamprea, 'Colombia's Right-to-Health Litigation in a Context of Health Care Reform' in C Flood and A Gross (eds), *The Right to Health at the Public/Private Divide: A Global Comparative Study* (CUP 2014).

[133] Further practical implications of progressive socio-economic rights jurisprudence is discussed by Sahu in the context of the Indian Supreme Court's development of the right to a healthy environment: G Sahu, 'Implications of Indian Supreme Court's Innovations for Environmental Jurisprudence' (2008) 4(1) *Law, Environment and Development Journal* 1.

[134] Sherman and Lehr, n42, 13.

but the need for corporations to engage in HRDD generally has already been agreed at international level, as has the need for MFCs to respect the right to health.[135] Despite some undesirable outcomes of South American right to health litigation, the fact remains that courts in those countries have recognized that the right to health can be horizontally enforced. Furthermore, courts around the world have been prepared to find in other fields that corporations have failed to perform adequate due diligence and have placed obligations upon them accordingly.[136] The leap from mandating due diligence in these fields to mandating right to health due diligence would not be an improbable one to make. Furthermore, if the appropriate implementation and tracking requirements from the UNGPs are also mandated, then it is likely that compliance with court ordered right to health due diligence could be effectively monitored.

5. CONCLUDING REMARKS

The fact that corporations should respect human rights has been established beyond doubt – what it means for a corporation to respect human rights in practice is, however, far from settled. The debate on how MFCs should be required to respect the right to health, in particular the child's right to health, is just beginning. This debate should be seen as part of the wider issue of how human rights are relevant to the NCD prevention agenda, and how both public and private actors should be responding to the NCD crisis. Important advances have been made in this regard by the recent Unicef report on *Food Marketing and Children's Rights*.[137]

This chapter has explored the extent to which MFCs can be legally compelled to take responsibility for the impact that their business practices have upon the obesogenic environment, and children's enjoyment of their right to health. It first outlined the current state of business and human rights law, and the concept of HRDD. It then illustrated how MFCs in particular could be expected to conduct right to health due diligence, particularly with regard to children's health. It then argued that the indirect and horizontal effects of the right to health provide sufficient legal grounding for States to adopt right to health due diligence legislation, and possibly for courts to impose right to health due diligence obligations upon MFCs in certain circumstances.

Some progressive legislatures have begun to recognize that the HRDD framework set out in the UNGPs will be more effective if it is translated

---

[135] See the Report of the Special Rapporteur, n82.
[136] See De Schutter et al., n84.
[137] Garde et al., n76. See also: A Garde et al., 'For a Children's Rights Approach to Obesity Prevention: The Key Role of an Effective Implementation of the WHO Recommendations' (2017) 8(2) *European Journal of Risk Regulation* 327.

into law. Progressive courts have recognized for some time that the right to health can be justiciable, and moreover can have the effect of placing legal obligations upon corporations in appropriate circumstances. Compulsory right to health due diligence would satisfy both the concern to avoid placing direct human rights obligations upon MFCs, and the concern to ensure that MFCs are sufficiently held to account for practices that contribute to obesogenic environments. It would build upon the international consensus that has already been reached on the most effective method for securing corporate accountability for human rights abuses, and would enrich the debate on the extent to which the economic freedoms of MFCs may be limited in order to protect the health of populations.

12. Bridging governance gaps with extraterritorial human rights obligations: Accessing home State courts to end childhood obesity

Joshua Curtis[1]

1. INTRODUCTION

Ending childhood obesity demands the control and direction of private agri-food corporations according to certain public values and regulatory rationales. However, adequate corporate accountability mechanisms must be operative not only within each State's territory but also, and crucially, across States' borders. This chapter argues that efforts to end obesity that only take a territorial approach to corporate accountability – confining each State's obligations to protect the vulnerable or provide redress to those within its own borders – will not be sufficient to achieve the given objective. An extraterritorial, or transnational, perspective on law and policy is required to coordinate activities between States, fill regulatory gaps, and inform robust global health governance. I argue that two specific aspects of this perspective are essential, though currently overlooked; the future importance of transnational civil litigation against multinational corporations (MNCs) in the agri-food industry,[2]

---

[1] For their valuable comments on earlier drafts I am very grateful to my co-editors, Amandine Garde and Olivier De Schutter, my colleagues, Padraig McAuliffe and Mike Gordon, and the many participants in the conference from which this collection has germinated. Any errors remain my own and all weblinks are valid as of 5 August 2020.

[2] See, e.g., S Joseph, *Corporations and Transnational Human Rights Litigation* (Hart 2004); M Eroglu, *Multinational Enterprises and Tort Liabilities: An Interdisciplinary and Comparative Examination* (Edward Elgar 2008); C van Dam, 'Tort Law and Human Rights: Brothers in Arms - On the Role of Tort Law in the Area of Business and Human Rights' (2011) 2 *Journal of European Tort Law* 221; H van Loon, 'Principles and Building Blocks for a Global Legal Framework for Transnational Civil Litigation in Environmental Matters' (2018) 28 *Uniform Law Review* 298.

and the potential of extraterritorial human rights obligations (ETOs)[3] to move States towards the changes in law and policy required to make such litigation effective. These entwined aspects are becoming centralized in the fields of human rights and environmental protection, yet they remain underappreciated in the broad field of global health governance (arguably due to the institutional separation of public health and human rights reflected in national governments and the UN),[4] and are yet to make any real impression in the more specific field of obesity prevention. However, they provide valuable insights, both structural and methodological, as well as key normative parameters and argumentative weight, in the search for solutions of law and governance, and the struggle to implement them through State action. This transnational perspective therefore provides an important corrective to the current approach to global governance on childhood obesity.

It is necessary to briefly recall the nature of the global agri-food system and its effects on local food environments to situate the following analysis.[5] The incidence of obesity and many of the factors contributing to its prevalence are directly related to the cross-border operations of agri-food MNCs, which, through their structured global value chains, have shaped food systems throughout the world. The agri-food industry is now highly concentrated, with

---

[3] For an overview see, W Vandenhole, 'Extraterritorial Human Rights Obligations: Taking Stock, Looking Forward' (2013) 5 *European Journal of Human Rights* 804. See further, discussion and references in section 4. For detailed treatment of the broader concepts of extraterritoriality and extraterritorial jurisdiction pertaining to corporate accountability, and the wider range of distinct measures and mechanisms contained therein, see, J Zerk, 'Extraterritorial Jurisdiction: Lessons for the Business and Human Rights Sphere from Six Regulatory Areas', Corporate Social Responsibility Initiative Working Paper No. 59, John F. Kennedy School of Government, Harvard University, Cambridge, 2010, 12–23; N Bernaz, 'Enhancing Corporate Accountability for Human Rights Violations: Is Extraterritoriality the Magic Potion?' (2013) 117 *Journal of Business Ethics* 493, 495–503.

[4] See, e.g., the chapter by Wenche Barth Eide and Asbjørn Eide in this volume.

[5] See generally, S Sell and O Williams (eds), Special Issue on Political Economies of Global Health, (2020) 27(1) *Review of International Political Economy*, especially S Gill and S Benetar, 'Reflections on the Political Economy of Global Health' therein; B Swinburn, et al. 'The Global Obesity Pandemic: Shaped by Global Drivers and Local Environments' (2011) 378 *Lancet* 804; B Popkin, 'Nutrition, Agriculture and the Global Food System in Low and Middle Income Countries' (2014) 47 *Food Policy* 91; M Qaim, 'Globalisation of Agrifood Systems and Sustainable Nutrition' (2017) 76 *Proceedings of the Nutrition Society* 12; C Hawkes (et al. eds), *Trade, Food, Diet and Health: Perspectives and Policy Options* (Wiley-Blackwell 2010); G Kennedy et al., *Globalization of Food Systems in Developing Countries: Impact on Food Security and Nutrition* (Food and Agricultural Organization 2004). For a full exposition of this context and an extended list of references see the introductory chapter by Garde, Curtis and De Schutter in this volume.

Nestlé, PepsiCo, Coca-Cola, ADM and Cargill together controlling 52.9 per cent of the food and beverage market in 2014,[6] and the four largest producers controlling 60 per cent of the baby food market.[7] The economic and political power of these MNCs is immense and even the most powerful States are apt to defer to their needs and seek their 'partnership' in designing food systems and overcoming public health crises. In short, we are experiencing a deep re-structuring of food systems in line with the demands of the global agri-food industry, strengthening the industrial and processed food model and intensifying obesogenic local food environments to the detriment of public health and human rights, especially in the developing countries of the global South. Such is the power, nature, scale and influence of this global industry.

To be successful, therefore, the global fight against childhood obesity must be fully cognisant of the associated challenges to effective corporate accountability in a transnational context. These challenges derive from the current structure of the global political economy[8] combined with a highly uneven transnational legal and normative framework,[9] marked by prevalent lacunae regarding the operation of MNCs across borders.[10] More than any other category of transnational actor, MNCs pursue their narrowly formulated

---

[6] *Too Big to Feed: Exploring the Impacts of Mega-Mergers, Consolidation and Concentration of Power in the Agri-Food Sector* (International Panel of Experts on Sustainable Food Systems 2017) 39.

[7] *Agrifood Atlas: Facts and Figures about the Corporations that Control What We Eat* (Heinrich Böll Foundation 2017) 29.

[8] See, e.g., B Van Apeldoorn et al., 'The Reconfiguration of the Global State-Capital Nexus' (2012) 9(4) *Globalizations* 471; M Babic et al., 'States versus Corporations: Rethinking the Power of Business in International Politics' (2017) 52(4) *International Spectator* 20; S Gill (ed.), *New Constitutionalism and World Order* (CUP 2014); K Irogbe, 'Global Political Economy and the Power of Multinational Corporations' (2013) 30(2) *Journal of Third World Studies* 223; L Sklair, *The Transnational Capitalist Class* (Wiley 2001).

[9] P Muchlinski, *Multinational Enterprises and the Law* (OUP 2007); J Dine and A Fagan (eds), *Human Rights and Capitalism: A Multidisciplinary Perspective on Globalisation* (Edward Elgar 2006) In legal and normative terms, this chapter employs a concept of transnational law that encompasses public and private international law as well as national procedural and substantive law that has significant effects across borders. The focus on transnational civil litigation in this chapter necessarily involves this breadth of legal and normative inclusiveness, rendering the overarching concepts of transnational law and transnational legal process the most fitting for the present discussion. See P Zumbansen (ed.), *The Many Lives of Transnational Law: Critical Engagements with Jessup's Bold Proposal* (CUP 2020).

[10] A de Jonge, *Transnational Corporations and International Law: Accountability in the Global Business Environment* (Edward Elgar 2011); J Zerk, *Multinationals and Corporate Social Responsibility: Limitations and Opportunities in International Law* (CUP 2006).

interests in a regulatory environment of near or 'effective' impunity.[11] This situation is now increasingly framed in human rights terms,[12] as addressed by others in this volume.[13] A recent survey of relevant public and private international law, as well as domestic tort and criminal law, concludes that from this transnational perspective 'the prospects for holding business actors to account for human rights abuses occurring in the context of their economic activity are quite bleak'.[14] John Ruggie, the progenitor of the UN Guiding Principles on Business and Human Rights,[15] memorably described the current transnational corporate accountability framework as deeply compromised by a plethora of

> governance gaps created by globalization – between the scope and impact of economic forces and actors, and the capacity of societies to manage their adverse consequences. ... How to narrow and ultimately bridge the gaps ... is our fundamental challenge.[16]

More than a decade later, little concrete progress has been made on the required bridges, and the fundamental challenge remains.

The most intractable root cause is the structural dependence of society in general on the location and distribution of highly mobile transnational capital and finance.[17] As a direct result, normative and ethical progress is repeatedly held hostage to what is perceived to be economic necessity.[18] Our global polit-

---

[11] C Coumans, 'Alternative Accountability Mechanisms and Mining: The Problems of Effective Impunity, Human Rights, and Agency' (2010) 30 *Canadian Journal of Development Studies* 48.

[12] N Bernaz, *Business and Human Rights: History, Law and Policy – Bridging the Accountability Gap* (Routledge 2017).

[13] See Bartlett's chapter in this volume.

[14] A Peters et al., 'Business and Human Rights: Making the Legally Binding Instrument Work in Public, Private and Criminal Law', MPIL Research Paper Series No. 2020-06, March 2020, at 20.

[15] 'Guiding Principles on Business and Human Rights: Implementing the United Nations "Protect, Respect and Remedy" Framework', Report of the Special Representative of the Secretary-General on the Issue of Human Rights and Transnational Corporations and Other Business Enterprises, John Ruggie, UN Doc. A/HRC/17/31, 21 March 2011 (UNGPs).

[16] Report of the Special Representative of the Secretary-General on the issue of human rights and transnational corporations and other business enterprises, John Ruggie, UN Doc A/HRC/8/5, 7 April 2008, para 3. See also, S Baughen, *Human Rights and Corporate Wrongs: Closing the Governance Gap* (Elgar 2015).

[17] See, e.g., the Special Issue on 'Financialisation and the New Capitalism?' (2019) 43(4) *Cambridge Journal of Economics*, filled with additional references to this phenomenon.

[18] See, e.g., J Curtis, 'The "Economics of Necessity", Human Rights and Ireland's Natural Resources' (2012) 7 *Irish Yearbook of International Law* 57.

ical economy, or what Ruggie terms 'globalisation', forces the vast majority of States into a position of heavy dependence on private foreign investment to finance economic growth and development.[19] It is now hard to overstate this dependence of the general public order on transnational private finance and the power of the actors that decide on its allocation and distribution, most notably MNCs.[20] This dependence is obviously far more of a constraint on policy and regulation in the poorer, so-called developing nations. However, increasingly all States are ever more dependent on transnational flows of private investment just to maintain their level of development, and tread water as it were, in what is now the 'new normal' for most wealthy countries of relative economic stagnation, recession and recurrent crisis.

This political economy viewpoint of systemic dependence is crucial to meet any global health challenge demanding the effective regulation of MNCs.[21] Yet to date, this perspective on transnational corporate accountability has not garnered sufficient attention in debates on global governance and childhood obesity. Territorialized, or nationally compartmentalized thinking is instead heavily dominant, producing approaches to governance that rely mainly, if not entirely, on effective domestic implementation of harmonized rules and standards set at the global level. To date, governance frameworks to end childhood obesity, broadly speaking, tend to rest on the application of discrete packages of uniform but largely hermetic national regulation. However, given the context above, domestic regulation may not have the capacity to control the activities of MNCs or provide an appropriate sanction in practice. In other words, this 'territorially compartmentalized approach' to global governance

---

[19] See, notably, S Lall and R Narula, 'Foreign Direct Investment and Its Role in Economic Development: Do We Need a New Agenda?' in S Lall and R Narula (eds), *Understanding FDI-Assisted Economic Development* (Routledge 2006). This is a dependence long pushed and facilitated by wealthy, capital exporting nations, by their design of the global economy, by manipulation of overseas development assistance and through the international organizations they control. See, e.g., OECD, *Foreign Direct Investment for Development: Maximising Benefits, Minimising Costs* (OECD 2002).

[20] See references above at n8. Additionally see, A Claire Cutler, *Private Power and Global Authority: Transnational Merchant Law in the Global Political Economy* (CUP 2003); S Strange, *The Retreat of the State: The Diffusion of Power in the World Economy* (CUP 1996).

[21] O De Schutter, 'The Role of Human Rights in Shaping International Regulatory Regimes' (2012) 79 *Social Research* 785. This dependence becomes stark when considering the clash of human development rationales and public health frameworks with regimes of international law designed specifically to protect MNCs and, nominally, to increase cross-border investment: O De Schutter et al. (eds), *Foreign Direct Investment and Human Development: The Law and Economics of International Investment Agreements* (Routledge 2013); V Vadi, *Public Health in International Investment Law and Arbitration* (Routledge 2012).

frameworks to end childhood obesity is out of touch with the operative modes of a global marketplace driven by de-territorialized MNCs that promote obesogenic environments.

Territorial limitations in fact plague the enforcement of most regimes of global governance. Hence, particularly in the fields of environmental protection and human rights, there is now a strong engagement with the required extraterritorial level of analysis, corporate regulation, and State obligation.[22] In general, this perspective provokes two types of response. One is to address the big picture directly and seek ways to change the situation at a systems-level. This is 'the big ask', involving extensive change in economics and politics, high levels of international cooperation and what are, correctly or incorrectly, perceived to be heavy losses for the powerful Northern States structurally advantaged by the status quo. The second is to identify promising paths of mitigation that do not demand large-scale structural change or incur the same extent of perceived costs – to identify the best 'next steps' on the path towards greater corporate accountability. The analytic and normative approach taken here, which combines critical political economy perspectives and gap analysis with selected normative elements of ETOs, is capable of informing both types of strategy. However, the following focuses on the latter mode of mitigation and incremental advance, in deference to political realism but nevertheless promising a level of change that would bring substantial benefits.

Against this background, the following section utilises a case study on the marketing of breast-milk substitutes (BMS) by Nestlé in the Philippines, to conduct a legal gap analysis identifying the most promising 'next step' toward greater accountability and effective governance in this area. The relevant governance regime is embodied in the International Code of Marketing of Breast-Milk Substitutes,[23] adopted by the World Health Assembly in and promulgated by the WHO, Unicef and various human rights bodies. However, as the case study demonstrates, the integrity of this global governance regime is deeply undermined by the holes in its territorially compartmentalized approach to implementation. The gap analysis highlights the need for increased access to the home State courts of agri-food MNCs for victims of commercial practices promoting obesogenic environments in host States. This would empower and

---

[22] See, e.g., A Parrish, 'Trail Smelter Déjà Vu: Extraterritoriality, International Environmental Law and the Search for Solutions to Canadian-U.S. Transboundary Water Pollution Disputes' (2005) 85 *Boston University Law Review* 363; W Vandenhole (ed.), *Challenging Territoriality in Human Rights Law: Building Blocks for a Plural and Diverse Duty-Bearer Regime* (Routledge 2015). See further discussion and references in section 4.

[23] Resolution WHA34.22, adopted by the Thirty-fourth World Health Assembly, 21 May 1981.

enable claimants bringing transnational tort or human rights-based civil claims capable of upholding the standards embodied in the Code, thereby contributing to the closure of the given governance gap.

Transnational civil litigation against MNCs is becoming an increasingly crucial element of global governance regimes in the areas of environmental protection and human rights.[24] Such litigation will no doubt become equally important to the governance of global health. Although transnational cases relating to obesity are yet to arise, nascent domestic civil litigation in this area,[25] and growing numbers of transnational claims seeking remedy for harms to human health resulting from the practices of MNCs,[26] strongly suggests that such cases are on the near horizon. An appreciation of the Nestlé case study will aid the necessary preparations for their fair hearing. Improved access to home State courts will inevitably increase the chances of enforcing global standards embodied in the Code. To this end, the major obstacles preventing effective access to home State courts are then presented, indicating the changes to law and policy required to remove them (section 3).[27]

---

[24] See, e.g., L Enneking, 'Transnational Human Rights and Environmental Litigation: A Study of Case Law Relating to Shell in Nigeria' in I Feichtner (et al. eds), *Human Rights in the Extractive Industries: Transparency, Participation, Resistance* (Springer 2019).

[25] M Dahm et al., 'Eating Behaviours, Obesity and Litigation: Should Casual-Food Restaurant Operators Heed the Warnings to their Fast-Food Counterparts?' (2010) 13(3) *Journal of Foodservice Business Research* 217; A Antler, 'The Role of Litigation in Combatting Obesity Among Poor Urban Minority Youth: A Critical Analysis of Pelman v. McDonald's Corp.' (2009) 15 *Cardozo Journal of Law and Gender* 275; C Miller, 'Obesity Litigation: Curbing America's Appetite through Court Action' (2008) 2 *Rivista di Diritto Alimentare* 3.

[26] A Marx et al., 'Access to Legal Remedies for Victims of Corporate Human Rights Abuses in Third Countries', Study Requested by the DROI Committee, European Parliament, February 2019; A Boyle, 'Human Rights and the Environment: Where Next?' (2012) 23(3) *European Journal of International Law* 613.

[27] The focus on procedure and effective court access in this chapter momentarily brackets off the substantive complexities of obesity-related litigation, either domestic or transnational. The substantive difficulties are serious and significant. Yet, they are in no way fatal to the prospects of obesity-related litigation. The argument here only requires the affirmation of the substantive viability of such cases, to which their factual existence adequately attests, despite their limited success to date (see references at n25). Therefore, the substantive issues may be appropriately compartmentalized for later analysis without prejudice to the present argument. Furthermore, as with all legal cases, there is clearly a positive correlation between the pre-requisite of court access and substantive viability. These claims, transnational or strictly domestic, are likely to become increasingly viable in line with the incidence of their hearing on the merits and the airing of progressive legal arguments in court, particularly those combining human rights and tort law; J Wright, *Tort Law and Human Rights* (Hart 2001); N Ferreira, *Fundamental Rights and Private Law in Europe: The Case of Tort Law and Children*

The key import of ETOs is then introduced (section 4), providing a first attempt to marry the previously separate literature on ETOs with that on childhood obesity and obesity-related litigation. The aim is to demonstrate the close fit in normative thrust and policy aim. ETOs offer compelling arguments for home States and their judiciaries to adopt the required changes in law and policy as a matter of obligation (section 5). They provide an important normative framework, capable of making a critical contribution to closing the gap in cross-border corporate accountability and informing a more adequate system of global health governance to end childhood obesity. Beyond improving the prospects of transnational litigation, some comments are offered, in conclusion, on the broader impact of ETOs on global health governance generally.

2. NESTLÉ, THE CODE, AND CHILDHOOD OBESITY IN THE PHILIPPINES

In 2018, an investigation by Save the Children and *The Guardian* uncovered potentially illegal marketing of BMS by employees of Nestlé to mothers and health professionals in the Philippines.[28] Nestlé allegedly targeted those in low socio-economic brackets in what is claimed to be a typical example of the 'aggressive, clandestine and often illegal methods' used to influence 'mothers in the poorest parts of the world to encourage them to choose powdered milk over breastfeeding'.[29] In addition, 'doctors, midwives and local health workers were offered free trips to lavish conferences, meals, tickets to shows and the cinema and even gambling chips' in return for the recommendation of their products to new mothers as 'essential elements' of motherhood.[30] Nestlé representatives were found constantly in hospitals distributing so-called 'infant

---

(Routledge 2011); V Trstenjak and P Weingerl (eds), *The Influence of Human Rights and Basic Rights in Private Law* (Springer 2016). Allied arguments are gaining ground in the field of business and human rights. A tighter web of transnational law, made up of strands of domestic tort and international human rights law, could be employed in home State courts to close corporate governance gaps – a prospect potentially facilitated by a future Binding Treaty on business and human rights; A Peters, et al., 'Business and Human rights: Making the Legally Binding Instrument Work in Public, Private and Criminal Law', MPIL Research Paper Series No. 2020-06, March 2020.

[28] H Ellis-Petersen, 'How Formula Milk Firms Target Mothers Who Can Least Afford It', *The Guardian,* 27 February 2018, https://www.theguardian.com/lifeandstyle/2018/feb/27/formula-milk-companies-target-poor-mothers-breastfeeding; For the broader study, addressing the same problem in a range of countries in the global South, see, Save the Children, *Don't Push It: Why The Formula Milk Industry Must Clean Up Its Act* (Save the Children 2018).

[29] H Ellis-Petersen, ibid.

[30] Ibid.

nutrition' pamphlets promoting their brand, together with discount coupons. Television advertisements portrayed BMS as leading to increased IQ and better future prospects for children. As a result, some impoverished mothers were found to be spending three-quarters of their income on BMS, while often going hungry themselves. Nestlé has rejected the allegations and denied any wrongdoing.[31]

There is a growing weight of evidence that the use of BMS promotes obesity.[32] In fact, as far as interventions to prevent childhood obesity go, the importance of ensuring breastfeeding (excluding the use of BMS except where paediatrically necessary) is probably paramount, occurring in 'a critical period of development associated with long-term consequences'.[33] The Commission on Ending Childhood Obesity states that '[b]reastfeeding is core to optimizing infant development, growth and nutrition'.[34] The UN Committee on the Rights of the Child has expressly linked the lack of BMS regulation in the UK to the country's high child obesity rate, noting this lack of regulation as a potential violation of the rights of UK children to the protection required by international human rights law.[35] If the allegations are true, therefore, Nestlé is creating, and/or exacerbating, an obesogenic environment for children in the Philippines. Yet this is nothing new. Global governance of BMS is in large part founded in reaction to Nestlé's practices.

2.1   The Establishment of the Code

Since 1969, when Nestlé's controversial operations were singled out by the UN Protein Advisory Group, the company has been consistently criticized for its forceful marketing aimed at entrenching its business model and expanding profits at the cost of children's and mothers' health, especially in developing

---

[31] See the response on Nestlé's website, https://www.nestle.com/ask-nestle/health-nutrition/answers/guardian-infant-formula-marketing-practices-nestle-philippines.

[32] S Uwaezuoke, et al., 'Relationship Between Exclusive Breastfeeding and Lower Risk of Childhood Obesity: A Narrative Review of Published Evidence' (2017) 11 *Clinical Medicine Insights: Pediatrics* 1; J Anttila-Hughes et al., 'Mortality from Nestlé's Marketing of Infant Formula in Low and Middle-Income Countries', NBER Working Paper No. 24452, March 2018.

[33] *Foresight, Tackling Obesities: Future Choices – Project Report* (2nd edn, UK Government Office for Science 2007) 62.

[34] WHO, 'Report of the Commission on Ending Childhood Obesity', WHO, Geneva, January 2016, 27.

[35] UN Committee on the Rights of the Child, Concluding Observations on the Fifth Periodic Report of the United Kingdom of Great Britain and Northern Ireland, UN Doc CRC/C/GBR/CO/5, 3 June 2016, paras 65–66.

countries.[36] Opposition consumer movements grew rapidly against the unconscionable tactics of the industry, including the Infant Formula Action Coalition and the International Baby Food Action Network, which organized transnational boycotts against Nestlé in the 1970s and 80s. This groundswell culminated in the adoption of the International Code of Marketing of Breast-Milk Substitutes (the Code) in 1981, providing the general framework for the global governance of this product, the successful implementation of which is integral to the vision of the Commission on Ending Childhood Obesity.[37]

The Code represents the global consensus on the standards the BMS industry should comply with. It is spearheaded internationally but is reliant on compartmentalized territorial implementation of its regulatory package through domestic law. Key aspects of the Code require each national government to regulate the provision of information and educational materials to reflect 'the benefits and superiority of breast-feeding' and 'the health hazards of unnecessary or improper use of infant formula'.[38] National authorities should ensure that mother's and the general public are not subjected to 'advertising or other form[s] of promotion' of BMS and that industry representatives may not, 'directly or indirectly', provide samples of such products.[39] There should be no 'special displays, discount coupons, premiums, special sales' or gift-giving and representatives should not be able to 'seek direct or indirect contact of any kind with pregnant women or with mothers of infants and young children'.[40] In addition, no 'financial or material inducements to promote [the relevant] products ... should be offered by manufacturers or distributors to health workers'.[41]

The leading international institutions on the Code are the WHO and Unicef, however it is also promulgated through the human rights treaty bodies. The Committee on the Rights of the Child (CRC), for example, ties the child's right to health to the avoidance of 'suboptimal breastfeeding practices', requiring States to 'introduce [the Code] into domestic law' and enforce it, together with 'the relevant subsequent World Health Assembly resolutions'.[42] The CRC repeated this requirement in its General Comment 16 on State obligations

---

[36] For a concise breakdown of public criticism and collective boycotts (1969–2015) of Nestlé's products stemming from this issue see, *Agrifood Atlas*, n7, 51.

[37] WHO, n34, 26–8.

[38] WHA Resolution, n23, Art 4.2.

[39] Ibid., Arts 5.1 and 5.2.

[40] Ibid., Arts 5.3–5.5.

[41] Ibid., Art 7.3.

[42] CRC, General Comment No. 15 on the Right of the Child to the Enjoyment of the Highest Attainable Standard of Health, UN Doc. CRC/C/GC/15, 17 April 2013, paras 18, 44, 55 and 81. The Convention on the Rights of the Child itself obligates States to ensure awareness of the 'advantages of breastfeeding'; 1577 UNTS 3 (1989), Art 24 2(e).

regarding the impact of business on children's rights.[43] Despite its relative tardiness, there is also indication that the Committee on the Elimination of Discrimination Against Women is becoming increasingly active in promulgating the Code in defence of the rights of both children and mothers.[44]

Nevertheless, for the last 40 years Nestlé has consistently refused to engage meaningfully with its critics or comply with the Code, instead maintaining and refining systematic practices of 'corporate political activity' to subvert governance frameworks pursuing clear public health goals.[45] Over decades, the Code, together with the guidelines, resolutions and injunctions that supplement this governance initiative, have been countered by the global economic realities of trade and investment liberalization, the extensive protection of (and dependence on) foreign investment and the sheer power and political influence of MNCs like Nestlé.[46] Despite the status and age of the Code the global market in BMS has grown by a factor of five over the last two decades, three times faster than the global economy, and is now said to be worth more than US$70 billion.[47] In 2016, Nestlé controlled 23.5 per cent of the global baby food market,[48] and the largest portion of the BMS market in most of the global South, including the Philippines. This is a phenomenal growth, reliant on a highly proactive marketing strategy 'driven from the most senior levels of each organisation'.[49] These senior actors are presumably seated in the home offices of these MNCs as they make their decisions, such as the home office of Nestlé in Switzerland.

---

[43] UN Doc. CRC/C/GC/16, 7 February 2013, paras 54 and 57.

[44] J Galtry, 'Strengthening the Human Rights Framework to Protect Breastfeeding: A Focus on CEDAW' (2015) 10:29 *International Breastfeeding Journal*.

[45] H Tanrikulu et al., 'Corporate Political Activity of the Baby Food Industry: The Example of Nestlé in the United States of America' (2020) 15(22) *International Breastfeeding Journal*. The point must be emphasized that the relative power and influence that Nestlé exercises over the government of the Philippines, compared to the US, is no doubt much higher.

[46] M Bader, 'Breast-Feeding: The Role of Multinational Corporations in Latin America' (1976) 6 *International Journal of Health Services* 609; T Waterson, 'Monitoring the Marketing of Infant Formula Feeds: Manufacturers of Breast Milk Substitutes Violate the WHO Code—Again' (2003) 326 *British Medical Journal* 113; S Forsyth, 'Non-Compliance with the International Code of Marketing of Breast Milk Substitutes is Not Confined to the Infant Formula Industry' (2013) 25 *Journal of Public Health* 185.

[47] Save the Children, n28, v.

[48] Ibid., 15.

[49] Ibid., vi.

2.2 Gaps in Enforcing the Code

If the reports are true, Nestlé's actions are a clear violation of Philippine law, which formally upholds the Code through interlocking acts and orders.[50] However, enforcement of the law is severely hampered in the Philippines for all the reasons discussed above. The Department of Health has reportedly initiated an investigation into the allegations that could inform a decision by the Food and Drug Authority, which can enforce a financial punishment.[51] However, officials emphasized that it is 'a struggle for government to crack down on all of these illicit practices of the milk companies', in part because of their 'stubborn and cunning tactics' and in part because 'a lack of resources meant the [Department] struggled to regulate the activities of milk formula companies and gathering evidence of violations was equally tough'.[52] Finally, powerful lobby groups associated with Nestlé and other industry MNCs were said to be working actively to block investigations and enforcement of the law.[53]

The situation in the Philippines, which is mirrored in many other developing countries,[54] stands as testimony to the inadequacy of the governance approach adopted. Worldwide, this industry has been found to systematically replicate the self-serving tactics of regulatory stifling and avoidance generally associated with tobacco MNCs: (1) hijacking the political and legislative process; (2) weaponizing their economic clout; (3) manipulating public opinion; (4) fabricating support through front groups; (5) attempting to discredit the scientific evidence; and (6) intimidating governments with litigation.[55] The unsatisfactory performance of this governance framework is largely due to the ability of companies like Nestlé to exploit gaps across borders and to escape accountability in both host and home States for their activities in the developing world.

---

[50] See, Executive Order 51 (The Philippine Milk Code, 1986); RA 7600 (Rooming-in and Breastfeeding Act, 1992); RA 10028 (Expanded Breastfeeding Promotion Act, 2009).
[51] H Ellis-Petersen, n28.
[52] Ibid.
[53] Ibid.
[54] K Vinje et al., 'Media Audit Reveals Inappropriate Promotion of Products Under the Scope of the International Code of Marketing of Breast-milk Substitutes in South-East Asia' (2017) 20 *Public Health Nutrition* 1333.
[55] S Ionata Granheim, et al., 'Interference in Public Health Policy: Examples of How the Baby Food Industry Uses Tobacco Industry tactics' (2017) 8(2) *World Nutrition* 288.

A legal gap analysis[56] reveals the need for an effective transnational or extraterritorial bridge. If the allegations against Nestlé in the Philippines are true, then the company is clearly exacerbating the obesogenic environment pertaining to children in this country. The relevant question to ask is how and where can misled mothers and obese Philippine children harmed by Nestlé's actions find an effective remedy and gain restitution or adequate compensation from the company, thereby also providing the Code with a credible sanction? The first option would be a domestic class action on behalf of the children or the mothers, taken against Nestlé's local subsidiary acting directly in the Philippines.[57] This claim could be based on several possible grounds under Philippine law; the breach of regulations implementing the Code, consumer protection, the tort of negligence or violation of the children's right to health, for example.[58] Yet, this domestic action in the Philippines will be subject to all the difficulties touched on above relating to the enforcement of regulations on MNCs in the Philippines.[59] In addition, Nestlé's local subsidiary, the target of the domestic action, may be made deliberately cash-poor by the parent company and therefore unable to pay the appropriate amount of compensation even if the domestic case is eventually successful.

---

[56] Gap analysis has long been employed as a useful analytic tool in the area of business management. See, e.g., L Goodstein et al., *Applied Strategic Planning: How to Develop a Plan that Really Works* (McGraw-Hill 1993) 261–82; C Fleischer and B Bensoussan, *Strategic and Competitive Analysis: Methods and Techniques for Analyzing Business Competition* (Prentice Hall 2002). A prime example relevant to the rights of the child can be found in Verité Research, *A Legal and Institutional Assessment of Sri Lanka's Justice System for Children* (UNICEF 2017) 5–18. The basic principle juxtaposes a clear assessment of the status quo with an ideal (here taken to be adequate sanction for the MNC and effective remedy for the victims), followed by identification of the differences or the gaps between the two and the formulation of applicable solutions to fill them.

[57] Philippine law does allow mass claims. See, Rules of Civil Procedure, 1997, Rule 3, section 12.

[58] On the overlap and possible combinations of the last two grounds, the broadest and most relevant to strengthening general structures of transnational corporate governance, see, E Engle, 'Tort Law and Human Rights' in M Bussani and A Sebok (eds), *Comparative Tort Law: Global Perspectives* (Edward Elgar 2015); E Engle, *Private Law Remedies for Extraterritorial Human Rights Violations*, PhD Thesis, University of Bremen, 2006, at https://elib.suub.uni-bremen.de/diss/docs/00010289.pdf.

[59] It has also been noted by a judge of the Supreme Court that 'Philippine courts have applied the rule on class suits with much caution and circumspection', which does not augur well for such a novel suit as this one. R Corona, 'Class Action, Public Interest Litigation and the Enforcement of Shared Legal Rights and Common Interests in the Environment and Ancestral Lands in the Philippines', Paper Presented at the 9th General Assembly of the ASEAN Law Association, 2006, 2.

If justice cannot be obtained in the Philippines, the next step, in the current absence of any other forum in which they could find an effective remedy,[60] would be for the plaintiffs to attempt to bring a case against the parent company in the courts of its home State, Switzerland. This transnational civil case could be based on the probable involvement of the parent in the harms wrought directly by the subsidiary, or a failure of due diligence to take proper steps to prevent the harm. It could be argued that due to the overall control exercised by the parent company over the subsidiary, the former should bear responsibility for the wrongful acts of the latter, especially where it has not been possible to extract justice directly from the subsidiary in the host State. Access to the Swiss courts is of utmost importance for the simple reason that, where agri-food MNCs are not held accountable in the host State, no other mechanism of effective justice or legal accountability exists, opening a large hole in the Code's governance framework.

The current territorial basis of international law allows for effective impunity with respect to the cross-border operations of agri-food MNCs and their subsidiaries, particularly in developing countries.[61] The international legal system remains limited by its traditional State-centric nature, where States are considered the primary, if not only, addressees of international legal obligations.[62] At present, and in general, international law does not impose direct human rights obligations on corporations, as reflected in the consensus around the non-binding UN Guiding Principles on Business and Human Rights (UNGPs).[63] The legal accountability of MNCs for human rights and

---

[60] For the sake of completeness, it must be mentioned that the claimants could challenge Nestlé in front of the Swiss National Contact Point (NCP) for possible breach of the OECD Guidelines on Multinational Enterprises. However, this procedure is conciliatory in nature, based on resolving a dispute through dialogue and mediation rather than applying law, and cannot result in the award of damages but at most the issuance of recommendations against the company. This in no way constitutes an *effective* remedy in most cases. See further, K Reinert et al., 'The New OECD Guidelines for Multinational Enterprises: Better but Not Enough' (2016) 26 *Development in Practice* 816.

[61] See, E Duruigbo, 'Corporate Accountability and Liability for International Human Rights Abuses: Recent Changes and Recurring Challenges' (2008) 6 *Northwestern Journal of International Human Rights* 226, 249–50; T Isiksel, 'The Rights of Man and the Rights of the Man-Made: Corporations and Human Rights' (2016) 38 *Human Rights Quarterly* 294.

[62] For in depth discussion of the State-centric nature of international law and the central concept of international legal personality see, L McConnell, *Extracting Accountability from Non-State Actors in International Law: Assessing the Scope for Direct Regulation* (Routledge 2016) 15–130.

[63] UNGPs, n15. There is a legitimate dispute over whether this consensus reflects an accurate statement of international human rights law. See D Bilchitz, 'A Chasm

other harms remains the preserve of domestic legal systems, based on the duty of each State to regulate those corporations operating within its territory.[64] Conservative, and increasingly outdated, interpretations of international law deny the existence of a general duty on home States to regulate their corporations in respect of their activities in other States – in other words, to actively protect the human rights and associated interests of people in other States from their own corporations, or to provide a remedy whenever their corporations infringe human rights abroad.[65] This is the position taken by the UNGPs. We will return to a discussion of this position in section 4. Here, we highlight the baseline consensus that the *primary* responsibility rests on the host State to ensure that MNCs operating in their territory are adequately regulated and held to account where necessary.

As we can see, however, this position will often effectively translate into concrete scenarios where the host State has the *sole* responsibility and justice falls through the cracks between national borders. It is then clear that this results in effective corporate impunity where the host State is either unwilling or unable to regulate or provide adequate sanction. In such cases, justice mandates effective access to home State courts.[66] This legal gap analysis could be replicated in many developing countries, highlighting a systemic defect in the compartmentalized approach. This is because, as things stand, a case against Nestlé in Switzerland would face numerous obstacles that currently close off

---

Between "Is" and "Ought"? A Critique of the Normative Foundations of the SRSG's Framework and the Guiding Principles' in S Deva and D Bilchitz (eds), *Human Rights Obligations of Business: Beyond the Corporate Responsibility to Respect?* (CUP 2013). Furthermore, sound competing theories exist for attaching direct human rights obligations to MNCs. See, e.g., S Ratner, 'Corporations and Human Rights: A Theory of Legal Responsibility' (2001) 111 *Yale Law Journal* 443.

[64] UNGPs, ibid., 83–91; O De Schutter, 'The Accountability of Multinationals for Human Rights Violations in European Law', Center for Human Rights and Global Justice Working Paper No.1, 2004, 7.

[65] L Bartels and C O'Brien, 'Submission to UN Committee on Economic, Social and Cultural Rights on its draft General Comment on State Obligations under the International Covenant on Economic, Social and Cultural Rights in the Context of Business Activities, 20 January 2016, http://www.ohchr.org/EN/HRBodies/CESCR/Pages/Submissions2017.aspx; C O'Brien, 'The Home State Duty to Regulate the Human Rights Impacts of TNCs Abroad: A Rebuttal' (2018) 3 *Business and Human Rights Journal* 47.

[66] Nevertheless, a sole reliance on litigation to 'solve' the obesity epidemic is by no means warranted or advocated. Litigation must be part of a wider public health strategy and a network of actions to regulate the agri-food industry. J Smith, 'Setting the Stage for Public Health: The Role of Litigation in Controlling Obesity' (2006) 28 *University of Arkansas Law Review* 443, 448.

home State courts as effective sites of justice and remedy for Philippine children and many others harmed by agri-food MNCs in the global South.

3. OBSTACLES PREVENTING EFFECTIVE ACCESS TO HOME STATE COURTS

While the success of transnational claims faces a range of obstacles, we will discuss the four main (largely procedural) ones: *forum non conveniens*; practical obstacles to funding and fact-finding; parent company liability for acts of subsidiaries; and the choice of law.[67]

3.1 An Inconvenient Forum?

The doctrine of *forum non conveniens* enables a court in the home State to refuse to take a case forward on the rationale that the courts of the host State would provide a more appropriate or more convenient forum.[68] Parent corporations can make this argument safely, in the knowledge that they may not, in practice, be so easily sued in the host State. Courts may also be tempted to employ it as a useful means by which to avoid politically controversial or otherwise 'sensitive' cases, descriptors often applying to transnational human rights claims. Yet the statistical likelihood of the case in fact being taken in the supposedly 'more convenient' forum is very low.[69]

Regarding claims filed against transnational corporations located in EU Member States, the national courts were effectively banned from reliance on the doctrine of *forum non conveniens* by the Brussels I Regulation.[70] The European Court of Justice upheld this position in the 2005 case of *Owusu*.[71] It

---

[67] For a full discussion of all the relevant obstacles see the seminal Third Pillar Report; G Skinner et al., 'The Third Pillar: Access to Judicial Remedies for Human Rights Violations by Transnational Business', International Corporate Accountability Roundtable, December 2013. In the EU context see, F Gregor, 'The EU's Business: Recommended Actions for the EU and Its Member States to Ensure Access to Judicial Remedy for Business-Related Human Rights Impacts', Access to Justice, Brno, December 2014.

[68] On the genesis and present inappropriateness of the doctrine and ways to move past it see, M Gardner, 'Retiring Forum Non Conveniens' (2017) 92 *New York University Law Review* 390.

[69] Skinner, et al., n67, 24.

[70] Council Regulation (EC) No 44/2001 of 22 December 2000 on Jurisdiction and the Recognition and Enforcement of Judgments in Civil and Commercial Matters.

[71] Case C-281/02, *Andrew Owusu v N. B. Jackson, trading as 'Villa Holidays Bal-Inn Villas' and Others*, Judgment of the Court (Grand Chamber) of 1 March 2005, ECLI:EU:C:2005:120, para 46. See, B Rodger, 'Forum Non Conveniens Post-Owusu' (2006) 2 *Journal of Private International Law* 1.

has since been affirmed and clarified by Article 4 of EU Regulation 1215/2012, which has since repealed the Brussels I Regulation.[72] Despite these relatively positive developments in EU law,[73] this doctrine still remains a serious obstacle to transnational claims brought elsewhere.

Swiss law has gone a step further, establishing a positive doctrine of *forum necessitatis* or 'jurisdiction by necessity',[74] whereby Swiss courts are obliged to accept jurisdiction over a case wherever it is not possible to bring the case in any other forum, or where it cannot reasonably be expected that the claimant can be given a fair hearing anywhere else.[75] However, there must still be a 'sufficient connection' between the facts of the case and Switzerland. In relation to our hypothetical case from the Philippines, Swiss law will, at a minimum, preclude arguments of *forum non conveniens* in the same manner as EU Regulation 1215/2012 even though it is not subject to it.[76] Indeed, if the claimant's access to justice has been effectively blocked in the Philippines, the Swiss courts may have to accept the case under the necessity doctrine. This will depend, however, on the claimant showing a sufficient connection, which might require a demonstration that the parent company was aware of those harmful actions and was in a position to stop them. Acquiring evidence to demonstrate this may be difficult due to obstacles related to information gathering and available finances, as well as difficulties posed by the separate legal personalities of the parent and subsidiary.

3.2   Information and Money

Prospective claimants face high barriers in accessing and collating the information needed to establish a sufficient connection between the transnational corporation and the harm inflicted.[77] For claimants located in remote areas,

---

[72]   EU Regulation No. 1215/2012 of the European Parliament and of the Council on Jurisdiction and the Recognition and Enforcement of Judgments in Civil and Commercial Matters, 12 December 2012, OJ L 351, Art 63.

[73]   Which, nevertheless, have still failed to definitively put paid to the doctrine in some national jurisdictions; G Holly, 'Vedanta v. Lungowe Symposium: A Non Conveniens Revival–The Supreme Court's Approach to Jurisdiction in Vedanta', Opinio Juris, 24 April 2019, https://opiniojuris.org/2019/04/24/vedanta-v-lungowe-symposium-a-non-conveniens-revival-the-supreme-courts-approach-to-jurisdiction-in-vedanta%EF%BB%BF.

[74]   C Nwapi, 'Jurisdiction by Necessity and the Regulation of the Transnational Corporate Actor' (2014) 30 *Utrecht Journal of International and European Law* 24.

[75]   Swiss Federal Code on Private International Law 1987, 8 December 1987, Art 3.

[76]   Ibid., Art 1; 'Unless this Code provides otherwise, the Swiss judicial or administrative authorities at the domicile of the defendant shall have jurisdiction.'

[77]   van Dam, n2, 228–9.

fact-finding is an arduous exercise often hampered by a lack of adequate technology. Where complicity is the basis of the claim it may be very difficult to find the evidence proving specific control by the MNC or the relevant intention of its directors and employees. Such information will typically be internal to the corporation. In the US the process of 'discovery' (the mandatory corporate disclosure of documents relevant to the case) is conducted liberally and broadly, often in favour of the plaintiff.[78] In the UK, discovery operates more restrictively.[79] This valuable process is often not available to litigants in European civil law systems, or, where a similar rule may apply, it is not generally effective due to various conditions attached.[80] In any event, the benefits of US-style discovery will not apply to claimants from the Philippines presenting a case in Switzerland.

Sufficient funds are also necessary for travel, lawyers' fees and other expenses. This is particularly true for claimants who would want to pursue their case in Switzerland, one of the most expensive countries in the world. High costs can be mitigated in various ways. State legal aid may be provided, systems of contingency fee payment enabled, collective claims or public interest claims encouraged, or law firms operating pro bono programmes may be subsidized. Yet, often these mechanisms will not be available or are highly vulnerable to removal, particularly in 'tight budget environments'.[81] In the EU, a 2003 Directive has attempted to establish minimum levels of legal aid in the interests of justice, in order to facilitate cross-border litigation between EU Member States.[82] However, this Directive is of very limited use to claimants from outside the EU.[83]

3.3 Piercing The Corporate Veil And The Parent Company's Duty of Care

The limited liability and separate legal personality of entities within a corporate group cause well-known problems of attribution and accountability, but these issues are greatly magnified in the case of transnational litigation. Under

---

[78] B Stephens, et al., *International Human Rights Litigation in U.S. Courts* (2nd Rev edn, Brill 2008) 470–503.
[79] Skinner et al., n67, 46.
[80] Ibid., 45.
[81] Ibid., 47–59.
[82] Council Directive 2002/8/EC of 27 January 2003 to improve access to justice in cross-border disputes by establishing minimum common rules relating to legal aid for such disputes, OJ L 026, 31/01/2003, P. 0041 – 0047.
[83] Ibid., Art 2(1) – requiring the claimant to be domiciled or habitually resident in a Member State of the EU.

corporate law, limited liability shields the shareholders in a corporation from having to assume all its debts or obligations, and separate legal personality affirms that the corporation itself is a legal entity (artificial person) distinct from its shareholders, directors and employees. The distinction between the corporate entity and its owners is often referred to as the 'corporate veil'. Although logical from some perspectives, once corporations themselves can be shareholders, often sole shareholders, the possibilities for abuse of these structures and the evasion of liability through iterations of what are often known as 'shell companies' become legion.[84]

Under certain circumstances courts may be prepared to 'pierce' the corporate veil, for instance where it can be proven that corporate groups have been structured for obviously abusive or fraudulent purposes. However, the jurisprudence on piercing is loose and inconsistent, and it remains a relatively exceptional practice.[85] Common law courts have on occasion either adopted or expressed openness to an alternative approach based on a 'duty of care' doctrine, under which the parent company may be held liable for harm done by its subsidiaries.[86] The parent is held to have an obligation to avoid undue risk to those affected by the actions of its subsidiary where three conditions are met: the damage is foreseeable; there is a strong connection or 'sufficient proximity' between the two companies; and imposition of a duty of care is fair, just and reasonable.[87] Analogous approaches can apply through tortious liability (otherwise known as the law of delicts or the law of obligations) for negligence (or quasi-delict) in civil law systems such as Switzerland.[88]

Assuming that Nestlé is operating through a local subsidiary, all the considerations above will apply to a prospective case. The likelihood of success will depend heavily on the degree of control that the parent can be proven to have

---

[84] P Blumberg, *The Multinational Challenge to Corporate Law: The Search for a New Corporate Personality* (OUP 1993) 56–9.

[85] R Thompson, 'Piercing the Veil Within Corporate Groups: Corporate Shareholders as Mere Investors' (1999) 13 *Connecticut Journal of International Law* 379; P Blumberg, 'Accountability of Multinational Corporations: The Barriers Presented by Concepts of the Corporate Juridical Entity' (2001) 24 *Hastings International and Comparative Law Review* 304.

[86] *Chandler v Cape plc* [2012] EWCA Civ 525 (UK); *Choc v Hudbay Minerals Inc* [2013] ONSC (Canada) 1414; *Vedanta Resources plc and another v Lungowe and others,*[2019] UKSC 20 (UK); *Akpan and others v Royal Dutch Shell and Shell Petroleum Development Company of Nigeria, Ltd* [2013] LJN BY9854 (Netherlands).

[87] *Chandler v Cape*, ibid., para 80.

[88] T Hubert-Purtschert, 'Law of Obligations' in M Thommen (ed.), *Introduction to Swiss Law* (Carl Grossmann Verlag 2018); P Känzig and J Stüssi, 'Switzerland' in N Bird (ed.), *The Professional Negligence Law Review* (2nd edn, Law Business Research 2019).

over the Philippine subsidiary and the amount of evidence that can be gathered to demonstrate the parent's intentions and level of awareness of potential harm, and the measures, if any, taken to mitigate it. As already mentioned, this will be made far more difficult by the absence of a US-style discovery process in Switzerland.

3.4 Which Law to Apply?

Transnational cases will inevitably involve a decision over which law should apply to all or parts of the case at hand; the law of the home State (forum), the law of the host State (site of the harm), or in some instances international law.[89] The choice may have a strong bearing on the prospects of the claim. Negative repercussions could arise for the claimant where the applicable law does not allow for secondary or vicarious liability; does not allow for group or class actions; does not recognize certain harms or bases for claims, or makes them harder to prove; contains prejudicial statutes of limitation; or provides immunity for the defendant.[90]

In the US a typical analysis will look first for any conflict between the law of the home and the host State. Where there is no conflict, the law of the forum (i.e., the home State) is applied. In the case of conflict, the court will generally apply the law of the host State 'unless the forum [State] has a greater interest in determining a particular issue, or if it has a more significant relationship to what occurred and to the parties'.[91] In the Member States of the EU, following the Rome II Regulation,[92] the law of the host State (the site of the harm) is the default choice in transnational cases.[93] Various exceptions exist, but they are

---

[89] G Virgo, 'Characterisation, Choice of Law and Human Rights' and Sandra Raponi, 'Grounding a Cause of Action for Torture in Transnational Law' in C Scott (ed.), *Torture as Tort: Comparative Perspectives on the Development of Transnational Human Rights Litigation* (Hart 2001).

[90] Ibid., 43. Immunities may relate, for example, to public corporations or corporations serving public functions. See, A Solé et al., 'Human Rights in European Business: A Practical Handbook for Civil Society Organisations and Human Rights Defenders', Tarragona Centre for Environmental Law Studies, September 2016, 41.

[91] Skinner et al., n67, 43.

[92] Regulation (EC) No 864/2007 of the European Parliament and of the Council of 11 July 2007 on the law applicable to non-contractual obligations (Rome II), OJ L 199, 31.7.2007, 40–49.

[93] L Enneking, 'The Common Denominator of the Trafigura Case: Foreign Direct Liability Cases and the Rome II Regulation' (2008) 16 *European Review of Private Law* 283.

interpreted narrowly.[94] Swiss law generally follows the EU principles in these regards.[95]

According to Save the Children, legal provisions based on the International Code are stronger in the Philippines than in Switzerland,[96] leading to an initial presumption that the application of Philippine law may be more favourable to the claimants. However, the range of possible tort actions may be more extensive and/or other benefits may be present in Swiss law. It could also be that more favourable rules are available through arguments based on Swiss mandatory provisions or public policy might be applicable to the claimants' benefit. Their position may also be strengthened by recent developments at the Council of Europe. In 2016, the Council's Committee of Ministers recommended that Member States 'should apply such legislative or other appropriate measures as may be necessary to ensure that their domestic courts refrain from applying a law that is incompatible with their international obligations, in particular those stemming from the applicable international human rights standards'.[97] In any event, we may conclude that the best scenario would be a mandatory rule in the home State's domestic system according to which the claimants could themselves choose the law that applied in cases where international human rights are implicated – a situation that does not currently pertain in the vast majority of domestic legal systems.

These procedural barriers are the first that need to fall, enabling effective *access* to home State courts, for this transnational mechanism to have a fighting chance of filling the observed gaps in corporate accountability and global health governance. The next sections demonstrate that the ETO framework provides a strong and increasingly accepted normative basis from which to demand the opening of home State courts, increasing the political weight on States to adopt the required policies through credible arguments of international legal obligation.

---

[94] van Dam, n2, 231–2.
[95] Swiss Federal Code on Private International Law 1987, 8 December 1987, Arts 13–19, 132, 133.
[96] Save the Children, n27, 9. Relative to the recommendations of the WHO Code, the Philippines is denoted as having 'full provisions in law' while Switzerland has 'few provisions in law'.
[97] Recommendation CM/Rec(2016)3 of the Committee of Ministers to member States on human rights and business, adopted by the Committee of Ministers on 2 March 2016 at the 1249th meeting of the Ministers' Deputies, para 40.

4. THE IMPORTANCE OF EXTRATERRITORIAL HUMAN RIGHTS OBLIGATIONS

It is now well recognized that States' international human rights obligations do not cease at their territorial borders.[98] The European Court of Human Rights provides a classic formulation of this principle, holding that States' human rights responsibilities can be engaged by 'acts and omissions of their authorities *producing effects outside their own territory*'.[99] Nevertheless, as noted earlier, the UNGPs hew to a somewhat anachronistic view, reifying territorial limits. According to this view, international law places no obligation on home States to protect populations in other States from the activities of their MNCs or to provide a remedy where such activities infringe human rights abroad, yet they may act to do so if they wish.[100]

This is an increasingly marginal and arguably incorrect interpretation of international law. Contrary to its voluntary tenor and substance, even a brief survey of the statements of the UN human rights treaty bodies shows a clear sense of hardening obligation.[101] Since the early 2000s the Committee on Economic, Social and Cultural Rights (CESCR) has devoted a section in each of its General Comments to State's extraterritorial obligations. The Committee states unequivocally that international cooperation 'is an obligation of all States'.[102] 'To comply with their international obligations' in relation to the Covenant 'States parties have to respect the enjoyment' of the stated rights 'in other countries ... [and] prevent third parties from violating [them] in other countries, if they are able to influence these third parties by way of legal or political means'.[103] The establishment of access to, and regimes of effective

---

[98] See generally, F Coomans and M Kamminga (eds), *Extraterritorial Application of Human Rights Treaties* (Intersentia 2004); M Salomon, *Global Responsibility for Human Rights: World Poverty and the Development of International Law* (OUP 2007); M Gondek, *The Reach of Human Rights in a Globalising World: Extraterritorial Application of Human Rights Treaties* (Intersentia 2009); M Langford (et al. eds), *Global Justice, State Duties: The Extraterritorial Scope of Economic, Social, and Cultural Rights in International Law* (CUP 2012).

[99] *Chiragov and Others v Armenia*, Application No. 13216/05, Judgment of 16 June 2015, para 167.

[100] UNGPs, n15, 7.

[101] R McCorquodale and P Simons, 'Responsibility Beyond Borders: State Responsibility for Extraterritorial Violations by Corporations of International Human Rights Law' (2007) 70 *Modern Law Review* 598.

[102] CESCR, General Comment 3, The Nature of the States Parties' Obligations, UN Doc. E/1991/23, 14 December 1990, para 14.

[103] CESCR, General Comment 14, The Right to the Highest Attainable Standard of Health, UN Doc. E/C.12/2000/4, 11 August 2000, para 39.

accountability within, home State courts clearly qualify as one such legal means of influence. In fact, this should be understood as a minimum expectation, as the measure would only provide a remedy in the event of wrongdoing, not a proactive strategy to prevent wrongdoing.

The Committee recently issued a General Comment on business and human rights, in which it clearly contradicts the UNGPs:

> The [State's] obligation to protect entails a positive duty to adopt a legal framework requiring business entities to exercise human rights due diligence ... Because of how corporate groups are organized, business entities routinely escape liability ... This *requires* States Parties to remove substantive, procedural and practical barriers to remedies, including by establishing parent company or group liability regimes.[104]

In relation to all of the obstacles to transnational liability discussed above, the Committee clarifies, in mandatory terms, that 'States parties have the duty to take necessary steps to address these challenges in order to prevent a denial of justice and ensure the right to effective remedy and reparation.'[105] Other treaty bodies have issued analogous statements.[106] Notably, the CRC has stated that:

> [h]ome States also have obligations ... to respect, protect and fulfil children's rights in the context of businesses' extra-territorial activities and operations ... States should enable access to effective judicial and non-judicial mechanisms to provide remedy for children and their families whose rights have been violated by business enterprises extra-territorially when there is a reasonable link between the State and the conduct concerned.[107]

The treaty bodies evidently utilize the concept of ETOs to invoke a context of clear and uniform obligation to provide effective access to home State courts.

However, this perspective is not limited to the treaty bodies. The UN Working Group on Business and Human Rights, tasked with implementing the UNGPs, has advocated that States should facilitate transnational claims '[a]s *part of their extraterritorial obligation* to respect, protect and fulfil human

---

[104] CESCR, General Comment 24, State Obligations under the International Covenant on Economic, Social and Cultural Rights in the Context of Business Activities, UN Doc. E/C.12/GC/24, 10 August 2017, paras 16, 42 and 44 (emphasis added).

[105] Ibid., para 44.

[106] CERD, Concluding Observations, United Kingdom of Great Britain and Northern Ireland, UN Doc. CERD/C/GBR/CO/18-20, 14 September 2011, para 29; CERD, Concluding Observations, Canada, UN Doc. CERD/C/CAN/CO/18, 25 May 2007, para 17; CERD, Concluding Observations, Canada, UN Doc. CERD/C/CAN/CO/19-20, 9 March 2012, para 14; HRC, Concluding Observations, Germany, UN Doc. CCPR/C/DEU/CO/6, 14 November 2012, para 16.

[107] CRC, General Comment 16, n43, paras 43 and 44.

rights'.¹⁰⁸ This could be an attempt by the Working Group to shift the normative standards of the UNGPs towards a more progressive alignment with those of the human rights treaty bodies.

Furthermore, providing clarification and systematization of international law in this respect, the Maastricht Principles on Extraterritorial Obligations of States in the Area of Economic, Social and Cultural Rights were adopted in 2011.¹⁰⁹ The Maastricht Principles provide an authoritative distillation of ETOs applicable to the present discussion. They set out a normative schema placing obligations on States, particularly Northern States, to regulate the activities of their corporations abroad where reasonable, and to influence them through the administrative, legislative and adjudicatory means at their disposal. They should give effect to such measures wherever corporations (including parent corporations and controlling companies) are domiciled on their territory, and they should ensure an effective remedy when people are harmed by these corporations, wherever the victims may be located.

According to Principle 24, all States:

> must take necessary measures to ensure that non-State actors which they are in a position to regulate, ... such as ... transnational corporations ..., do not nullify or impair the enjoyment of economic, social and cultural rights. These include administrative, legislative, investigative, adjudicatory and other measures.

States therefore 'must adopt and enforce' such measures in relation to the right to health wherever the parent or controlling company is domiciled on their territory.¹¹⁰ Furthermore, where violations and abuses occur all States 'must cooperate ... to ensure an effective remedy for those affected'.¹¹¹

In light of these normative developments and the depth of theoretical grounding now provided in the literature,¹¹² authors such as Augenstein and Kinley therefore assert that an outdated territorial focus is being replaced with

---

[108] Report of the Working Group on the Issue of Human Rights and Transnational Corporations and Other Business Enterprises, UN Doc. A/72/162, 18 July 2017, para 64 (emphasis added).
[109] Published with full commentary in (2012) 34 *Human Rights Quarterly* 1084.
[110] Ibid., Principle 25.
[111] Ibid., Principle 27.
[112] See references at n98. See also, V Tzevelekos, 'In Search of Alternative Solutions: Can the State of Origin be Held Internationally Responsible for Investor's Human Rights Abuses that are Not Attributable to It?' (2010) 35 *Brooklyn Journal of International Law* 155; A Berkes, 'Extraterritorial Responsibility of the Home States for MNC's Violations of Human Rights' in Y Radi (ed.), *Research Handbook on Human Rights and Investments* (OUP 2018).

a focus on the inherently universal rights of the victims of MNCs,[113] and home States 'may find that they are bound under international human rights laws to provide a forum in which to entertain' disputes, discipline corporations and provide transnational remedies for victims.[114] Kirshner calls, in particular, for European acceptance of an enlightened responsibility in this regard,[115] a call that is buttressed and enlivened by the favourable positions of the European Parliament and the Council of Europe. As elaborated in the next section, this support is indicative of a growing public demand for Northern States to take a leadership role in defence of human rights by acting to restructure frameworks of global governance and corporate accountability, necessitating the removal of barriers to home State courts.

5. ETOS AS NORMATIVE GROUNDING FOR IMPROVED ACCESS TO HOME STATE COURTS

The European Parliament has validated the Maastricht Principles by reliance on them in a resolution directly on the present issue of transnational corporate liability.[116] In the view of the Parliament, States 'have a duty to protect human rights, including against abuses committed by companies, even if they operate in third countries'.[117] The Parliament 'strongly recalls that, where human rights abuses occur, the States must grant access for the victims to an effective remedy'.[118] The resolution:

> [c]alls for the Member States to legislate in a coherent, holistic, effective and binding manner in order to fulfil their duty to prevent, investigate, punish and redress human rights violations by corporations acting under their jurisdiction, including those perpetrated in third countries.[119]

---

[113] D Augenstein and D Kinley, 'Beyond the 100 Acre Wood: In Which International Human Rights Law Finds New Ways to Tame Global Corporate Power' (2015) 19 *International Journal of Human Rights* 828.

[114] Ibid., 842.

[115] J Kirshner, 'A Call for the EU to Assume Jurisdiction over Extraterritorial Corporate Human Rights Abuses' (2015) 13 *Northwestern Journal of Human Rights* 1. For analogous reflections see also, S Besson, 'The European Union and Human Rights: Towards a Post-National Human Rights Institution?' (2006) 6 *Human Rights Law Review* 323.

[116] European Parliament Resolution of 25 October 2016 on corporate liability for serious human rights abuses in third countries (2015/2315(INI)), P8_TA(2016)0405.

[117] Ibid., para 13.

[118] Ibid.

[119] Ibid., paras 17 and 18.

Likewise, but with direct relevance to Switzerland, the Council of Europe's Committee of Ministers has called for Member States to 'apply such measures as may be necessary to require, as appropriate, business enterprises domiciled in their jurisdiction to respect human rights throughout their operations abroad'.[120] It has recommended the establishment of civil liability for the wrongdoing of subsidiaries 'wherever they are based' and measures ensuring that transnational claims are 'not unduly restricted', especially through the 'application of a law that is incompatible with ... applicable international human rights standards', or through an inequality of arms, lack of legal aid, or barriers to information.[121]

Building on these developments, a current process of multilateral negotiations is underway at the UN seeking the elaboration of a Binding Treaty on business and human rights.[122] This treaty process[123] offers a promising and influential forum for civil society and willing States to press for clear and binding rules on effective access to home State courts and the removal of the obstacles detailed above.[124] This, in effect, would simply be a formalization of the obligations to do so already expressed by the human rights treaty bodies and the UN Working Group, and the expectations conveyed by international bodies such as the European Parliament and the Council of Europe. Despite initial disengagement or active opposition, the willingness of the traditional home States of MNCs to engage constructively with the treaty process had increased significantly.[125] There is now a relatively broad consensus among stakeholders that the treaty process is complementary to and supportive of

---

[120] Recommendation CM/Rec(2016)3, n97, para 13. See also, Explanatory Memorandum to Recommendation CM/Rec(2016)3 of the Committee of Ministers to member States on human rights and business, 1249 Meeting, CM(2016)18-addfinal, 2 March 2016.

[121] Recommendation CM/Rec(2016)3, ibid., paras 31–43; Explanatory Memorandum to Recommendation CM/Rec(2016)3, ibid., paras 55–66.

[122] Human Rights Council, Resolution 26/9, Elaboration of an international legally binding instrument on transnational corporations and other business enterprises with respect to human rights, UN Doc. A/HRC/RES/26/9, 14 July 2014. See further, S Deva and D Bilchitz (eds), *Building a Treaty on Business and Human Rights: Context and Contours* (CUP 2017).

[123] H Cantu Rivera, 'Negotiating a Treaty on Business and Human Rights: The Early Stages' (2017) 40 *University of New South Wales Law Journal* 1200.

[124] Among other mechanisms by which victims' access to a remedy might be enhanced through the treaty process. See, E George and L Laplante, 'Access to Remedy: Treaty Talks and the Terms of a New Accountability Accord' and B Stephens, 'Making Remedies Work' in S Deva and D Bilchitz (eds), *Building a Treaty on Business and Human Rights: Context and Contours* (CUP 2017).

[125] D Blackburn, 'Removing Barriers to Justice: How a Treaty on Business and Human Rights Could Improve Access to Remedy for Victims', Centre for Research on

the UNGPs. The European Parliament has called specifically for constructive engagement in the treaty process by the EU and the Member States,[126] and has itself expressly demanded 'the establishment of a legally binding framework for companies, including transnational corporations', complete with effective remedial mechanisms.[127]

A Revised Draft of the Binding Treaty was released in July 2019,[128] and as currently framed it would effectively codify the CESCR's statements and the Maastricht Principles, applying ETOs to the removal of all of the described obstacles to home State court access. For example, the draft obliges prospective State Parties to provide their domestic judicial and other competent authorities with the jurisdiction necessary to routinely admit transnational civil claims, circumventing the doctrine of *forum non conveniens* and even perhaps going so far as demanding a form of *forum necessitatis*.[129] The treaty would oblige States to 'provide for a comprehensive and adequate system of legal liability for human rights violations or abuses in the context of business activities, including those of transnational character'.[130] States would have to provide 'proper and effective legal assistance to victims', circumventing obstacles of information and money.[131] They would be obliged to establish in their domestic legislation that their MNCs take appropriate preventive actions to avoid human rights abuses abroad and undertake effective due diligence,[132] also establishing a duty of care on parent MNCs where there is a 'failure to prevent … [subsidiaries] from causing harm to third parties' in a transnational

---

Multinational Corporations (SOMO), Amsterdam, August 2017, 65; H Cantu Rivera, n123, 1212.

[126] European Parliament, Resolution on the EU's Priorities for the UN Human Rights Council in 2015 (2015/2572(RSP)), 12 March 2015, para 32.

[127] European Parliament, Resolution on Financing for Development (2015/2044(INI)), 19 May 2015, para 36. See also, European Parliament resolution of 12 September 2017 on the impact of international trade and the EU's trade policies on global value chains (2016/2301(INI)), P8_TA-PROV(2017)0330, para 9.

[128] UN Open-Ended Intergovernmental Working Group, Legally Binding Instrument to Regulate, in International Human Rights Law, the Activities of Transnational Corporations and other Business Enterprises, Revised Draft, 16 July 2019,

https://www.ohchr.org/Documents/HRBodies/HRCouncil/WGTransCorp/OEIGWG_RevisedDraft_LBI.pdf. Multiple links to commentary on the Revised Draft are available here, https://www.business-humanrights.org/en/about-us/blog/debate-the-treaty/reflections-on-the-revised-draft-treaty.

[129] Revised Draft, ibid, Arts 4(8), 6(1), 6(4), 6(6) and 7.
[130] Ibid., Art 6(1).
[131] Ibid., Art 4(12).
[132] Ibid., Art 5.

context.[133] Obstacles of applicable law are addressed,[134] and States would also have to enable the 'reversal of the burden of proof for the purpose of fulfilling the victim's access to justice' where needed.[135]

This treaty, targeted at the provision of an effective regime of transnational corporate liability, could result in increased harmonization of national laws and policies from a sense of legal obligation that would help to significantly normalize ETOs or 'to reconfigure the appropriate legal theory such that extraterritoriality ceases to be an issue'.[136] And finally, if the treaty as currently drafted was ratified and implemented by Switzerland, there would be no significant procedural obstacle to our hypothetical case against Nestlé, providing a fighting chance for justice for the children and mothers harmed by its practices in the Philippines, and helping to close a gaping hole in the global fight against childhood obesity.

6. CONCLUSION – ETOS AND THE BROADER CONTEXT OF GLOBAL HEALTH GOVERNANCE

This chapter has presented three main arguments: (1) the obesity epidemic cannot be properly addressed without a fundamental appreciation of the cross-border or extraterritorial context of relative legal impunity in which agri-food MNCs operate; (2) effective access to home State courts for transnational litigants pursuing claims against these MNCs for creating or exacerbating obesogenic environments across borders is an essential element in combatting the global obesity epidemic; and (3) ETOs provide a crucial normative framework supporting calls for the mandatory opening of home State courts thereby closing a large gap in the accountability of agri-food MNCs.

The case study of Nestlé in the Philippines demonstrates some of the systemic problems inherent in programmes of global health governance that do not include effective legal mechanisms that adequately address the reality of the global political economy. ETOs provide a compelling framework and 'the appropriate departure point' from which to approach a diverse range of issues requiring improved global governance and the 'reshaping [of] the international economic environment'.[137] Beyond the issue of obesity, ETOs require action and can inform models of just global governance in a broad spectrum of

---

[133] Ibid., Art 6(6).
[134] Ibid., Art 9.
[135] Ibid., Art 4(16).
[136] V Curran, 'Harmonizing Multinational Parent Company Liability for Foreign Subsidiary Human Rights Violations' (2017) 17 *Chinese Journal of International Law* 403, 408.
[137] O De Schutter, 'The Role of Human Rights', n21, 785.

fields directly affecting the health of people worldwide, and especially those regularly left to bear the brunt of the pathologies of our global order in the poorer countries. As discussed in previous chapters, the fields of trade and investment are crucial in this regard. ETOs have a great deal of potential to positively shape global governance in both these fields,[138] by mandating the conduct of human rights impact assessments in the process of negotiations on trade and investment agreements,[139] or even earlier in the formulation of initial negotiating positions and directives.[140] In these and many other ways the framework of ETOs can help to reorient the structure of incentives that States and corporations face and to re-form the models, institutions and regimes of global governance.[141]

However, ETOs remain politically contested and are yet to gain significant purchase on policymaking in these larger fields. On the more circumscribed issue of access to home State courts it is arguable that the logic of ETOs has much greater purchase. Access to home State courts could therefore be a very useful issue through which to press for the further development of ETOs. Establishing this set of obligations firmly as the normative basis for opening home State courts to transnational litigants would support their international acceptance and implementation in broader fields, aiding the principled resolution of other pressing issues of global governance and raising the 'problem-solving capacity' of our international order.[142]

This could ultimately have deep ramifications for the politics of global justice. In our case study, it would have the effect of beginning to enfranchise poor and marginalized sections of the Philippine population within a more expanded and inclusive process of global governance. In the grand scheme, next to the expanding power of agri-food MNCs, access to the Swiss courts to claim against Nestlé, would be a small victory. Much more needs to be done in the crucial areas of international trade, finance, investment and health governance. Nevertheless, justice may have been attained on this issue for future generations of poor Philippine children. Their 'distant' human plight and their substantive political presence will have been felt in the heart of Europe, amid

---

[138] Ibid., 796–7.

[139] Maastricht Principles, n109, Principles 17 and 14; Report of the Special Rapporteur on the Right to Food, Olivier De Schutter, Addendum, Guiding Principles on Human Rights Impact Assessments of Trade and Investment Agreements, UN Doc. A/HRC/19/59/Add.5, 19 December 2011.

[140] J Curtis, *Human Rights and Foreign Investment: Cooperation and Coherence in Global Law-Making* (CUP forthcoming 2021).

[141] O De Schutter, 'The Role of Human Rights', n21, 797, 808–10. For further discussion see Curtis and Garde's chapter in conclusion to this volume.

[142] T Altwicker, 'Transnationalizing Rights: International Human Rights Law in Cross-Border Contexts' (2018) 29 *European Journal of International Law* 581, 582.

the seats of numerous MNCs affecting the lives of local populations in the global South. As Augenstein extrapolates:

> extraterritorial human rights protection holds out the promise of recovering the politics of human rights beyond the international order of states. International legal obligations to provide access to justice for extraterritorial human rights violations are the counterpart of legal entitlements of third country victims to stake a public and political claim in the home states of multinational corporations.[143]

If this vision of transnational politics and public space comes closer to reality it could ramify positively throughout international society, aiding our perception of the governance structures we all need and wish to build in the future.

---

[143] D Augenstein, 'Paradise Lost: Sovereign State Interest, Global Resource Exploitation and the Politics of Human Rights' (2016) 27 *European Journal of International Law* 669, 690.

13. Overcoming the legal challenge to end childhood obesity: Pathways towards positive harmonization in law and governance

Joshua Curtis and Amandine Garde

This book has built on three broad and relatively uncontroversial premises. First, childhood obesity is among the most complex and pressing global problems facing the international community.[1] Second, the national policies required to overcome this problem are increasingly well defined.[2] Third, the law has a pivotal role to play in implementing these policies.[3] Yet, more law does not necessarily bring a better outcome.

'The law' is as multifaceted as obesity. It holds the potential to help the solution materialize, but it can hinder it too. One of the central aims of this book was not just to discuss the most relevant aspects of the law pertaining to the challenge of childhood obesity, but also to demonstrate this fundamental ambiguity in the law itself, the effect of which is dependent on the dominant intention animating it. To summarize somewhat crudely, the foregoing chapters revolve around two such intentions. On the one hand, a desire to build and protect an economic system, dependent on an acceptance of neoliberal or mainstream economic theory, ostensibly for the greater good. On the other, a desire to realize, establish and protect basic levels of universal human rights, again, arguably for the greater good. The choice of intention permeates the law – informing its structure, determining its interpretation and application, and setting political priorities. The overall balance struck between these two intentions and the legal regimes built on their basis ultimately determines the

---

[1] UN General Assembly Resolution 73/2 of 10 October 2018 (A/73/L.2) adopting the Political declaration of the third high-level meeting of the General Assembly on the prevention and control of NCDs; B Swinburn et al., 'The Global Syndemic of Obesity, Undernutrition, and Climate Change: The Lancet Commission Report' (2019) 393 *The Lancet* 791.
[2] WHO, *Report of the Commission on Ending Childhood Obesity* (WHO 2016).
[3] Ibid., p. 38; B Swinburn et al., n1, pp. 793, 802, 803, 808, 811, 817, 818–21, 836.

net effect of law and its ability to contribute to effective obesity prevention strategies.

This is an important part of, and perspective on, the 'legal challenge' referred to in our title. The book has sought to clarify this challenge by marking out the choices we face at the intersection of human rights and economic legal regimes in relation to childhood obesity, highlighting the potential conflict between the intentions animating each regime. The clarity gained helps to inform the way forward. To overcome this challenge, and to maximize the law's beneficial effects, human rights must govern the formulation and operation of economic law: the *intention* to provide universal human rights to all should ultimately hold sway. This does not mean that human rights can or should necessarily override every instance in which they are in tension with international economic law. Nor does it mean that human rights can provide an answer to every dilemma we face in the drive to end childhood obesity, when this objective must be balanced against other legitimate interests. However, it does send a message about where priorities should lie: human rights should ultimately shape, contain, inform or limit the overall design and function of the economy. Conversely, the drive to maintain, protect and expand the economic status quo should not justify overriding human rights or establishing obstacles to their full realization.

These conjoined viewpoints – on the ambiguity of the law, the intention behind the law and the drive towards its overall harmonization – will infuse this concluding discussion, which proceeds through three sections. We first recap the 'vertical' structure of the book, weaving together the chapters in each of its three parts to tell its 'originally designed' story. Next, we draw out and sharpen the 'horizontal' themes that emerge from the book taken as a whole. We then close by looking to the future and beyond the book, applying these horizontal themes to the proposal for a Global Framework Convention on Obesity Prevention.

1. RECAPPING THE STRUCTURE

Discussions on human rights and international economic law typically begin with economic law. They first seek to delineate the precise terms of the economic regime and then identify the possible entry points for human rights. This approach tends to automatically accord conceptual and ontological primacy to the economic regime, and could be viewed as conceding the 'high ground' from the outset.[4] This ordering may stem from the recognition that the enforce-

---

[4] For example, this priority is represented by the 'in' in the title of Dupuy, Petersmann and Francioni's early edited collection in the field of human rights and

ment mechanisms of international economic law are more robust than those on which the human rights regime relies. It is anomalous, however, from the point of view of the harmonization advocated here. This book therefore takes a different approach. Its starts with an in-depth look at the relevance of the human rights regime to childhood obesity. It sees the role of human rights not simply as seeking to 'fit in' with international economic law, but as reshaping or redirecting it where possible.

1.1 Part I

The central concern of Part I was to delineate the precise terms of the human rights regime. The authors presented the rationale for a human rights-based approach to NCD prevention and the added value that this approach yields for the prevention of childhood obesity, beyond but complementary to existing approaches grounded in public health, behavioural science and economics. Human rights are often seen as vague aspirational standards in comparison to supposedly well-defined and 'concrete' rules of economic law.[5] The chapters in Part I dispel the myth of human rights' excessive vagueness, establishing and grounding their inherent ability to clearly direct policy and law making by

---

investment law, *Human Rights in International Investment Law and Arbitration* (OUP 2009). The ontological order is clear in the title of the book and most of the contributions reflect this order. Part II of the book even asks the question, in its title, 'Is there a role for human rights in investor-State arbitration and international economic adjudication?' Despite subsequent divergence to some degree, this early seminal text has set the overall methodological tone for investigation in the field ever since, deeply skewing the debate towards the maintenance, or at best the slow and piecemeal reform, of the investment regime in light of its evident failure to adequately account for human rights and other public interests. An analogous order had already been set up in relation to trade, through the 'trade and …' or 'trade linkage' debates initiated in the late 1990s, which tended to reify and reproduce, rather than contest, the basic principles of economic law at issue. See A Lang, 'Reflecting on 'Linkage': Cognitive and Institutional Change in The International Trading System' (2007) 70(4) *Modern Law Review* 523, for an identification of this methodological tone. For a historiographic effort to overcome it see, A Lang, *World Trade Law after Neoliberalism: Reimagining the Global Economic Order* (OUP 2011) chapter 2: 'Trade and Human Rights' in Historical Perspective, 23–60.

[5] This fallacious commonplace is often asserted in order to reify economic law and denigrate human rights as any sort of 'viable competitor', capable alternative or robust method for re-interpreting economic rules or re-designing their content. In Part II, the chapters by Foster, Messenger and Sattorova highlight the fact that many of the core components of economic law (such as 'fair and equitable treatment', 'non-discrimination', 'likeness' and 'necessity') are themselves quite vague, representing standards that are difficult for States to implement consistently and could also be described as aspirational.

drawing on the now extensive content given to these rights by decades of elaboration by courts and international bodies, as well as the provision of evidence based guidance from the WHO and other relevant agencies.

Roache and Cabrera detail the implications of the rights most relevant to the fight against childhood obesity, with a focus on the right to health and the right to food. They show how a good faith implementation of these rights would result in significant reform that would drastically reshape obesogenic environments. They demonstrate the benefits of rights framing for public health advocates working in this area, also highlighting the need to combat the prevalent use of rights-talk by food industry actors who strategically confuse commercial and non-commercial freedoms in order to co-opt the human rights discourse.

Ó Cathaoir and Hartlev deepen the analysis and implications of child rights. Distilling the work of the Committee on the Rights of the Child (CRC), they advocate for a rights-based approach that imposes three sets of duties: to establish an enabling environment, to empower actors, and to ensure government and industry accountability. They highlight the deep synergies between State obligations under human rights law and the detailed policy framework of the Ending Childhood Obesity (ECHO) Commission, and suggest that human rights bodies such as the CRC should make more explicit use of WHO policy recommendations and reports, including them in their own dialogues with States, thus adding depth, detail and better guidance on States' human rights obligations in the area of child health and strengthening the institutional complementarity between the WHO and the human rights system.

Finally, Friant-Perrot and Gokani draw out the ramifications of human rights for deep-seated social inequalities and the attendant skewing of childhood obesity rates. They show how prioritizing the substantive and equal dignity of all children allows the identification of pitfalls in alternative policy formulations aimed at ending childhood obesity, which would otherwise remain invisible. We cannot effectively address child obesity, they argue, while remaining blind to socio-economic disadvantage, and the non-discrimination norm of human rights law provides a principled means of avoiding this trap.

In concert, the chapters in Part I establish the importance of framing child obesity as a human rights issue, explaining how it can help ensure that States account for their failure to effectively protect and fulfil the child's right to health and other related rights. They also demonstrate the under-appreciated detail and substance of a human rights approach to ending childhood obesity, showing that adopting such an approach is both feasible and effective. Health advocates and human rights lawyers need to work more closely together, drawing on each other's knowledge base and expertise to shape and inform effective obesity prevention strategies.

1.2   Part II

As discussed in the introduction, the global rise of childhood obesity is closely linked to economic liberalization through its catalytic effect on the fundamental drivers of obesogenic environments, through in particular the increasing concentration and power of agri-food multinationals (MNCs) and the emergence of a transnational agri-food industry, the westernization of diets and the growing consumption of processed foods, via global sourcing, production and marketing. It is increasingly established that economic liberalization and obesogenic food systems have been both propelled and institutionalized by the development of modern trade and investment law. By noting the consonance between the obesity epidemic and international economic law we do not suggest primary or in any way 'conscious' causation. However, we do stress that the chief aim of international economic law has never been to protect public health and human rights: these objectives are at best an indirect effect of, or an allowed *exception* to, the core intention of this body of law.

Against this background, the chapters in Part II assess the actual regulatory space provided by international economic law for States to better prevent obesity as a major public health and human rights concern, specifically the extent of the exceptions allowed for the pursuit of this goal. This is a highly contentious area, rife with controversies and unsettled doctrinal disputes. As Sattorova clearly points out with respect to investment law, this lack of legal certainty can be a strong inhibitor when States are considering public health and human rights measures, particularly as the financial costs of getting it wrong may be high. In the trade context, Foster highlights a lack of political will to implement obesity prevention measures in the Caribbean, which could derive from the same 'chilling' effect of economic law on States' efforts to implement obesity prevention laws. There is an urgent need for clarity so that State action to end childhood obesity is not unduly, or automatically misconceived as contrary to economic law.

Trade agreements routinely include general exception clauses, enabling certain State actions in pursuit of various public interests. To qualify as an allowed exception under trade law obesity prevention measures must comply with three core standards: they must be necessary for the protection of human health, they must not involve arbitrary or unjustifiable discrimination, and they must not amount to disguised restrictions on international trade.

Foster recalls how initial decisions by the Appellate Body of the WTO defined necessity quite narrowly, allowing exceptional measures only when there was no alternative. However, she also shows that more recent decisions have lowered the threshold of necessity to an extent, somewhat expanding the scope of permissible exceptions. She argues that WTO members have not been seriously constrained by these standards when pursuing bona fide policy objectives such as public health protection. Messenger also notes a progressively nuanced approach by the Appellate Body towards States' public health policies, suggesting that such concerns have been an important driver in the more inclusive development of trade law, describing a dynamic learning process between the trade regime and representatives of non-trade concerns. Ultimately, Messenger also agrees that, through its established interpretation of exceptions, the trade regime is sufficiently flexible in general to accommodate State measures to address childhood obesity.

Focusing on trade in the EU system, MacMaoláin strikes a more pessimistic and cautious tone when looking specifically at the introduction of food labelling regulations. He argues that the EU trade regime curtails the manner in which EU Member States can implement food labelling schemes due primarily to the existence of harmonized rules that prevent States from making front-of-pack labelling systems mandatory. He nonetheless concludes that, despite the constraints deriving from EU internal market law, certain food labelling formats may still be designed in such a way as to comply with both EU and WTO rules, and yet also inform healthier choices. MacMaoláin's chapter is a helpful reminder of the risk that the current lack of congruence between States' trade obligations and their desire to promote public health may be a source of legal uncertainty, and have a chilling effect on the adoption by States of obesity prevention measures.

Mirroring a certain shift toward lenience in the WTO Appellate Body, Sattorova shows that the investment regime has also become somewhat more accepting of public health measures. Arguably, and taken in the aggregate, investment tribunals have expanded the scope for State action primarily motivated by a bona fide public health objective.[6] Yet these same tribunals remain largely unreceptive to human rights arguments that potentially support, or even obligate, such objectives.[7]

Collectively, Foster and Sattorova compile a useful list of guiding principles that States should follow when formulating, enacting and implementing obesity prevention measures in order to minimize the risk of violating trade and investment rules. They should: ensure proportionality, reasonableness and rationality; avoid discrimination; ensure that any necessary differential treatment is justified on health grounds and underpinned by scientific evi-

---

[6] M Langford and D Behn, 'Managing Backlash: The Evolving Investment Treaty Arbitrator?' (2018) 29 *European Journal of International Law* 551.

[7] S Schadendorf, 'Human Rights Arguments in Amicus Curiae Submissions: Analysis of ICSID and NAFTA Investor-State Arbitrations' (2013) 10 *Transnational Dispute Management*; J Harrison, 'Human Rights Arguments in Amicus Curiae Submissions: Promoting Social Justice?' in PM Dupuy (et al. eds), *Human Rights in International Investment Law and Arbitration* (OUP 2009).

dence; and ensure due process, transparency and inclusiveness (although industry participation should be carefully limited). Sattorova also clarifies an additional standard in international investment law that has no corollary in international trade law: obesity prevention measures should not contravene the 'legitimate expectations' of foreign investors. States should therefore be prepared to establish that investors cannot legitimately expect not to be subject to such measures. It is crucial they avoid making either explicit or implicit representations, communications or commitments to foreign investors that the regulatory environment will not change or that relevant public health measures will not be implemented, as doing so will create a legitimate expectation. Finally, due to the more ad hoc and disparate nature of investment law and its dispute resolution process, States should keep in mind that investment law involves significantly less legal certainty than trade law, increasing the risk of violations. As such, these principles should be adhered to strictly in situations of potential investment arbitrations.

Considered together, the chapters in Part II suggest that most obesity prevention measures (such as those recommended, for instance, by the ECHO Commission) would satisfy the criteria for valid exceptions or legitimate government measures under trade and investment law, even where they restrict trade or negatively affect foreign investors. This position is strengthened if States endeavour to follow the principles outlined above. In general, States retain a sufficient margin of discretion to adopt effective regulatory strategies to protect public health and combat childhood obesity. This implies that States should not be allowed to hide behind their obligations under trade or investment regimes as an excuse for failing to implement the recommendations of the ECHO Commission or other necessary measures to prevent child obesity. The caveat is that States must also be prepared to justify their actions before a variety of international adjudicatory bodies (e.g. CJEU, WTO Dispute Settlement and Appellate Bodies, and investment arbitration tribunals) in a manner that is cognisant of, and sensitive to, the terms of the relevant treaties. This preparation is crucial: the more robust a regulatory intervention, the more likely it is to be challenged by MNCs and their home States.[8]

Two points should be underscored here. First, trade and investment law have a negative background effect in exacerbating the fundamental drivers of obesity. The second is that obesity prevention measures – even where backed solidly by evidence, public health arguments and the requirements of human rights law – will often be implemented by States in a negative or defensive

---

[8] The international challenges mounted against tobacco control laws in Uruguay (large graphic health warnings) and Australia (tobacco plain packaging), or against minimum unit pricing of alcoholic beverages in Scotland, are all well documented.

environment created by the current structure of international economic law: the onus is on States to justify measures that may restrict trade or impinge on the rights of foreign investors. The structure and substance of economic law do not actively *encourage* States to pursue public health objectives such as ending childhood obesity. Instead, international economic law may be understood as setting important, and in some ways defining, terms of engagement on a battleground between entrenched economic interests and increasingly acute public interests. These terms of engagement should be redefined. Considering the negative effects of liberalization, public health and human rights should be given at least equal, if not governing, status together with economic concerns. Upholding public health and human rights should be at the core of public policy driving international economic law, not awkward or tangential exceptions to its general direction of travel.

1.3 Part III

Part III focuses on the identification of a range of normative tools and processes that States should rely upon more extensively to respond effectively to obesity and ensure greater compliance with their human rights obligations to protect children and establish healthier food environments. States should not only seek to act within the allowed confines of economic law, they should also prioritize institutional, procedural and technical methods of tackling childhood obesity that are inherent in the structure and substance of human rights. This Part highlights additional modalities, mostly drawn from progressive understandings of human rights law, by which States might more effectively regulate the agri-food industry and which remain largely unexplored in the literature and public health advocacy.

Wenche Barth Eide and Asbjørn Eide expand the imperative towards greater inter-institutional integration and cooperation between human rights and public health into the functioning of the larger UN system. They illustrate the disappointing results of cooperation within this system to date, highlighting the poor coordination between the WHO, FAO, UN Secretariat and human rights bodies, as a major obstacle to an effective and coherent public health *and* human rights-based approach. A debilitating gulf between public health and human rights actors exists, involving signal failures to establish a basis of interlinked, coherent policy framing and a collaborative reform agenda. Nevertheless, Barth Eide and Eide remain optimistic that more coherent institutional collaboration could result from the framework of the UN Decade of Action on Nutrition, with better and more targeted communication and cross-fertilization between the various agencies and actors, that could lead to more than semantic alignment between human rights and public health in the drive to end childhood obesity.

The next three chapters tease out some of the vital ways in which progressive human rights norms can, and indeed must, move the fight against childhood obesity beyond a defensive posture, working within the extant structure of agri-food industry corporate power and business-friendly legal arrangements, into the active opening of new spaces and mandates that move beyond these present structures.

Garde and Byrne explore the tension within the human rights paradigm between the rights of the child and the supposed 'human rights' of corporations, as earlier touched upon by Cabrera and Roache, through which the agri-food industry attempts to capture the discourse of rights for their own benefit. In particular, they argue that the 'best interests of the child' principle, enshrined in Article 3(1) of the CRC, provides a valuable though much under-utilized balancing tool that should be relied upon throughout the policy cycle to reconcile the imperatives of human rights, public health and international economic law. In particular, illustrating the argument with the regulation of food marketing, they reflect on the role that the 'best interests principle' can play when State regulatory measures intended to prevent childhood obesity are challenged by powerful economic actors on the ground that such measures would infringe the rights of these actors to freedom of (commercial) expression or (intellectual) property. They argue that the 'best interests of the child' principle should be used in litigation not only as a shield to defend evidence-based regulatory measures against industry-led challenges, but also as a sword allowing States and civil society to challenge in court unfair commercial practices that harm the rights of the child. Looking beyond the confines of the courtroom, Garde and Byrne also consider the role that the 'best interests of the child' principle could play in the development and implementation of legal measures intended to prevent childhood obesity, focusing specifically on how *ex ante* impact assessments can help promote the enjoyment of the highest attainable standard of health by all children.

The other two chapters focus directly on the corporate accountability of agri-food MNCs, drawing on recent and emergent human rights norms capable of concretely constraining the potential negative effects of these actors through mandating the State imposition of credible legal sanctions against them. Bartlett builds on the international consensus established in 2011 by the UN Guiding Principles on Business and Human Rights that corporations have a responsibility to respect all human rights, including the right to health. Detailing a conceptual approach according to which corporations fail to respect the right to health if they contribute knowingly to the creation and/or maintenance of an obesogenic environment, he argues that States are obliged to ensure that all corporations active within their territory or jurisdiction carry out appropriate right to health due diligence to reduce the likelihood that they impair the right to health in their business activities. States would be obliged to do so under human rights obligations to protect the rights of their citizens. Sanctions for a failure to undertake right to health due diligence could be applied through national legislation or by the progressive application of national law by courts drawing on doctrines pertaining to the horizontal or indirect effect of human rights in the legal system. Agri-food MNCs would then be obliged to assess their product development, marketing and distribution practices for potential contributions to an obesogenic environment (particularly in relation to products consumed by or marketed to children) and adjust their actions accordingly for fear of a legal sanction.

Taking comparable arguments to the international plane, Curtis draws on work in the field of extraterritorial human rights obligations (ETOs) to delineate duties on States to cooperate in the construction of effective transnational civil liability for agri-food MNCs that contribute to obesogenic environments and thereby impinge on the right to health across borders. Given that many host States in which agri-food MNCs operate are often developing countries and may not have the wherewithal to hold such actors accountable in their legal systems for negative effects on the human rights of the local population, the courts of the MNC's home State, most often a developed country, may be the only possible forum in which justice might be sought. Yet, due to the combination of domestic rules that tend to have a limited extraterritorial reach, and to the structure of MNCs, access to home State courts for transnational litigants may be blocked, resulting in effective impunity for transgressive actions of MNCs in host States. When interpreted progressively and applied in accord with its true purpose, human rights law does place duties on home States to remove such obstacles and open their courts to bona fide transnational litigants. ETOs mandate such action by the home States of powerful agri-food MNCs in order to establish the transnational element in a more robust and effective system of corporate accountability, giving effect to universal human rights, removing the specter of impunity, and shoring up gaps in governance.

As Part III demonstrates, the progressive development of human rights law, particularly through increased and explicit reliance on the 'best interests of the child' principle, human rights due diligence, and ETOs, offers an adaptable and universal normative framework capable of responding to systemic governance gaps arising from the pathologies of our global economic order, aiding the construction of adequate systems of global health and human rights governance.

2. HORIZONTAL OR EMERGENT THEMES

From these contributions, four main horizontal themes emerge which are closely interlinked and deserve strategic focus: (1) legal fragmentation; (2) the importance of legal capacity building and interdisciplinarity; (3) the integration of the evidence-base into law and policy; and (4) the under-explored potential of human rights law.

2.1 Responses to Legal Fragmentation

The fragmentation of modern international law into a plethora of segmented and semi-autonomous regimes has for some time been central to international legal practice and discourse.[9] This book underscores the complexity of moving various bodies of law towards the establishment of a coherent, joined-up and effective approach to the global challenge of child obesity. Human rights lawyers and bodies will by nature advocate for a human rights approach, pushing for certain policies and legal solutions, perhaps without adequately framing their advocacy in light of existing economic concerns, or sufficiently accounting for an evidence base and an agenda developed by public health professionals. Trade and investment lawyers may approach the issue solely through the lens of economic rules and market-based priorities without sufficient consideration for State obligations under human rights law or sensitivity to the non-economic evidence base. Public health actors may take an approach that is not alive to the constraints or opportunities of economic and human rights law. In bringing all these perspectives together, we hope that this book goes some way towards piecing the fragments together.

There is a need to move economic law from the inside, from the perspective of its dispute resolution processes and the interpretation of its terms. The WTO Appellate Body has moved somewhat towards a greater appreciation of non-trade concerns in response to its need to grapple with environmental and public interest issues. Similarly, there is some evidence that investment tribunals have created more space for State regulation for similar reasons and in response to significant public opprobrium. This shows the inherent flexibility of any set of substantive rules and the importance of always pushing just causes within these fields of law in order to encourage them to adapt from inside. However, this may not be enough considering pressing public health crises, so we should be prepared to also move economic law from the outside. This will involve changes to the substantive content and procedures of economic law through alteration, renegotiation and redesign of economic agreements. Foster, for example, indicates the desirability of a change in the standard required for exceptions to economic law regimes, from 'necessity' to a more permissible

---

[9] At least since the publication of a seminal report from the International Law Commission; 'Fragmentation of International Law: Difficulties Arising from the Diversification and Expansion of International Law', UN Doc A/CN.4/L.682, 13 April 2006.

standard of a 'rational connection' or 'logical relation' to a given public interest. Another desirable move is to expressly include provisions on the achievement of sustainable development objectives in economic agreements, which could significantly broaden the scope of allowed regulation. Although not yet undertaken in international economic agreements, this scope could also be explicitly extended to cover all reasonable measures for the realization and protection of human rights. Some of the desirable changes to the substance and structure of investment law could include the greater use of trade-style general exceptions clauses, more restrictive definitions of 'investor' and 'investment', greater textual space for social policy measures or dedicated carveouts for specific public interest issues, or the imposition of investor obligations and responsibilities in the form of a 'clean hands' doctrine making the invocation of investors' rights conditional upon compliance with human rights.

International economic law is not the only regime that needs to evolve. As our three final chapters suggest, the international human rights law regime needs to evolve too. Currently, it is subject to considerable criticism for a supposed inability to adequately regulate or challenge global economic processes and actors, especially MNCs. Human rights law needs to evolve through bolder State action and more progressive and teleological interpretation and advocacy, paying closer attention to structural inequalities and imbalances. This, in turn, requires that human rights lawyers become far more fluent in the operation of economic systems and principles. They need to engage closely with economic law instead of relying on the sheer moral force of human rights to overcome obstacles from outside their immediate sphere of specialization. They must also become better acquainted with the knowledge base and working methods of public health professionals, to build a collaborative, normative and practice-oriented foundation that would inform and heighten political will for all these systemic moves.

2.2 Building Legal Capacity and Interdisciplinarity

For issues of legal fragmentation to be addressed through better communication we need to increase legal capacity and forge genuinely interdisciplinary collaborations; for it is well established that an interdisciplinary approach to the prevention of child obesity is paramount.[10]

While there is clear international recognition of the seriousness of obesity as a major global health challenge, insufficient attention is still paid to the

---

[10] S Mariana, et al., 'Interdisciplinary Approach to Obesity' in A Lenzi (et al. eds), *Multidisciplinary Approach to Obesity: From Assessment to Treatment* (Springer 2015).

legal aspects of the response it requires, especially the international or transnational legal aspects. There is significant attention given to needed domestic legal reforms, but this is rarely contextualized in light of the constraints and demands of international trade, investment and human rights law, knowledge of which is crucial to the effectiveness of domestic legislation and regulation. Furthermore, the legal and regulatory questions raised are inherently international issues, as the agri-food industry is organized at a global level, requiring not only national or local responses, but also international and regional legal responses. At the same time, it is necessary to build the capacity of the legal community as a whole so that they can more fully engage with public health perspectives and agendas and better grasp the details of the evidentiary base on which effective obesity prevention measures should rest. As we highlighted in our introduction, the law must be informed by other disciplines. Finally, it is crucial that lawyers specialized in one area of law become aware of the relevance of how the law in other fields affects their work.

In addition, cross-sectoral collaborations across governmental departments should be strengthened. A whole-of-government approach is required to end childhood obesity and spur political will. This implies that some departments should better understand the relevant legal obligations and become better aware of the expectations of civil society. We hope that this book has contributed – to some extent at least – to filling existing gaps in awareness and capacity.

2.3 Evidence-based Law and Policy

This book has also highlighted the importance of generating greater integration between the evidence base underpinning obesity prevention policies and the legal medium and techniques used either to promote or discourage their implementation. The science underpinning relevant policies should be taken seriously by the law, even motivate the law. We hope that the analysis in this book allows for a deeper understanding of this relationship, enabling a more refined approach to the use of law and legal instruments.

Human rights lawyers and mechanisms should rely more explicitly on the growing body of knowledge concerning childhood obesity when considering the programmatic content of the child's right to health and related rights, as it provides the technical foundation upon which obesity prevention policies should be included in State programmes to realize and protect these rights. It provides the fundamental connection between rational public health measures and effective programmes for the realization and protection of human rights.

The evidence base should be equally important when adjudicators consider the compatibility of obesity prevention policies with economic law. It should heighten the sensitivity of adjudicators to view such policies as necessary for the pursuit of a valid public health aim, as outside the bounds of investors' legitimate expectations of regulatory stability, and as appropriate restrictions on trade. It should also weigh heavily for a legal balancing in favour of the rights of the child, and in accordance with the principle of the best interest of the child, when these rights point in different policy directions to those indicated by expansive interpretations of corporate rights. In short, the evidence attests to the elevated status of national obesity prevention measures when they are in tension with obligations to protect economic interests.

The science behind obesity is also highly relevant for national courts when applying tort law and should be given due weight when courts assess notions of causation and personal responsibility. The evidence is also fundamental when constructing a legal concept of an obesogenic environment. The accurate construction and application of this concept in law making and adjudication is set to be a crucial aspect of success in ending childhood obesity. The legal application of the concept holds especially high relevance for the potential of human rights law to address the challenge, as is reflected throughout this book.

Part of the problem with generating political will on obesity is the systemic nature of the issue: it cuts across policy areas; it concerns different constituencies; it must be addressed through the lenses of several scientific disciplines. The weight and the nature of evidence necessary to sufficiently focus and direct the will required to tackle the problem is unwieldy. In this respect, the Lancet Commission's approach should help to better frame the search for, and packaging of, that evidence. It analyses this challenge in terms of five intertwined feedback loops driving the harm we encounter:[11]

- governance loops of political power reinforcing corporate power;
- business loops creating food and natural environments centred on financial profit;
- supply and demand loops doing the same;
- ecological loops destroying the environment; and
- human health loops determining the effects of all of these systems on our wellbeing.

All of these are well-researched independently, but it is now their synchronous, overlapping and reinforcing operation that needs better understanding, clear exposition, focused messaging, and effective integration into the overall evidence base. Grasping the importance of the law as both an explanatory and connective factor in these feedback loops, and the role that it must play in ending their harmful cycles, is crucial to this process. This interlinked perspective also provides a basis for better understanding of how the law can

---

[11] B Swinburn et al., n1, 802–4.

facilitate increased harmonization between the economic, health, human rights and environmental fields and their respective legal regimes, as well as overall improved global governance.

2.4 Potential of Human Rights Law

Better integration of a legal perspective brings awareness of the obstacles and contributing factors presented by economic law, but it also brings the promise of an increased reliance on human rights law. This may give rise to expectations which, if they are too high, can only be disappointed. Human rights law is regularly criticized for its seeming ineffectiveness in curbing the excesses, inequities and social damage of so-called free markets, high capital mobility and unregulated corporations,[12] as well as for its inability to gain traction within the formulation and adjudication of economic law.[13] Yet, this is not an inherent failure of human rights as a tool. Rather, it is an important, though perhaps temporary, shortcoming in how we understand and use human rights law, and in the professional awareness, imagination and dedication of human rights lawyers and human rights bodies.[14] The underutilization of the potential of human rights might not be so surprising when it is acknowledged that the relevance of human rights to economics has only recently been perceived as an important subject of in-depth study. In addition, though rarely noted by human rights critics, powerful State and private forces have also long been at work directly undermining the full conceptual, normative and procedural realization of human rights law. When viewed objectively and purposively, and if faithfully implemented in a conducive environment, human rights law yields much untapped potential and can disrupt the status quo. Human rights law provides a number of positive tools to address the deficiencies of economic processes and economic law that are not yet being used.[15] As Alston states, in light of strong political and economic opposition, human rights have always faced an

---

[12] See, e.g., S Moyn, *Not Enough: Human Rights in an Unequal World* (Harvard University Press 2018).

[13] In the investment law context see, M Hirsh, 'Investment Tribunals and Human Rights: Divergent Paths' in PM Dupuy (et al. eds), *Human Rights in International Investment Law and Arbitration* (OUP 2009); and in the trade law context, S Joseph, *Blame it on the WTO? A Human Rights Critique* (OUP 2011).

[14] See in particular, P Alston, 'The Populist Challenge to Human Rights' (2017) 9 *Journal of Human Rights Practice* 1; UN, 'Report of the Special Rapporteur on Extreme Poverty and Human Rights', UN Doc A/HRC/29/31, 27 May 2015.

[15] See, e.g., G MacNaughton and D Frey (eds), *Economic and Social Rights in a Neoliberal World* (CUP 2018); R Balakrishnan (et al. eds), *Rethinking Economic Policy for Social Justice* (Routledge 2016); A Nolan (ed.), *Economic and Social Rights After the Global Financial Crisis* (CUP 2014); R Balakrishnan and D Elson (eds),

uphill battle. The current adverse situation does not spell the irrelevance of human rights. However, it does indicate that, to realize their positive potential, 'human rights proponents need to urgently rethink many of their assumptions, re-evaluate their strategies, and broaden their outreach, while not giving up on the basic principles'.[16]

3. PERSPECTIVES ON A FRAMEWORK CONVENTION ON OBESITY PREVENTION

The adoption of an international, legally binding instrument under the auspices of the WHO may be the best way forward to address these four main themes and associated imperatives. While we are acutely aware that the adoption of a Framework Convention on Obesity Prevention (FCOP) will be difficult to achieve, we nonetheless believe that it is a feasible, desirable and indeed necessary pursuit. The relative success of the 15-year-old Framework Convention on Tobacco Control (FCTC) should provide inspiration for an analogous FCOP. Before we reflect on the lessons that can be learnt from the FCTC for the development and implementation of a FCOP, we first address the objections that could be made to the adoption of an international convention.

3.1 Confronting Fragmentation in the Construction of New International Conventions

An important preliminary question is whether international law reform is advisable – that is, whether the aim of ending childhood obesity should be pursued, at least partly, by further action at the global level, notwithstanding its imperfect structures. Miller has argued that progressive social movements are ill-served by attempts to work through global structures, and in fact risk increasing overall levels of harm, due essentially to the control over existing global institutions exercised by the dominant Sates and economic actors with a vested interest in maintaining the status quo.[17] They will either circumvent an institution that succeeds in passing rules that significantly disrupt normal operations by abandoning it, by starving it of resources, or by obstructing its functioning, or they will otherwise hijack the implementation process and blunt the effect of the rules or turn them into means to further entrench extant

---

Economic Policy and Human Rights: Holding Governments to Account (Zed 2011); M Couret Branco, *Economics Versus Human Rights* (Routledge 2009).

[16] P Alston, 'Human Rights Under Siege' (2017) 14 *SUR International Journal on Human Rights* 267, 268.

[17] R Miller, 'Global Institutional Reform and Global Social Movements: From False Promise to Realistic Hope' (2006) 39 *Cornell International Law Journal* 501.

patterns, 'making matters worse for humanity'.[18] He argues instead that progressive social movements should focus on mitigating the harm done by the global order through better and more effective local organization.[19]

The dual prospects of circumvention, on the one hand, or co-option, on the other, are both real. Yet, it is also true that an increasing majority of global institutional interactions play out somewhere between these poles. For our purposes, the most relevant example is the FCTC, which has contributed to real gains in tobacco control, ultimately saving many lives.[20] This indicates the propriety of a more nuanced assessment of the contribution of global institutional reform. Dynamics in international relations evolve, as do interactions between the local and the global: the power of various States, actors and interest-based coalitions is fluid, waxing and waning with time and changed circumstance; the personalities and preferences of particular key policy figures also change; and it is important to note that with respect to certain issues, including child obesity, the interests of powerful and weak States may converge more readily than in others.

A movement towards a FCOP will need to be alive to the form and nature of global institutions, the 'interests, motivations and capabilities of those who enjoy positions of authority within them', the politics of the major State actors, and their incentives to circumvent and especially to co-opt institutional reform and process.[21] Yet, these considerations do not outweigh the benefits of pursuing the establishment of global norms to prevent obesity, as has been done for tobacco control and as this book calls for.[22] Tackling the incoherence

---

[18] Ibid., 503.

[19] This position reflects a strongly 'realist' perspective on international relations, and is thus vulnerable to the usual responses and counter arguments from a contextualized, more empirical and broadly 'constructivist' position: see R Jackson (et al. eds), *Introduction to International Relations: Theories and Approaches* (7th edn, OUP 2019) 69–106 and 234–61.

[20] 'Impact Assessment of the WHO FCTC: Report by the Expert Group', Conference of the Parties to the WHO Framework Convention on Tobacco Control, Seventh Session, WHO Doc FCTC/COP/7/6, 27 July 2016. 'Evidence from the scholarly literature, reports from Parties, WHO and other health authorities, and further sources show that the FCTC has made a powerful contribution to tobacco control policy development and implementation, strengthening existing strategies, and contributing to denormalising smoking.' Ibid, para 23. See also, S Gravely et al., 'Implementation of Key Demand-reduction Measures of the WHO Framework Convention on Tobacco Control and Change in Smoking Prevalence in 126 Countries: An Association Study' (2017) 2 *Lancet Public Health* e166.

[21] C Barry, 'Is Global Institutional Reform a False Promise?' (2006) 39 *Cornell International Law Journal* 523, 524.

[22] This is in line with a strong current in the academic literature: 'Editorial: Why a Global Convention to Protect and Promote Healthy Diets is Timely' (2014) 17 *Public*

of the global order and the imbalance between various regimes by actively harmonizing each regime and ensuring their coherence at the national and the international levels, making them more supportive of national democratic processes and social movements, requires more international cooperation, not less, and more global governance, albeit of a different type.[23] An appropriately designed FCOP could play an important role, not just in delivering better health outcomes but also in building better systems of global governance.

3.2 From the FCTC to the FCOP

A future FCOP holds the promise of establishing an internationally agreed approach to the prevention of childhood obesity capable of guiding and coordinating national efforts and creating a global level playing-field for the agri-food industry, and agri-food MNCs more specifically. A Convention could thereby mandate and empower government and civil society action and set global minimum standards of accountability, measurement and progress review. Reflecting on the lessons learnt from the FCTC provides a useful starting point for the promoters of a FCOP.

The FCTC, the first (and to date the only) global health treaty adopted under the auspices of the WHO, entered into force in February 2005. It is one of the most rapidly and widely embraced treaties in UN history, with 181 Parties covering more than 90 per cent of the world population.[24] Some features of the FCTC could inspire the design of the FCOP. First, the FCTC promotes a comprehensive approach to tobacco control, calling on States to adopt a broad range of measures, including price measures, particularly taxation, the protection from exposure to tobacco smoke, the regulation of tobacco pack-

---

Health Nutrition 2387; G Lien and K DeLand, 'Translating the WHO Framework Convention on Tobacco Control (FCTC): Can We Use Tobacco Control as a Model for other Non-communicable Disease Control?' (2011) 125 *Public Health* 847; D Yach et al., 'The World Health Organization's Framework Convention on Tobacco Control: Implications for Global Epidemics of Food-related Deaths and Disease' (2003) 24 *Journal of Public Health Policy* 274; L Gostin, 'Meeting Basic Survival Needs of the World's Least Healthy People: Toward a Framework Convention on Global Health' (2008) 96 *Georgetown Law Journal* 331; Consumers International and World Obesity Federation, *Recommendations Towards a Global Convention to Protect and Promote Healthy Diets* (2014). For arguments to the contrary see, S Hoffman et al., 'Assessing Proposals for New Global Health Treaties: An Analytic Framework' (2015) 105 *American Journal of Public Health* 1523.

[23] T Schrecker, 'Globalization and Health: Political Grand Challenges' (2020) 27(1) *Review of International Political Economy* 167.

[24] 180 States and the European Union: http://www.who.int/fctc/cop/en/ (accessed 17 August 2020).

aging, labelling, advertising and other forms of marketing, tobacco contents measures, measures relating to cessation programmes (demand side[25]), as well as measures covering illicit trade in tobacco products, sales to and by minors, and the provision of support for economically viable alternative activities (supply side[26]). The FCTC therefore acknowledges that only a coordinated, multisectoral approach can effectively prevent smoking related NCDs.[27] Similarly, obesity prevention also requires 'strong political commitment' to 'develop and support, at the national, regional and international levels, comprehensive multisectoral measures and coordinated responses'.[28] As the ECHO Commission report shows, there is a growing international consensus regarding the measures required to this effect, which centre on improving labelling and nutrition information, restricting unhealthy food marketing, reformulating food, promoting breastfeeding, raising standards for food available in schools and other public institutions through public procurement, and using economic tools such as tax measures to influence consumption patterns. As for tobacco, States should adopt a mix of regulatory measures which should be complemented by education and public awareness campaigns, as well as healthy weight programmes.

Secondly, the FCTC sets minimum requirements.[29] As such, it allows for a potentially effective compromise. On the one hand, the minimum requirements bind all Parties, therefore establishing a global level-playing field within which all business actors must operate. This, in turn, limits unfair competition by making it clear that some commercial practices are not acceptable anywhere in the world. On the other hand, a minimum harmonization approach does not stifle national initiatives in countries where there is enough political will to adopt more ambitious tobacco control strategies. Whilst some countries have failed to effectively implement (or even become a party to) the FCTC, others have shown leadership and exceeded its minimum requirements, as discussed further below. The FCTC therefore recognizes that if taken by all States, the minimum requirements it lays down will contribute to achieving its objectives, without purporting to mandate a uniform tobacco control strategy for all Parties.

---

[25] FCTC, Arts 6–14.
[26] Ibid., Arts 15–17 and the additional protocol.
[27] In practice, however, one of the major ongoing challenges that the FCTC has experienced is a continuing lack of intersectoral cooperation between policy domains at the national and global levels. 'Impact Assessment of the WHO FCTC', n20, para 26. Most governments still lack an effective recognition that the provisions of the FCTC apply to all public sectors and government departments, not just those related to health.
[28] Art 4.2.
[29] Art 2.1.

The FCTC is also – as its name indicates – a Framework Convention. As such, it lays down the principles, objectives and the general institutional set-up and rules of governance.[30] Further specific commitments and time-bound targets are concluded in more detailed agreements or protocols, which are implemented in national legislation. The Framework approach therefore allows for the development of an increasingly detailed governance regime over time as greater consensus is achieved within the overall framework. It is particularly well suited to situations where initial political will on an issue remains patchy, setting up flexible institutional mechanisms for confidence to grow, information to be more efficiently shared, the evidence base to develop, existing policies to be fine-tuned and evaluated, trust to be built and commitments to steadily deepen.

This Framework approach establishing minimum requirements is all the more appropriate as the FCTC has been supplemented by a range of evidence-based guidelines and policy options and recommendations which facilitate its dynamic interpretation. They help States adapt their national regulatory frameworks to the latest available evidence regarding the commercial practices employed by the tobacco industry, the appearance of new products on the market (e.g., heated tobacco), the effectiveness of existing tobacco control policies to reduce the burden of smoking and exposure to second-hand smoke, etc. In practice, these guidelines have proven influential and have given food for thought to States willing to exceed the minimum requirements the FCTC provides (e.g., enlarged tobacco warnings) or to adopt measures that the FCTC does not specifically mention. For example, the FCTC itself does not explicitly refer to the contribution that tobacco plain packaging can make to effective tobacco control strategies. However, the FCTC Guidelines on Articles 11 on packaging and labelling[31] and 13 on advertising, promotion and sponsorship[32] identify the importance of packaging as a marketing tool and the need for States to take measures intended to reduce the appeal of tobacco pack-

---

[30] See generally, D Bodansky, 'The Framework Convention/Protocol Approach', Doc WHO/NCD/TFI/99.1, WHO 1999.

[31] 'Parties should consider adopting measures to restrict or prohibit the use of logos, colours, brand images or promotional information on packaging other than brand names and product names displayed in a standard colour and font style (plain packaging). This may increase the noticeability and effectiveness of health warnings and messages, prevent the package from detracting attention from them, and address industry package design techniques that may suggest that some products are less harmful than others.'
(at para 46).

[32] 'The effect of advertising or promotion on packaging can be eliminated by requiring plain packaging …' (at para 16).

aging and curb the uptake of smoking by young people.[33] As a result, several States have successfully implemented tobacco plain packaging schemes from 2010 onwards.

Thirdly, while the FCTC emphasizes the necessity of involving both State and non-State actors from a range of sectors, providing institutional support for civil society participation,[34] it also explicitly calls on States to ensure that the development and implementation of tobacco control policies are effectively protected from industry interference. Article 5(3) of the FCTC requires that 'in setting and implementing their public health policies with respect to tobacco control, Parties shall act to protect these policies from commercial and other vested interests of the tobacco industry in accordance with national law'. As mentioned in our introduction, this provision takes as its starting point 'what may fairly be described as an expression of profound distrust about the motives of the tobacco industry' and 'assumes a history of deliberate subversion by the industry of governmental health policies'.[35] Notwithstanding the repeated calls of the WHO and the international community to draw this red line,[36] the primary obstacle identified by the FCTC's Expert Group working on impact assessment remains the '[a]ggressive action by the global tobacco industry to oppose tobacco control measures and to undermine Article 5.3'.[37] As discussed in this book, there is a similar need to ensure that any interference with public policy by agri-food MNCs (and other relevant business actors) is averted for meaningful progress to be made towards the globally agreed objective of halting the rise in obesity by 2030.

Fifteen years after its adoption, the FCTC is largely considered a success. Parties to the FCTC have made significant progress in adopting new tobacco control laws and action plans as a result of the international regulatory framework in place to control tobacco.[38] Overall, health advocates point to the

---

[33] For evidence supporting tobacco plain packaging, see in particular: *Standardised Packaging of Tobacco: Report of the independent review undertaken by Sir Cyril Chantler*, King's College London, April 2014; and *Post-Implementation Review Tobacco Plain Packaging*, Australian Government, Department of Health, 26 February 2016.

[34] M Sparks, 'Governance Beyond Governments: The Role of NGOs in the Implementation of the FCTC' (2010) 17 *Global Health Promotion* 67.

[35] *BAT and Others v Secretary of State for Health* (High Court decision of 19 May 2016: [2016] EWHC 1169 (Admin), at para 170.

[36] See recently para 22 of the UN General Assembly Resolution 73/2 of 10 October 2018 (A/73/L.2) adopting the Political declaration of the third high-level meeting of the General Assembly on the prevention and control of NCDs.

[37] 'Impact Assessment of the WHO FCTC', n20, para 26.

[38] In 2015, the WHO estimated that 80 per cent of the Parties had strengthened their existing or adopted new tobacco control legislation after ratifying the Convention.

significant benefits the FCTC has had in raising the profile of tobacco control worldwide, activating and strengthening civil society networks, supporting governments – both politically and legally – in taking action against the tobacco industry, contributing to the de-normalization of smoking, facilitating increased information flows and mobilizing greater political and financial resources.[39] A key success of the FCTC in influencing broader global governance processes has indeed been its utility in helping public bodies defend legal challenges from the industry. In particular, the FCTC and its accompanying Guidelines, have been extensively relied on in recent high-profile disputes at national, regional and global levels. When national laws imposing tobacco plain packaging have been challenged, the FCTC as supplemented by its Guidelines has been invoked by courts of law or tribunals as authoritative both before national courts[40] or before international dispute settlement bodies.[41] Even though they are not legally binding, the Guidelines have been adopted by consensus; they are based on the best available scientific evidence and the

---

Some Parties are aiming to reach less than 5 per cent prevalence of tobacco use, including Finland, Ireland and New Zealand, while the Pacific island countries are aiming to become 'tobacco-free islands' by 2025: *10th Anniversary of the WHO Framework Convention on Tobacco Control – Saving Lives for a Decade*, WHO, Geneva, 2015; and England published a tobacco control plan in 2017 whose vision is 'to create a smoke-free generation': *Towards a Smokefree Generation – A Tobacco Control Plan for England*, Department of Health, London, 2017.

[39] The WHO refers to the FCTC as '[t]he most powerful tool at our disposal ... which effectively protects people from the many harms of tobacco'. 'WHO World No Tobacco Day: Three Ways to Save Lives', WHO 2011. 'The treaty demonstrates the role and strength of international law as a tool for achieving global public health goals.' G Lien and K DeLand, 'Translating the WHO Framework Convention on Tobacco Control (FCTC): Can We Use Tobacco Control as a Model for other Non-communicable Disease Control?' (2011) 125 *Public Health* 847, 849.

[40] See, e.g., the unsuccessful challenge against the imposition of tobacco plain packaging in the UK: *BAT and Others v Secretary of State for Health* (High Court decision of 19 May 2016: [2016] EWHC 1169 (Admin), and Court of Appeal decision of 30 November 2016: [2016] EWCA Civ 1182). Similarly, on graphic health warnings, the CJEU has given significant weight to the FCTC and its Guidelines in upholding the validity of Directive 2014/40 on tobacco products (OJ 2014 L 127/1): see in particular, Case C-547/14 *Philip Morris* ECLI:EU:C:2016:325, at paras 111–113.

[41] Very prominent international law disputes include the international investment law challenge Philip Morris mounted against Uruguay's tobacco warning legislation and its WTO law challenge against Australia's plain packaging legislation. On the evidentiary value of the FCTC in these two disputes, see L Gruszczynski and M Melillo, 'The FCTC and its Role in WTO Law: Some Remarks on the WTO Plain Packaging Report' (2018) 9 *European Journal of Risk Regulation* 564; and M Melillo, Evidentiary Issues in Philip Morris v Uruguay: The Role of the Framework Convention for Tobacco Control, and Lessons for NCD Prevention, (2020) *21 Journal of World Investment and Trade* 724.

experience of the Parties to the FCTC; and they are intended to have a decisive influence on the content of the rules adopted in the area under consideration.[42] More generally, the FCTC has supported governmental litigation strategies in six key ways: (1) providing a legal basis for measures; (2) demonstrating the measure's public health purpose; (3) demonstrating the evidence in favour of a measure; (4) demonstrating international consensus; (5) demonstrating that a measure promotes or protects health-related human rights; and (6) demonstrating whether or not a measure is reasonable, proportionate or justifiable.[43] The FCTC has facilitated the harmonization of global norms and has demonstrated its potential to significantly reduce the fragmentation of the international legal order, bringing different bodies of law more closely together, from public health and human rights to economic law. Its full implementation is integral to the commitments States have made to achieving a 25 per cent reduction in premature deaths from NCDs by 2025, including a 30 per cent reduction in the prevalence of tobacco use in persons aged 15 years and over.[44]

Many believe a FCOP could replicate these benefits with a view to ending obesity.[45] Nearly ten years ago, Lien and DeLand concluded their study into the prospects of translating the achievement of the FCTC into a similar convention on healthy diets by highlighting the 'sea of scientific evidence and political will' that propelled the former into reality.[46] At that time, they doubted that there was sufficient of either for a convention on healthy diets. However, as detailed in this book, much has changed over the last decade to sustain a successful bid for a second global health treaty, and several proposals have since been made by scholars and civil society representatives alike. In particu-

---

[42] One study into 96 court judgements involving industry challenges to restrictive regulations notes that the FCTC was cited in 45 decisions, 'with 80 per cent of WHO-FCTC-citing and 67 per cent of non-WHO-FCTC-citing cases upholding the measure in its entirety and on every ground': S Zhou, J Liberman and E Ricafort, 'The Impact of the WHO Framework Convention on Tobacco Control in Defending Legal Challenges to Tobacco Control Measures' (2018) *Tobacco Control* 1, 1.

[43] Zhou, Liberman and Ricafort, ibid.

[44] WHO Global Action on the Prevention and Control of NCDs 2013-2020. Reducing tobacco use is also integral to global efforts to achieve the SDG target to reduce premature deaths from NCDs by one-third by 2030 (SDG 3).

[45] As an editorial in the journal of *Public Health Nutrition* puts it: 'As dietary risk factors have recently overtaken tobacco as the leading risk factor for disease, a similar powerful tool as the WHO Framework Convention on Tobacco Control is needed to help reduce the global burden of obesity and diet-related NCDs'. 'Why a Global Convention to Protect and Promote Healthy Diets is Timely' (2014) 17 *Public Health Nutrition* 2387.

[46] G Lien and K DeLand, 'Translating the WHO Framework Convention on Tobacco Control (FCTC): Can We Use Tobacco Control as a Model for other Non-communicable Disease Control?' (2011) 125 *Public Health* 847, 852.

lar, inspired by the precedent of the FCTC, Consumer International and World Obesity Federation proposed a Convention on Unhealthy Diets in 2014.[47] While that proposal did not get much political support at the time, the Lancet Commission's Global Syndemic report has called for a Framework Convention on Food Systems. The Commission's report makes a series of broad recommendations supporting and weaving through the idea of a Convention, most of which echo the themes of this book, calling in particular for efforts to 'join up the silos of thinking and action to create platforms to work collaboratively on common systemic drivers', and to 'strengthen national and international governance levers' to implement agreed guidelines and policy responses such as those of the ECHO Commission and enable better accountability when they are not implemented.[48] The Summit on Food Systems and Nutrition convened under the auspices of the UN for the Fall of 2021 may provide an opportunity to cement a consensus in favour of such an instrument.

3.3 For a Human-rights Based FCOP

When it was negotiated, the FCTC was presented as an evidence-based demand reduction strategy that was in the economic and public interests of all countries. In particular, the FCTC was designed as a treaty emphasizing sovereign State economic interests, global interdependence and the necessity for intergovernmental cooperation, which then were issues of primary concern.[49] As discussed throughout this book, such concerns are equally prevalent in obesity prevention debates and should therefore be invoked in advocacy strategies for the adoption of a FCOP.

The FCTC may be seen as supportive of a human rights-based approach to tobacco control.[50] There was nonetheless little explicit consideration of

---

[47] Consumers International and World Obesity Federation, *Recommendations Towards a Global Convention to Protect and Promote Healthy Diets* (CI and WOF 2014). For the sake of completeness, one should also refer to Gostin's seminal article setting out the rationale and justification for a Framework Convention on Global Health, and formulating a relatively detailed framework for its substantive content: L Gostin, 'Meeting Basic Survival Needs of the World's Least Healthy People: Toward a Framework Convention on Global Health' (2008) 96 *Georgetown Law Journal* 331.

[48] B Swinburn et al., n1, 792.

[49] A Taylor and A McCarthy, 'Human Rights in the Origins of the FCTC', in ME Gipsen and B Toebes (eds), *Human Rights and Tobacco Control* (Elgar, 2020), chapter 10. See also A Taylor, 'Governing the Globalization of Public Health' (2004) 32 *Journal of Law, Medicine & Ethics* 500: 'The domestic and international spheres of health policy were becoming more intertwined and inseparable.'

[50] O Cabrera and L Gostin, 'Human Rights and the Framework Convention on Tobacco Control: Mutually Reinforcing Systems' (2011) 7 *International Journal of Law in Context* 285.

human rights commitments when the FCTC was negotiated in the 1990s and, ultimately, a human rights framework was not incorporated in the final text of the Convention that was adopted in 2003.[51] As Taylor and McCarthy note, the decision to exclude human rights as part of the treaty dialogue was both deliberate and strategic, not least because views on the intersection between human rights and tobacco control have evolved significantly since the 1990s.

> Up to that point, the tobacco industry had co-opted the language of human rights to promote its own interests, specifically portraying tobacco control as an infringement on personal autonomy and economic rights. Countervailing human rights considerations had not yet entered the mainstream dialogue among proponents of tobacco control. Therefore, using human rights as the foundation of the FCTC would have, at the time, made the instrument vulnerable to the industry's biased messaging on human rights and tobacco, and would have required an additional educational and consensus-building effort that could have seriously impaired progress on the instrument.[52]

Since then, however, and as discussed in our introduction, human rights have been placed more firmly on the NCD prevention agenda. This book, which is part of the efforts made to better integrate human rights to the prevention of obesity and related NCDs, demonstrates the potential and added value of human rights to obesity and NCD prevention policies. When taken seriously and applied rigorously in political processes, and when viewed holistically to include the valence of socio-economic rights and ETOs, human rights law comes into sharp relief as a central connecting factor and an important repository of obligations and guidance. Time is ripe to put human rights at the heart of a FCOP. We have argued that the current production and maintenance of obesogenic environments is a breach of State's obligations to protect the right to health and related human rights. We have also argued that, to improve the situation and develop a global consensus, clear evidence-based policies have been developed by the WHO and other bodies, and that these policies have been collectively endorsed by governments through successive World Health Assemblies and other fora, which makes it necessary for States to take these commitments seriously. We have finally argued that international action in the form of a new legally binding instrument is essential to the effectiveness of those policies and therefore the realization of human rights. If each premise is true, then it follows that all States are under an obligation to pursue the adoption and implementation of a FCOP in good faith, not only for the benefit of their own population but also for those adversely affected by obesity and related NCDs all over the world.

---

[51] Taylor and McCarthy, n49.
[52] Ibid.

Galvanizing Political Will for a FCOP

Human rights obligations contained in relevant treaties and the principles referred to in section 2.4 above should be mobilized to push States towards the negotiating table. There is a distinct added value in the concerted adoption of a human rights framework for those advocating a FCOP and seeking to generate the requisite political will. While not all States can be expected to endorse the idea that, by cooperating towards setting up a multilateral framework, they are discharging human rights duties, even States denying the existence of such duties may be convinced to join the negotiating table, due to forces of socialization.[53] The normative weight of international human rights law is increasingly difficult for States to avoid. It holds the potential of becoming an effective way of shaming or socializing States into action if utilized on a sufficient scale.

A human rights approach to child obesity can also create powerful alliances between, for example, public health and consumer experts – as is often the case – but also child rights experts. Civil society was a crucial driving force in the FCTC negotiations and remains a central element of its successful implementation and future development.[54] This is why it is important that civil society be directly empowered. Studies show that States are often sensitive to civil society reports portraying them as insufficiently supportive of public health,[55] and as such institutional or earmarked funding needs to be supplied for their work to be effective. In furtherance of this goal, the Lancet Commission's Global Syndemic report has called for a global fund of US$1 billion to be set up to support civil society advocacy.[56] By embracing human rights, civil society advocates could arguably make up for the difference in political will surrounding the issue of tobacco control.

The powerful alliances required from civil society and States are all the more necessary for the success of a FCOP as they will need to counter the ever more powerful alliances forged by agri-food MNCs and their allies to oppose the initiative. In particular, the civil society alliances will need to ensure that the FCOP lays down minimum standards that are sufficiently robust to promote the realization of human rights. The process must be guided by the best available evidence with a view to ensuring the enjoyment of the highest

---

[53] R Goodman and D Jinks, *Socializing States: Promoting Human Rights through International Law* (OUP 2013).

[54] H Mamudu and S Glantz, 'Civil Society and the Negotiation of the Framework Convention on Tobacco Control' (2009) 4 *Global Public Health* 150; Framework Convention Alliance, '2018 Annual Report', FCA 2018.

[55] H Wipfli, 'The FCTC Turns 10: Lessons from the First Decade' (2016) 26 *Journal of Epidemiology* 279, 282; Mamudu and Glantz, ibid.

[56] Swinburn et al., n1, 793–4.

attainable standard of health for all. Minimum standards should not be minimal standards. Indeed, there may be one outcome worse than having no FCOP: it is to have one that establishes only minimal standards, less protective even than international human rights law in its present state. A new instrument thus conceived would lock in the status quo and become an instrument in the hands of agri-food MNCs to argue against evidence-based, more robust legislation intended to promote healthier diets and thus contribute to the prevention of child obesity: the minimum standard, in such a scenario, could end up defining the maximum that States would be allowed to do in the name of public health.

Promoting Participation in the Negotiation Process of a FCOP and Reducing Fragmentation

The normative imperatives of human rights law also provide a compelling set of procedures that should be followed in negotiations. Human rights law should therefore be utilized to inform appropriate modalities of negotiation that will ensure attention to the full scope of connected issues. As discussed in section 2 above, the need to bridge and connect the factually enmeshed concerns now artificially siloed in the separate regimes of health, human rights, investment and trade will require the construction and faithful employment of appropriately designed negotiating procedures.[57] Otherwise, the necessary cross-regime understanding and interdisciplinary learning will be left to sheer political chance and no doubt blocked or subverted by the power of entrenched interests in protection of existing fragmented arrangements.

As stressed in section 2.4 above, the full structure of human rights law, understood to include relevant ETOs of international cooperation, provides important guidance in the construction of negotiating modalities. In the most general sense, the negotiations must adhere to the core principles of human rights, ensuring equity, wide participation, non-discrimination, transparency and access to information. Equitable participation must cover not only the regularly marginalized lower and middle-income countries but also the full range of affected social groups, especially, with respect to a future FCOP, children, women and indigenous people, for whom current patterns of land use and unsustainable production processes are of central concern.[58]

More concretely, negotiating modalities will need to effectively implement clear normative demands to ensure convergence and coordination between States' obligations under the right to health and other related rights, on the

---

[57] One should also add the environment, following the Lancet Commission's Global Syndemic Report.

[58] See further, O De Schutter, 'The Specter of Productivism and Food Democracy' (2014) *Wisconsin Law Review* 199.

one hand, and commitments in the areas of trade and investment, on the other. These demands are sourced from the UN Guiding Principles on Business and Human Rights,[59] numerous human rights treaty bodies and the Maastricht Principles on the Extraterritorial Duties of States in the Area of Economic, Social and Cultural Rights.[60]

Such modalities would be given appropriate form through the implementation of human rights impact assessments (HRIAs) to inform negotiating mandates, during the process of negotiations and in review of final texts and treaty implementation. Concrete templates for the nature and operation of HRIAs are given in the detailed guidelines produced by various special rapporteurs of the Human Rights Council.[61] HRIAs not only provide a means by which to link economic, health and environmental regimes through the right to health and other related rights, they also follow a methodology that should ensure broad participation. They do so in two ways: (1) by virtue of their built-in requirement for exhaustive participation; and (2) through their requirements for full information on all relevant impacts on all relevant rights, necessitating the sourcing of that information from rights-holders far and wide. Some may object that these procedures might become too onerous or convoluted to fit within traditional negotiating routines and meet pressing negotiating timetables. However, this could simply reflect the inadequacy of extant negotiating processes and the rush to push forth inadequate and narrow frameworks of agreement, helping to explain the current fragmentation of international agreements. In addition, there are ways to simplify broad-based HRIAs so that they do not lose their integrity. One option is greater reliance on the coordinating power of National Human Rights Institutions to act as clearing houses for information collection and impact assessment. The Global Alliance of National Human Rights Institutions, based in Geneva, could similarly be involved in coordinating the process of HRIAs and targeting input into the negotiations.

Human rights are especially well suited to act as a desirable overarching medium for the process of negotiations, where complex issues must be focused without loss of meaning, where trade-offs and balancing must be engaged in

---

[59] 'Guiding Principles on Business and Human Rights: Implementing the United Nations "Protect, Respect and Remedy" Framework', Report of the Special Representative of the Secretary-General on the Issue of Human Rights and Transnational Corporations and Other Business Enterprises, John Ruggie, UN Doc. A/HRC/17/31, 21 March 2011, Principle 9 and commentary.

[60] Published with full commentary in (2012) 34 *Human Rights Quarterly* 1084.

[61] Report of the Special Rapporteur on the Right to Food, Olivier De Schutter, Addendum, Guiding Principles on Human Rights Impact Assessments of Trade and Investment Agreements, UN Doc. A/HRC/19/59/Add.5, 19 December 2011.

and where a wide range of diverse interests must be reconciled.[62] Such conception embraces the political potential of human rights as devices of coordination and empowerment in the process of decision-making.[63] While recognizing that rights should not seek to over-determine outcomes, their relative ethical and normative importance must still give them a certain extra weight in balance with other factors and interests. Human rights have the potential to give substance to a 'global public standard' capable of facilitating assessment of the normative legitimacy and propriety of the institutional and substantive decisions the complex process of negotiations demands. They can provide such a standard due to three key features. First, human rights are sufficiently concise to provide concrete guidance in deliberations, yet they are also sufficiently broad to avoid the over-determination of outcomes and the pre-emption of those deliberations. Here the regular charge of vagueness becomes a relative strength of human rights, allowing for contestation and debate, with the purpose of attaining nonetheless distinct goals. Secondly, they are both legal rights, with attendant normative force, and moral ideals, perpetually allowing for future progressive developments. This gives them a unique legitimizing weight that avoids structural petrification. Finally, their universal nature mandates the required moral, political and institutional cosmopolitanism,[64] which provides the right ethos on which to build necessary future structures of international cooperation and global governance.

A human rights-based approach would open avenues for the design of the FCOP to better harmonize health, human rights and economic regimes through its substance and operation. For example, greater harmonization could be pursued through directions to trade and investment panels on how to interpret the FCOP (through further legal capacity building efforts) and the weight to give its obligations if it is raised in specific disputes. There could also be a clause mandating a referral to public health bodies or human rights bodies for advisory opinions or for the provision of relevant expert evidence in such cases.

---

[62] O De Schutter, 'The Role of Human Rights in Shaping International Regulatory Regimes' (2012) 79 *Social Research* 785, 805–6.

[63] C Bietz, *The Idea of Human Rights* (OUP 2009). This conception of human rights departs from the more popular vision of 'rights as trumps': R Dworkin, 'Rights as Trumps' in J Waldron (ed.), *Theories of Rights* (OUP 1984).

[64] W Werner and G Gordon, 'Kant, Cosmopolitanism and International Law' in A Orford and F Hoffmann (eds), *The Oxford Handbook of the Theory of International Law* (OUP 2016).

Promoting Better Accountability Mechanisms
The institutional structure of human rights law provides valuable potential additions to the accountability framework that may develop out of a future FCOP. With a tight interweaving of health policy and human rights norms, the Convention could include dedicated procedural clauses requiring States to report on progress at regular intervals not only to health bodies but also to human rights treaty bodies. This would extend the scope and add to the imperative of good faith implementation of the Convention. In addition, it would help to motivate greater coordination and dialogue between health and human rights bodies at the international level. It would also help to mobilize domestic civil society advocates in the human rights field, including national human rights institutions, incorporating them into the wider effort to monitor and drive the Convention forward and similarly facilitating greater convergence with public health advocates.

The task of building political momentum for a FCOP is not to be underestimated. It will unavoidably require sustained, long-term efforts. Relevant governance mechanisms need to be instituted, coupled with broad participation. As the Report of the Lancet Commission suggests, it will be important, despite the urgency of the initiative, to allow adequate space and time for the expansion of the evidence-base to better inform policy and law. Time and conceptual space will also be needed to facilitate the necessary dialogues between multiple, diverse disciplines and sectoral and departmental representatives, so that they may translate insights and learn from each other's perspectives in order to properly build collaborative and genuinely coordinated responses.

Language within the FCOP should establish, as explicitly as possible, the inherent, universal and ethical nature of human rights (and the necessary public health measures for their attainment) as fundamentally different to the particular, instrumental and functional nature of economic rights. It should be made clear that wherever these prior rights are implicated in economic processes or disputes, at the very least, due account must be given to the weight of public health and human rights law, including the guidance offered by principles and soft law developed in their furtherance. Additionally, provision should be made for the necessity of expanding future regulation in this area in line with a developing understanding of the inter-connectedness of policy fields and the complexities of achieving the Convention aims. Decision-makers in economic regimes should be increasingly aware that the claims of economic actors based on the supposedly static character of the FCOP or the broader field cannot be legitimate.

4.   CODA

We hope that this book has provided further grist for the mill of such debates on a future FCOP as well as the broader drive to end childhood obesity. As a coda, we choose to gesture towards the need for present economic regimes of law and policy, together with the ideologies underpinning them, to begin to reimagine themselves. As a growing number of scholars are noting,[65] the very purpose of trade and investment law is coming in for ever-deeper questioning, a trend spurred by recurrent economic crises and the disintegrating legitimacy and explanatory power of mainstream economic theory. The quasi-exclusive focus on liberalization and protection of global capital, which we inherit from the neoliberal era, is no longer tenable. More fundamental concerns and values (not least public health, environment and climate change, labour and human rights) demand to be integrated into the *very purpose and intent* of economic law, not just to ask for its permission. Efforts to date are limited to a loose accommodation of these concerns to some extent, at the fringes and limits of economic law and policy. Such efforts are ineffective in blunting the existential imperative of non-economic demands. They fail even to maintain general acceptance of a current economic structure that so often operates in direct opposition to them. In this context, the kind of harmonization between regimes that is advocated here becomes something that is not just in the interests of human rights, public health and environmental advocates. It becomes a survival mechanism for economic law and policy itself. This brings us back to the underlying purpose or intention of legal regimes stressed at the start of this Conclusion. While economic law may be said to be 'losing its religion', if not its church, genuine openness to peoples of another persuasion may offer a means of re-vitalization and a new, albeit it markedly different, conviction and message – one that is aligned with a healthy population living on a planet with a future.

---

[65] Notably, Andrew Lang, *World Trade Law After Neoliberalism: Reimagining The Global Economic Order* (OUP 2011); O De Schutter, *Trade in the Service of Sustainable Development: Linking Trade to Labour Rights and Environmental Standards* (Hart 2015); R Sakr, 'Beyond History and Boundaries: Rethinking the Past in the Present of International Economic Law' (2019) 22 *Journal of International Economic Law* 57; H Cohen, 'What is International Trade Law For?' (2019) 113 *American Journal of International Law* 326; L Chiussi, 'The Role of International Investment Law in the Business and Human Rights Legal Process (2019) 21 *International Community Law Review* 35; H Mann, 'Reconceptualising International Investment Law: Its Role in Sustainable Development (2013) 17 *Lewis and Clarke Law Review* 521; P Martinez-Frega and C Rega, *Public Purpose in International Law: Rethinking Regulatory Sovereignty in the Global Era* (CUP 2015); M Fakhri, *Sugar and the Making of International Trade Law* (CUP 2014) 211–14.

Index

adequate and nutritious foods, access to 35
adult obesity, likelihood of 72
advergames 260
advertising
    children's vulnerability to 46–7
    constitutional protection of 266–9
    as dissemination of information 267
    as form of expression 266–9
    legality of rights-infringing measures 45
    outdoor advertising 107
    role in free market economy 267
    of tobacco products near schools 45, 173
    of unhealthy food and beverage products 53, 75, 262
Agenda for Sustainable Development 2030 5, 7–8
agricultural goods, liberalization of 118
agri-food industry 10–19, 309, 356
    corporate power of 347
agri-food privatization 13
alcohol, global recommendations on 42
Alma-Ata Declaration (1978) 108, 226
animal-source foods 188
Annual Report of the EU Platform on Diet, Physical Activity and Health (2016) 294

balanced diet, importance of 153
BAT v Secretary of State for Health 303
behavioural economics, research in 104
behavioural research 70
'best interests of the child' principle 254–64, 347
    application of 265
    from defensive to strategic litigation 269–77
    and exposure to unhealthy food marketing 254–64

objections to food marketing regulation and 265–80
protection of children from exposure to unhealthy food marketing 258–64
Bill of Rights (US) 45, 71
biodegradability, issue of 44
brain's reflective system 104
breastfeeding
    benefits and superiority of 318
    importance of 317
    promotion of 7, 60, 75
breast-milk substitutes (BMS)
    commercial marketing of breast-milk substitutes 16
    global governance of 317
    illegal marketing of 316
    impact on childhood obesity 317
    International Code of Marketing of Breast-milk Substitutes *see* International Code of Marketing of Breast-Milk Substitutes (1981)
    Nestlé's illegal marketing of 316, 320
Brussels Convention (1902) 115
Brussels I Regulation 324–5
Business and Human Rights Resource Centre database 291

caffeine 115, 285
calorie consumption 106
Canada – Certain Measures Concerning Periodicals 194
Canadian Charter of Rights and Freedoms 45
cardiovascular diseases 3–4, 70, 72, 187
Caribbean Community (CARICOM) 26, 185
    current childhood obesity regional responses 208–16

'whole of society' approach to combating childhood obesity 217
food energy availability/guidelines 188
food import quantity index 189
front-of-package labelling and taxation initiatives 208–16
Port of Spain Declaration (2007) 190–92, 217
prevalence of obesity and NCDs in 186–7
Regional Organisation for Standards and Quality (CROSQ) agency 209, 210
Caribbean Court of Justice (CCJ) 204–5
Caribbean Public Health Agency (CARPHA) 186, 205
leadership on the issue of childhood obesity 191
Plan of Action for Promoting Healthy Weights in the Caribbean 190
policies for priority action 191
CARIFORUM-EU Economic Partnership Agreement 177, 185, 193, 200–203
provisions and trade in unhealthy foods 200–203
cash-crops 114
Child and Adolescent Statute 54
child-directed marketing 262
childhood obesity
calls from the international community to end 4–5
cross-border dimension of 15
evidence-based intervention to reduce 105
global rise of 2–3
as a growing public health challenge 2–5
human rights-based approach to 8–10
inequalities in 87
international economic law on 19–22
obesity prevention program 82, 88
prevention of
children's rights-based approach to 106

human rights and 31–4
rights and duties of parents 78–80
right to health and 71–8
risks associated with 3
shared responsibility to end 78–80
children's access to adequate nutrition 75
children's consumer socialization, stages of 258
Child Rights Impact Assessments (CRIAs) 266, 277–80
Child Rights Impact Evaluation (CRIEs) 266, 277–80
child, rights of 34, 84
to access to a healthy diet 101
accountability of 68
to adequate food 69
assessments of 266, 277–80
to be heard and participate 62
breach of 68
empowerment 67–8
freedom of expression 69
fundamental interpretative legal principle 253
to health/a healthy life 40, 71–8
impact evaluations 266, 277–80
infringement of 67, 251
interpretation of 62–71
civil society organizations/alliances 36, 53, 364
Codex Alimentarius Commission 15, 138, 156
Codex Guidelines on Nutrition Labelling 139, 156, 205, 209, 211
definition of nutrition labelling 157
Guideline 3.4. of 157
Guideline 4.2. of 157
Committee on Economic, Social and Cultural Rights (CESCR) 74, 223, 244, 330
General Comment 12 of 223–4
General Comment 14 of 95, 284–5, 302
General Comment 15 of 285
General Comment 20 of 94–5
Committee on World Food Security (CFS), UN 231, 232–4
consumer behaviour 151–2, 161, 228, 259
determinants of 104
consumer empowerment 90, 100, 103

consumer protection laws 53–4, 275
  consumer's health, protection of 45
  Consumer Protection Code 54
consumer sovereignty 23
consumer's right to information 103
Convention on the Rights of the Child
    (CRC) 8–10, 57, 71, 88, 244, 252,
    285, 342
  child rights-based approach 66, 252
  general principles 62
  Articles 2, 23, 24, 25, 27 95–6
  recommendations to regulate
      unhealthy food marketing
      73–4
  risk of stigmatization 82
Convention on Unhealthy Diets (2014)
    362
corporate accountability 306, 309, 314
corporate capture, risk of 15
corporate-driven economic globalization
    241, 243
Corporate Human Rights Benchmark 291
corporate social responsibility 178, 243,
    297
costs associated with obesity 3
costs-benefit analysis (CBA) 279
Council of Europe 329, 333
  Committee of Ministers 329, 334
Court of Justice of the European Union
    (CJEU) 145, 147, 267, 303

Dassonville case 145
Decade of Action on Nutrition
    (2016–2025) 5, 219–20, 222,
    230–32, 246, 249, 346
  governance and accountability 231
  human rights-based approach 231
  integrative action areas 230
  leadership for action in 231
diet-related diseases 228, 235 *see also*
    non-communicable diseases
diets, westernization of 11
digital marketing, of unhealthy food 107,
    255, 271
  regulation of 262

eating habits, determinants of 98
EC – Asbestos dispute 130, 194, 195
economic liberalization 87, 121, 128

economic liberty, concept of 126
  obesity and 19–21
EDF v Romania 181
empowering of consumers, through
    information 105
empowerment of children 82
Ending Childhood Obesity Commission
    (ECHO) 1, 58–60, 83–4, 236
  recommendations 6, 7, 72, 80, 345
    Comparison of ECHO and
        Human Rights' Bodies
        Recommendations 78
  standardized global nutrient
      labelling system 15
energy-dense diets 86, 91–2, 102, 105
  energy imbalance 6, 91
environmental tax legislation
  chilling effect on the adoption of
      174
equality, principle of 87, 89, 93, 97–8
European Commission 140, 149, 167,
    301
  concerns about the use of
      traffic-light nutrition labels
      154
  Green Paper on promoting healthy
      diets and physical activity
      140
European Convention on Human Rights
    and Fundamental Freedoms
    (ECHR) 30, 267
European Court of Human Rights
    (ECtHR) 64, 267, 330
European legislation
  Charter of Fundamental Rights 44
  directive prohibiting labels on
      tobacco products 44
  Food Information Regulation
      139–42
  Internal Market 268
  Non-Financial Reporting Directive
      300
  Renewable Energy Directive 167
  Tobacco Products Directive (2014)
      44, 302
European Parliament 333–5
  Environment, Public Health and
      Food Safety Committee 144
evidence-based intervention, to reduce
    obesity 105

evidence-based law and policy, for prevention of child obesity 351–3
evidence-based regulatory measures, against industry-led challenges 347
extraterritorial human rights obligations (ETOs) 310, 316, 330–33, 348
   concept of 331
   impact on global health governance 316, 336–8
   for improved access to home state courts 333–6
   leadership role in defence of 333

family unity, impact on growth of child 69
fast food
   chains 13
   placement of outlets 107
   children's exposure to 75, 285
Food and Agriculture Organization (FAO) 5, 27, 188, 220
   human rights-based development 222–6
   links between food systems and obesity 240–41
   reduction of human rights capacity in 225
food and beverage industry 40, 43, 52, 207
   personal freedoms and commercial interests 43
food and subsidies, distribution of 97
food business operators 144, 148–9
food commodities 11
food corporations 11, 35, 236
food environment
   equal access to healthy food 98
   role in development of nutrition-based diseases 98
food imports 13, 20, 188–9
food information 141, 150
Food Information Regulation (2011) 138, 141, 142–5, 149
   adoption by Member States 144
   Article 7 of 150
   Article 33(1) of 151
   Article 35 of 144, 148, 153
food labelling laws
   adoption of 138

   aim of 144
   colour-coded reading 148, 149
   to combat childhood obesity 138
   framework directives 140
   guidelines on food labelling 26
   Codex Guidelines on Nutrition Labelling 139
   Nutrition Labelling Directive (1990) 143
   for health-promoting labels 152–6
   international obligations 156–8
   public education campaigns 160
   'use by' date for highly perishable foods 140
food marketing 248
   association with growing rates of child obesity 254–7
   best interests principle 254–64, 347
   of breast-milk substitutes (BMS) see breast-milk substitutes
   establishment of the code for 317–19
   'micro-targeting' of marketing messages 255
   objections to regulation of
   balancing of competing rights and interests 266–9
   child rights impact 277–80
   responding to free expression and trade challenges 269–73
   unfair commercial practices 273–7
   'predatory' marketing system 256
   promotion of overconsumption 259
   protection from manipulative 285
   regulation of 7, 161, 347
   scope of marketing restrictions 256
   WHO recommendations on 256–7
food procurement 7
food provision, inequalities in 108
food security 35, 97, 189, 222, 225
   Food Security Compact 223
   global crisis 232
   global debate on 232
   as a human rights issue 223
food stuffs, reformulation of 38, 50, 150, 159, 208, 297
Framework Convention on Obesity Prevention (FCOP) 340

adoption and implementation of 363
design of 367
human-rights based FCOP 362–8
perspectives on 354–69
Framework Convention on Tobacco Control (FCTC) 15, 42, 49, 59, 122, 303
impact on approach to the prevention of childhood obesity 356–62
Framework for Action on Nutrition (2014) 230
Francis Mullin case 304
French National Assembly
LOI n° 2017-399 du 27 Mars 2017 bill 298
vigilance plan 298

General Agreement on Tariffs and Trade (GATT) 21, 116–17, 119, 192, 202
Article I of 193
Article III of 130, 133, 135, 193
Article XI of 194
Article XX of 127–30, 131, 133, 136, 196, 198–9, 202, 204
dispute settlement panels 196
EC – Asbestos dispute 130, 132
environmental protection policies 124
interpretation of 'likeness' under 130–32
national treatment obligation under 193
Report of the Working Party on Border Tax Adjustments 193
US – Clove Cigarettes dispute 132, 136
US–Mexico dispute over dolphin-safe tuna 124, 127–9
US – Shrimp dispute 131–2
General Agreement on Trade in Services 119
Global Alliance of National Human Rights Institutions 366
globalization of food systems
impact on food affordability 20
through international cooperation 15
Global NCD Action Plan 238
global North 12

global obesity crisis 33, 336
driving force behind 106
in relation to sugar 113
global South 311, 319, 324, 338
global value chains (GVCs) 14, 114, 310
cross-border 14
good life, concept of 70

Havana Charter 116
health care
privatization of 35
quality of 35
healthy food
access to 101
in child-centred institutions 75
health conscious food choices 141
health inequalities and childhood obesity 86, 88, 90–99
in high-income countries 91
impact of environmental factors to 92
interventions to reduce 97, 99
in low- and middle-income countries 91
non-discrimination and equality 96–9
socioeconomic position 90
health-promoting environment, creation of 87, 92, 291
health-promoting labels 152–6
international examples 154–6
horizontal effect of human rights 27, 284, 304–7
Hospital Britanico case 305
human dignity of the child, principle of 37, 69, 93
human rights
abuses by non-State actors 286
case law
industry litigation 47–51
rights-based litigation 52–5
children's rights 34, 364
childhood obesity implications for 8–10, 31–4
duties of States 24
extraterritorial obligations *see* extraterritorial human rights obligations (ETOs)
infringement of 102

obligations to protect the rights of citizens 348
relationship with obesity prevention 39–42
right to food 33–4
right to health 32–3, 93, 228
State duty to protect against abuse of 37
as a tool for exploiting trade flexibilities 214–16
UN Commission on Human Rights 37
UN Framework on 37
UN Guiding Principles on Business and Human Rights (UNGP) 27, 37, 76, 240, 242–3, 246, 284, 312, 322, 347, 366
Universal Declaration of Human Rights (UDHR) 30, 32–3, 71, 93
violations of 36
Human Rights Council (HRC) 33, 50, 165, 241, 286, 366
Working Group on Business and Human Rights 243
human rights due diligence (HRDD) 283, 289
human rights impact assessments (HRIAs) 277, 337, 366
human rights law
institutional structure of 368
obligations of
corporations 36–8
states to respect, protect, and fulfil human rights 35–6
on public health 368
potential to prevent child obesity 353–4, 363
principal subjects of 36–7

import-substitution policies 117
India-Singapore FTA 175
individual responsibility, in addressing obesity 42–3
industry-sponsored investment law 47
infectious diseases 2
insulin resistance 72
interdisciplinarity, in prevention of child obesity 350–51
International Bill of Rights 71

International Code of Marketing of Breast-Milk Substitutes (1981) 16, 60, 240, 244, 246, 314
in defence of the rights of both children and mothers 319
establishment of 317–19
gaps in enforcing 320–24
key aspects of 318
international commodity agreements 116–17
International Conference on Nutrition (ICN) 223, 235
International Court of Justice 64
International Covenant on Civil and Political Rights (ICCPR) 30, 63, 93
International Covenant on Economic, Social and Cultural Rights (ICESCR) 30, 33, 71, 93, 215, 222, 226, 231
right to food in 97
International Fund for Agricultural Development (IFAD) 232
international human rights law see human rights law
international investment agreements (IIAs) 161, 164
investor obligations and responsibilities 176–9
international investment law 168
key aspects of 169
objectives of 163
international public health governance 59
international trade law 112
public policy concerns as a driver of 124–32
exceptions under Art XX GATT 127–30
interpretation of 'likeness' under the GATT 130–32
regulatory autonomy of WTO members 124–6
role of judicial interpretation 124–6
international trade, liberalization of 189
International Trade Organization (ITO) 116
investment treaties 183
negative effect on national childhood obesity 176

negative effect on public health measures 176–9
pre-empting the negative effects of 179–83
public policy-making and 172
reforms in 174–6
investor behaviour
   claim of breach of the fair and equitable treatment 180–81
   effects on government decision-making 173
   investor-State disputes 163, 168
   obligations and responsibilities 176–9
Irwin Toy v. Quebec (Attorney General) 45–6, 48

Kirloskar Brothers v Employees State Insurance 305
KnowTheChain 291

legal capacity, for prevention of child obesity 350–51
legal fragmentation, responses to 349–50
legal gap analysis 314, 321, 323
life expectancy 3, 87, 92
litigation, based on human rights
   to advance obesity prevention 52
   against advertising of unhealthy food and beverage products to children 53
   challenges associated with 48
   proportionality test 48
local food systems, re-structuring or viability of 12, 20
Lorillard Tobacco Company v Reilly 45

Maastricht Principles on the Extraterritorial Duties of States in the Area of Economic, Social and Cultural Rights (2011) 332, 333, 366
malnutrition 2, 5, 62, 108
   children's vulnerability to 94
market economics 118
marketing, notion of 256
Marketing to Children Road Test 293
market-oriented agricultural trading system 118

Mehta case 305
Methanex v. United States 180
Mexico
   anti-obesity plan 41
   General Guidelines for the Sale or Distribution of Food and Drinks 40–41
   National Health and Nutrition Surveys 41
   national obesity strategy 40
   rates of obesity 40
   tax on sugar-sweetened beverages (SSB tax) 41
Millennium Development Goals 5, 221
Most Favoured Nation (MFN) obligations 115, 192–3, 195
multinational agricultural and food corporations (agri-food MNCs) 11, 22, 309, 356, 365
   alliances forged by 364
   ambiguous status of 15–19
   corporate accountability of 347
   cross-border operations of 310, 322
   and human rights 322, 335
   impact on the development of obesity and NCDs 15–19
   in the global South 324
   power of 343
   transnational impact of 15
multinational food corporations (MFCs)
   creation of obesogenic environments 283
   digital and personalized marketing campaigns 292
   economic freedoms of 308
   food decision-making 296
   obligations of 282
   product and promotional development 293
   product reformulation 297
   responsibility campaigns 295
   responsibility to respect the right to health 302
   and right to health
      due diligence 289–98
      in international law 284–9
Murli S. Deora v. Union of India and Others 53

nanny State 23
National Council for the Rights of
    Children and Adolescents 54
National Human Rights Institutions 9,
    366, 368
National Social Responsibility Levy 195
neoliberal economics 117
Nestlé
    case in Switzerland 323
    consumer movements against 318
    Department of Health 320
    Food and Drug Authority 320
    illegal marketing of BMS 316
    infant formula, health hazards of
        improper use of 318
    'infant nutrition' pamphlets 316–17
    profits at the cost of children's and
        mothers' health 317
    transnational boycotts against 318
    violation of Philippine law 320
New International Economic Order 117
New Work Item Proposal (NWIP) 209
non-communicable diseases (NCDs) 3–4,
        23, 155, 220, 255, 302, 307
    'NCD promoting' environments 8
    obesity and diet-related 31, 186
    prevention of
        agenda for 363
        human rights-based approach
            to 341
    risk factors identified by the WHO
        188
    WHO NCD Global Action Plan 8
non-discrimination, right to 21–2, 87, 88,
        92–3, 109
    under Article 2 ICESCR 94
    child's rights and 109
    and equality 96–9
    State's duties to respect, protect and
        fulfil 100
nutrient content in a food product,
        measurement of
    'teaspoon' measurement 151
    use of portion sizes as 151
nutritional declarations 109
nutritional information 89, 103
    and health messages 104
    PAHO Nutrient Profile criteria 211
    per portion of food 104
Nutrition Facts Panels (NFP) 209

obesity *see* childhood obesity
obesity epidemic *see* global obesity crisis
        135
Owusu case 324

personal autonomy
    ban on smokers' rights to 49
    notion of 42
pharma mafia 173
Philip Morris v. Uruguay 47, 164–6,
        176, 182, 206, 303
Philippines 329
    childhood obesity in 316–24
    Nestlé's illegal marketing of BMS
        see *Nestlé*
    obesogenic environment pertaining
        to children 321
physical activity 76–7
plastic bags, tax on 158
Population Nutrient Intake Goals
        (PNIGs) 211
primary goods
    export of 116
    production of 114
processed and ultra-processed food 3, 11,
        34, 188–9, 228
    processed food markets
        expansion of 20, 343
        in developing countries 20
public-private partnership
    with food and alcohol industries 19
    food 'partnerships' 17

Quebec Charter of Human Rights and
    Freedoms 45

Recommended Population Food Goals
    (RPFGs) 188
rights see *human rights*
Right to Food Guidelines 225, 233, 240
risk nutrients 155, 159
Rome Declaration on Nutrition (2014) 5,
        108, 223
Rome II Regulation 328

Save the Children investigation 316, 329
smoking
    ban in public places 53, 173

Murli S. Deora v. Union of India and Others 53
    stigma associated with 82
    tobacco *see* tobacco
social justice 25, 90–99, 108
social protection 108
social wellbeing 71
societal values, hierarchy of 271
soda tax 50–51
sponsorship, of unhealthy food 264
standardization of diets 99
stigmatization, of childhood obesity 81–3
    risk and consequences of 83
sugar
    from commodity to public health concern 120–24
    consumption of 134
    global production of 112
    global sugar market 113, 121, 123, 136
    health effects of 136
    relation to the global obesity crisis 113
    taxes on 135, 196, 211–14
Sugar and the Making of International Trade Law 112
sugar-sweetened beverages (SSBs)
    health impacts of 55
Sustainable Development Goals (SDGs) 5, 39, 58, 119, 187, 219, 228, 245
    for ending childhood obesity 60–62
sustainable food systems, promotion of 108

taxation
    to influence consumer behaviour 120, 161, 357
    of sugar-sweetened beverages (SSB tax) 41, 50–51, 208, 212–13
    of unhealthful foods 75
Technical Barriers to Trade (TBT) Agreement 132–3, 158, 194, 200, 205, 268
tension, between commercial interests and individual rights 42–7
    consumers rights relating to receiving information about products 42

Thailand – Restrictions on Importation of and Internal Taxes on Cigarettes 196–7
tobacco
    ban/restrictions on advertising 55, 173
    exposure to tobacco smoke 49
    harms and dangers of 44
    tobacco control 59
    Framework Convention on Tobacco Control (FCTC) 15, 49, 59, 359–60
    human rights-based approach to 362
    tobacco industry 15, 50, 55, 122, 173, 279, 302, 358–60, 363
trade liberalization 136, 228, 266
    and increasing rates of obesity 20
trademark, illegal expropriation of 48
transnational corporations *see* multinational agricultural and food corporations
Treaty on the Functioning of the European Union (TFEU) 138
    Article 34 of 145
    conflict between national measures and 147
    on free movement of food 144–8

ultra-processed foods *see* processed and ultra-processed food
UNICEF 244–5
United National Conference on Trade and Development (UNCTAD) 117, 177
United Nations (UN)
    Codex Alimentarius Commission 15, 138, 156
    Commission on Ending Childhood Obesity 39
    Commission on Human Rights 37
    Committee on Economic, Social, and Cultural Rights (CESCR) 32
    Committee on World Food Security (CFS) 231, 232–4
    Convention on the Rights of the Child (CRC) 8–10, 317
    Council of Human Rights 37

Decade of Action on Nutrition
 (2016–2025) 5, 219–20, 222,
 230–32, 346
Development Group (UNDG) 221
Forum on Business and Human
 Rights 243
General Assembly 4–5, 30, 65, 187,
 219, 222
 Agenda 2030 5, 7–8
 Political Declaration on
  Prevention and Control
  of NCDs 42
 Universal Declaration of
  Human Rights 32
 Global Strategy on Women and
  Children's Health (2010) 227
 Guiding Principles on Business and
  Human Rights 37, 76, 240,
  284, 312, 322, 347, 366
 Interagency Task Force on NCD
  (UNIATF) 8, 236
 Protein Advisory Group 317
 System Standing Committee on
  Nutrition (UNSCN) 231, 234
*United States – Measures Affecting the
 Cross Border Supply of Gambling
 and Betting Services* 197
US – Clove Cigarettes dispute 132, 136
US–Mexico dispute, over dolphin-safe
 tuna 124, 127–9
US – Shrimp dispute 129, 131–2, 199

value added tax (VAT) 195, 212
Vienna Declaration (1993) 108
Voluntary Guidelines on Policy
 Guidance for Food Systems and
 Nutrition (VGFSN) 233

war capitalism 117, 122
Washington Consensus 118–19
World Food Programme (WFP) 232
World Food Summit (WFS) 223
World Health Assembly (WHA) 1, 39,
 58, 60, 105, 236, 256, 314, 318,
 363

World Health Organization (WHO) 4,
 21, 57, 220
 Cluster of Family, Women and
  Children 227
 Department of Nutrition for Health
  and Development (NHD) 239
 Ending Childhood Obesity
  Commission (ECHO) *see*
  Ending Childhood Obesity
  Commission
 'Fact sheets' website 229
 Framework Convention on Obesity
  Prevention 28
 Gender, Equity and Human Rights
  Team (GER) 227
 Global Action Plan for the
  Prevention and Control of
  Noncommunicable Diseases
  2013–2020 (GAP) 4, 6, 230,
  237
 Global Monitoring Framework on
  NCDs 39
 Global Strategy on Diet, Physical
  Activity and Health 16, 208
 human rights-based development
  226–30
 Partnership on Newborn, Children
  and Maternal Health
  (PNCMH) 227
 Population Nutrient Intake Goals
  (PNIGs) *see* Population
  Nutrient Intake Goals
 on right to health 32–3
 Set of Recommendations on the
  Marketing of Foods and
  Non-Alcoholic Beverages to
  Children 105
World Obesity Federation 362
World Summit for Children 244
World Trade Organization (WTO) 48,
 112, 138, 185

Zero Hunger Programme (Brazil) 225